Buddhist
handbook

THE SALAMANDER SERIES

The salamander is an ancient symbol of emerging awareness—
similar to the archetypal meaning of Hermes in Greek mythology.
This logo marks a series of publications reflecting the presently
growing new consciousness.

Buddhist *handbook*

Salamander  *Series*

POMEGRANATE ARTBOOKS • SAN FRANCISCO

May this emanation reach all the beings
on earth to bestow endless peace,
merit and happiness.

Thru L. Lissi

In memory of James Lane Prior,
friend, mentor and publisher
of the Salamander Series.

Born 1928, De Land, Florida.
Died 1990, Kathmandu, Nepal.

Originally published in Eugene, Oregon, 1981, by Salamander Publications
Published by Pomegranate Artbooks, Box 6099, Rohnert Park, California 94927
© 1981 Salamander Publications © 1993 Pomegranate Artbooks
ISBN 1-56640-593-9
Printed in U.S.A.

Firmly tie the mind, resembling a mad elephant,
 To the strong pillar of its perceptual content
 With the rope of contemplative inspection,
 And gradually tame it with the hook of discrimination.

HANDBOOK OF BUDDHISTS

By
H. Saddhatissa Thera
(*Tripitakacarya*)

Maha Bodhi Society of India
Sarnath, Banaras.

$$\frac{\text{B E. 2500}}{\text{C. E. 1956}}$$

Reproduction of the title page of the original translation edition from which these excerpts are taken.

CONTENTS

Homage	11
The Three Refuges	11
Salutation to the Buddha	12
Salutation to the Dharma	13
Salutation to the Sangha	14
The Ten Precepts	15

The Main Teachings

The Noble Attitudes	18
The Four Noble Truths	20
The Law of Dependent Origination	22
The Three Characteristics	24
The Four Boundless States	25
Ten Perfections Leading to Buddhahood	25
Roots of Unwholesome Action	26
Roots of Wholesome Action	26
The Five Hindrances	26
The Seven Links of Enlightenment	27
The Threefold Dispensation	27
The Ten Fetters of Existence	28
The Seven Stages of Purity	30
Meditation on Death	31

PREFACE

We are dependent for the translation of the following material on a small book, now out of print, which was published in India in 1956. The publisher of this early book, H. Saddhatissa Thera, gave credit to several others for their aid in bringing these subtle concepts across the language barrier. We feel their names should not be lost:

Nyanatiloka Maha Thera
Narada Maha Thera
Sister Vajira
Bhikkhu U Dhammaratana
S.G.M. Weerasingha

With a scholar's care, the crucial terms were reproduced in the original language of the text next to the English translation. We, being more pilgrim than scholar, accept the translation here at "face value." Although strange to the Western ear, it might be noted that the rhythms of repetition have a particular psychological value.

In a very few cases, we considered it necessary to alter a term to more closely match Western usage. Despite every effort to present these teachings in familiar vernacular, a few terms have had to be retained for want of an appropriate English equivalent. Each of

PREFACE

The Three Refuges, for example, are terms allowing several levels of meaning:

The term *Buddha* can range in meaning from the most common image of seated meditation to the formless "body" of the Essence of Being.

The term *Dharma* can range in meaning from the literal teachings, such as reflected in this book, to the direct experience of the Void.

The term *Sangha* can range in meaning from the company of one's fellow aspirants to the communion of Bodhisatvas.

On the other hand, the term *Nirvana* implies a state beyond all conception and has no English equivalent. The term *Mahaparinarvana* implies an omniscient penetration of the Essence that is even less translatable.

HOMAGE

Homage to Him, the Blessed One, the Exalted One,
  the Fully Enlightened One

THE THREE REFUGES

I go to the Buddha as my Refuge.
I go to the Dharma as my Refuge.
I go to the Sangha as my Refuge.
For the second time, I go to the Buddha as my Refuge.
For the second time, I go to the Dharma as my Refuge.
For the second time, I go to the Sangha as my Refuge.
For the third time, I go to the Buddha as my Refuge.
For the third time, I go to the Dharma as my Refuge.
For the third time, I go to the Sangha as my Refuge.

SALUTATION TO THE BUDDHA

- Such, indeed, is that Blessed One:
  Exalted, Omniscient, Endowed with
  knowledge and virtue, Auspicious,
  Knower of the worlds, a Guide incomparable for
  the training of individuals, Teacher
  of gods and men, Enlightened and Holy.
- To life's end, my Refuge is the Buddha.
- The Buddhas of the ages past,
  The Buddhas that are yet to come,
  The Buddhas of the present age,
  Lowly, I each day adore!
- No other Refuge do I seek.
  Buddha is my matchless Refuge;
  By might of truth in these my words,
  May joyous victory be mine!
- With my brow I humbly worship,
  The blest dust on His Holy Feet;
  If Buddha I have wronged in aught,
  May the Enlightened forgive me!

SALUTATION TO THE DHARMA

- Well-expounded is the Dharma (Doctrine) by the Blessed One, to be self-realized: with immediate fruit; to be but approached to be seen; capable of being entered upon; to be attained by the wise, each for himself.
- To life's end, my Refuge is the Dharma.
- The Dharmas of the ages past,
  The Dharmas that are yet to come,
  The Dharmas of the present age,
  Lowly, I each day adore!
- No other Refuge do I seek,
  Dharma is my matchless Refuge,
  By might of Truth in these my words,
  May joyous victory be mine!
- With my brow, I humbly worship
  The Dharma threefold and supreme,
  If Dharma I have wronged in aught,
  May Dharma's acquittance be mine!

SALUTATION TO THE SANGHA

- ◆ Of good conduct is the Order of the Disciples of the Blessed One, of upright conduct is the Order of the Disciples of the Blessed One, of wise conduct is the Order of the Disciples of the Blessed One, of dutiful conduct is the Order of the Disciples of the Blessed One. This Order of the Disciples of the Blessed One—namely, these Four Pairs of Persons, the Eight Kinds of Individuals—is worthy of offerings, is worthy of hospitality, is worthy of gifts, is worthy of reverential salutation, is an incomparable field of merit to the world.
- ◆ To life's end, my Refuge is the Sangha.
- ◆ The Sanghas of the ages past,
  The Sanghas that are yet to come,
  The Sanghas of the present age,
  Lowly, I each day adore!
- ◆ No other Refuge do I seek,
  Sangha is my matchless Refuge,
  By might of Truth in these my words,
  May joyous victory be mine!
- ◆ With my brow, I humbly worship,
  The Sangha triply unrivaled,
  If Sangha I have wronged in aught,
  May Sangha forgive me that ill!

THE TEN PRECEPTS

1. I take the precept to abstain from killing.
2. I take the precept to abstain from stealing.
3. I take the precept to abstain from incelibacy.
4. I take the precept to abstain from lying.
5. I take the precept to abstain from liquor that causes intoxication and heedlessness.
6. I take the precept to abstain from taking food at an unseasonable time.
7. I take the precept to abstain from dancing, singing and unseemly shows.
8. I take the precept to abstain from the use of garlands, perfumes, unguents, and from things that tend to beautify and adorn (the person).
9. I take the precept to abstain from the use of high and luxurious seats.
10. I take the precept to abstain from accepting gold and silver.

THE MAIN
TEACHINGS

THE NOBLE ATTITUDES

- ◆ He who is skilled in his goodness
  Who wishes to attain that Calm State, should act thus:
  He should be able, upright, yea perfectly upright,
  Of noble speech, gentle and humble.
- ◆ Contented, easily supportable, with few duties,
  Of light livelihood, controlled in senses.
  Discreet, not impudent,
  Not greedily attached to families.
- ◆ He should not pursue anything trifling
  Such that other wise men might censure him.
  May all Beings be happy and secure;
  May their hearts be wholesome.
- ◆ Whatever living Beings there be—
  Feeble or strong, tall, stout or medium,
  Short, small or large, without exception.
- ◆ Seen or unseen,
  Those dwelling far or near,
  Those who are born, or who are to be born,
  May all Beings be happy!

- Let none deceive another
  Nor despise any person whatsoever in any place,
  Let him not wish any harm to another
  Out of anger or ill will.
- Just as a mother would protect her only child
  At the risk of her own life,
  Even so let him cultivate a boundless heart
  Toward all Beings.
- Let his thoughts of boundless love
  Pervade the whole world,
  Above, below and across without any obstruction,
  Without any hatred, without any enmity.
- Whether he stands, walks, sits,
  Lies down, as long as he is awake
  He should develop this mindfulness,
  This they say is the noblest living here.
- Not falling into Error (self-illusion),
  Being Virtuous and endowed with insight,
  By discarding attachment to sense desires,
  Never does he come again for conception
  in a womb.

THE FOUR NOBLE TRUTHS

1. The Noble Truth about suffering:

   Birth is suffering; decay is suffering; disease is suffering; death is suffering; to be conjoined with things which we dislike is suffering; to be separated from things which we like is suffering; not to get what one wants—that also is suffering. In short, these five aggregates* which are based on grasping are suffering.

2. The Noble Truth about the cause of suffering:

   It is this craving that leads back to birth, along with the lure and the lust that finds pleasure now here, now there, namely, the craving for sensual pleasure, the craving to be born again, the craving for annihilation.

---

*Five aggregates, viz: 1. Matter, 2. Feeling, 3. Perception, 4. Tendencies, 5. Consciousness.

3. The Noble Truth about the cessation of suffering:

Truly it is the utter passionless cessation of, the giving up, the forsaking, the release from, the detachment for, this craving.

4. The Noble Truth about the path leading to the cessation of suffering:

That is the Middle Path, popularly known as the Noble Eightfold Path:

Right View
Right Aspiration
Right Speech
Right Action
Right Livelihood
Right Endeavor
Right Mindfulness
Right Concentration

[Extracted from the first sermon of the Buddha delivered at the Deer-Park (Banaras).]

THE LAW OF DEPENDENT ORIGINATION

Dependent on Ignorance arise Activities (moral and immoral);

Dependent on Activities arises (Rebirth) Consciousness;

Dependent on Consciousness arise Mind and Matter;

Dependent on Mind and Matter arise the Six Spheres of Sense;

Dependent on the Six Spheres of Sense arises Contact;

Dependent on Contact arises Sensation;

Dependent on Sensation arises Craving;

Dependent on Craving arises Attachment;

Dependent on Attachment arise Actions;

Dependent on Actions arises Birth;

Dependent on Birth arise decay, death, sorrow, lamentation, pain, grief and despair.

Thus does this entire aggregation of suffering arise.

Of a truth, the complete separation from, and cessation of, Ignorance leads to the cessation of Activities;

The cessation of Activities leads to the cessation of Consciousness;

The cessation of Consciousness leads to the cessation of Mind and Matter;

The cessation of Mind and Matter leads to the cessation of the Six Spheres of Sense;

The cessation of the Six Spheres of Sense leads to the cessation of Contact;

The cessation of Contact leads to the cessation of Sensation;

The cessation of Sensation leads to the cessation of Craving;

The cessation of Craving leads to the cessation of Attachment;

The cessation of Attachment leads to the cessation of Actions;

The cessation of Actions leads to the cessation of Birth;

The cessation of Birth leads to the cessation of decay, death, sorrow, lamentation, pain, grief and despair.

Thus does the cessation of this entire aggregate of suffering result.

THE THREE CHARACTERISTICS

1. Transiency

    "All conditioned things are transient"—when one comprehends this Truth by one's own wisdom, then does one get appalled at this Misery (i.e., the Body and Mind): this is the Path to Purity.

2. Sorrowfulness

    "All conditioned things are sorrowful"—when one comprehends this Truth by one's own wisdom, then does one get appalled at this Misery (i.e., the Body and Mind): this is the Path to Purity.

3. Soullessness

    "All Dharmas (conditioned and unconditioned states) are soulless"—when one comprehends this Truth by one's own wisdom, then does one get appalled at this misery (i.e., the Body and Mind): this is the Path to Purity.

THE FOUR BOUNDLESS STATES

1. Kindness
2. Compassion
3. Altruistic Joy
4. Equanimity

TEN PERFECTIONS LEADING TO BUDDHAHOOD*

1. Perfection in Almsgiving and Liberality
2. Morality
3. Renunciation
4. Wisdom
5. Energy
6. Forbearance
7. Truthfulness
8. Resolution
9. All-embracing Kindness
10. Equanimity

---

*More commonly used are the Six Perfections of: Generosity, Discipline, Patience, Perseverance, Concentration and Appreciation.—(Ed.)

ROOTS OF UNWHOLESOME ACTION

- ◆ Greed
- ◆ Hate
- ◆ Delusion

ROOTS OF WHOLESOME ACTION

- ◆ Greedlessness
- ◆ Hatelessness
- ◆ Delusionlessness

THE FIVE HINDRANCES

These five qualities are obstacles to the mind and are blinding our mental vision, and at whose presence mind will not be able to discern the truth:

1. Sensuous lust
2. Ill will
3. Torpor and Languor
4. Restlessness and Worry
5. Skeptical doubt

THE SEVEN LINKS OF ENLIGHTENMENT

1. Attentiveness
2. Investigation of Law
3. Energy
4. Rapture
5. Tranquility
6. Concentration
7. Equanimity

THE THREEFOLD DISPENSATION

1. Learning of the Wording of the Doctrine
2. Practicing it
3. Penetrating it and realizing its goal

THE TEN FETTERS OF EXISTENCE

"There are ten Fetters, by which beings are bound to the Wheel of Existence:

1. Self-delusion
2. Doubt
3. Clinging to mere Rule and Ritual
4. Sensual lust
5. Ill Will
6. Greed for Fine Material Existence
7. Greed for Immaterial Existence
8. Conceit
9. Restlessness
10. Ignorance

"One who is freed forever from the first three fetters is called a Stream-Enterer, i.e., one who has entered the stream leading to Nirvana. He has unshakable faith in the Buddha, His Doctrine and His Holy Order, and is incapable of breaking the five moral rules, i.e., abstaining from killing, stealing, adultery, lying and drinking of alcoholic drinks. He will be reborn seven times at the utmost, and not in a state lower than the human world.

"One who has overcome the fourth and fifth fetters in their grosser form is called a Once-Returner, i.e., he will be reborn only once more in the Sensuous Sphere and thereafter reach Holiness.

"The Non-Returner is wholly freed from the first five fetters, which bind one to rebirth in the Sensuous Sphere; after death, while living in the Fine Material Sphere, he will reach the goal.

"The perfectly Holy One is freed from all the Ten Fetters.

"Each of the aforementioned four stages of Holiness consists of the 'Path' and the 'Fruition.'

"The 'Path' consists of the single moment of entering the respective attainment. With 'Fruition' is meant those moments of consciousness which follow immediately thereafter as the result of the Path and which, under circumstances, may repeat for innumerable times during a lifetime."*

---

*Word of the Buddha.

THE SEVEN STAGES OF PURITY

1. The Purity of Morality
2. The Purity of Mind
3. The Purity of Understanding
4. The Purity of Escape from all Doubt
5. The Purity of the Eye of Knowledge with regard to Path and Non-Path
6. The Purity of the Eye of Progressing Knowledge
7. The Purity of the Eye of Knowledge

MEDITATION ON DEATH

Transient, alas! are all component things,

    Subject are they to birth—and then decay;

    Having gained birth to death the life-flux swings—

    Bliss truly dawns when unrest dies away.

Uncertain is life, certain is death.

    Without a shadow of a doubt I must die.

    My life has death for its goal.

    Life is indeed precarious, but sure, sure indeed is death!

I am in the power of the passions, like a fish in
> the hands of the fisherman, for I am in the net of
> re-births, threatened by death and by the guardians
> of the hells.

Thou hast boarded this vessel, which is the human
> state; cross the river of suffering; thou fool, this is
> no time to sleep; when and at what cost wilt thou
> find this vessel again?

LIST OF FIGURES

2 Sensory Pathways of Pain and Acute Versus Chronic Pain

The affective-motivational pathway and the
sensory-discriminative pathway. 17

3 Evaluation of the Pain Patient

Components of the pain history 36
Pain assessment instruments. 52
MMPI profile of a male patient with chronic pain
demonstrating the Conversion-V pattern 60

4 Common Psychiatric Comorbidities and Psychiatric Differential Diagnosis of the Pain Patient

Relationship between anxiety and pain 71

6 Psychotherapy

Approach of cognitive-behavioral therapy 135

INTRODUCTION

to the Concise Guides Series

The Concise Guides Series from American Psychiatric Publishing, Inc., provides, in an accessible format, practical information for psychiatrists, psychiatry residents, and medical students working in a variety of treatment settings, such as inpatient psychiatry units, outpatient clinics, consultation-liaison services, and private office settings. The Concise Guides are meant to complement the more detailed information to be found in lengthier psychiatry texts.

The Concise Guides address topics of special concern to psychiatrists in clinical practice. The books in this series contain a detailed table of contents, along with an index, tables, figures, and other charts for easy access. The books are designed to fit into a lab coat pocket or jacket pocket, which makes them a convenient source of information. References have been limited to those most relevant to the material presented.

Robert E. Hales, M.D., M.B.A.
Series Editor, Concise Guides

INTRODUCTION

The magnitude of human pain is profound. Estimates suggest that more than 34 million Americans have chronic, nonmalignant pain (Leitman and Binnisk-Unni 1994). The impact of pain is far reaching, adversely affecting vocational endeavors and contributing significantly to disability (Andersson 1999; White and Gordon 1982). Economically, the impact of chronic pain is enormous in terms of the costs of absenteeism, reduced productivity, medical care, and workers' compensation (Fordyce 1995; Waddell 1996). In addition, pain interferes with people's activities, interests, and relationships and limits enjoyment of life.

Significant losses can accompany chronic pain (e.g., income and autonomy). Patients may experience guilt, blaming themselves for their inability to overcome or master pain. In the home, the patient's role, and consequently the roles of others, may require modification, leading perhaps to strained relationships.

Pain is a common complaint among patients seeking medical attention. Despite the pervasiveness of pain and its multiple ramifications, the management of pain has often been elusive to clinicians. This is particularly true when one considers the diversity of pain disorders that lack clear identifiable etiologies, or when pain exceeds expectations given the underlying medical condition. Complex pain in a patient (i.e., pain that has not responded to common pain medications and interventions) can present an enormous burden to medical services.

Increasing attention has been directed to the issues of pain management, mobilized in part by the efforts of organizations such as Compassion in Dying Federation that educate the public about

2

pain management and by standards of the Joint Commission on Accreditation of Healthcare Organizations (JCAHO). Pain management has received increased attention from the medical community as a result of societal demands for more effective and comprehensive treatment. JCAHO requires that physicians consider pain as *the fifth vital sign* and that pain severity be documented using a standardized pain scale and appropriately managed. Pain management also has received greater legal attention. Charges of abuse and negligence have been raised against physicians found to have inadequately treated pain (Albert 2001; Charatan 1999). External pressures are increasing to ensure that physicians become current in effective pain management.

■ PAIN MANAGEMENT

Pain management first emerged as a subspecialty of anesthesiology. The need for the development of the science underlying pain and the skills for its treatment prompted efforts to refine training strategies and provide specialized pain clinics. Since the first pain clinic was established in 1951, approximately 1,700 pain clinics have been established in the United States. This expansion points to the enormous need for specialized settings and specialists to work toward the amelioration of pain.

However, it became readily apparent that the knowledge and skills required of pain practitioners far exceeded those skills available to traditional anesthesiology training models. In addition to physical discomfort, patients with pain experience marked emotional distress. Emotional factors (e.g., depression and anxiety) not only emerge as a consequence of pain but also can contribute to pain, exacerbating and maintaining it. In addition, psychological factors can likewise interfere with treatment adherence and efficacy. Patients' frustration caused by ongoing pain, the effects on functioning, and the impact on families and relationships can contribute significantly to psychiatric morbidity. As a result, leaders in pain management training declared traditional medical models of pain to be too shortsighted and required a

modification in traditional training conceptualizations (Loeser 2001).

■ INTERDISCIPLINARY PAIN MEDICINE

As a result, *pain medicine* has emerged as a medical subspecialty in its own right. Although not yet universally accepted, the term *pain medicine* is intended to encompass the principles of pain management and embody an interdisciplinary approach. Currently, specialists in pain medicine view pain as a distinct multifactorial illness (Gallagher 1999). Thus, no one discipline embodies the skills and mastery required to address pain. Rather, management and treatment of pain require the joint efforts of multiple clinical specialties, each of which can contribute to the effective treatment of pain. Hence, the skills of the anesthesiology expert can be complemented by the rehabilitation skills of the physiatrist and the psychotherapeutic and psychopharmacologic skills of the psychiatrist.

In 1998, the American Board of Psychiatry and Neurology (ABPN) and the American Board of Physical Medicine and Rehabilitation (ABPMR) joined the American Board of Anesthesiology (ABA) in recognizing pain management as an interdisciplinary subspecialty. Regardless of the primary discipline, pain medicine subspecialists need to understand the anatomy and physiology of pain perception, the psychological factors modifying the pain experience, and the basic principles of pain management.

Eligibility for the certifying examination in pain medicine requires that the applicant possess a medical license. The applicant must also be board certified in one of the aforementioned disciplines and must have completed residency training in pain medicine approved by the Accreditation Council for Graduate Medical Education (ACGME) or 24 months (full-time equivalent) of practice in pain medicine. After 2003, all applicants will also need to have completed a fellowship in pain medicine in order to meet eligibility requirements.

Currently, the ACGME is refining fellowship training in pain medicine to reflect multiple disciplines. Toward this end, efforts are

4

currently under way to specify the training experiences, didactics, and rotations in anesthesiology as well as psychiatry, neurology, and physical medicine and rehabilitation. Parameters for specialty tracks in pain medicine for each of these disciplines will also be available.

ABPN diplomates were first eligible to sit for the subspecialty certification examination in 2000. Subspecialty certification is appropriate for psychiatrists whose practices are largely devoted to pain management. Invariably, given the pervasiveness of pain complaints, the general psychiatrist will encounter pain management issues among his or her patients. The general psychiatrist should also have the training and experience to recognize and treat basic psychiatric issues associated with pain. This text provides a concise guide to the psychiatric aspects of the management of pain.

■ TRADITIONAL MEDICAL MODELS OF PAIN VERSUS BIOPSYCHOSOCIAL PARADIGMS

In traditional medical models of pain management, pain is seen as a signal of underlying disease or a pathophysiologic state. The physician is proactive in undertaking pharmacologic and other treatment interventions to treat the underlying disease state or relieve pain. The focus is on the disorder rather than on the person with the disorder. Consequently, the physician enlisted to treat the patient with pain first makes a determination as to the cause, or etiology, of the pain. In ambiguous cases, there is often an exhaustive search for biomedical causes and treatment. When such efforts fail, such patients are dismissed as being "untreatable." The patient, in turn, is often left to persist in pain, with no improvement in functional adaptations.

In these models there is a dualistic notion of pain, dividing it by *organic* versus *psychogenic* causes. Thus, there is a tendency to attribute to psychic factors any pain process in which the physical causes cannot be fully delineated. Similarly, if the pain complaints

seem disproportionate to the underlying disease or if the pain fails to respond to treatment as expected, there is a belief that psychological processes underlie the pain. For many patients with chronic pain, such dualistic notions are inadequate (Boissevain and McCain 1991; Lynch 1992).

Frustrated by the inability to account for or explain pain or by a feeling of futility or defeat when faced with a patient who persistently experiences pain despite the clinician's best efforts, the clinician may cease to take the patient's complaints seriously. For such patients, psychiatry becomes the treatment of last resort, prompted by resignation that the pain is psychic rather than somatic. Pain patients do not often think of themselves as needing to see a psychiatrist. So often, physicians are accustomed to hearing patients ask, "Why do I have to see a *psychiatrist*?" The implication that the pain could be psychogenic can contribute to patients' distress. They may perceive that their doctors have given up on them, that their pain complaints are no longer taken seriously, or that they are being blamed for their persistent pain despite treatment (Gamsa 1994). (See Table 1–1 for a summary of the traditional pain model.)

Current conceptualizations of pain medicine adopt a *biopsychosocial* perspective (Engel 1977) (see Table 1–1). This model contends that the health status of individuals with chronic illnesses, the course of the illness, and the outcome of treatment are influenced by the interaction of biological, psychological, and social factors. The model provides a useful paradigm in which to view chronic pain states. The focus is on the rehabilitation and reclamation of the pain patient in the context of the pivotal doctor–patient relationship. Pain is not viewed exclusively as a signal of disease but as an experience with biological, psychological, and social derivatives. The treatment hinges on patient participation, and the physician serves as a guide, teacher, and interventionist to facilitate the rehabilitation process. The goal, therefore, is not necessarily cure, because in many cases, pain can be a chronic or even lifelong process. The biopsychosocial paradigm addresses relief from pain, while simultaneously addressing the impact of the pain condition

6

TABLE 1–1.	Traditional versus biopsychosocial models of pain	
	Traditional pain model	**Biopsychosocial model**
View of pain	As an illness	As an experience
Determinants of pain	Disease	Biological, social, and psychological factors
Responsibility for treatment	Physician	Patient
Role of clinician	Expert on pain relief	Educator, motivator, physician-healer
Role of patient	Passive	Proactive
Goal of treatment	Cure or pain relief	Increased function
		Improved quality of life
		Restored or improved relationships
Methods	Pharmacologic	Educational
	Technical	Motivational
		Interpersonal
		Psychological
		Pharmacologic
		Technical
Focus of attention	Somatic complaints	Reciprocal relationship between somatic complaints and emotion, psychological processes, and interpersonal functions
	Pain as corresponding to pathology; if pain does not correspond, it is not real	
	Disregard for patient's beliefs related to pain	Regard for patient's beliefs
	Focus on cause of pain	Focus on widespread impact of pain on life

on other aspects of one's functioning, relationships, vocational adaptations, and emotional well-being. The patient's emotional experiences, beliefs, and expectations can determine the outcome of treatment and are fully emphasized as the focus of treatment intervention. The biopsychosocial perspective pursues and examines psychological and social facets of the patient's pain experience without discounting the pain based on the presence of such facets. The goal is to identify and rectify any impediments to recovery and rehabilitation.

■ THE ROLE OF PSYCHIATRISTS IN MULTIDISCIPLINARY PAIN MEDICINE

General psychiatric training renders the psychiatrist particularly well suited for the treatment of pain (Leo et al. 2003). Traditionally, psychiatrists view patients holistically and adopt a biopsychosocial perspective. Psychiatrists are trained in communication skills and are familiar with an array of pharmacologic agents that can reduce pain.

The psychiatrist enlisted to care for the pain patient can perform a variety of functions pivotal to the biopsychosocial approach (Table 1–2). Psychiatrists may choose the roles they wish to assume in pain treatment as defined by their skills, training, and expertise and the collaborative efforts of other clinicians. Thus, psychiatrists might serve a role in diagnosing and managing discrete psychiatric disorders that accompany pain or interfere with treatment. Psychiatrists might be involved in facilitating the patient's adaptation after trauma or injury resulting in pain (e.g., motor vehicle crashes, work-related injuries); in interventions to treat pain (e.g., after an amputation); or in fostering improved quality of life, including social and vocational factors. Naturally, the psychiatrist can be involved in facilitating communication between the patient and clinicians with whom the patient interacts. (In some circumstances, the patient's perceptions of how he or she is being treated, believed, or construed may adversely affect therapeutic alliances and compromise the pain treatment team.)

8

TABLE 1–2.	Role of psychiatrists in pain management (biopsychosocial approach)

Assess pain

Assess intervening variables that affect pain

Prognosticate (consider factors that might influence pain, treatment compliance, and effects of treatment)

Determine problem areas for the patient

Establish a treatment approach

Delineate goals of treatment

Reassess treatment efficacy

Make modifications in the treating plans as necessary

Psychiatrists may be involved in the direct assessment and treatment of pain, in coordinating referrals to other pain specialists, and in all facets of the treatment plan. Conversely, psychiatrists may respond to referrals from specialists in other disciplines to complement existing treatment strategies in which psychological factors are thought to be complicating recovery.

Psychiatrists can offer pharmacologic interventions for pain. They also can address emotional and cognitive sequelae of pain or its treatment and factors interfering with treatment (e.g., treatment adherence). The patient with chronic pain can become dependent on opiate analgesics, requiring psychiatric intervention. In some cases, the care of the pain patient may be entirely delegated to the psychiatrist.

Psychiatric intervention is sought to help in treating patients who have acute pain or painful terminal disorders, especially to address the psychological consequences and psychiatric comorbidities. More frequently, physicians seek consultation for patients with chronic pain with whom they are frustrated by lack of treatment response. Often, such patients are pejoratively labeled as noncompliant, uncooperative, attention seeking, medication seeking, or malingering (Gallagher 1999). Deciphering the relative contribution of biological and psychological variables to pain complaints requires the evaluation of a psychiatrist with skills in the biopsycho-

social assessment of pain. The patient's frustration caused by ongoing pain, the effects on functioning, and the impact on relationships contributes to significant psychiatric morbicity. It is not surprising, therefore, that the presence of chronic pain is a significant risk factor for suicide (Breitbart 1993; Breslau et al. 1991). Thus, there is a great demand for psychiatrists to assist with pain management.

■ REFERENCES

Albert T: Doctor guilty of elder abuse for undertreating pain. Am Med News, July 23, 2001, pp 1, 4

Andersson GBJ: Epidemiological features of chronic low-back pain. Lancet 354:581–585, 1999

Boissevain MD, McCain GA: Toward an integrated understanding of fibromyalgia syndrome, I: medical and pathophysiologic aspects. Pain 45:227–238, 1991

Breitbart W: Suicide risk and pain in cancer and AIDS patients, in Current and Emerging Issues in Cancer Pain: Research and Practice. Edited by Chapman CR, Foley KM. New York, Raven, 1993, pp 49–65

Breslau N, Davis GC, Andreski P: Migraine, psychiatric disorders, and suicide attempts: an epidemiologic study of young adults. Psychiatry Res 37:11–23, 1991

Charatan F: Doctor disciplined for "grossly undertreating" pain. Br Med J 319:728, 1999

Engel GL: The need for a new medical model: a challenge for biomedicine. Science 196:129–136, 1977

Fordyce WE: Back Pain in the Workplace: Management of Disability in Nonspecific Conditions. Seattle, WA, International Association for the Study of Pain, 1995

Gallagher RM: Treatment planning in pain medicine: integrating medical, physical and behavioral therapies. Med Clin North Am 83:823–849, 1999

Gamsa A: The role of psychological factors in chronic pain, II: a critical appraisal. Pain 57:17–29, 1994

Leitman R, Binnisk-Unni A: National Pain Survey. New York, Louis Harris and Associates, 1994

Leo RJ, Pristach CA, Streltzer J: Incorporating pain management training into the psychiatry residency curriculum. Acad Psychiatry 27:1–11, 2003

Loeser JD: Multidisciplinary pain programs, in Bonica's Management of Pain, 5th Edition. Edited by Loeser JD, Butler SH, Chapman CR, et al. Philadelphia, PA, Lippincott Williams & Wilkins, 2001, pp 255–264

Lynch M: Psychological aspects of reflex sympathetic dystrophy: a review of the adult and pediatric literature. Pain 49:337–347, 1992

Waddell G: Low back pain: a twentieth century health care enigma. Spine 2:2820–2825, 1996

White AA, Gordon SL: Synopsis: workshop on idiopathic low-back pain. Spine 7:141–149, 1982

SENSORY PATHWAYS OF PAIN AND ACUTE VERSUS CHRONIC PAIN

Pain is a multidimensional concept (Loeser 1982) (Table 2–1). First, there is a sensory component of the pain experience—an unpleasant sensation detected in the body and processed in the central nervous system (CNS). This process, referred to as *nociception*, relies on the transfer of information about the sensory experience from receptors in the periphery through nerves to the spinal cord and on to the brain.

Second, there is an assessment of the unpleasant sensory experience. This assessment involves a cognitive awareness of the sensation arising from the periphery that the person labels as *pain*. Not all sensations are painful; some can be construed as unusual, uncomfortable, or irritating, but not painful. Thus, the common pins-and-needles sensation in one's foot might be described as the foot "falling asleep," but not as pain. Similarly, one may experience an itch, a twitch, or other noxious sensation that is labeled as painful (e.g., burning, throbbing).

TABLE 2–1.	Dimensions of pain and the biopsychosocial model	
Nociception		Biological
Pain		
Suffering	}	Psychological
Pain Behavior		Social

The third dimension involves the perception that the discomfort is associated with suffering. This subsumes not only the sensation and awareness of pain but also the reactions to the experience (e.g., distress, dysphoria, anxiety, hopelessness). The experience of pain may connote various experiences for the individual, including many unpleasant emotional states.

The final dimension of pain consists of the pain behaviors displayed by the patient in response to the unpleasant experience. Here the person conveys to others how much distress he or she is experiencing. These behaviors can be verbal ("Wow, this really hurts!"), paraverbal (moaning), or nonverbal (guarding of an affected limb, splinting, wearing a neck brace, taking medication, reclining).

The neurophysiologic substrates of the pain experience are discussed in this chapter. The first part of the chapter comprises a discussion of the sensory pathways and mechanisms. The second portion focuses on distinctions between acute and chronic pain.

■ SENSORY PATHWAYS

Pain-Relaying Pathways and Mechanisms

In their most basic aspects, the pain relay pathways involve three sets of neurons. First-order neurons relay noxious information from the periphery or viscera to the spinal cord. Second-order neurons relay sensory information from the spinal cord to the thalamus. Third-order neurons arising from the thalamus send information to higher brain regions where complex processing of the pain experience occurs.

First-Order Neurons

The detection of pain requires that information regarding injury, trauma, and noxious stimulation be detected by a *transducer*. Transducers serve the purpose of taking information (e.g., changes in temperature, chemical irritation, pressure) from some location on the body surface, muscles, or internal organs and converting it into

neurochemical information that is interpretable by the brain. The transducers for pain include the free nerve endings of the first-order neurons in the pain pathway (i.e., the A-δ and C neurons). These neurons have long dendrites with fine terminal arborizations present in the skin, muscle, connective tissue, joints, bone, and internal organs. When stimulated, action potentials extend from the dendrites to the cell body (in the dorsal root ganglion) and from the axon to the spinal cord.

Information relayed about other, nonnoxious, sensory modalities (e.g., pressure, touch, proprioception) are detected by other types of sensory transducers. These include pacinian corpuscles, Meissner's corpuscles, and other transducers. When sufficiently stimulated, these receptors in turn pass information along another set of first-order neurons, the A-β neurons.

The neurons differ in their diameter, myelination, and therefore, electrical conduction rates (Table 2–2). Miscalculating the intended alignment of a hammer to the intended target (i.e., the head of the nail), one can quickly appreciate the pain relay process once the swift blow of the hammer makes inadvertent contact with the fingers of the hand holding the nail in place. First, A-β fibers, responding to low-threshold touch receptors, relay information about the blunt object making contact with the hand. Simultaneously (when the stimulus is disconcertingly high, as in this example), high-threshold mechanoreceptors and heat receptors are activated. This information is conducted quickly and robustly, via A-δ fibers, immediately after the injury. A-δ fiber information is well localized, sharp, pricking, and pulsating, but very short lived. Shortly thereafter, C fibers relay information from the injured hand, information that is less definitive or localized than that of the A-δ fibers (Besson and Chaouch 1987). These C fibers mediate the slowly emerging, more persistent, dull, aching, and burning pain that is experienced. All three types of fibers relay information to the dorsal horn of the spinal cord, where they synapse directly, or indirectly through interneurons, on the second-order neurons involved in the nociceptive pathway (Byers and Bonica 2001).

14

TABLE 2–2.	**Sensory neural fiber types**		
	A-β	**A-δ**	**C**
Diameter	Large (5–15 μm)	Intermediate (1–4 μm)	Thin (0.5–1.5 μm)
Myelination	Yes	Yes	No
Conduction rate	Fast (30–70 m/s)	Fast (12–30 m/s)	Slow (0.5–2.0 m/s)
Sensory information	Cutaneous touch and pressure	Well localized Sharp pain	Poorly localized Dull, aching pain

Viscera are also supplied by C fibers and A-δ fibers. These are activated by inflammatory processes, ischemia, disease, rapid distention, and contraction. These events trigger free nerve endings to transduce the noxious information into electrical information that is eventually transmitted to the dorsal horn.

Pain from the face is relayed to the CNS through the fifth cranial (i.e., the trigeminal) nerve. Noxious information from the face is relayed via dendrites of one of the three branches of the trigeminal nerve, passes through to the trigeminal ganglion (containing the cell bodies of the trigeminal nerves), and passes to the second-order neurons in the pons and medulla. In a pattern that parallels that of spinal cord pathways, information is ultimately relayed to the thalamus and higher brain structures (Dubner and Bennett 1983). The face and mouth have a high density of pain transducers and pain fibers, thus rendering them exquisitely sensitive to stimulation. Similarly, the representation of the face and mouth in the somatosensory cortex of the brain is extensive, suggesting that processing and encoding of sensory information from the face and mouth is quite elaborate.

Dorsal Horn Anatomy

The gray matter of the spinal cord is classified by histological characteristics into 10 layers or laminae (referred to as *Rexed layers*). The dorsal horn contains six of these. Those layers that are essential

in the pain processing pathways include laminae I, II, and V, primarily where A-δ and C fibers terminate (Terman and Bonica 2001). Cells within the dorsal horn include those that are nociceptive specific (i.e., respond to noxious stimulation). Other cells respond only to innocuous stimuli, whereas others, referred to as *wide dynamic range* (WDR) cells, respond to noxious and innocuous stimuli but discharge at a higher frequency to noxious stimuli.

The *substantia gelatinosa*, contained within lamina II, has a significant role in modulating pain. This substance involves small interneurons that serve as control switches or gates through which sensory information from the periphery is either enhanced or depressed. Certain of these interneurons (i.e., islet cells) are inhibitory, whereas others (i.e., stalked cells) are excitatory. The substantia gelatinosa receives extensive serotonergic and noradrenergic input from nerve fibers emanating from higher brain centers, which likewise influences the gating process.

When one experiences pain from a joint, massage of the overlying skin may reduce some of that discomfort. This phenomenon, referred to as counterirritation, is attributed to the gating mechanism of the substantia gelatinosa. Massaging, thereby stimulating the tactile receptors of the skin, activates A-β fibers. These, in turn, activate interneurons within the substantia gelatinosa that serve to inhibit pain-mediating pathways (Melzack and Wall 1965; Wall 1980). Counterirritation has been offered as an explanation to account for why certain therapeutic modalities can be effective in mitigating pain—for example, use of liniment or transcutaneous electrical nerve stimulation (TENS) units.

Lamina V contains WDR cells with large receptive fields (i.e., they receive extensive inputs from multiple sources). For example, A-δ and C fibers arising from visceral structures enter lamina V. The WDR cells receiving the neural input from visceral organs simultaneously receive input from other sites. This process is the basis for referred pain (i.e., the interpretation of unpleasant sensory input arising from viscera as emanating from peripheral sites) (Pomeranz et al. 1968). Thus, hypoxic injury to the heart is perceived as pain in the left arm, because the afferents from the heart synapse on those

lamina V cells of the left lower cervical and upper thoracic segments. The brain interprets the stimulation of those cells as pain originating in the left upper chest and arm.

Second-Order Neurons: The Spinothalamic Tract

The axons arising from neurons making up the spinothalamic tract emanate from the entire gray matter of the spinal cord. Most of these fibers cross to the other side of the spinal cord through the ventral commissure in the midline and ascend in the anterolateral aspect of the white matter (myelinated) portion of the spinal column. These fibers ascend without interruption through the spinal column and brain stem and terminate in the contralateral thalamus (Besson and Chaouch 1987; Dennis and Melzack 1977). However, a small number of fibers project to the ipsilateral thalamus.

The pain relay pathways become divergent (Figure 2–1). There are two pathways within the spinothalamic system: the neospinothalamic and the paleospinothalamic pathways. The latter is considered to be a phylogentically older pathway.

Third-Order Neurons: The Thalamus and Beyond

The thalamus is the primary relay station for sensory information from the spinal cord to the cortex (Chudler and Bonica 2001; Rome and Rome 2000). The second-order neurons from the neospinothalmic tract terminate in the lateral aspect of the ventral posterior nucleus (VPN). Third-order neurons from the VPN relay information to the somatosensory cortex (parietal lobe). Through this pathway, discriminative aspects of pain, its localization, and coordinated motor responses to the pain are possible (Rome and Rome 2000).

Simultaneously, from the paleospinothalamic pathway, information is relayed through a parallel pathway to the reticular formation, medial thalamus, hypothalamus, and prefrontal cortex (Giesler et al. 1994). The nociceptive system thereby influences affect, attention, cognition, and memory that relate to painful sensory information (Chudler and Bonica 2001). A stress reaction develops to

17

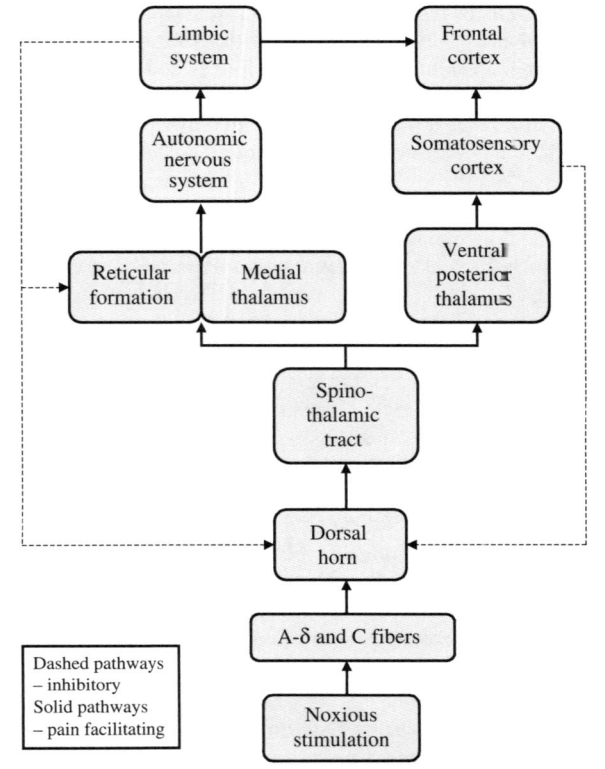

FIGURE 2–1. **The affective-motivational pathway** *(left)* **and the sensory-discriminative pathway** *(right)*.

noxious sensation, involving the hypothalamic-pituitary axis and autonomic nervous system (Giesler et al. 1994). Ultimately, this information is relayed to both cortices. As a result, the affective quality and coloring of the pain experience are possible. In addition, affective influences mediated by limbic involvement are likely to

modulate pain. Thus, one's surprise (*I can't believe I hit my hand with the hammer!*), alarm (*I didn't see that coming!*), anger (*That was so stupid!*—along with use of expletives), and fear (*My hand is damaged for good!*) are likely to shape the experience of pain. Mood states (e.g., a predisposition to anxiety or depression) can shape the cognitive strategies one employs to deal with the pain, one's sense of efficacy in dealing with the injury, and one's expectations for the future. The relay of pain information to the bilateral cortices adds a cognitive component to the pain experience. Thus, the mutual influences of mood, cognition, expectation, and pain are mediated.

The frontal cortex mediates the cognitive processes underlying pain. These involve the identification and evaluation of, and decision making pertaining to, the noxious sensory information input from the periphery. Hence, immediate short-term problem solving can be undertaken (e.g., ignoring the hammering, preferring instead to tend to the injured hand). Other cognitive processes—such as one's expectations, along with the attributions, beliefs, and meanings ascribed to the painful experience—are likewise derived from cortical processes and influence both the pain experience and the decision making around the pain. In addition, memory of the painful experience is established and encoded for further referral and to guide subsequent behaviors—for example, how (and whether) one tries carpentry again.

The Autonomic Nervous System's Role in Pain

The autonomic nervous system plays a significant role in pain. Signals of threat and danger are relayed to the hypothalamus. From there, specifically the posterior portion, information is relayed to the spinal cord (i.e., the thoracic and lumbar regions) by sympathetic neural pathways (McMahon 1991). Ultimately, fibers from the thoracolumbar regions innervate a number of end organs producing activation (i.e., a state of heightened arousal). Those end organ activities that are necessary for fight-or-flight responses are promoted, whereas those that are not are suppressed. Thus, the in-

formation signaling threat or danger results in elevated heart rate and blood pressure, increased oxygen use, sweating, dilation of pupils, and increased glycogen utilization within muscles. Other organ functions are inhibited (e.g., peristalsis).

The effects of sympathetic nervous system activity are relatively brief in duration because of the rapid release and degradation of norepinephrine and acetylcholine released in the mediation of the fight-or-flight response. More sustained reactions to stressors or threat are mediated by neuroendocrine effects, a product of adrenal medulla activation. Sympathetic nervous system activation of the adrenal gland results in release of norepinephrine and epinephrine, mimicking sympathetic activity.

Pain-Modulating Processes Within the Central Nervous System

Several factors influence pain intensity apart from stimulus intensity, including pain-reducing and pain-augmenting processes. These are discussed briefly in the following sections.

Pain-Reducing Pathways

Several structures serve to diminish the pain sensory information coming into the CNS. Intuitively, pain-modulating mechanisms prevent one from being overcome by unbridled pain, thereby allowing the organism an opportunity to escape and tend to the injury. The four regions in the CNS that can function to reduce pain sensation and control pain awareness include 1) the cortex and limbic structures, 2) the midbrain (the periaqueductal gray area [PAG], 3) the rostroventral medulla (RVM), and 4) the spinal dorsal horn (Besson and Chaouch 1987; Terman and Bonica 2001). The gating mechanism of the substantia gelatinosa within the dorsal horn is described earlier in this chapter. The cortex and reticular formation can influence attention, arousal, expectations of pain, and psychological factors that can, in turn, influence pain experiences. The specific mechanisms by which these structures influence pain have yet to be clarified.

The PAG is a midbrain structure with an abundance of opiate receptors. Neural connections extend from the PAG to neighboring serotonergic structures (e.g., the RVM) and noradrenergic structures (e.g., the dorsolateral pons). The pain-modulating influences of the PAG are conducted largely, if not exclusively, through the RVM. The RVM in turn projects onto the cells of the dorsal horn in laminae I, II, and V (Terman and Bonica 2001). If morphine is injected into the PAG, RVM, or amygdala, analgesia results. In μ opiate receptor–deficient mice, morphine injection into the PAG, RVM, and amygdala is completely ineffective in mitigating pain. The μ receptor, therefore, is responsible for the supraspinal analgesia produced by opiates, mediated through the PAG and RVM.

Pain-Augmenting Mechanisms and the Emergence of Chronic Pain

When acute pain is inadequately treated, there is an increased risk of emergence of chronic pain. Several mechanisms are postulated to play a role in the development of chronic and enduring pain (Table 2–3).

Ongoing abnormalities in peripheral tissues, with resultant inflammation, can result in activation of nociceptive pathways, rendering pain chronic. In such cases, treatment is best directed at the inflammatory mechanisms (e.g., aspirin or nonsteroidal anti-inflammatory agents). Peripheral nerves may become dysfunctional due to injury or disease (e.g., diabetes, infection, or toxin exposure). Damaged neurons may fire spontaneously. Nociceptive fibers firing in this way are perceived in the CNS as signaling pain; yet, in the peripheral tissues there may be no current injury. In such cases, antidepressants and anticonvulsants might be the most helpful treatment.

Trauma and injury can produce reflex motor activity in the vicinity of the injury, producing spasm. This process may initially serve a protective function in acute pain states, but in chronic pain states it can lead to aggravated muscle tension that exacerbates painful states (Zimmerman 1979).

21

TABLE 2–3.	**Causes of chronic pain**

Ongoing activation of pain pathways from the periphery can cause pain to become chronic

Peripheral nerves may be dysfunctional

Motor reflexes may potentiate pain

Dorsal horn can become sensitized

Sympathetic nervous system can become a major contributor to ongoing pain

Cortical and limbic activity can contribute to pain

The dorsal horn can become sensitized by a number of mechanisms that can potentiate chronic pain. Changes that occur within the dorsal horn may account for the maintenance of pain sensation that loses its relevance in its ability to signal danger. This sensitization appears to be related to changes mediated by CNS neurotransmitters, especially the excitatory neurotransmitter glutamate. With repeated stimulation (e.g., in poorly treated acute pain or in reinjury), glutamate activity can expand to include other receptors, including N-methyl-D-aspartate (NMDA) receptors. With expansion of glutamate activity, a series of intracellular processes occurs that results in the heightened activation of dorsal horn cells, referred to as *wind up*. Such processes become difficult to interrupt from a therapeutic standpoint; however, NMDA receptor blockers (e.g., ketamine) can be helpful.

Ongoing NMDA activation can result in cell death. Death of neurons leaves areas of deafferentation in the spinal cord pathways. As a result, nearby sensory neurons often sprout collaterals into the deafferentated area to replace the synaptic connections lost after cell death. This replacement results in an innervation of pain pathways corresponding to the injured areas stimulated or activated by nearby undamaged areas.

The sympathetic nervous system can become a major contributor to ongoing pain (Zimmerman 1979). Trauma and injury trigger a sympathetic response that can effectively alter the neurochemical

22

milieu of nociceptors in the periphery, along with causing changes in the microcirculation. This situation can alter the sensitivity of peripheral pain receptors, thereby augmenting pain sensitivity.

Pain can be maintained—despite lack of injury or even after effective healing—by the actions of the sympathetic nervous system. In such cases, protracted painful conditions can arise, such as reflex sympathetic dystrophy and complex regional pain disorder. Some of these disorders can be alleviated by blockade of sympathetic activity (i.e., sympatholysis); however, not all respond to sympatholytic techniques. Treatment for such disorders can include nerve blocks, sympathetic nerve blocks, and psychotropic medications (e.g., antidepressants and anticonvulsants).

Commensurate alterations in the thalamus and somatosensory cortex can occur after peripheral nerve injury. Thus, even after amputation, the area of the somatosensory cortex corresponding to the amputated limb increases. Other cortical and limbic events can contribute to pain. The experience of pain can be shaped and influenced by the diffuse interconnections of the pain pathways with limbic and cortical pathways. In such cases, psychotropic medications, psychotherapy, and adjunctive therapeutic approaches such as relaxation training may be helpful modes of treatment.

Neurochemicals in Pain Processing

Pain-augmenting neurotransmitters. In the periphery, tissue injury results in the activation of a number of cellular processes that release algogenic substances—chemical compounds that can activate free nerve endings for pain transmission (Snyder 1980). These substances include acetylcholine, bradykinin, histamine, potassium ion, and serotonin (Levine et al. 1993). They are produced and released from disease processes or cellular damage.

Prostaglandins (of the E series) are likewise produced from arachidonic acid released from damaged cellular membranes. These agents can activate nociceptors and potentiate pain transmission.

Substance P is a major neurotransmitter of C fibers. Although direct application of substance P to peripheral nerves does not trig-

ger firing, the presence of substance P can activate central neurons mediating the pain pathway and processing. Unlike most neurotransmitters, substance P is slowly degraded in the dorsal horn and thus may account for the sustained aching pain associated with C-fiber activation. Substance P may also play a role in the regulation of affect; inhibitors of substance P are being invoked in the treatment of depression and anxiety (Mantyh 2002).

Glutamate is an excitatory neurotransmitter involved in the mediation of pain. It may be responsible for activation of cellular processes that promote chronic pain.

Inhibitory neurotransmitters (pain-modulating). The inhibitory neurotransmitters (neurotransmitters that modulate pain) include endogenous opiates, serotonin, norepinephrine, and neurotensin (Snyder 1980).

Endogenous opiates. The endogenous opiates consist of β-endorphins, enkephalins, and dynorphin (Sewell and Lee 1980). These are found abundantly distributed throughout the CNS, thereby modulating pain transmission. Enkephalin is an endogenous opiate found in the interneurons of the substantia gelatinosa, mediating the effects of inhibitory interneurons within the dorsal horn. Binding to opioid receptors, enkephalin can inhibit the release of substance P from nociceptors. In fact, intraspinal application of opiates (e.g., morphine) is thought to influence the enkephalin receptors, thereby mitigating pain transmission from the spinal cord. Enkephalin and dynorphin are extensively distributed throughout the CNS. Cells producing β-endorphin arise from the hypothalamus and are thought to exert their influence within the limbic system and midbrain.

Nonopiate endogenous inhibitory neurotransmitters. *Serotonin (5-HT).* Serotonin (5-HT) is contained in the raphe nuclei in the medulla and pons. 5-HT is released by neurons projecting onto neurons in the dorsal horn laminae. Fibers from the raphe nuclei also extend to the diencephalon and forebrain. The activity of 5-HT

24

appears to be inhibitory. Depletion of serotonin diminishes the analgesic effects of systemically applied opiates in the CNS.

Norepinephrine. Norepinephrine is contained in the locus coeruleus, which sends extensive projections throughout the CNS. In addition, there are descending norepinephrine-containing projections within the spinal dorsal horn. Norepinephrine, like 5-HT, appears to be essential for opiate-induced analgesia. Blockade of norepinephrine (e.g., by phentolamine) reduces the effectiveness of systemically applied opiates.

Neurotensin. Neurotensin is another potent neurotransmitter involved in descending inhibition of spinal neurons. Some cells of the PAG contain neurotensin, and these in turn project onto raphe nuclei in the medulla and pontine nuclei. The action of neurotensin may produce analgesia.

Opiate Receptors and Descending Inhibition of Pain Pathways

There are four classes of opiate receptors recognized to date (Terenius 1985). The mu (μ) receptor is responsible for supraspinal analgesia. It also produces euphoria from opiate use and is responsible for physical dependence. Physical effects of opiates (e.g., hypotension, decreased respirations, hypothermia, pruritus, and decreased gastrointestinal [GI] motility) are all attributed to μ receptor activation from opiate use.

Analgesia on a spinal level is a result of the opiate activation of the kappa (κ) receptor. Activation results in pupil constriction and sedation. Delta (δ) receptors also produce analgesia; these receptors are activated by endogenous opiates. The role of the sigma (σ) receptor is more controversial. It produces no analgesia but is responsible for the dysphoria, and possibly hallucinations, associated with opiate use. Because of these disparate effects, as compared with other opiate receptors, there is controversy about whether the sigma receptor is actually an opiate receptor.

The μ receptor produces more analgesia than the other types of receptors. It is also responsible for changes in respiratory activity, GI motility, and sphincter tone produced by opiates. The μ receptor is abundantly present in the dorsal horn, medulla, and the PAG. It is also responsible at the peripheral nerve endings. Its abundance in the myenteric plexus is likely responsible for the effects of the opiates on GI motility and sphincter tone.

■ ACUTE VERSUS CHRONIC PAIN

The sensation of pain serves an adaptive function. Specifically, nociceptive pathways serve to alarm the organism that some damage or injury has been sustained, that efforts may need to be directed at tending to the injury and avoiding further injury. Consider a disorder such as Hansen disease, also known as leprosy, which is characterized by dysfunction in pain-mediating pathways. Persons infected with *Mycobacterium leprae,* the agent that causes the disease, have deficits in pain perception. On the surface, this seems quite desirable; however, over the course of the illness, these patients sustain marked deficits in self-care and are exposed to hazards brought on by physical injury and infection. Death can result from the lack of appropriate awareness of the bodily warning mechanisms that would otherwise motivate treatment.

Problems arise when pain takes on a life of its own. Certainly, in medical conditions in which there is ongoing tissue damage—arthritis, for example—pain may likewise be ongoing. One might question the utility of such pain, because one certainly is aware of the trauma that warrants medical attention. On the other hand, and perhaps more troubling, are situations in which pain persists despite healing (e.g., post-herpetic neuralgia) or situations in which pathologic processes emerge within the CNS or the peripheral nervous system (or both) to produce aberrant activity that is interpreted and experienced as pain—as in Dejerine-Roussy syndrome (a pain syndrome related to thalamic stroke).

26

Classifications of Acute and Chronic Pain

Pain is classified in several ways, including the familiar categories *acute* and *chronic*. For example, it can be classified based on its temporal aspects, its etiology and its associated features from differing sources, and its functional significance (see Table 2–4). Acute pain has been customarily defined as pain that is less than 6 months in duration. Chronic pain is defined as pain persisting beyond 6 months (Crue 1983). There are always problems with arbitrary definitions such as these. For example, it becomes difficult to classify some painful conditions (e.g., migraine or osteoarthritis) based on temporal aspects. Migraine is a recurrent painful disorder that can persist for years, but the specific episodes of pain are relatively short-lived. Osteoarthritis, on the other hand, is a chronic, progressive medical condition that is accompanied by a mixture of acute and chronic pain components. Acute pain can be precipitated by new injury, whereas chronic pain features can arise from prior injuries and sensitization of peripheral nervous system involvement.

Generally, acute pain is considered to be pain that serves self-protective functions. The value of the alarm functions of pain brought on by the inadvertent slamming of one's thumb with a hammer is obvious. Such pain, it is hoped, is discrete and mobilizes the person to take measures to minimize pain and prevent further injury. Conversely, chronic pain is considered to have lost such meaningful aspects. One is hard pressed to arrive at any adaptive function gleaned from chronic neuropathic pains or fibromyalgia.

Acute pain arises from tissue injury, trauma, or inflammation. Chronic pain extends beyond the period of healing and can be brought on by pathophysiologic processes within the nervous system. Some pain states can be mediated by the ongoing barrage of peripheral pain sensors (i.e., nociceptors). The pathologic firing of peripheral or CNS pathways that mediate pain can also trigger chronic pain.

Another distinction between acute and chronic pain states is based on the presence of psychological and psychiatric conditions

27

TABLE 2–4.	Features distinguishing acute and chronic pain	
	Acute pain	**Chronic pain**
Duration	< 6 months	> 6 months
Cause	Tissue damage, injury, inflammation	Pathophysiologic processes in the peripheral or CNS pathways
		Psychogenic factors
Biological utility	Yes	No
Psychological factors contributing	No	Yes

Note. CNS = central nervous system.

that accompany or aggravate the pain. The pain brought on by fracture or another traumatic injury is not necessarily accompanied by the personality changes and psychiatric disturbances that can accompany chronic pain states. Psychological sequelae of acute pain are likely to be discreet and obvious.

The long duration and pervasive effects of chronic pain states likely have an impact on a person's functioning. Naturally, pain can have profound effects on social, interpersonal, and emotional functioning. By virtue of the long-term course, there may be changes in mood, thought patterns, perceptions, and personality that accompany the pain. One's life experiences and ability to adapt to ongoing demands and stress are affected. Therefore, it is incomprehensible to address chronic pain without considering psychological and social functioning.

Categories of Chronic Pain

Chronic pain has been categorized as *nociceptive*, *neuropathic*, or *psychogenic* (Table 2–5). These classifications differ with respect to their characteristics and responsiveness to varying types of treatment interventions (Leo and Singh 2002; Portenoy 1989). For example, nociceptive pain responds to anti-inflammatory agents and

28

TABLE 2–5.	**Categories of chronic pain**

Nociceptive: somatic

Source	Damage to tissue, soft tissue, or bone; inflammation; trauma
Localization	Well localized
Features	Aching, sharp
Examples	Pain of arthritis, cancer
Effective medication	Aspirin, NSAIDs, COX-2 inhibitors, opiates

Nociceptive: visceral

Source	Injury or damage to visceral structures, organs
Localization	Referred pain, fairly well localized
Features	Aching, sharp
Examples	Pain of angina, kidney stones, appendicitis
Effective medication	Opiates, other analgesics

Neuropathic

Source	Damage to nerve tissue, either peripheral or CNS
Localization	Nerve distributions, poorly localized with CNS sources
Features	Paresthetic, numb, burning, pins-and-needles
Examples	Postherpetic neuralgia, trigeminal neuralgia
Effective medication	Antidepressants, anticonvulsants

Psychogenic

Source	No clear underlying cause; psychological distress
Localization	Poorly localized
Features	Vague, sweeping
Examples	Somatization disorder
Effective medication	Psychotropic medications, psychotherapy

Note. CNS = central nervous system; COX-2 = cyclooxygenase-2; NSAIDs = nonsteroidal anti-inflammatory drugs.

Source. Reprinted by permission of *Annals of Long-Term Care: Clinical Care and Aging*, 10(2):37–45, 2002, p. 38; Leo RJ, Singh A: "Pain Management in the Elderly: Use of Psychopharmacologic Agents."

opiate analgesics, whereas neuropathic pains respond to antidepressants, anticonvulsants, and possibly neuroleptics.

"Patienthood" as a Psychosocial State: The Patient With Simple Versus Chronic Pain

An array of factors can become central to the life experiences of the patient with chronic pain (Table 2–6). As a result of these factors, a number of emotional and psychological sequelae are associated with the chronic pain state. Physicians have long noted a puzzling discrepancy between physical disease status and progression and the patient's subjective experiences (Weisberg and Clavel 1999). Some patients with severe disease present few complaints and report less disability and emotional distress. Yet some others with little documented disease report severe symptoms and experience marked distress and disability.

Despite the pervasiveness of chronic pain, most individuals with chronic pain can nonetheless maintain basic functioning, work, and interests. They are able to work with their clinicians and other care providers and can respond with some relief to medications or interventions. At times, psychotherapeutic interventions may be required to address mood disturbances, stress, and coping. This cluster of patients is sometimes referred to as having *simple* chronic pain. A small proportion of patients with chronic pain are entirely debilitated by the pain and are sometimes referred to as having *complex* chronic pain (see Table 2–7 for a comparison of the two categories). In this subset, patients have a notable preoccupation with pain. For these persons, life revolves around the pain. Activities are forestalled, and work is not pursued. The patients may be thrust into positions of marked dependency on others. Several, perhaps all, aspects of their lives are made contingent on pain experiences or are put off because the patients fear their pain might get worse (Sternbach 1974). For such persons, being a patient is a primary psychosocial state. Life experiences become centered on doctors' visits. If these visits are unsatisfying, patients may develop a history of "doctor shopping." They may seek invasive and diagnostic procedures to confirm the

30

TABLE 2–6.	Common problems encountered by patients with chronic pain
Medical	Problems with access to appropriate care
	Difficulties in establishing a working relationship with practitioner skilled in pain management
Psychological	Comorbid mood disturbances
Physical	The pain itself
	Deconditioning resulting from inactivity
	Medical complications from use of multiple medications
Vocational	Job loss
	Restrictions from usual types of job activities
Financial	Financial problems arising from job loss, loss of medical coverage, or the cost of medical care
Legal	Litigation related to injuries, workers' compensation, or disability issues
Family	Pain's interference with customary role of the patient, causing others within the family to adopt new roles
	Limited reserves of energy and time left for other family members' needs (e.g., children's needs, their activities, their school work, etc.) because so much is taken up with pain and the pain patient
Sociocultural	Pain's interference with one's ability to engage in customary activities and maintain social ties, resulting in significant losses in the patient's social support network

existence of the pain or alleviate their distress. Such patients may display increasing preoccupation with medication use and, possibly, abuse. Numerous psychological factors beset the patient with complex pain, many of which can exacerbate and maintain pain (Weisberg and Clavel 1999).

Patients with simple chronic pain may do well with a single pain specialist, with referral as needed to services provided by practitioners in other specialties (e.g., psychiatrists, therapists). Patients

31

TABLE 2–7.	Simple versus complex chronic pain
Simple pain	**Complex pain**
Pain is clearly defined	Multiple pain complaints are present
Patient is easily enlisted into treatment	Difficulty can be encountered enlisting patient into treatment
Patient's support systems are stable	Patient has unstable social systems
Comorbid psychological factors are easily defined	Severe complicating psychological factors can be present
Patient's pain shows some response to medications and treatment	Patient's pain shows poor response to medications and treatment
Patient may require short-term psychotherapy or psychological interventions	Patient may require multidisciplinary treatment approaches, including psychiatric treatment
Litigation is not central to the patient's presentation	Litigation is apt to be central to the patient's presentation

with complex pain, on the other hand, can overwhelm a single practitioner. Clearly, such patients need a multidisciplinary approach to their pain, involving the coordinated joint efforts of practitioners in medical, surgical, physical, neurologic, or psychiatric services.

Multi-Axial Pain Classification

The International Association for the Study of Pain has advocated a multi-axial classification of chronic pain, comparable to that used in psychiatric diagnosis (International Association for the Study of Pain, Subcommittee on Taxonomy, 1986). The intention behind the classification system is to standardize diagnosis and facilitate research endeavors in pain treatment. Axis I refers to the body region that is the source of pain (e.g., lower back); Axis II refers to the systemic source whose abnormal functioning produces

pain (e.g., neurologic system); Axis III characterizes the pattern of the pain and its temporal characteristics (e.g., 6 months of continuous pain that radiates to the lower extremity); Axis IV refers to the patient's rating of pain intensity and pain duration (e.g., severe); and Axis V refers to the etiology (e.g., intervertebral disk rupture). This classification approach may be useful if it is systematized and employed uniformly. However, the multi-axial system has not yet been required by insurers nor universally accepted in clinical circles.

■ REFERENCES

Besson JM, Chaouch A: Peripheral and spinal mechanisms of nociception. Physiol Rev 67:67–186, 1987

Byers MR, Bonica JJ: Peripheral pain mechanisms and nociceptor plasticity, in Bonica's Management of Pain, 3rd Edition. Edited by Loeser JD, Butler SH, Chapman CR, et al. Philadelphia, PA, Lippincott Williams & Wilkins, 2001, pp 26–72

Chudler EH, Bonica JJ: Supraspinal mechanisms of pain and nociception, in Bonica's Management of Pain, 3rd edition. Edited by Loeser JD, Butler SH, Chapman CR, et al. Philadelphia, PA, Lippincott Williams & Wilkins, 2001, pp 153–179

Crue BL: The neurophysiology and taxonomy of pain, in Management of Patients with Chronic Pain. Edited by Brena SF, Chapman SL. New York, Spectrum, 1983, pp 21–31

Dennis SG, Melzack R: Pain-signaling systems in the dorsal and ventral spinal cord. Pain 4:97–132, 1977

Dubner R, Bennett GJ: Spinal and trigeminal mechanisms of nociception. Annu Rev Neurosci 6:381–418, 1983

Giesler GJ, Katter JT, Dado RJ: Direct spinal pathways to the limbic system for nociceptive information. Trends Neurosci 17:244–250, 1994

International Association for the Study of Pain, Subcommittee on Taxonomy. Classification of chronic pain: descriptions of chronic pain syndromes and definitions of pain terms. Pain Suppl 3:S1–12, 1986

Leo RJ, Singh A: Pain management in the elderly: use of psychopharmacologic agents. Annals of Long-Term Care: Clinical Care and Aging 10:37–45, 2002

Levine JD, Fields HL, Basbaum AI: Peptides and the primary afferent nociceptor. J Neurosci 13:2273–2286, 1993

Loeser JD: Concepts of pain, in Chronic Low Back Pain. Edited by Stanton-Hicks M, Boas R. New York, Raven, 1982, pp 145–148

Mantyh PW: Neurobiology of substance P and the NK_1 receptor. J Clin Psychiatry 63(suppl 11):6–10, 2002

McMahon SB: Mechanisms of sympathetic pain. Br Med Bull 47:584–600, 1991

Melzack R, Wall PD: Pain mechanisms: a new theory. Science 150:971–979, 1965

Pomeranz B, Wall PD, Weber WV: Cord cells responding to fine myelinated afferents from viscera, muscle and skin. J Physiol 199:511–532, 1968

Portenoy RK: Mechanisms of clinical pain: observations and speculations. Neurol Clin 7:205–230, 1989

Rome H, Rome J: Limbically augmented pain syndrome (LAPS): kindling, corticolimbic sensitization, and the convergence of affective and sensory symptoms in chronic pain disorders. Pain Medicine 1:7–23, 2000

Sewell RDE, Lee RL: Opiate receptors, endorphins and drug therapy. Postgrad Med J 56:25–30, 1980

Snyder SH: Brain peptides as neurotransmitters. Science 209:976–983, 1980

Sternbach RA: Pain Patients: Traits and Treatment. New York, Academic Press, 1974

Terenius L: Families of opioid peptides and classes of opioid receptors, in Advances in Pain Research and Therapy, Vol 9. Edited by Fields HL, Dubner R, Cervero F. New York, Raven, 1985, pp 463–477

Terman GW, Bonica JJ: Spinal mechanisms and their modulation, in Bonica's Management of Pain, 3rd Edition. Edited by Loeser JD, Butler SH, Chapman CR, et al. Philadelphia, PA, Lippincott Williams & Wilkins, 2001, pp 73–152

Wall PD: The role of the substantia gelatinosa as a gate control. Res Publ Assoc Res Nerv Ment Dis 58:205, 1980

Weisberg MB, Clavel AL Jr: Why is chronic pain so difficult to treat? Psychological considerations from simple to complex care. Postgrad Med 106:141–142, 145–148, 157–160, 163–164, 1999

Zimmerman M: Peripheral and central nervous mechanisms of nociception, pain and pain therapy: facts and hypotheses, in Advances in Pain Research and Therapy. Edited by Bonica JJ, Liebeskind JC, Albe-Fessard DG. New York, Raven, 1979, pp 3–32

35

3

EVALUATION OF
THE PAIN PATIENT

Comprehensive assessment of the pain patient involves judicious use of history, physical examination, pain assessments, diagnostic testing, and psychological testing. This chapter focuses on the elements of comprehensive history gathering. Given that pain is a subjective experience, a number of measurement indices have been employed as part of the assessment, allowing for grading the quantity, extent, or severity of the pain. The elements of the history are the focus of the first portion of this chapter, and pain assessments are discussed in the second portion.

The neural processing of pain is quite complex, involving more than just sensory processes. In fact, pain processing involves neurologic substrates common to emotion and cognition (i.e., limbic and cortical systems). The experience of pain and the appreciation of, and reactions to, pain information involve cognitive and emotional factors. The behaviors displayed by the pain patient can likewise have an impact on social and adaptive functioning. It follows, then, that pain assessment can be quite complex, considering somatic and psychological factors (cognitive, emotional, and motivational), as well as adaptive and social functioning (Figure 3–1).

■ CONDUCTING AN INTERVIEW

The patient should be encouraged to speak freely during the course of verbal evaluation. Open-ended lines of inquiry should be

36

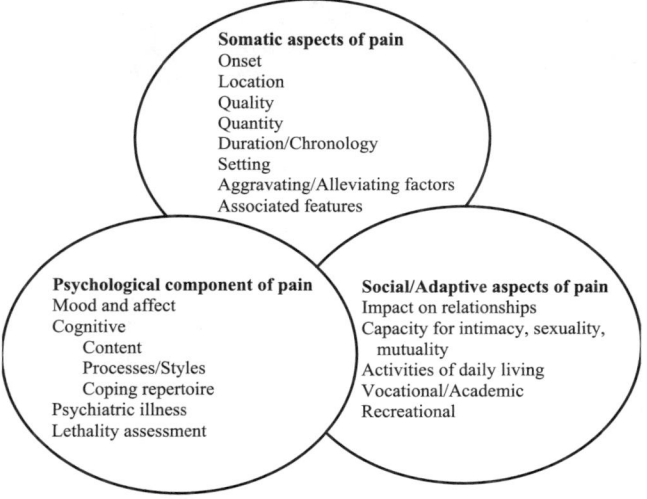

FIGURE 3–1. **Components of the pain history.**

employed, so as to prompt the patient to elaborate (e.g., "Tell me more about the pain," or "How has the pain affected your lifestyle?"). Very specific lines of inquiry (e.g., "Is the pain aggravated by movement?") often restrict the free elaboration of the patient, can prematurely limit the patient's willingness to provide information, and can confine the patient's reporting of history to the examiner's persuasion and biases. Open-ended lines of inquiry communicate that the patient is listened to, whereas running through a litany of questions can suggest that the patient's impressions and experiences of pain are of less importance.

Occasional paraphrased recapitulation of the patient's report allows the interviewer to clarify what was conveyed. If aspects of the history are missing, the practitioner can quickly insert clarifying inquiries—for example, "Let me see if I got this right. You indicated that you have been experiencing dull, aching pain in your

lower back. It seems to radiate down your right leg, and it makes you feel unsteady when you walk. Is that right?" If the paraphrasing is confirmed, the practitioner might consider redirecting and clarifying questions—"I am still unclear about something. What seems to bring on the pain?" With those patients who have difficulty articulating characteristics of the pain, encouraging the use of metaphor could facilitate capturing the features of the pain experience (Fishman and Loscalzo 1987).

Patients appear for psychiatric evaluation with varying agendas. For example, a patient might seek out psychiatric assessment at the recommendation of a clinician who is concerned about the patient's adherence to treatment or about psychological issues that might be contributing to or exacerbating pain. On the other hand, the patient might have agendas that are quite different from those of the clinician (e.g., the impact of pain on relationships, employment, and quality of life). The open-ended line of inquiry allows for exposure and examination of the more covert aspects of the patient's reasons for seeking evaluation or treatment. Ascertaining the patient's agenda can be helpful in guiding the interview and arriving at a reasonable treatment plan that reflects the patient's needs. An example: a patient sought help on the recommendation of her physician, who presumed that depression was complicating her chronic back pain. During the evaluation, it became apparent that she had concerns about marital issues arising from role modifications within the home as a result of her pain (e.g., "My husband doesn't understand my pain."). To mitigate both the depression and the back pain, it seemed that more direct attention to facilitating effective patterns of communication, problem solving, and coping within the marriage would be required.

■ OBTAINING THE PAIN HISTORY

Somatic Component

Essential to the diagnosis of pain disorders is information about the somatic components of the pain: its duration, course, intensity, and precipitating and mitigating factors. The more detailed this history,

38

TABLE 3–1. **Obtaining a pain history**

Onset: When did the pain begin?

Location: Where is the pain located? Does it radiate? If so, where? What factors influence the radiation?

Quality: What is the pain like?

Quantity: How intense is the pain?

Duration and chronology: How long has the pain been going on? What has the course of your pain been like? Is it getting better? Worse?

Setting: Under what circumstances does the pain occur?

Aggravating and alleviating factors: What factors aggravate the pain? What brings about relief or attenuation of pain?

Associated features: What other symptoms are associated with the pain? How does it affect your sleep? Your appetite? Your energy level?

Source. Adapted from Morgan ML, Engel GL: *The Clinical Approach to the Patient.* Philadelphia, PA, WB Saunders, 1969.

---

the more likely the psychiatrist will arrive at an understanding of the pain features amenable to treatment. In addition, clarity of these features allows the clinician to determine whether the interventions and treatments used are effective, because one should be able to detect changes and improvements in some or all of these parameters. Table 3–1 summarizes the somatic components to be obtained in the pain history (Morgan and Engel 1969).

Chronic disorders of any sort, by virtue of their occurrence over time, will produce changes in a person's emotional and psychological state, influence adaptive functioning, and affect social roles and relationships. Thus, evaluation of such patients naturally prompts inquiry into the factors that predispose, activate, and perpetuate the pain and disability. These factors may possibly involve psychosocial stressors. Examination of the factors that render treatment ineffective is also warranted. Once all of these factors are evaluated and addressed, appropriate treatment, rehabilitation, and reclamation of the patient will be possible (Aronoff et al. 2000). Having established the history of pain complaints, the physician can direct attention to the psychological and social correlates of the pain.

Psychological Component

Certainly, any focus on somatic concerns should prompt the psychiatrist to consider psychiatric comorbidities in which pain or other related somatic concerns might be a feature or focus (Fishbain 1999). Careful inquiry will need to be made into common psychiatric comorbidities associated with pain (Table 3–2).

The psychiatrist should inquire into the relationship of emotional and psychological states to subjective pain complaints and exacerbations. Inquiry should be conducted in a manner that does not trigger defensiveness on the part of the patient. Often, patients have become accustomed to being rejected by physicians who use traditional medical approaches and have felt as though their pain complaints have been dismissed as being "all in their head." Consequently, patients with chronic pain can be exquisitely sensitive to inquiry that suggests even the most remote aspects of psychological and emotional dysfunction. They may well fear that attention could be directed away from the physical aspects of treatment. Nonetheless, they could respond favorably to the comprehensiveness of an assessment—including the possible emotional and psychological effects of chronic pain—and the prospect that treatment directed at the psychological factors accompanying pain might also have pain-mitigating effects.

The essential components of the psychological variables related to pain are summarized in Figure 3–1. These items are interrelated, so there will be considerable overlap in a person's moods, cognitive appraisals, and coping strategies. Thus, flexibility will be required when assessing each of these components.

Mood and Affect

Careful examination of mood states can begin with inquiry into the patient's pervasive mood over recent weeks and whether this represents a change from his or her baseline mood. Concerned primarily about illness, disability, functioning, and treatment, the patient may well dismiss his or her own mood or affective states as being natural

TABLE 3–2. **Psychiatric disorders accompanying acute and chronic pain**

Anxiety disorders
Delirium
Depression
Sexual dysfunction
Sleep disorders
Somatoform disorders
    Conversion disorder
    Hypochondriasis
    Pain disorder
    Somatization disorder
Substance abuse/dependence

reactions to the pain state. Consequently, inquiry might be directed at how other people in the patient's life have commented on the patient's recent mood and whether they have construed the recent mood as a distinct change from the patient's usual mood.

Inquiry into mood and affective states is likely to reveal the emotional factors related to the pain experiences among chronic pain patients. Among inpatients with chronic pain, pain ratings were linearly correlated with anger, fear (or anxiety), and depression. On the other hand, the presence of joy, interest, and surprise were predictive of lower pain states. Other emotional states (e.g., shame, disgust, and contempt) were only weakly correlated with pain complaints (Fernandez and Milburn 1994).

It might be possible to determine in the interview that certain affective states are temporally related to pain levels. Discrete, situational emotions are important determinants of pain ratings (Gaskin et al. 1992). Thus, for example, it could become apparent that certain emotional states precede pain, whereas other emotional states arise after the experience of pain. Exacerbations of pain could possibly predispose a person to certain affective states (e.g., dysphoria, anxiety, and anger) (Huyser and Parker 1999). On the other hand,

the presence of affective states (e.g., anger) could possibly result in exacerbations of pain. Thus, dysphoria can arise as a reaction to the pain experience, as a result of the lack of satisfactory treatment, in response to the sequelae of pain, or as an independent disorder (i.e., depression) warranting treatment. It might be helpful to discern whether such relationships exist, because these relationships can have implications for possible treatment interventions.

Anger can be an important component of the experience of the patient with chronic pain (Wade et al. 1990). The presence of anger in and of itself is not a problem. Rather, problems arise when there is a conflict around the expression of anger, there is difficulty around the expression of anger, or there are high levels of hostility. In these circumstances, there is likely to be activation of autonomic nervous system and endocrine systems (e.g., increased cortisol levels) and other physiologic effects of anger (Fernandez and Turk 1995). Patients incapable of diffusing anger or channeling it into appropriate avenues are prone to resentment, suspicion, mistrust, and heightened levels of arousal. Likewise, inability to modulate unpleasant emotional states are likely to heighten levels of pain (Kinder and Curtiss 1988).

Anxiety disorders are accompanied by an increased incidence of somatic symptoms and pain complaints (Beidel et al. 1991). Anxiety can lower pain thresholds and predispose one to heightened somatic concerns (Barsky et al. 1988).

More important than the mere presence of a particular affective state are the ways in which unpleasant emotional states are managed. Thus, inquiry into coping strategies would be warranted (see "Coping Strategies" later in this chapter). Naturally, the repertoire of strategies one employs to comfort him- or herself and the effectiveness of those strategies would be of interest.

Cognitive Patterns

The psychiatrist needs to examine the patient's cognitions about pain—that is, the beliefs held by the patient about the meaning of the pain, expectations about future pain, and interpretation of the impact the pain has on his or her life, functioning, and relationships.

Cognitive appraisal of pain depends on the individual's perspective of the consequences of pain on his or her well-being, the importance he or she assigns to the pain, and his or her view of the measures available to cope with the pain and its ramifications.

Questions arise as to the role the pain plays in the patient's life. This aspect of inquiry might naturally follow from discussions of the medical conditions and evaluations underlying the pain. The topic can be introduced by asking patients what they were told about the cause of the pain and what their reactions were to these explanations. For example, for some patients the explanations offered by clinicians are reassuring; for others, they are met with incredulity. This line of inquiry can reveal the sorts of preoccupation and concerns about the pain that might not have been overtly expressed to other clinicians. For example, in patients with cancer, this line of inquiry might unveil thoughts the patients have about fears that the cancer is spreading or that it now renders them "terminal." It also can reveal misconceptions about the pain or distortions of what has been disclosed to them and, therefore, a need for clarification and education. When there is no clear etiology for the pain, the interviewer can gain insight into the patient's disease conviction. *Disease conviction* refers to the extent to which patients maintain that they are ill, how much they are bothered by symptoms, and the extent to which they would accept the reassurances of the physician. Disease conviction is notably present among depressed patients with somatic concerns (Pilowsky 1975).

Attention needs to be directed to listening for the distorted cognitive patterns and styles that can be manifested by the patient with pain (Table 3–3). These patterns and styles may be influenced by one's prevailing emotional state. On the other hand, such cognitive patterns can influence one's emotional state. Thus, the relationships are likely to be reciprocal. Such cognitive styles are likely to reduce self-efficacy, hamper development of effective coping, drain one's support systems, accentuate unpleasant emotional states (e.g., anger, anxiety, and depression), and exacerbate pain. The presence of such patterns, therefore, could signal the need for psychotherapeutic interventions.

43

TABLE 3–3. **Problematic cognitive patterns in pain**

Catastrophizing: the tendency to view and expect the worst (e.g., "If I don't get rid of this pain, I will be miserable forever!")

Helplessness: the belief that nothing that one does matters, that there is no benefit despite one's best efforts (e.g., "My doctor says that I should exercise to improve my osteoarthritis. I know it won't help!")

Help-rejecting: rejection of the efforts of well-meaning others as a means of expressing anger, securing ongoing support or attention, or even manipulating others

Labeling: ascribing a behavior of a person to a characteristic or nature of the person. The patient who is disappointed with the ineffectiveness of a medication might need to discount the qualifications of the clinician (e.g., "The medication the doctor gave me didn't help. What a quack!")

Magnification: the exaggeration of the significance of a negative event (e.g., "My pain got worse at work yesterday. I had to leave an hour early. I might as well come to grips with the fact that I am totally disabled!")

Overgeneralization: expanding one adverse event or setback to many or all aspects of one's life

Personalization: the interpretation that an event or situation is indicative of something about oneself (e.g., "There must be something wrong with me.")

Selective abstraction: the propensity to attend selectively to negative aspects of one's life while ignoring satisfying and rewarding aspects

Self-fulfilling prophecies: effectively creating life scenarios so as to fulfill expectations of adverse outcomes (e.g., the patient who expects that her spouse will not take her pain complaints seriously behaves toward him in a manner that is short-tempered and supercilious; in the process he may possibly withdraw and avoid her, confirming her expectations)

In a recent interview, a distressed patient reported, "The pain—it's always there. It ruins my entire life. There is absolutely nothing that gives me relief." The patterns reflected in these statements signal the presence of catastrophizing ("It ruins my entire life"), overgeneralizing ("it's always there"), and

44

helplessness ("absolutely nothing that gives me relief"). Recognition of these features might prompt further inquiry into similar beliefs about other aspects of the patient's life. Using this line of inquiry, the evaluator can determine how pervasive these patterns of beliefs are, how rigidly they are maintained, and how malleable the person is in terms of alternative ways of looking at his or her condition.

Coping Strategies

Identification of problematic emotions and cognitive patterns should signal a need for inquiry into the coping strategies used by the individual to self-soothe, self-comfort, reduce distress, and modulate unpleasant states. Inquiry should again be open-ended (e.g., "When you get to feeling [or thinking] this way, how do you cope?"). Attentive listening to active and passive strategies is required. Some patients can have a propensity to retreat and withdraw from other people (thus affecting social functioning). Other patients might have a need to enlist and secure the support of others (an approach that can be adaptive or maladaptive). Still other patients have a tendency to engage in passive coping strategies (e.g., hoping for relief, praying, sleeping, etc.). For still others, there might be a tendency to distract oneself with other activities, engage in self-statements that can produce relief, and so forth (Rosenstiel and Keefe 1983).

Some patients are apt to focus on somatic complaints and pain, as opposed to dealing with the distress and emotional responses. They can have a propensity to amplify somatic complaints. Others might cope with unpleasant emotions and cognitive patterns by self-medicating with analgesics or even by abusing substances. Somatic amplification is a strategy commonly employed by a person in distress. Emotionally laden distress can be difficult for patients to tolerate or to address directly. Some patients tend instead to focus on, embellish, or magnify somatic complaints and concerns so as to enlist the support of others and to communicate to others their level of distress.

Coping strategies that involve the support of other people can be healthy, or they can be overdemanding and exasperating to members of the patient's social support network. Patients' cognitive processes can serve to put up barriers to addressing and dealing with problem areas in their lives. Statements such as "This pain will be the ruin of me! It will never get better, no matter what they tell me to do!" might actually serve to foster passivity and buffer the patient from taking any responsibility in the rehabilitation process.

It is critical to assess lethality. Patients with chronic pain and unremitting or terminal illnesses are particularly prone to despair. Suicide rates are quite high among such individuals (Breslau et al. 1991; Fishbain 1996). It is imperative to carefully inquire into thoughts of despair, hopelessness, suicidal ideas, and intent and whether plans are present. To ascertain the severity of these issues, it is important to determine the following: Is there a history of prior suicide attempt? If so, did the attempt occur within recent months? Is there a family history of suicide? What support systems are in place to ensure the patient's safety? Does the patient make use of those available supports?

Social and Adaptational Component

The patient's social history can be especially important in understanding the profound impact of pain (see Figure 3–1). An important feature to consider is the patient's adaptive functioning. Inquiry should be focused on what the patient is able to do and what activities are avoided due to the pain. A thorough evaluation of the following factors is indicated: the patient's day-to-day activities and interests, loss of (or decline in) activities due to the pain, the patient's occupation, how work is affected, how the patient is supported (if not by work), concerns over the accessibility and cost of medical care, whether litigation related to the cause of pain is pending, and whether applications for disability are under review. Inquiry into the patient's general life satisfaction is critical (e.g., how free time is spent, pursuit of interests, how the patient comforts

him- or herself, how the patient manages pleasant and unpleasant emotions). The interviewer needs to listen for elements that suggest the patient assumes an invalid role in all or most aspects of his or her life and assess the function that role serves for the patient.

Especially pertinent is the identification of significant persons in the patient's life and how the pain has influenced relationships with those persons. Inquiry into how pain is communicated to others, the expected responses, the responses generated and from whom, and how the patient perceives those responses is germane. Pain patients and their spouses or significant others can experience losses in intimacy and sexual dissatisfaction due to the impact of pain on sexual functioning. Inquiry should be directed to how the patient's pain influences the behaviors of others. To avoid defensiveness on the part of the patient, the examiner should avoid implying that such influence on others is intentional or manipulative. However, the interviewer should always recognize the possibility that such influences are unconsciously driven.

Careful histories of alcohol and drug use are imperative. Abused agents can include medications prescribed for the patient's use (e.g., opiate analgesics), and patients may become defensive if they fear that analgesics provided to them—even if not fully effective in eradicating pain—might be withdrawn or withheld. Patients might require assurance that this line of inquiry is part of a comprehensive approach. This inquiry is also important in determining what types of medical and pharmacologic approaches best suit the patients' needs.

Longitudinal Approach

A historical perspective of the pain history can be quite helpful in understanding the evolution of the present pain experience. Thus, it can be useful to evaluate the patient's early pain complaints, history of medical interventions, and response to treatment. There can be indications of the quality of previous doctor–patient interactions; how proactive or passive a role the patient took; and the patient's history of adherence to medical treatment, including physical or occupational therapy, medications, diet, exercise, and other components.

Earlier history can constitute a backdrop against which the current pain experiences can be evaluated. Previous experiences can influence the patient's expectations of current treatment, his or her current doctor–patient relationships, and the patient's participation and follow-through with treatment.

Other longitudinal aspects include developmental life experiences. The presence of early childhood illnesses (e.g., diabetes) can have a profound impact on family interactions and shaping early relationships. These experiences can shape current relationships as well. Family history of medical illnesses, particularly those involving pain, and how these were experienced by the family—and by the patient in particular—can reveal patterns of pain behaviors that the patient grew up with and that influence current experiences (Fishman and Loscalzo 1987). These patterns may have an impact on how the patient currently manages his or her pain. Degree of impairment and disability arising from painful medical or surgical conditions can also have been "learned" by the patient in such early experiences. Responses of family members to treatment endeavors might have shaped the patient's expectations and beliefs about the utility and effectiveness of pain interventions, whether or not those early experiences bear directly on the type of pain (or the source of pain) the patient experiences in his or her own current medical condition.

Other developmental factors may have an impact on a person's current social and adaptive functioning. For example, history of sexual abuse is present in a number of patients with chronic pelvic pain, abdominal pain, and even disorders such as fibromyalgia (Gross et al. 1980). Accessing this information can relay significant history about the dynamics within the home, how crises were managed, what support systems were available to the patient while growing up, and whether the patient has a support system in place to actually support, nurture, and protect him or her. This inquiry should be conducted in a sensitive and respectful manner. Patients may well be reluctant to confide such information, fearing that it could reflect adversely on them. They may feel a need or a desire to protect family members, despite the abuse itself or the family's failure to intervene on their behalf

48

even in the face of evidence or suggestion of abuse. Patients may need to be informed that such experiences can influence how they approach their world, can affect the patients' expectations regarding the reliability and goodwill of treating sources (authority figures), and have been related to certain chronic pain disorders.

Evaluation of Treatment Suitability

At times, psychiatric evaluation is requested to assess the factors that contribute barriers to effective pain treatment. Evaluation can determine whether psychopharmacologic treatment, psychotherapeutic modalities, or both should be employed. Sometimes psychiatric evaluation is requested when psychological factors are mediating the pain experience or when psychiatric disorders more completely explain the origin of the pain. Psychiatric evaluation can be conducted to assess the patient's suitability to other interventions (e.g., surgery). Table 3–4 lists the factors that predict a poor surgical outcome for pain disorders. Once such factors are addressed in psychiatric treatment, however, a patient could possibly be considered for surgical interventions.

■ PAIN ASSESSMENT INSTRUMENTS

Pain assessment tests and scales are useful adjuncts to the evaluation of the pain patient. These instruments allow the examiner to ascertain the severity and intensity of the pain experience. A number of scales are available, and the selection of the assessment instrument to be used is determined in part by the characteristics of the pain and the elements gleaned from the interview (see Table 3–5 for a list of psychometric scales used in assessing chronic pain). In acute pain states, certain types of assessments are desirable that are of limited utility in assessing chronic pain states (see Table 3–6 for a summary of the instruments used in acute versus chronic pain). On the other hand, multidimensional pain assessments and complex behavioral assessments can be invoked when complex interactions between pain states and psychosocial factors are implicated in mediating pain.

TABLE 3–4.	Factors that suggest poor surgical outcome for pain disorders

Emotional factors
    Anger
    Anxiety
    Depression
Cognitive factors
    Catastrophizing
    Perception of loss of control
Vocational factors
    Financial settlement or pending litigation
    Job dissatisfaction
    Workers' compensation
Social factors
    Marital dissatisfaction
Historical factors
    History of physical abuse
    History of sexual abuse
    Prior psychological treatment
    Substance abuse or dependence

Patients with acute pain (e.g., postoperative pain) are preoccupied with the situational characteristics of the pain. The pain is expected to be time limited. Conversely, for those with chronic pain, their day-to-day, interpersonal, academic, and vocational functioning is overshadowed by the pain experience. Therefore, assessments used in acute pain settings will be fundamentally different from those used in chronic pain. Measures for acute pain, summarized in Table 3–6, focus on the experience and intensity of pain and assess responsiveness to treatment interventions. Chronic pain assessments focus on broader aspects of patients' pain experiences, functioning, and psychological adaptation.

The pain assessments described in the following sections serve a number of functions, including assessment of pain intensity, quality, and duration. In addition, such scales can assist the physician in making treatment selections and assessing the efficacy of treatment.

50

TABLE 3–5.	Psychometric pain scales used in assessing chronic pain

Coping Strategies Questionnaire: Assesses the coping strategies in patient's repertoire to deal with chronic pain. May predict the level of activity, physical impairment, and psychological functioning associated with pain.

Fear Avoidance Beliefs Questionnaire: Assesses beliefs characterized by danger, threat, or harm associated with pain. The degree to which patients assign threat to activities can limit their participation in, and lead to avoidance of, activities related to work.

McGill Pain Questionnaire: Assesses the features of pain severity and intensity. Allows patients to qualify pain in emotional, cognitive-evaluative, and sensory terms.

Minnesota Multiphasic Personality Inventory: Provides personality profile and pathologic assessment of patient with chronic pain

Quality of life indices: Assesses the impact of chronic pain states on various aspects of a person's life, activity, recreation and leisure activities, social interactions, work, and adaptive self-care

West Haven–Yale Multidimensional Pain Inventory: Assesses patient's appraisal of pain, its impact on his or her functioning, and the patient's perceived responses of others to his or her pain

TABLE 3–6.	Pain assessment instruments for acute and chronic pain

Acute pain	Recurrent/Chronic pain
Visual analog scale or numeric rating scale	Visual analog scale, McGill Pain Questionnaire
Medication use	Medication use
Observer rating	Observer rating
	Pain diary
	West Haven–Yale Multidimensional Pain Inventory
	Psychological measures

Single Dimension Scales

The most commonly used pain scales involve single-dimension ratings of pain intensity. Such scales are appealing because of their ease of administration and interpretation. Patients also find them easy to complete (e.g., requiring little in the way of time commitment or concentration). However, single-dimension scales have been criticized for oversimplifying pain ratings and for ignoring factors that contribute to or exacerbate the pain experience (e.g., emotional and cognitive factors).

Verbal Descriptor Scale

Verbal descriptor scales (VDS) require that a patient rate the pain experienced according to one of five to seven verbal descriptors. Only limited types of responses are permitted. Such scales can be used in clinical and experimental settings. Of course, use of a VDS assumes that the patient has intact verbal skills (i.e., reading and comprehension). Thus, these measures may not be useful for patients who have significant language barriers or cognitive impairments or for young children. The scoring of VDSs correlates with pain ratings of other scales (e.g., visual analog scale [VAS]). The VDS included in Figure 3–2 ignores the emotional, cognitive, and behavioral components of pain.

Numeric Rating Scale

A numeric rating scale (NRS) is often used to measure pain experience and intensity. Patients are asked to rate their pain on an 11-point scale, from 0 (No Pain) to 10 (Worst Pain). A variation of this scale shows a rating of pain from 0 to 100, with similar anchors (Jensen et al. 1986). These scales are reliable and correlate with other simple assessment measures. Use of an NRS requires that the patient have intact language and cognitive skills. One drawback of the NRS is that the patient's rating of pain (i.e., the number selected) has no intrinsic meaning. Thus, if a patient rates his pain as a "5," this rating cannot be assumed to be one-half that of another patient who rates her pain

52

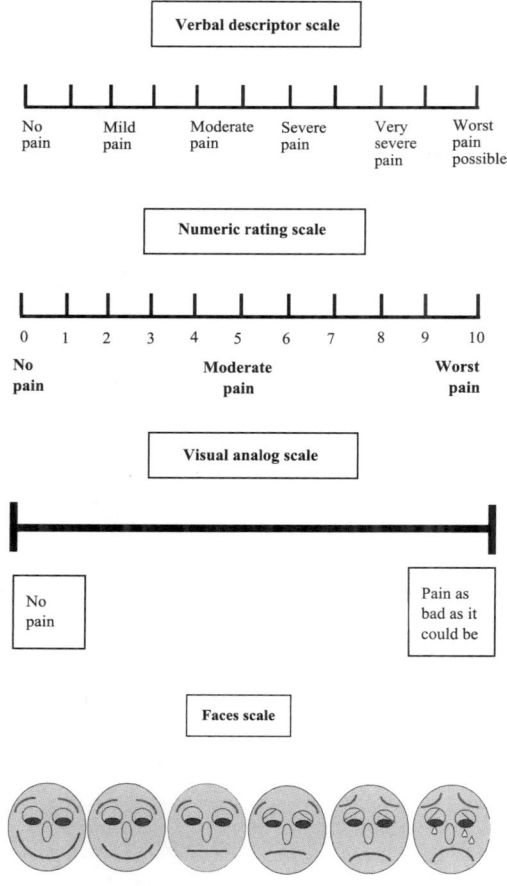

FIGURE 3–2. **Pain assessment instruments.**

as a "10." Furthermore, the transition from one rating (e.g., from "5" to "4") might not mean the same, even within the same patient, as a transition at another point in the scale (e.g., from "9" to "8").

Visual Analog Scale

An extension of the NRS, the VAS consists of a 10-cm line with anchors at 0 and 10 or verbal anchors (see Figure 3–2). The patient is asked to draw an X along the line that best denotes his or her level of pain. The VAS has been used in clinical as well as experimental settings. The denoted pain levels for an individual can be compared over time to quantify levels of pain worsening or improving. These serial comparisons, unlike those employed with repeated use of the NRS, are proportional. However, the use of the VAS for clinical comparisons has been questioned (Carlsson 1983). The VAS might not be suitable for elderly patients or patients who have difficulty understanding its abstract concept. In such cases, pain can be erroneously denoted and can impede the appropriate characterization of the pain and its treatment.

Faces Scale

With the faces scale, the patient is asked to rate pain intensity according to printed facial expressions conveying varying amounts of distress (see Figure 3–2). This is an easily understood rating instrument and one that has appeal for children. The faces scale allows the examiner to bypass issues related to language barriers (Frank et al. 1982).

Behavioral Measures

Behavioral measures are instruments that assess pain in a manner vastly different from the simple rating scales. Although some professionals in the field have questioned the utility and reliability of observer ratings of pain behavior, those ratings are often used by clinicians and nursing staff. Thus, when someone complains of distress, the clinician often examines the overt behavior

of the patient to look for corroborating behaviors that substantiate the allegation of pain. The clinician might look for evidence of distress, facial grimacing or wincing, guarding of an affected area, limping, splinting, and similar behaviors. The problem with observer ratings is that the results are contingent upon the skill of the observer in detecting pain symptoms. However, observer ratings are also subject to a great deal of bias. For instance, a nurse observing a patient with chronic pain who is able to smile or make puns periodically might dismiss the patient's allegations of pain ratings because of the bias that such behaviors would be entirely inconsistent with pain.

Medication Use

Reviews of the patient's use of medications can be an indicator of the patient's pain experience and severity. It is useful to assess the patient's adherence to treatment, appropriateness of medication use, and excess medication use. Pain patients can be unreliable about medication use and can significantly underestimate the extent of their opioid use (Ready et al. 1982). Thus, the support of collateral informants (e.g., from a spouse or other family member) to provide information about the use of medications can be helpful.

Pain Diary

A pain diary can be as simple or as detailed as the clinician deems necessary. However, the more complex the entries are, the less inclined the patient might be to reliably make entries, because the task can seem overwhelming. Completion of pain diaries can be quite time consuming for patients. In addition, clinicians need to devote some time to review the diary contents to look for trends in the pain ratings and associated temporal features. Pain diaries can be very useful. They can reveal patterns of pain intensity, exacerbations of pain, and mitigating factors. They can likewise reveal varying psychological states temporally related to episodes of pain or pain relief. This information can be particularly useful when patients are resistant to the idea that psychological states could be related to the

pain experience. Also, diaries can be a source of information about the extent to which patients engage in activities (e.g., reclining, pursuing their interests).

For the diary to be maximally effective, patients must be committed to maintaining it. Completion of the entire diary for a week in the hour preceding the doctor's appointment limits the utility of the diary, as the entries will be based on the patient's memory and recollections. Instead, the utility of the diary is best derived when the patient maintains the diary reliably and consistently during the periods of study. Categories that might be included in a pain diary include the date and time; the pain rating; the situation; the patient's emotions, behavior, and thoughts; and the response of others to the patient's pain.

Multidimensional Pain Scales

McGill Pain Questionnaire

Commonly used to characterize pain, the McGill Pain Questionnaire (MPQ; Melzack 1975) is a verbal rating scale. Subjects are asked to select verbal descriptors for their pain among sets of categories of descriptors. A long form and short form are available for use. The long form contains 20 sets of categories. The first 10 refer to the sensory-discriminative aspects of the pain. Sets 11–15 contain items that characterize the affective-emotional components of the pain. Set 16 contains descriptors that correspond to the evaluative components of pain, and the remaining 17–20 sets of descriptors contain miscellaneous items. The short form (see Table 3–7) contains 15 items. The patient is asked to rank the extent to which each item corresponds to the intensity of his or her pain (Melzack 1987). The short form offers the advantage of being easier to complete. The scoring in the short form correlates with results obtained in the longer form. The MPQ has been translated into a number of different languages, useful for those patients for whom language barriers impede the reading or understanding of the English version.

56

TABLE 3–7.	**Short form of the McGill Pain Questionnaire**			
	None	**Mild**	**Moderate**	**Severe**
Throbbing	0)_____	1)_____	2)_____	3)_____
Shooting	0)_____	1)_____	2)_____	3)_____
Stabbing	0)_____	1)_____	2)_____	3)_____
Sharp	0)_____	1)_____	2)_____	3)_____
Cramping	0)_____	1)_____	2)_____	3)_____
Gnawing	0)_____	1)_____	2)_____	3)_____
Hot-burning	0)_____	1)_____	2)_____	3)_____
Aching	0)_____	1)_____	2)_____	3)_____
Heavy	0)_____	1)_____	2)_____	3)_____
Tender	0)_____	1)_____	2)_____	3)_____
Splitting	0)_____	1)_____	2)_____	3)_____
Tiring- exhausting	0)_____	1)_____	2)_____	3)_____
Sickening	0)_____	1)_____	2)_____	3)_____
Fearful	0)_____	1)_____	2)_____	3)_____
Punishing-cruel	0)_____	1)_____	2)_____	3)_____

Source. Reprinted from *Pain*, Volume 30, Melzack R: "The Short-Form McGill Pain Questionnaire," pp. 191–197, Copyright 1987, with permission from Elsevier Science.

Quality of Life Assessment

Any assessment of pain level—or of pain relief resulting from treatment—is less meaningful without a consideration of the patient's quality of life. Thus, any reductions in pain ratings that suggest an intervention is successful mean little without commensurate changes in the patient's psychological and social well-being and changes in adaptive functions. Clinicians often allude to the term *quality of life*; yet, there is controversy as to what elements constitute the means to quantify and establish parameters for this concept (Ferrell et al. 1989). Indices of quality of life are explored with patients with terminal disorders, and

these can be easily adapted to the patient with chronic and unremitting pain. Factors included in such indices include ratings of life satisfaction, life enjoyment, ability to perform activities of daily living, ability to engage others, and satisfaction with one's appearance. These issues can be the basis for modifications in pain treatment and can be the focus of psychotherapeutic endeavors as well.

Psychological Assessments

West Haven–Yale Multidimensional Pain Inventory

The West Haven–Yale Multidimensional Pain Inventory (WHYMPI; Kerns et al. 1985) is a 52-item inventory developed for the assessment of a patient's idiosyncratic appraisals of chronic pain. The instrument relies on components of the cognitive-behavioral approach to help understand and conceptualize pain. The instrument is used to examine a person's perceptions, appraisals, and emotions and behaviors associated with pain. Coping strategies used by the individual patient are also assessed, as are the patient's reactions to the responses of others to pain complaints. Not only does the examiner come to understand the patient's view of his or her own pain but the WHYMPI can also serve as a basis for the development of treatment interventions (e.g., to be used in psychotherapy).

Response patterns can reveal patient profiles that might become a focus of clinical attention. The dysfunctional profile reveals high levels of perceived pain, life interference from the pain, low levels of perceived life control, and subjective distress. An interpersonally distressed profile is likewise characterized by high levels of perceived pain and life interference, and patients with this profile perceive themselves to have low levels of social support. Last, an adaptive profile is one in which the patient perceives high levels of self-control, along with low levels of perceived pain and perceived life interference from the pain. The profiles summarized here can have predictive value in terms of

58

treatment approaches and treatment outcomes (Bradley and McKendree-Smith 2001).

Fear Avoidance Beliefs Questionnaire

The Fear Avoidance Beliefs Questionnaire (FABQ; Waddell et al. 1993) is a 16-item instrument that assesses the beliefs and fears a patient associates with back pain. Each item is ranked along a 7-point Likert scale ranging from *strongly agree* to *strongly disagree*. The patient's beliefs and fears can have an impact on the patient's range and extent of activity. The scale assesses fears the patient has about eliciting pain through behaviors required at work and in general activity. The higher the level of fear, the higher the level of the patient's perceived disability.

Coping Strategies Questionnaire

The Coping Strategies Questionnaire (CSQ; Rosenstiel and Keefe 1983) is useful in assessing *active* (e.g., diverting one's attention, increasing the level of activity) and *passive* (e.g., praying, hoping, ignoring pain) coping strategies used by patients dealing with chronic pain. The instrument measures the extent to which maladaptive strategies (e.g., catastrophizing) or more adaptive strategies (e.g., reinterpreting the meaning of the pain and using coping self-statements) are employed. Thus, the scale can illustrate those strategies that are effective and, therefore, should be maximized when dealing with pain. In addition, those strategies that are ineffective and maladaptive can be the focus of therapeutic interventions to foster modification of those strategies.

Minnesota Multiphasic Personality Inventory

The Minnesota Multiphasic Personality Inventory (MMPI; Hathaway et al. 1989) has been used extensively as an assessment tool for a variety of psychological disturbances. It is also among the most widely used assessment instruments in pain syndromes. The MMPI consists of 566 statements requiring *true* or *false* responses. The MMPI comprises 10 standard clinical scales assessing psycho-

pathologic states, 3 validity scales, and 4 additional scales evaluating ego strength and other factors. Consultation with a psychologist trained in the administration and interpretation of the MMPI can be very helpful in the use of this instrument.

The strength of the MMPI lies in the fact that it is useful for assessing psychological personality measures that can be pertinent to pain states. Initial study suggested that patients with chronic pain displayed a uniform personality profile, with elevated ratings in the Hypochondriasis, Hysteria, and Depression scales (Love and Peck 1987). These elevated ratings form a V shape when represented on an MMPI graph—a pattern often referred to in the literature as the "Conversion V" (Figure 3–3). It was believed that this pattern characterized patients with chronic pain. Despite use of the term *conversion*, it was never maintained that the pain complaints were conversion or characterized features of a conversion disorder. Rather, the pattern revealed a tendency to be somatically preoccupied (hypochondriasis), to develop somatic complaints when stressed (hysteria), and to develop the dysphoria accompanying pain (depression).

In fact, when back pain patients were followed up over the course of their illnesses, a gradual change in MMPI profiles that eventually reflected the Conversion-V profile emerged over time. This finding suggested that as a patient makes the transition from acute to chronic pain, commensurate changes occur in his or her psychological state over time. The MMPI patterns can be modified with successful treatment (Naliboff et al. 1988).

One argument against the interpretation of the chronic pain profile rests with the contention that use of the MMPI has intrinsic biases in this population. The items endorsed by chronic pain patients corresponding to the Hypochondriasis, Hysteria, and Depression scale items would be endorsed simply by virtue of the fact that the person is in pain (i.e., the items of the MMPI scales are biased) (Smythe 1984). The endorsed items might simply replicate the patient's pain complaints and might not fundamentally characterize a personality prototype of the chronic pain patient

Nonetheless, the MMPI has utility in identifying personality features that could predict responsiveness to various treatment

60

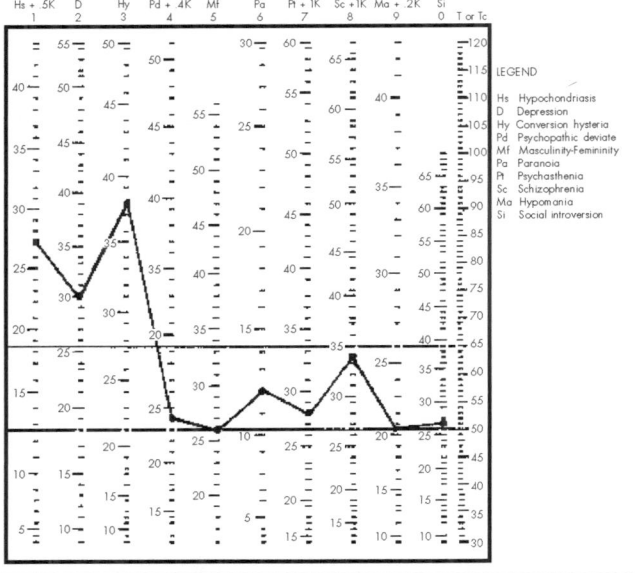

FIGURE 3–3. **MMPI profile of a male patient with chronic pain demonstrating the Conversion-V pattern.**

Elevations are noted in the Hypochondriasis, Depression, and Hysteria scales.

approaches. It can also be useful in drawing attention to those personality characteristics of the chronic pain patient that might present barriers to treatment and that ultimately could require psychotherapeutic intervention.

■ REFERENCES

Aronoff GM, Tota-Faucette M, Phillips L, et al: Are pain disorder and somatization disorder valid diagnostic entities? Curr Rev Pain 4:309–312, 2000

Barsky AJ, Geringer E, Wool CA: A cognitive-educational treatment for hypochondriasis. Gen Hosp Psychiatry 10:322–327, 1988

Beidel DC, Christ MAG, Long PJ: Somatic complaints in anxious children. J Abnorm Child Psychol 19:659–670, 1991

Bradley LA, McKendree-Smith NL: Assessment of psychological status using interviews and self-report instruments, in Handbook of Pain Assessment, 2nd Edition. Edited by Turk DC, Melzack R. New York, Guilford, 2001, pp 292–319

Breslau N, Davis GC, Andreski P: Migraine, psychiatric disorders, and suicide attempts: an epidemiologic study of young adults. Psychiatry Res 37:11–23, 1991

Carlsson AM: Assessment of chronic pain, I: aspects of the reliability and validity of the visual analogue scale. Pain 16:87–101, 1983

Fernandez E, Milburn TW: Sensory and affective predictors of overall pain and emotions associated with affective pain. Clin J Pain 10:3–9, 1994

Fernandez E, Turk DC: The scope and significance of anger in the experience of chronic pain. Pain 61:165–175, 1995

Ferrell BR, Wisdom C, Wenzl C: Quality of life as an outcome variable in the management of cancer pain. Cancer 63:2321–2327 1989

Fishbain DA: Current research on chronic pain and suicide. Am J Public Health 86: 1320–1321, 1996

Fishbain DA: Approaches to treatment decisions for psychiatric comorbidity in the management of the chronic pain patient. Med Clin North Am 83:737–760, 1999

Fishman B, Loscalzo M: Cognitive-behavioral interventions in management of cancer pain: principles and applications. Med Clin North Am 71:271–287, 1987

Frank AJM, Moll JMH, Hort JF: A comparison of three ways of measuring pain. Rheumatol Rehabil 21:211–217, 1982

Gaskin ME, Greene AF, Robinson ME, et al: Negative affect and the experience of chronic pain. J Psychosom Res 36:707–713, 1992

Gross RJ, Doerr H, Caldirola D, et al: Borderline syndrome and incest in chronic pelvic pain patients. Int J Psychiatry Med 10:79–96, 1980

Hathaway SR, McKinley JC, Butcher JN, et al: Minnesota Multiphasic Personality Inventory–2: Manual for Administration. Minneapolis, MN, University of Minnesota Press, 1989

Huyser BA, Parker JC: Negative affect and pain in arthritis. Rheum Dis Clin North Am 25:105–121, 1999

Jensen MP, Karoly P, Braver S: The measurement of clinical pain intensity: a comparison of six methods. Pain 27:117–126, 1986

Kerns RD, Turk DC, Rudy TE: The West Haven–Yale multidimensional pain inventory (WHYMPI). Pain 23:345–356, 1985

Kinder BN, Curtiss G: Assessment of anxiety, depression and anger in chronic pain patients: conceptual and methodological issues, in Advances in Personality Assessment. Edited by Speilberger CD, Butcher JN. Hillsdale, NJ, Erlbaum, 1988, pp 161–174

Love AW, Peck CL: The MMPI and psychological factors in chronic low back pain: a review. Pain 28:1–12, 1987

Melzack R: The McGill Pain Questionnaire: major properties and scoring methods. Pain 1:277–299, 1975

Melzack R: The Short-Form McGill Pain Questionnaire. Pain 30:191–197, 1987

Morgan ML, Engel GL: The Clinical Approach to the Patient. Philadelphia, PA, WB Saunders, 1969

Naliboff BD, McCreary CP, McArthur DL, et al: MMPI changes following behavioral treatment of chronic low back pain. Pain 35:271–277, 1988

Pilowsky I: Dimensions of abnormal illness behaviour. Aust N Z J Psychiatry 9:141–147, 1975

Ready LB, Sarkis E, Turner JA: Self-reported vs. actual use of medications in chronic pain patients. Pain 12:285–294, 1982

Rosenstiel AK, Keefe FJ: The use of coping strategies in chronic low back pain patients: relationship to patient characteristics and current adjustment. Pain 17:33–44, 1983

Smythe HA: Problems with the MMPI. J Rheumatol 11:417–418, 1984

Waddell G, Newton M, Henderson I, et al: A Fear-Avoidance Beliefs Questionnaire (FABQ) and the role of fear-avoidance beliefs in chronic low back pain and disability. Pain 52:157–168, 1993

Wade JB, Price DD, Hamer RM, et al: An emotional component analysis of chronic pain. Pain 40:303–310, 1990

4

COMMON PSYCHIATRIC COMORBIDITIES AND PSYCHIATRIC DIFFERENTIAL DIAGNOSIS OF THE PAIN PATIENT

The psychiatrist enlisted to care for the patient with chronic pain will have to consider an enormous psychiatric differential diagnosis. The psychiatric diagnosis can be carefully extracted based on the patient's symptoms, the notable signs during evaluation and interview, the longitudinal course, and supporting evidence provided by laboratory investigations and physical examination.

■ PAIN DISORDER

Pain disorder requires that pain is a primary symptom and is severe enough to warrant clinical attention. Marked disability might be alleged, and the patient's life becomes centered on the pain.

Earlier versions of DSM required that clinicians infer whether psychological underpinnings or conflicts precipitated pain complaints. Thus, if it was evident from physical examination and diagnostic evaluation that a physical cause could not fully account for the pain, psychiatric labels were invoked reflecting the psychological origins of the pain—for example, *psychogenic pain disorder* from DSM-III (American Psychiatric Association 1980) and

64

somatoform pain disorder from DSM-III-R (American Psychiatric Association 1987) (King and Strain 1992).

In DSM-IV (American Psychiatric Association 1994) there was a transition in the thinking underlying diagnosis. The terms *somatoform* and *psychogenic* were dropped. There is no longer a requirement for exclusion of a physical cause for the pain, and the primacy of psychological factors (i.e., conflicts, defenses, and emotional states) underlying and accounting for pain was de-emphasized. DSM-IV-TR (American Psychiatric Association 2000) leaves open the possibility that psychological factors can contribute to the pain experience by precipitating, exacerbating, or maintaining pain but do not necessarily have to fully account for the pain. This approach is more consistent with current views of the interrelationships between pain and psychological factors. The diagnostic criteria of pain disorder are summarized in Table 4–1.

Pain disorder can be associated with a general medical condition, psychological factors, or both. Pain disorder associated with a general medical condition is recorded solely on Axis III, because psychological factors are thought to have minimal or no involvement in the pain experience. When psychological factors are implicated and believed to have a significant contributory role in the pain, one of the two other types of pain disorder would be encoded on Axis I. An inference is still required on the part of the clinician to determine whether and to what extent psychological factors are involved in the patient's plight.

Pain Disorder Versus Other Somatoform Disorders

Discrepancies arise among diagnosticians when it comes to the psychiatric differential diagnosis accompanying pain. In one review of chronic pain patients, somatoform disorders were diagnosed in 16%–53% (Dworkin and Caligor 1988); in another series, approximately 40% of 283 chronic pain patients received a diagnosis of conversion disorder (Fishbain et al. 1986). Part of the discrepancy may be due to the diagnostic criteria employed—that is, some diagnoses may have been based on earlier DSM versions in which dis-

65

TABLE 4–1.	**DSM-IV-TR diagnostic criteria for pain disorder**

A. Pain in one or more anatomical sites is the predominant focus of the clinical presentation and is of sufficient severity to warrant clinical attention.

B. The pain causes clinically significant distress or impairment in social, occupational, or other important areas of functioning.

C. Psychological factors are judged to have an important role in the onset, severity, exacerbation, or maintenance of the pain.

D. The symptom or deficit is not intentionally produced or feigned (as in factitious disorder or malingering).

E. The pain is not better accounted for by a mood, anxiety, or psychotic disorder and does not meet criteria for dyspareunia.

Code as follows:

307.80 Pain Disorder Associated With Psychological Factors: psychological factors are judged to have the major role in the onset, severity, exacerbation, or maintenance of the pain. (If a general medical condition is present, it does not have a major role in the onset, severity, exacerbation, or maintenance of the pain.) This type of pain disorder is not diagnosed if criteria are also met for somatization disorder.

Specify if:

Acute: duration of less than 6 months
Chronic: duration of 6 months or longer
307.89 Pain Disorder Associated With Both Psychological Factors and a General Medical Condition: both psychological factors and a general medical condition are judged to have important roles in the onset, severity, exacerbation, or maintenance of the pain. The associated general medical condition or anatomical site of the pain (see below) is coded on Axis III.

Specify if:

Acute: duration of less than 6 months
Chronic: duration of 6 months or longer

Note: The following is not considered to be a mental disorder and is included here to facilitate differential diagnosis.

66

TABLE 4–1.	DSM-IV-TR diagnostic criteria for pain disorder *(continued)*

Pain Disorder Associated With a General Medical Condition:
a general medical condition has a major role in the onset, severity, exacerbation, or maintenance of the pain. (If psychological factors are present, they are not judged to have a major role in the onset, severity, exacerbation, or maintenance of the pain.) The diagnostic code for the pain is selected based on the associated general medical condition if one has been established or on the anatomical location of the pain if the underlying general medical condition is not yet clearly established—for example, low back (724.2), sciatic (724.3), pelvic (625.9), headache (784.0), facial (784.0), chest (786.50), joint (719.40), bone (733.90), abdominal (789.0), breast (611.71), renal (788.0), ear (388.70), eye (379.91), throat (784.1), tooth (525.9), and urinary (788.0).

tinctions among the psychiatric conditions might have been less clear. In addition, sampling bias (i.e., studying patients from very distinct subsets of the population) may possibly have contributed to the diagnostic inconsistencies (Fishbain 1999).

Any pain complaint would not necessarily invoke a diagnosis of pain disorder; rather, it must be considered among a number of other psychiatric disorders (see Table 4–2). Distinguishing pain disorder from other psychiatric disorders is pertinent to determining appropriate pharmacologic and psychotherapeutic treatment.

Distinguishing pain disorder from other somatoform disorders can be quite difficult. For example, certain pain disorders—central pain states and fibromyalgia, for example—can mimic somatoform disorders. It is possible that a medical condition that is as yet unrecognized can lead, by default, to the erroneous conclusion that the pain associated with that condition is psychogenic. Patients with persisting pain, particularly pain with no clear etiology, might, like the person with hypochondriasis, insist on finding a cause. This insistence might be grounded in the effort to convince the clinician of the legitimacy of the pain complaints and the need for treatment.

67

TABLE 4–2.	Psychiatric disorders in which pain can be a prominent complaint

Pain disorder
    Pain complaints the focus of clinical attention
    Associated psychological features (can be present or absent)
Somatization disorder
    At least four pain complaints
    Other somatic concerns (genitourinary or gastrointestinal)
    Pseudoneurologic disturbance
Hypochondriasis
    Preoccupation with fears of having a serious medical condition
    Based on a misinterpretation of bodily sensations, which can include discomfort or pain
Conversion disorder
    Loss of voluntary motor function or sensory function other than pain
Dyspareunia
    Pain arising exclusively during intercourse
Factitious disorder
    Deliberate deceit or feigning of symptoms (can include complaints of pain)
    No obvious secondary gain

Somatic Amplification and Its Function

Pain disorder is included under the rubric of somatoform disorders. In some patients with pain, as with other somatoform disorders, amplification of somatic symptoms (including pain) may be a manifestation of psychological distress. For some persons, this amplification might reflect a strategy to cope with or manage psychological distress (Lipowski 1988). For others, somatic amplification may result from the distress associated with unpleasant affective states such as depression or anxiety. These emotional states may lead to heightened self-consciousness and a propensity to attend to bodily signals that might otherwise be ignored. Influenced by the distress of the prevailing emotional state combined with cognitive distortions (e.g., catastrophizing and magnification), the individual is likely to

misinterpret the bodily sensations as signaling a significant health- or pain-related disorder.

Somatic amplification can serve a number of psychological "functions" for the patient. For some patients, it can serve to secure and enlist the support of others. For other patients, it can serve to distance others, express discontent or anger, or avoid interpersonal conflicts. There may also be benefits derived, such as avoidance of unpleasant tasks and responsibilities.

Somatic amplification and the focus on somatic symptoms can serve to mask other psychological symptoms. Depression in a patient presenting with somatic concerns is quite common. For example, patients might wish to deny depressive symptoms entirely, because to acknowledge them may incur the stigma of a psychiatric disorder or imply something about their character (e.g., weakness in the face of adversity). Still, for other patients, the propensity to present with somatic complaints may be based on the belief that somatic concerns will be taken more seriously than will emotional factors (Lipowski 1990).

Pain and Deceit

Both factitious disorder and malingering involve the voluntary production or exaggeration of symptoms. Pain can be invoked with either condition. Although deceit is essential for both conditions, the motives for the two conditions differ. In factitious disorder, the motive is to assume the "sick role"—that is, to gain something from the association with medical treatment; the motive does not include a concrete secondary gain. Malingerers, on the other hand, derive a clear secondary gain that could be understandable from the person's environmental circumstances. Examples of secondary gains can include financial gain (e.g., from litigation or disability compensation), seeking a haven (e.g., in the case of one who is homeless), and acquiring psychoactive substances (e.g., opiates). Factors that suggest possible malingering are summarized in Table 4–3. Ailments claimed by patients seeking opiate analgesics typically include those not readily verifiable (e.g., renal colic, tic douloureux, and sickle cell crisis, among others). Thus, the patient might allege se-

69

TABLE 4–3.	**Factors that raise suspicion of malingering**

Patient presentation to medical attention has a medicolegal context

Marked discrepancy exists between claims of disability or distress and objective findings

Patient's reports may be vague, may be loaded with overgeneralizations, or may seem rehearsed. History may fall apart when examiner's questions are reframed. Patient's responses to questions may be cryptic, and there is a tendency to hedge statements

Once patient's objective is achieved, symptoms seem to take on less significance

Patient rejects all forms of treatment that do not include psychoactive medications

Patient exhibits lack of cooperation with medical diagnostic interventions

Patient shows poor compliance with treatment interventions

Antisocial personality disorder is present

vere flank pain and provide a urine sample into which a drop of blood was deliberately placed. In the busy emergency department, such complaints can be met with a tendency to placate the patient with provision of the sought-out narcotic.

■ DEPRESSION

Among chronic pain patients, depression prevalence rates were estimated at 30%–54%, much higher than in the general population (Banks and Kerns 1996). A number of studies demonstrated that the severity of depressive symptoms predicted the number and severity of pain complaints (Dworkin et al. 1990; Faucett 1994). The causal relationships between depression and pain are unclear. Depression may develop as a consequence of pain (Gamsa 1990) or medical treatment (Massie and Holland 1990). Alternatively, depression may precede the pain and may be related to the maintenance of pain. The biopsychosocial approach to pain assessment recognizes that the relationship between pain and emotional disturbances (e.g., depression) is likely to be reciprocal.

Chronic pain patients are often plagued with distress related to unremitting pain, life changes, modifications in lifestyle and adaptive functioning, loss of rewarding activities, and decline in social reinforcements. The potential pitfall is that clinicians might assume the depression is expected, given the pain, and overlook a potentially treatable disorder. Conversely, depression may be assumed to be present when physical examination and diagnostic interventions fail to account for the severity of the pain or if treatment measures are unsuccessful in mitigating pain. In such cases, the clinician can be misled into ignoring the pain complaints in the attempt to address the presumed depression. The patient may well construe this lack of attention to the pain complaints as devaluing the pain, confrontations can arise, and treatment measures ultimately may be thwarted.

When assessing depression, it is important to keep in mind that neurovegetative symptoms such as sleep disturbances, appetite changes, and fatigue can overlap considerably with symptoms of medical and surgical conditions associated with pain. Thus, reliance on these features may lead to the erroneous diagnosis of a depressive disorder.

To effectively diagnose depression in the medically ill, it may be best to focus on psychological symptoms of depression, which are unlikely to be influenced by medical conditions or their complications. Thus, any loss of interests; lack of mood reactivity; lack of concentration; indecisiveness; and preoccupation with guilt, worthlessness, death, dying, suicide, despair, and hopelessness are more suggestive of an underlying depression (Cavanaugh 1984). Similarly, items in diagnostic scales (e.g., the Beck Depression Inventory; Beck and Steer 1987) can overlap considerably with medical symptoms, exaggerating depression severity in certain pain patients.

■ ANXIETY

The model presented in Figure 4–1 depicts a theory linking anxiety with musculoskeletal pain (e.g., fibromyalgia). In this model,

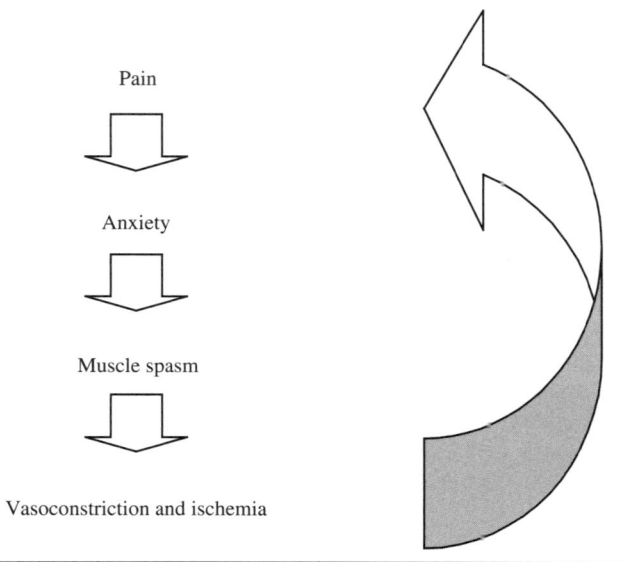

FIGURE 4–1. **Relationship between anxiety and pain.**

pain can heighten anxiety, which in turn can result in muscle strain and spasm. If the strain and spasm are severe enough, localized ischemia and muscle cell damage can arise, resulting in the release of pain-producing substances that then can potentiate pain. Heightened responses of lower back muscles, as shown by electromyography (EMG), were observed among patients discussing personal anxiety-provoking stressors (Flor et al. 1985). Similarly, heightened tension in frontal muscles, associated with personal distress, was noted among patients with tension headaches. This anxiety-pain model makes intuitive sense, but it has not been consistently borne out in evaluations using EMG. One reason for this is that although EMG can reflect activity in superficial muscles, it may not measure the recordings of deeper muscles from which pain may actually originate. Also, a time lag is expected between

the experience of distress and the production of muscle contraction and release of pain-producing substances (Flor and Turk 1989). If EMG recordings are not measured for a sufficient duration to account for this lag time, it is conceivable that negative results would be yielded.

Anxiety is common among chronic pain patients. Anticipatory anxiety (e.g., preoperative anxiety) predicts increased rates of postoperative pain reporting and distress (Thomas et al. 1998). However, other researchers have questioned the impact of anxiety on pain states (Arntz et al. 1991). Anxiety related to precipitating pain can lead to restriction of movement and avoidance of physical therapy. This situation can further exacerbate pain by contributing to deconditioning and muscle weakness. Anxiety disorders are accompanied by an increased incidence of somatic symptoms and pain complaints (Beidel et al. 1991). Anxious patients may experience higher than expected pain levels, mediated by limbic system activation. The limbic system activity during anxiety may nullify the pain-inhibiting processes that might normally emerge from the midbrain and descending inhibitory pathways (Mersky 1989). Thus, the pain experience is potentiated.

Patients with posttraumatic stress disorder (PTSD) often present with multiple physical ailments and complaints (McFarlane 1986). PTSD may accompany and perhaps exacerbate pain associated with traumatic injuries, warranting treatment. Patients with PTSD are prone to somatization, affective dysregulation, and dissociation. Such patients lack the ability to differentiate between relevant and irrelevant information, predisposing them to focus attention on and misinterpret somatic experiences (van der Kolk et al. 1996).

Terminal cancer patients and others with chronic pain may experience existential anxiety, whereby a person questions the quality and meaning of life. Distress arises as one reflects on unaccomplished goals, time remaining to achieve goals, deriving meaning out of one's life, leaving a legacy, and so on. The interruption of hoped-for life achievements can lead to marked dysphoria, anxiety, and narcissistic injury, requiring psychotherapy.

■ SUBSTANCE-RELATED DISORDERS

Fear of drug addiction is often offered as an explanation of why clinicians manage pain suboptimally. Such concerns are particularly heightened when treatment of chronic, nonmalignant pain is required. Patients with somatoform pain disorders may be more prone to dependence on psychoactive substances than patients with more serious physical illnesses (Streltzer et al. 2000). However, some studies indicate that among chronic pain patients with substance use disorders, the substance use disorder preceded the onset of the pain disorder (Brown et al. 1996).

One feature of substance dependence suggestive of a pathological state is the desire for acquisition of such substances (e.g., opiates) for something other than just pain relief (i.e., for psychological relief). Behaviors suggestive of substance abuse or dependence include "problematic" behaviors such as solicitation of medications from multiple sources, forgery of prescriptions, theft of medications, and acquisition of psychoactive substances from illegal sources.

Clinicians can be apt to misinterpret some behaviors of pain patients as being indicative of an underlying substance-related disorder. Referred to as *pseudoaddiction*, such behaviors are likely to arise when patients are undertreated with analgesics (i.e., with inadequate dosage or inadequately spaced doses) (Weissman and Haddox 1989). To acquire more analgesics, such patients may manipulate clinicians, embellish symptoms, and use up prescribed medications in excess of the intended rates. In such cases, optimizing the analgesic treatment may eliminate future manipulative behaviors. If the manipulative behaviors cease once the analgesics are optimized, the presumption is that the behavior is indeed a reflection of an underlying pseudoaddiction. Deciphering between addiction and pseudoaddiction can be somewhat difficult, however, and has been a source of controversy, in part because often no direct correlation can be found between objective medical findings or assessments and the degree of subjective pain complaints (Streltzer et al. 2000; Streltzer 2001). Use of psychoactive substances should enhance treatment adherence (e.g., participation in

physical therapy) and improve adaptive functioning. Misuse of such medications will exacerbate maladaptive functioning.

■ PERSONALITY DISORDERS

Common personality disorders associated with chronic pain include histrionic, dependent, paranoid, and borderline types (Fishbain 1999). *Personality disorders* refers to long-standing, pervasive patterns of behavior, including patterns of relating to others, relating to emotions, and viewing the world (reality testing). Diagnosis of such Axis II disorders should facilitate treatment, for example, by identifying those features of the personality that may interfere with treatment. Thus, the identification of a personality disorder should heighten the clinician's awareness of the patient's needs, the meanings of the illness to the patient, and the coping repertoire of the patient (Weisberg and Keefe 1997). Unfortunately, for the patient with complex pain, the identification of Axis II disorders can be employed pejoratively to cast aspersions on the difficult-to-treat patient and does little in the way of facilitating or complementing treatment.

One problem that frequently arises is whether the behaviors observed (those suggesting a personality disorder) are reflective of a long-standing pattern of functioning or whether they arise from the chronic pain experience. The patient may have a biological and environmental or developmental predisposition toward the expression of a particular personality trait characteristic of a disorder. Under ordinary circumstances, the predisposition might never be fully actualized. However, in a person who is under the stress of a chronic pain state—with its ensuing social, occupational, financial, and legal ramifications—such traits may be heightened and expressed in a manner that, on the surface, might suggest a personality disorder.

■ SCHIZOPHRENIA

The literature on pain among patients with schizophrenia has suggested that these patients demonstrate an insensitivity or indifference

to pain associated with serious medical conditions. A number of experimental paradigms have demonstrated that patients with schizophrenia tend to have reduced pain sensitivities and higher thresholds for pain compared with patients who do not have schizophrenia (Dworkin 1994). Reduced pain sensitivity was found to be a familial trait present among healthy relatives (i.e., without schizophrenia) of patients with schizophrenia (Hooley and Delgado 2001).

A number of mechanisms for these findings have been postulated. Higher pain thresholds have been correlated with higher levels of endogenous opioids within the cerebrospinal fluid in patients with schizophrenia as compared with those without schizophrenia. These endogenous opioids might mitigate awareness of and sensitivity to pain. In addition, altered cortical evoked potentials during noxious stimulation has been demonstrated, suggesting alterations in the perception and processing of painful sensory information. Finally, disturbances in affective (limbic) systems accounting for the negative symptoms of schizophrenia may likewise interfere with the processing of pain and reactions to pain (Dworkin 1994).

Preliminary genetic studies revealed that allelic variants of the delta (δ) opiate receptor prevail among people with schizophrenia. The δ receptor is normally responsive to endogenous opiates; however, the allelic variants observed among people with schizophrenia could be less sensitive to endogenous opiates (Xu et al 2002). Thus, a feedback mechanism accounting for increased endogenous opiates in the cerebrospinal fluid might be explained. Further investigations are required to clarify the pathophysiology of pain insensitivity in schizophrenia.

■ REFERENCES

American Psychiatric Association: Diagnostic and Statistical Manual of Mental Disorders, 3rd Edition. Washington, DC, American Psychiatric Association, 1980

American Psychiatric Association: Diagnostic and Statistical Manual of Mental Disorders, 3rd Edition, Revised. Washington, DC, American Psychiatric Association, 1987

76

American Psychiatric Association: Diagnostic and Statistical Manual of Mental Disorders, 4th Edition. Washington, DC, American Psychiatric Association, 1994

American Psychiatric Association: Diagnostic and Statistical Manual of Mental Disorders, 4th Edition, Text Revision. Washington, DC, American Psychiatric Association, 2000

Arntz A, Dreessen L, Merckelbach H: Attention, not anxiety, influences pain. Behav Res Ther 29:41–50, 1991

Banks SM, Kerns RD: Explaining high rates of depression in chronic pain: a diathesis-stress framework. Psychol Bull 119:95–110, 1996

Beck AT, Steer RA: Beck Depression Inventory Manual. San Antonio, TX, Psychological Corporation, 1987

Beidel DC, Christ MAG, Long PJ: Somatic complaints in anxious children. J Abnorm Child Psychol 19:659–670, 1991

Brown RL, Patterson JJ, Rounds LA, et al: Substance abuse among patients with chronic back pain. J Fam Pract 43:152–160, 1996

Cavanaugh SVA: Diagnosing depression in the hospitalized patient with chronic medical illness. J Clin Psychiatry 45:13–16, 1984

Dworkin RH: Pain insensitivity in schizophrenia: a neglected phenomenon and some implications. Schizophr Bull 20:235–248, 1994

Dworkin RH, Caligor E: Psychiatric diagnosis and chronic pain: DSM-III-R and beyond. J Pain Symptom Manage 3:87–98, 1988

Dworkin SF, von Korff M, LeResche L: Multiple pains and psychiatric disturbance: an epidemiologic investigation. Arch Gen Psychiatry 47:239–244, 1990

Faucett JA: Depression in painful chronic disorders: the role of pain and conflict about pain. J Pain Symptom Manage 9:520–526, 1994

Fishbain DA: Approaches to treatment decisions for psychiatric comorbidity in the management of the chronic pain patient. Med Clin North Am 83:737–760, 1999

Fishbain DA, Goldberg M, Meagher BR, et al: Male and female chronic pain patients categorized by DSM-III psychiatric diagnostic criteria. Pain 26:181–197, 1986

Flor H, Turk DC: Psychophysiology of chronic pain: do chronic pain patients exhibit symptom-specific psychophysiologic responses? Psychol Bull 105:215–259, 1989

Flor H, Turk DC, Birbaumer N: Assessment of stress-related psychophysiological reactions in chronic back pain patients. J Consult Clin Psychol 53:354–364, 1985

Gamsa A: Is emotional disturbance a precipitator or a consequence of chronic pain? Pain 42:183–195, 1990

Hooley JM, Delgado ML: Pain insensitivity in the relatives of schizophrenic patients. Schizophr Res 47:265–273, 2001

King SA, Strain JJ: Revising the category of somatoform pain disorder. Hosp Community Psychiatry 43:217–219, 1992

Lipowski ZJ: Somatization: the concept and its clinical application. Am J Psychiatry 145:1358–1368, 1988

Lipowski ZJ: Somatization and depression. Psychosomatics 31:13–21, 1990

Massie MJ, Holland JC: Depression and the cancer patient. J Clin Psychiatry 51(suppl 7):12–17, 1990

McFarlane AC: Posttraumatic morbidity of a disaster: a study of cases presenting for psychiatric treatment. J Nerv Ment Dis 174:4–14, 1986

Merskey H: Psychiatry and chronic pain. Can J Psychiatry 34:329–336, 1989

Streltzer J: Pain management in the opioid-dependent patient. Curr Psychiatry Rep 3:489–496, 2001

Streltzer J, Eliashof BA, Kline AE, et al: Chronic pain disorder following physical injury. Psychosomatics 41:227–234, 2000

Thomas T, Robinson C, Champion D, et al: Prediction and assessment of the severity of post-operative pain and of satisfaction with management. Pain 75:177–185, 1998

van der Kolk BA, Pelcovitz D, Roth S, et al: Dissociation, somatization, and affect dysregulation: the complexity of adaptation to trauma. Am J Psychiatry 153:83–93, 1996

Weisberg JN, Keefe FJ: Personality disorders in the chronic pain population: basic concepts, empirical findings, and clinical implications. Pain Forum 6:1–9, 1997

Weissman DE, Haddox JD: Opioid pseudoaddiction: an iatrogenic syndrome. Pain 36:363–366, 1989

Xu J, Leo RJ, DiMartino S, et al: Linkage studies of delta opioid receptor gene and pain insensitivity in schizophrenia. Paper presented at the annual meeting of the American Psychiatric Association, Research Colloquium for Junior Investigators, Philadelphia, PA, May 2002

5

PHARMACOLOGY OF PAIN

Familiarity with the range of medications employed in the treatment of pain is essential. This chapter focuses on the utility of such agents and the disorders in which they may be employed, as well as dosing and side effects.

■ OPIATE ANALGESICS

Opiates have largely been the mainstay of treatment in acute pain states and terminal disorders. Long-term use in chronic, nonmalignant states has raised significant concerns for many clinicians about predisposing patients to functional impairments, dependence, and poor treatment response (Buckley et al. 1986; Finlayson et al. 1986; Maruta 1978; McNairy et al. 1984). A knowledge of opiate activity in the management of pain is essential. Familiarity with the dosing and duration of effects is required, as well as a knowledge of the ceiling effects (i.e., the maximal dose beyond which no further analgesic effect would be obtained) (Inturrisi 1984) (Table 5–1).

Guidelines for Use

The affinity of the opiates for the μ receptors within the central nervous system (CNS) determines their effectiveness in mitigating pain. Certain opiates, such as codeine and propoxyphene, are considered to be weak opiates, useful in mild to moderate pain. For more severe pain, stronger opiates such as morphine are required. Morphine is the agent against which all other opioids tend to be

TABLE 5–1. Opiate dosing and use

Agents	Equianalgesic doses, mg		Starting dose, mg	Duration, hours	Affinity for μ receptors	Ceiling effect
	Oral	Parenteral				
Morphine-like						
Morphine	30	10	15–30 (oral)	4–5	+++	No
Codeine	200	120	30–60 (oral)	4–6	+	Yes
Hydromorphone	7.5	1.5	4–8 (oral)	4–5	+++	No
Meperidine	300	75	50–100* (oral)	2–5	++	No
Oxycodone	20	NA	15–30 (oral)	4–6**	++	No
Methadone	20	10	5–10 (oral)	3–8	+++	No
Levorphanol	4	2	2–4 (oral)	4–5	+++	No
Fentanyl***	—	0.1	0.1 (iv)	4–6	+++	No
Partial agonist						
Buprenorphine	—	0.4	0.3–0.6 (iv)	4–6	Partial	Yes
Agonist-antagonist						
Nalbuphine	—	10	10–20 (iv)	3–6	Antagonist	Yes
Butorphanol	—	2	0.5–2 (iv)	3–4	Antagonist	Yes
Dezocine	—	10	5–20 (iv)	3–6	Antagonist	Yes
Pentazocine	—	30	30–60 (iv)	3–4	Antagonist	Yes

TABLE 5–1. **Opiate dosing and use** *(continued)*

*Higher starting doses may be required for moderate to severe pain.
**Sustained-release form available.
***Fentanyl transdermal patch not listed here.

Note. Dash (—) indicates not available in oral form. iv = intravenous; NA = not applicable.

Source. Adapted from Rundell JR, Wise MG: "Pain and Analgesics," in *Concise Guide to Consultation Psychiatry,* 3rd Edition. Washington, DC, American Psychiatric Publishing, 2000, p. 213. Copyright 2000 American Psychiatric Publishing. Used with permission; Jaffe JH, Martin WR: "Opioid Analgesics and Antagonists," in *The Pharmacological Basis of Therapeutics.* Edited by Gilman AG, Rall TW, Nies AS, et al. New York, Pergamon, 1990; Bouckoms A: "Psychiatric Aspects of Pain in the Critically Ill," in *Problems in Critical Care.* Edited by Wise MG. Philadelphia, PA, JB Lippincott, 1988. Copyright 1988, JB Lippincott; Cassem NH: "Pain (Current Topics in Medicine, Vol. 2)," in *Scientific American Medicine.* Edited by Rubenstein E, Federman DD. New York, Scientific American, 1989.

compared. Fentanyl is a very potent analgesic with greater affinity for the μ receptor than morphine.

The doses recommended in Table 5–1 are offered as a guideline; the optimal analgesic dose may vary widely among patients. Opiate rotation—that is, sequential trials of analgesic—may be required to identify the opiate that optimally addresses pain while offering the most favorably tolerated side effects. Equianalgesic doses of opiates must be a consideration.

Side Effects

Selection of an opiate to be employed can be based upon several factors (Table 5–2). For example, the patient's prior experiences (efficacy of a drug or its untoward effects) might influence analgesic choice. Affinity for the μ receptor also determines the severity of the side effects encountered with opioids, influencing respiratory rate, gastrointestinal (GI) motility, sphincter tone, and so forth. Side effects of opiate analgesics can include constipation, nausea, vomiting, excess sedation, pruritus, and respiratory depression. Laxatives are required for constipation. Stimulants can be used for excess sedation. Pruritus can be addressed with concomitant use of antihistamines (e.g., hydroxyzine). Respiratory depression is rare in patients who receive chronic opiate treatment, but it can arise with excess doses and in opiate-naïve patients. Reversal of respiratory depression may require the use of low doses of an opiate antagonist (e.g., naloxone). If opiate antagonists are used judiciously, it is possible to avoid precipitating pain or significant withdrawal symptoms.

To avoid some of the side effects associated with morphine-like opioids, a mixed agonist-antagonist is sometimes selected. The agonist-antagonist class of opioids consist of pentazocine, butorphanol, nalbuphine, and dezocine. These agents are agonists at κ receptors, but antagonists at μ receptors. These agents have less influence on the μ receptors of the GI tract, producing less nausea, vomiting, and constipation than pure opiate agonists. Because of their antagonist properties, employing higher doses may actually

83

TABLE 5–2.	Opioid therapy guidelines for chronic nonmalignant pain

Consider opiates after other reasonable alternatives have failed

Consider contraindications for opiate use

Prescription of opiates should be managed by a single practitioner

Select opiates based on:

    Ease of administration (oral, transdermal, other)

    Cost

    Duration of analgesic effect

    Tolerability of side effects

    Potential risk of drug interactions

Administer opiates around-the-clock, instead of as needed

Adjust or increase opiate dose gradually, contingent on:

    Degree of pain relief

    Degree of functional improvement

    Side effect profiles

Address side effects

Formalize treatment and document well

Consider use of patient contract

Consider making opiate therapy contingent on participation in other aspects of treatment (e.g., physical therapy, occupational therapy, psychotherapy)

Follow up weekly to monthly until patient is stable; once patient is stabilized, less frequent follow-up may be possible

---

depress analgesia. Ceiling effects limit the utility of such agents among certain patients.

Drug Interactions

Choice of opiate analgesic might be determined by other concurrently administered medications. Toxic reactions occur when meperidine is administered to patients taking monoamine oxidase inhibitors (MAOIs). When these medications are coadministered, a serotonin syndrome can result, producing diaphoresis, rigidity, hyperreflexia, hypertension or hypotension, tachycardia, delirium, seizures, hyperthermia, and occasionally, death (Gratz and Simpson

84

1993; Rundell and Wise 2000; Sternbach 1991). More selective MAOIs—for example, selegiline, a monoamine oxidase B inhibitor used to treat parkinsonism—can also interact with narcotic analgesics to produce toxic reactions. To avoid toxicity, the MAOI should be discontinued approximately 2 weeks prior to anticipated opiate initiation. When this is not possible, codeine, fentanyl, oxycodone, and morphine might be safer alternatives. Additionally, the analgesic effects of the opiates can be potentiated by the interference of the hepatic metabolism caused by the MAOIs. Consequently, the opiates should be dosed substantially lower than usual.

The analgesic effects of the opioids can be augmented by the coadministration of several other psychotropic medications, including fluoxetine, tricyclic antidepressants (TCAs; e.g., amitriptyline, imipramine, clomipramine), and antipsychotics (e.g., promethazine, chlorpromazine, haloperidol) (Keeri-Szanto 1974; Maltbie et al. 1979; Stambaugh and Wainer 1981). Lower opiate doses may be required if coadministered with these agents, to avoid untoward effects. Opioids (e.g., propoxyphene) can inhibit the metabolism of TCAs (e.g., doxepin), leading to marked sedation and anticholinergic and α-adrenergic effects (Abernethy et al. 1982). Cigarette smoking diminishes the effectiveness of opiate analgesics (e.g., propoxyphene and pentazocine) by potentiating their metabolism.

Medical Conditions

Concurrent medical conditions might influence opiate selection. Among patients with renal failure, metabolites of selected opiates (i.e., morphine, meperidine, and propoxyphene) can produce significant untoward effects. The metabolites of these agents, which depend on renal clearance, can accumulate, producing prolonged sedation. In the case of meperidine, seizures and CNS toxicity can arise, whereas with propoxyphene, cardiac conduction abnormalities can develop. Doses have to be reduced significantly in patients with renal compromise. Alternatively, hydromorphone lacks metabolites with significant activity and is a safer choice.

Route of Administration

The selected route of administration of the analgesic can be influenced by several factors, including ease of administration, degree of desired patient control, and tolerability or preference of the administration route. The oral route of administration is convenient, flexible, and nonintrusive. The drawback is that 1.5–2 hours must be allowed for peak drug effects of most opiates. If patients have difficulty swallowing pills, liquid formulations are available. Some agents (e.g., hydromorphone) can be crushed and added to liquids for ingestion. For patients who are too incapacitated to swallow oral medications, alternative routes (transmucosal, transdermal, intramuscular, subcutaneous, intravenous, or intraspinal) would have to be explored. Oral transmucosal fentanyl citrate is available. This formulation allows for rapid absorption of fentanyl for rapid pain relief (in 5–10 minutes) and is useful for patients with breakthrough pain despite optimal analgesic treatment. The peak analgesic effect with intramuscular administration has a faster onset but also dissipates faster than with oral administration; however, intramuscular administration is intrusive and painful. Repeated intramuscular opioid administration can lead to abscess formation and muscle fibrosis. Subcutaneous administration is an alternative to intramuscular injections and may be better tolerated. Intravenous administration of opiates is less intrusive, convenient, and quick-acting. One variant of the intravenous infusion is patient-controlled analgesia (PCA), whereby the patient self-administers and regulates opiate administration (Table 5–3). When patients control the rate of opiate administration, they often require less opiate than when they have to rely on dosing prescribed on an as-needed basis.

Transdermal fentanyl is slowly released through a reservoir, transfers through subcutaneous tissue, accumulates in subcutaneous fat tissue, and slowly diffuses into the blood stream. A slow concentration gradient develops between the fat and neighboring blood vessels. Normally, fentanyl has a 3-hour half-life, but with the slow release from the subcutaneous reservoir the effective half-life increases to 17 hours. Because of the delay in movement to the

86

bloodstream, transdermal fentanyl will not have immediate analgesic effects for approximately the first 24 hours. Consequently, during this time, supplemental analgesics are required. Once the effectiveness of the fentanyl patch has been appreciated, the supplemental analgesics can be discontinued. The patch needs to be replaced every 3 days. Both PCA and transdermal administration offer the advantage of reduced demand on staff time for administering as-needed opiates.

TABLE 5–3. **Dosing guidelines**

---

1. Converting from conventional immediate-release oral morphine (or equivalent) to controlled-release morphine
   a. Calculate the total amount of conventional immediate-release oral morphine (or equivalent) used in a 24-hour period
   b. Divide this amount by 3
   c. The resulting amount is the dose of controlled-release morphine to be administered three times daily
2. Converting from oral morphine (or equivalent) to transdermal fentanyl
   a. Calculate the total amount of oral morphine (or equivalent) employed in a 24-hour period
   b. Divide total oral morphine dose by 3
   c. Select the nearest patch strength in µg/h (i.e., 25, 50, 75, or 100 µg/h)
   d. Continue to administer the scheduled oral morphine for the first 12–24 hours after the first patch is in place
3. PCA specifications
   a. Administer loading dose, generally 1–2 mg of morphine (or equivalent)
   b. Decide the hourly rate of the opiate that will be administered continuously (e.g., 1–2 mg morphine [or equivalent] hourly)

The patient-requested rate needs to be determined. The PCA has lockout periods, during which no opiate will be administered even if the patient presses the button to administer the medication. The lockout period is generally determined to be 6–12 minutes. The patient will be able to self-administer 1–2 mg morphine (or equivalent) when the button is pressed beyond the preestablished lockout period.

Note. PCA = patient-controlled analgesia.

In some cases, switching from one route to another can require significant dose modifications. For example, oral meperidine has approximately one-fourth the analgesic efficacy of similar parenteral doses. Thus, when switching from intramuscular to oral meperidine, four times the parenteral dose is generally required.

Continuous pain, present most of the day, requires analgesics administered around the clock as opposed to as needed (Portenoy and Hagen 1990). When medications are dispensed as needed, higher doses of the opiate may be required to relieve pain. Furthermore, a longer period of time might elapse before sufficient relief is attained. Scheduled analgesics might avoid both of these difficulties.

When treated with short-acting agents (see Table 5–1), patients may experience recurrence of pain at the end of the dosing interval, when levels of the analgesic agent are reduced. Such effects, including interference with sleep, may be difficult for patients to tolerate. Longer-acting agents, therefore, are preferred. With these agents, pain recrudescence at the end of the dosing interval is less likely to occur. Agents such as levorphanol have long durations of action, as compared with morphine, and might be useful in this regard. Longer-acting formulations of other agents (e.g., controlled-released morphine, controlled-release oxycodone, and transdermal fentanyl) have become available for sustained analgesia (see Table 5–3). Such formulations allow for more gradual release through the GI tract and can be dosed at 5- and 12-hour intervals. Crushing of the slow-release formulations (e.g., to be administered via nasogastric tube) will result in release of all of the opioid and eliminates any long-acting effects.

As with transdermal fentanyl, long-acting formulations do not produce immediate relief. Thus, supplementation with short-acting agents may be required until the analgesic effects of the long-acting agent are appreciated.

Agents With Multiple Uses

Methadone has been used primarily for opioid detoxification and maintenance treatment of individuals with opioid dependence. Its

utility in such situations is that it has a long half-life and binds preferentially to opiate receptors. Methadone has analgesic ability as well. Its analgesic effects are short-lived, however; thus, more frequent dosing is required. For patients already receiving methadone maintenance therapy, their usual doses can be divided to optimize pain relief. Patients requiring methadone maintenance acquire the drug on an outpatient basis by appearing at the methadone clinics daily. If a patient simultaneously required pain management—that is, more frequent dosing with smaller doses— the patient would have to appear at the clinic several times daily, which could prove to be logistically difficult. A federal license is required to prescribe methadone for detoxification or maintenance treatment related to opioids but is not required for purposes of pain management.

Methadone is available in two isomeric forms, the l- and d- isomers. Although the d-isomer does not bind the opiate receptor, it does bind to N-methyl-D-aspartate (NMDA) receptors. It is thought that this action may exert an analgesic effect independent of μ receptor binding. Thus, the methadone is likely to be more potent than expected by conventional opiate pharmacokinetics. When switching from one opiate to methadone, some clinicians advocate a reduction of as much as 75%–90% in the dose due to the unexpectedly high potency of the methadone.

Buprenorphine is a partial agonist, binding preferentially to μ receptors. It is not easily reversed by antagonists (e.g., naloxone). It is administered intravenously for pain control in moderate to severe pain. There is an analgesic ceiling effect; thus, for pain persisting beyond optimal dosing, the clinician may have to explore alternatives. Buprenorphine is beginning to have appeal for detoxification and maintenance treatment of patients addicted to opioids. It is administered orally for this purpose. It is available only in research settings testing the effectiveness of buprenorphine for opiate detoxification and maintenance. Oral administration may eventually provide an alternate route of analgesia at some point.

Tolerance, Dependence, and Pseudoaddiction

Tolerance can emerge with the long-term use of opiate analgesics—that is, higher doses are required to achieve the same level of analgesia previously achieved at lower doses. Because of this propensity, opiate rotation has been advocated. To rotate from one opiate analgesic to another, refer to the equianalgesic doses shown in Table 5–1. Because the cross-tolerance among opioids is incomplete, the equianalgesic dose of the newer agent is reduced by 25%–50% of its usual prescribed dose. Alternatively, supplementation with adjunctive agents (e.g., non-opioid analgesics) may augment the analgesic effect of the opiate without requiring significant opiate dose increments.

If a patient presents with increases in pain despite analgesic use, it is inappropriate to assume that this increase reflects tolerance without first examining the patient and determining if another health condition has emerged that warrants attention. It is possible that disease progression or a secondary illness or physical process is emerging, aggravating the pain despite analgesic use and requiring alternative treatment interventions (Portenoy 1996).

A common misconception is that the development of tolerance might signal dependence. Physical dependence is probable with the long-term use of opiate analgesics. It is likely manifest if the patient develops signs of opiate withdrawal when the dosage is suddenly reduced or the agent is abruptly discontinued. Signs can include lacrimation, rhinorrhea, gooseflesh, irritability and anxiety, nausea, vomiting, abdominal cramping, lower extremity cramping, and other features. If the opioid needs to be discontinued after long-term use, the process should be undertaken gradually to avoid the unnecessary discomfort that accompanies abrupt withdrawal. Because of their antagonist properties, the clinician must be cautious about administering agonist-antagonists to patients with opiate dependence or to those previously treated with full agonist opiates. Agonist-antagonists can likewise precipitate withdrawal, adding significant distress to the pain already experienced. Alternatively, methadone can be employed to successfully detoxify the patient while minimizing withdrawal symptoms. Use of adjunctive agents (e.g.,

transdermal clonidine) may also reduce some of the autonomic symptoms that can accompany withdrawal.

As discussed in Chapter 4, patients who are inadequately treated with opiate analgesics may display behaviors (i.e., pseudoaddiction) that, on the surface, appear to be manipulative and characteristic of drug seeking (Weissman and Haddox 1989). These behaviors generally cease once opioids are dosed appropriately to mitigate pain. However, distinguishing substance dependence from pseudoaddiction can be difficult.

Opiate Abuse

Crushing the tablets of Oxycontin SR and taking in the crushed material intranasally or intravenously will result in release of all of the oxycodone at once; this activity has become popular with persons in the drug underground for its euphoric effects. It was earlier thought that by antagonizing μ receptors, less abuse liability would be associated with the opioid agonist-antagonists. Unfortunately, these expectations were not borne out. However, it had been discovered that some persons would pulverize the medication pentazocine and inject it intravenously for its euphoric effects. To counter this, the manufacturer has added naloxone (an opiate antagonist) to the tablet. When taken orally, as intended, the naloxone is poorly absorbed and, therefore, does not interfere with the intended analgesic effects. However, if pulverized and injected, the naloxone would then be fully effective and would mitigate any euphoric effect produced by the abuse of this medication. The same approach might soon be employed to reduce abuse liability with Oxycontin SR. Butorphanol has been made available as a nasal spray formulation to facilitate ease of administration, particularly in patients with difficulty swallowing. When combined with inhaled antihistamines, butorphanol can produce a euphoric effect similar to that of heroin.

Patient Contracts

Clinicians may be uncomfortable about prescribing opioids (or other controlled substances) for the long term, especially in chronic

nonmalignant pain, because of concerns about federal regulations and the risks of substance abuse. To ease their concern, a patient contract can be established (Table 5–4). In the contract, the responsibilities of the patient and the physician are defined. In this way, both the clinician and the patient are clear about the treatment and are protected on issues pertaining to the use of controlled substances. The contract provides for the appropriate disclosure of these issues and the parameters for treatment—including the use and acquisition of analgesics and other treatment responsibilities. The patient is made aware of his or her responsibilities with regard to use of the medication. The patient's responsibilities regarding the other facets of treatment (e.g., physical therapy, smoking cessation, avoidance of alcohol, weight loss) can also be delineated. The patient is informed that violation of the conditions of the contract can allow the physician to terminate the use of controlled substances. The contract can also stipulate the requirement that the patient participate in psychotherapy, substance abuse treatment, or other therapy. The contract can specify limitations regarding the acquisition of controlled substances (e.g., that prescriptions will not be provided for "running out early," prescription loss, or spilled or misplaced medications) and can state that prescriptions should not be acquired from other clinicians, emergency departments, or after-hours facilities. A copy of the contract, signed by the clinician and the patient, can be given to the patient; the original should be filed in the patient's chart.

■ TRAMADOL

Tramadol is unique in its pharmacologic effects. It has opiate effects (approximately 1/15 the potency of morphine) and influences other neurotransmitter pathways (i.e., it inhibits the reuptake of norepinephrine [NE] and serotonin [5-HT]). Both NE and 5-HT are thought to inhibit the influence of pain-mediating neurotransmitters (i.e., substance P) within the dorsal horn of the spinal cord. Newer variants combining the anti-inflammatory effects of acetaminophen with tramadol are available (e.g., Ultracet). The abuse and dependence

TABLE 5–4.	Items to be factored into patient contract for use with controlled substances

Physician responsibilities

Disclose that the substances prescribed are controlled by local, state, and federal agencies

Specify that prescriptions for controlled substances will be made only during regular office hours—not at night, on weekends, on holidays, and so forth

Specify that unknown risks may be associated with long-term use of controlled substances and that the patient will be kept apprised of any advances in the field that call attention to such risks

Disclose information regarding potential development of tolerance and physical dependence

Specify the grounds for termination of prescription of controlled substances

Patient responsibilities

To prevent loss, misplacement, or theft of controlled substances, understanding that controlled substances will not be readily replaced

To be present, in person, to pick up prescriptions for controlled substances

To take the medication in the dose, and at the intervals, prescribed

To keep track of the amount of medication remaining

To comply with random urine or blood testing in order to document the proper use of medications and confirm adherence

To comply with the laws of the state regarding use of medications and operation of motorized vehicles

To work with physician in developing better health habits

To not divert or dispense controlled substances to others

liability of tramadol was once thought to be quite low. However, several reports have emerged that indicate that tramadol is an agent on which patients can become quite dependent. In one case, a patient had been using such dramatic daily amounts that inpatient methadone detoxification was required (Leo et al. 2000).

■ NONOPIOID ANALGESICS

Aspirin, other salicylates, acetaminophen, nonsteroidal anti-inflammatory drugs (NSAIDs), and cyclooxygenase-2 (COX-2)

inhibitors are useful for treating acute and chronic pain. These non-opioid agents act by interfering with prostaglandin synthesis and disrupting pain by reducing inflammation at peripheral sites. (However, the mechanism of analgesia produced by acetaminophen is unclear.) Some of these are also useful as antipyretic agents. The efficacy of these agents is limited by a ceiling effect, and their usefulness is limited by the risks of side effects.

Aspirin produces irreversible platelet aggregation, a concern if surgery is anticipated in the near future. Other salicylates (e.g., choline magnesium trisalicylate and salsalate) have fewer GI side effects and less effect on bleeding time. Reye's syndrome is associated with aspirin use in children who have a viral illness (varicella). Aspirin hypersensitivity is of two types: one involving respiratory reactions (observed in patients with rhinitis, asthma, nasal polyps); and the second involving rapid development of urticaria, angioedema, hypotension, shock, or syncope.

Acetaminophen does not produce GI distress, nor does it produce platelet inhibition. However, when combined with warfarin, it can predispose patients to marked anticoagulation and bleeding. Severe hepatotoxicity can arise with excessive use of acetaminophen and in persons who ingest alcohol concurrent with acetaminophen use. Patients should therefore restrict their alcohol use when taking acetaminophen.

NSAIDs have efficacy comparable with that of the salicylates and are viable alternatives for persons with hypersensitivities to aspirin. However, there are occasional cross-sensitivities to NSAIDs in aspirin-sensitive individuals. Some NSAIDs have significantly more analgesic efficacy than salicylates (e.g., parenteral ketorolac has analgesic efficacy comparable with 6–12 mg of morphine). NSAIDs are nonselective inhibitors of the cyclooxygenase enzyme responsible for the prostaglandin synthesis in peripheral tissues that results in inflammatory pain. Because of their lack of selectivity, NSAIDs have inhibitory effects on the cyclooxygenase-1 enzyme, interfering with prostaglandins that mediate beneficial physiologic effects in the GI tract and renal tubules.

The most problematic side effects of NSAID use include gastric irritation and ulceration, bleeding due to reduced platelet aggregation, and renal dysfunction. NSAIDs do not produce irreversible platelet inhibition as is the case with aspirin. Patients at risk for GI disturbances are those of advanced age, those with histories of prior ulcers, and those simultaneously receiving steroids. To reduce the risk of GI complications, the lowest doses possible should be used. Use of misoprostol or omeprazole may be efficacious in preventing ulcers. Ranitidine and cimetidine are not useful in preventing ulceration, but they can be employed to treat the gastric ulcers produced by NSAID use. NSAIDs can reduce renal blood flow and glomerular filtration. As a consequence, there is increased water and electrolyte reabsorption in the proximal tubule, predisposing vulnerable persons to increased blood pressure and congestive heart failure (CHF). Other toxic effects of NSAIDs include hepatotoxicity and acute renal failure.

Concomitant use of NSAIDs and lithium can lead to lithium toxicity. Aspirin, acetaminophen, and perhaps the NSAID sulindac may be safely employed in patients concomitantly treated with lithium (Ragheb and Powell 1986).

Cyclooxygenase-2 Inhibitors

COX-2 inhibitors (i.e., celecoxib, rofecoxib, and valdecoxib), because of their selectivity for COX-2, are less likely than NSAIDs to produce any adverse GI or renal effects. These agents have been useful in reducing pain associated with rheumatoid arthritis and osteoarthritis. Celecoxib (100 mg twice daily) or rofecoxib (25 mg/day) are used for osteoarthritis. The doses are doubled for rheumatoid arthritis. Valdecoxib dose is 10 mg/day for both osteoarthritis and rheumatoid arthritis. Use is contraindicated in patients with sensitivities to COX-2 inhibitors or allergies to sulfonamides or NSAIDs.

■ ANTIDEPRESSANTS

Antidepressants have long been advocated for the treatment of several chronic pain disorders. Uses include the following:

- Direct pain-mitigating effects (independent of effects on mood)
- Treatment of comorbid depression and anxiety that can accompany and exacerbate pain
- Ameliorating sleep and appetite disturbances accompanying pain

Pain reduction with use of antidepressants has been demonstrated among nondepressed pain patients. Among depressed pain patients, antidepressants can produce analgesia faster and at doses far lower than those required for antidepressant effects.

Analgesia produced by antidepressants is thought to be mediated by enhancing the inhibitory neurotransmitters (e.g., NE and 5-HT) present within descending pain-mediating pathways. In the spinal cord, the synthesis and release of pain-promoting neurotransmitters (e.g., substance P and glutamate) is reduced by these agents. Certain antidepressants may augment opiate effects within the spinal cord. Morphine analgesia is potentiated by amitriptyline, imipramine, clomipramine, fluoxetine, sertraline, and nefazodone (Larson and Takemori 1977; Lee and Spencer 1980; Pick et al. 1992; Taiwo et al. 1985). On the other hand, within the brain, the antidepressants reduce the extent of limbic output, which might otherwise contribute to depression and anxiety that exacerbate underlying pain.

Tricyclic Antidepressants

The bulk of the evidence pertaining to the use of antidepressants in pain states has been directed at the utility of TCAs (Table 5–5). Neuropathic and idiopathic pains may respond better to TCA use than do nociceptive pains. However, these agents can be effective in nociceptive pain states when there is a comorbid depression or anxiety that complicates the disorder. The efficacy of TCAs appears to be related to the reuptake inhibition of NE and 5-HT. Those TCAs with a broad spectrum of activity may have more efficacy in pain reduction than those with neurotransmitter-specific effects.

TABLE 5–5.	Antidepressant use in chronic pain

Tricyclic antidepressants	**Selective serotonin reuptake inhibitors**
Neuropathy	Diabetic neuropathy
Diabetic-type	Tension headache
Postherpetic	**Venlafaxine**
Post-stroke	Fibromyalgia
Nondiabetic peripheral	Chronic headache
neuropathy	Peripheral neuropathy
Headache	**Bupropion**
Tension	Peripheral neuropathy
Migraine	**Trazodone**
Rheumatologic disorders	Diabetic neuropathy
Fibromyalgia	**Nefazodone**
Osteoarthritis	Headache
Rheumatoid arthritis	Tension
Other	Migraine
Atypical facial pain	**Mirtazapine**
Phantom limb pain	? (Unclear utility)
Complex regional pain	
syndrome	
Monoamine oxidase inhibitors	
Peripheral neuropathy	
Migraine headache	

Thus, amitriptyline and imipramine appear to be more effective than desipramine or clomipramine (Max et al. 1992).

Generally speaking, TCAs are initiated at a dose of 10–25 mg at bedtime. Analgesia appears to be dose dependent. The dose can be increased slowly (e.g., increased in increments of 10–25 mg every 3–7 days) until analgesia or intolerable side effects occur. Specific analgesic serum levels for the TCAs are unknown. However, if a dose of 150 mg/day is achieved without significant pain relief, assessment of serum levels may be prudent. This may help to ascertain whether there is poor adherence to the medication regimen, poor absorption, rapid metabolism of the TCA, or all of these. If the

patient is adherent to the regimen, but due to metabolic factors has seemingly low serum levels, the dose of the TCA can be increased beyond 150 mg/day if the side effects are not prohibitive. Serum levels should be checked to assess for toxic ranges, particularly for nortriptyline. However, if side effects preclude dose advancement, alternatives need to be considered.

Unfortunately, the adverse effects of the TCAs can limit their utility (Table 5–6). Amitriptyline and imipramine have more troublesome side effects than the secondary amine TCAs (e.g., nortriptyline and desipramine). TCAs are contraindicated in some patients: those with closed-angle glaucoma, recent myocardial infarction, cardiac arrhythmias, poorly controlled seizures, or severe benign prostatic hypertrophy.

Monoamine Oxidase Inhibitors

The MAOI phenelzine has been found to be effective in the treatment of selected pain disorders. However, MAOI use has been limited by medication side effects, the need for a tyramine-free diet, and the potential risk of drug interactions (e.g., serotonin syndrome arising from coadministration with meperidine).

TABLE 5–6. **Tricyclic antidepressant side effects**

Anticholinergic	Cardiac
Dry mouth	Palpitations
Constipation	Sweating
Memory impairments	Tachycardia
Blurred vision	Prolonged QT interval
Urinary retention	Neurologic
Delirium	Myoclonus
Antihistamine	Tardive dyskinesia
Sedation	Parkinsonism
Weight gain	Seizures
α-Adrenergic	
Orthostatic hypotension	

98

Selective Serotonin Reuptake Inhibitors

The selective serotonin reuptake inhibitors (SSRIs) offer the advantages of greater tolerability of side effects and relative safety in overdose as compared with TCAs. However, the literature on SSRI effectiveness is limited by the small sample sizes and small dosage ranges employed in the studies (Ansari 2000). SSRIs found to be effective for one type of pain do not necessarily have efficacy in other types (e.g., fluoxetine can be useful for chronic daily tension headaches, but might not be effective for diabetic neuropathy) (Diamond and Freitag 1989; Saper et al. 1994). Similarly, the effectiveness of the SSRIs does not generalize (i.e., if one SSRI is effective for a certain type of pain, this does not mean that other SSRIs will show similar efficacy). For example, paroxetine appears to be effective for neuropathic pain, but fluoxetine does not (Max et al. 1992; Sindrup et al. 1990, 1991).

There is some question whether the reduced efficacy of the SSRIs as compared with TCAs is related to the 5-HT selectivity of the SSRIs. As noted in the section on TCAs, those TCAs with broader spectra of neurotransmitter activity tend to be more effective than those with more selective 5-HT activity (Max et al. 1992). In one study, fluoxetine was less effective than amitriptyline and desipramine and fared no better than placebo.

The doses of SSRIs are increased slowly as tolerated and as warranted by the need for analgesic, antidepressant, or anxiolytic efficacy. Side effects associated with their use include nausea, diarrhea, insomnia or sedation, tremors, and sexual dysfunction.

Other Antidepressants

Both venlafaxine and bupropion (which have a broad spectrum of activity, including NE, 5-HT, and dopamine) display some promise with respect to efficacy in certain pain disorders (Barkin and Fawcett 2000) (see Table 5–5). These agents lack significant cardiac or anticholinergic side effects and have fewer risks of drug interactions. There is a risk of seizure associated with higher doses of

bupropion; venlafaxine may be associated with nervousness, insomnia, weight loss, and elevations in diastolic blood pressure. If TCAs are intolerable, these agents may prove to be workable alternatives for the pain patient. A new antidepressant, duloxetine, is pending U.S. Food and Drug Administration (FDA) approval. It shares with venlafaxine NE and 5-HT reuptake inhibition. Because of these properties, it will be marketed specifically for use with chronic pain patients.

A number of other antidepressants with prominent 5-HT effects have utility in depressive disorders (e.g., trazodone, nefazodone, and mirtazapine). Only one case report involving mirtazapine in pain reduction exists in the literature (Brannon and Stone 1999). Two studies—one involving patients with neuropathy and the other involving chronic headache patients—found pain-mitigating effects with nefazodone. Patients with migraine and tension headache experienced marked reductions in the frequencies, severity, and durations of recurrent headache when treated with daily nefazodone (Goodnick et al. 2000; Saper et al. 2001). Additional clinical trials investigating the roles of these antidepressants are warranted.

Trazodone appears to be minimally, but not conclusively, efficacious in pain. Although two double-blind studies demonstrated efficacy of trazodone in diabetic neuropathy and pain resulting from deafferentation of nerves (Khurana 1983; Ventafridda et al. 1988), the effects on patients with headache, fibromyalgia, rheumatoid arthritis, and chronic low back pain seemed less promising (Ansari 2000). Trazodone has been employed for its sedative properties. Some patients, particularly those taking opiates or other sedating agents, may find the sedative effects too incapacitating. The analgesic properties of trazodone appear to be independent of its sedative effects (Ansari 2000). Caution concerning other potential adverse effects associated with trazodone use (e.g., orthostasis and priapism) is warranted; doses should be kept to a minimum, and increased only gradually, to reduce the risk of incurring adverse effects.

■ ANTICONVULSANT DRUGS

Anticonvulsant drugs (ACDs) historically have demonstrated efficacy in neuropathic pain (McQuay et al. 1995) (Table 5–7). Analgesia produced by ACDs is presumed to be related to the influences of the ACDs on slowing the peripheral nerve conduction of primary afferent fibers, thereby dampening the painful sensory information relayed to the CNS. In addition, the ACDs influence γ-aminobutyric acid (GABA) activity responsible for inhibiting pain processes within the spinal cord and brain. They also function to inhibit the production of pain-promoting neurotransmitters (Swerdlow 1984).

Because of the differences in the pain-relieving effects of ACDs as compared with antidepressants, it is plausible that ACDs would be workable alternatives for patients with persisting pain despite optimal antidepressant use or patients for whom antidepressant use proved intolerable. Alternatively, simultaneous administration of antidepressants and ACDs could be used, because the analgesic mechanisms of these classes of agents complement each other. When coadministered, lower doses of the antidepressant, the ACD, or both, are possible, perhaps allowing analgesia while circumventing the higher doses of either agent that predispose a person to adverse effects.

ACDs have mood-stabilizing effects and are useful for pain patients with psychiatric comorbidities, such as bipolar disorder, schizoaffective disorder, and impulsivity arising from dementia (Leo and Narendran 1999). Thus, patients with mood disturbances, impulsivity, and unpredictable aggression along with coexistent chronic pain may be ideal candidates for ACD selection. Adverse effects common with ACDs include sedation, fatigue, and GI and motor side effects.

Gabapentin has received FDA approval for use in the treatment of neuropathic pain. Gabapentin offers numerous advantages over other available ACDs. It is unlikely to produce serious side effects associated with the use of other anticonvulsants (e.g., hyponatremia associated with carbamazepine, or hepatic effects

101

TABLE 5–7.	Uses of anticonvulsants in various pain conditions

Carbamazepine	Oxcarbazepine
Trigeminal neuralgia	Trigeminal neuralgia
Neuropathy	Tiagabine
Gabapentin	Diabetic polyneuropathy
Neuropathy	Peripheral neuropathy
Atypical facial pain	Phantom limb
Reflex sympathetic dystrophy	Phenytoin
Central pain	Trigeminal neuralgia
Valproate	Diabetic neuropathy
Migraine prophylaxis	Topiramate
Neuropathy	Neuropathy
Lamotrigine	
Trigeminal neuralgia	
Peripheral neuropathy	
Central neuropathy	

associated with valproate). Patients taking gabapentin do not require serum drug, hematologic, electrolyte, or hepatic enzyme monitoring as is often required with other ACDs. The most common adverse events reported with its use were somnolence, dizziness, ataxia, tremor, fatigue, and nystagmus. Gabapentin is excreted unchanged from the kidneys; plasma clearance is proportional to creatinine clearance (McLean 1994). Dose reductions are required for patients with compromised renal functioning and those who require dialysis.

Carbamazepine is approved by the FDA for use in trigeminal neuralgia; valproate has been indicated for migraine prophylaxis. Along with phenytoin, carbamazepine and valproate have been shown to be efficacious in chronic neuropathic pain (Galer 1995; Maciewicz et al. 1985; Swerdlow 1984).

Emerging evidence suggests the potential roles of newer ACDs (e.g., lamotrigine, oxcarbazepine, and topiramate). Although these agents demonstrate some promise with regard to potential utility in neuropathic states (Remillard 1994; Solaro et al. 2001;

Zakrzewska et al. 1997), their utility and safety among pain patients requires further investigation. They may offer better tolerability over other ACDs (e.g., carbamazepine) and may be useful for patients with intractable pain or pain that is poorly responsive to other agents.

As with most psychopharmacologic agents, initial doses should be reduced or increased gradually while monitoring for any intolerance or adverse events. Pain-mitigating doses are comparable with those employed for anticonvulsant efficacy. Common side effects (Leo and Narendran 1999; Swerdlow 1984) encountered with several ACDs are provided in Table 5–8.

■ ANTIHISTAMINES

Histamines have been implicated in a number of pain states (e.g., headache and inflammatory pains) because of their role in facilitating inflammatory processes (e.g., prostaglandin production). Antihistamine effects, therefore, could be expected to reduce pain mediated by inflammatory processes. Furthermore, antihistamine effects appear to augment opiate receptor binding of opioid analgesics (Rumore and Schlichting 1986). Thus, antihistamines might be seen both as augmenting agents to further the effects of other analgesics (e.g., opiates) and as solitary agents on their own. Used alone, antihistamines such as diphenhydramine and hydroxyzine appear to have a ceiling effect. Additionally, these agents may be particularly useful in patients given their sedative, antiemetic, and anxiolytic properties. They are fairly well tolerated, with few respiratory or GI side effects. These agents can be sedating, however, and can intensify appetite. Thus, they can be problematic in patients for whom excess weight might exacerbate current pain disorders (e.g., obese patients with low back pain) and in those with musculoskeletal pains for whom weight loss might reduce discomfort and deconditioning. An additional concern is that confusion and delirium can arise from use of antihistamines. Antihistamines may need to be initiated at low doses, with dose increases as warranted to address pain,

103

TABLE 5–8.	Side effects of anticonvulsants

Carbamazepine	Valproate
Sedation	Nausea, heartburn, indigestion
Nystagmus, diplopia, ataxia	Vomiting, diarrhea
Nausea, vomiting	Sedation
Myoclonus	Weight gain
Elevated liver enzymes	Tremor
Hyponatremia, SIADH	Rash
Rash	Hair loss
Leukopenia, neutropenia	Thrombocytopenia
Aplastic anemia	Hepatotoxocity
Gabapentin	Pancreatitis
Sedation	Phenytoin
Dizziness, ataxia	Nausea/vomiting
Fatigue	Ataxia
Nystagmus, diplopia	Diplopia
Headache	Hirsutism
Tremor	Gingival hyperplasia
Nausea, vomiting	Confusion
Lamotrigine	
Dizziness	
Ataxia, diplopia, blurred vision	
Sedation	
Headache	
Vomiting	
Rash, Stevens-Johnson syndrome	

Note. SIADH = syndrome of inappropriate diuretic hormone.

sleep, and so forth as tolerated. For example, hydroxyzine can be initiated at 25 mg/day and increased slowly as tolerated.

■ BENZODIAZEPINES AND ANXIOLYTICS

Benzodiazepines have been employed to mitigate pain arising from muscle spasm (e.g., fibromyalgia). The presumption is that patients with marked anxiety are prone to heightened muscle tension, which

can exacerbate musculoskeletal pain. Clonazepam, a long-acting benzodiazepine, might be effective in patients with neuropathic pain in which allodynia (painful sensations elicited by normally non-noxious stimuli, such as a bedsheet pulled up along the legs) appears to be a prominent feature (Bouckoms and Litman 1985). Use of benzodiazepines must be undertaken cautiously, because these agents can contribute to excess sedation, gait instability, and memory impairments.

Some researchers have questioned whether benzodiazepines are useful to the patient with chronic pain. Benzodiazepines are GABA agonists. They inhibit 5-HT neurotransmitter release, which may in turn increase pain sensitivity. Some of the controversies associated with benzodiazepine use in chronic pain states are summarized in Table 5–9 (Fishbain et al. 1992; King and Strain 1990).

Buspirone is an anxiolytic agent that differs from benzodiazepines, mediating an antianxiety effect through the serotonin type 1A receptor (5-HT_{1A}) receptor. One study reported that patients with neuropathic pain tend not to respond favorably to buspirone treatment (Kishore-Kumar et al. 1989). However, in patients with severe anxiety that may aggravate pain experiences, a trial of buspirone to mitigate anxiety may be warranted.

■ STIMULANTS

Stimulants may have analgesic effects when combined with opioids (Forrest et al. 1977; Laska et al. 1984). Dextroamphetamine (5–15 mg two or three times daily) or methylphenidate (5–15 mg two to four times daily) has been used to augment opiate analgesia. These drugs have been also used to reduce the sedation, dysphoria, and cognitive inefficiency that can accompany opiate use. Both pemoline (up to 75 mg/day) and caffeine (65 mg two or three times daily) have likewise been used for such purposes. However, use of stimulants may be limited by intervening adverse effects, including overstimulation (e.g., anxiety, insomnia, and even paranoia), appetite

TABLE 5–9. Controversies associated with benzodiazepine use in chronic pain

Against	For
Lack of definitive benefit in chronic pain	Efficacy as:
Risk of dependence	Anxiolytics
Potential cognitive impairment	Sedatives
Depression associated with benzodiazepine use	Detoxifying agents

suppression (problematic in patients who are undernourished and cachectic), and confusion. Additionally, in persons who are predisposed to motor abnormalities, tics and other dyskinetic movements may be exacerbated. When these drugs are taken in overdose, an extreme form of these adverse effects can occur, resulting potentially in hypertension, arrhythmias, seizures, hallucinations (including formication), delirium, and death. Contraindications for stimulant use include glaucoma, poorly controlled hypertension, arrhythmias and cardiovascular disorders, anorexia, seizure disorders, hyperthyroidism, and (in the case of pemoline) liver dysfunction.

The use of stimulants has been limited because of fears regarding abuse and addiction. Caution is advised in patients with current or preexisting substance use disorders, especially prior stimulant abuse (e.g., cocaine). Both dextroamphetamine and methylphenidate are Schedule II medications under federal regulatory control. Physicians may be reluctant to make use of these agents because they fear possible misinterpretation by government agencies and punitive measures that may be taken when these agents are prescribed.

Pemoline has often been the stimulant selected first by physicians. Reports suggest a lower abuse potential associated with pemoline use, and there are no regulatory controls over its use (Chiarello and Cole 1987). Pemoline offers an additional advantage in that it is available in a chewable tablet and is easily absorbed from the buccal mucosa. The chewable form may well be a desirable option for patients who have difficulties swallowing (e.g., dysphagia or candidiasis of the esophagus). Pemoline use requires

periodic evaluation of liver function, however, because there is a
risk of hepatotoxicity (Nehra et al. 1990).

■ NEUROLEPTICS

There have been limited studies demonstrating the efficacy of various neuroleptics (e.g., fluphenazine) in chronic pain states. These
agents have been found to be useful in certain cases of neuropathic
pain (Gomez-Perez et al. 1985). In animal models, clozapine and
risperidone were found to have analgesic effects, but olanzapine
had only a modest antinociceptive influence (Schreiber et al. 1997,
1999). In a small clinical case series, olanzapine was effective in reducing the severity ratings of recurrent migrane and tension headache refractory to other interventions (Silberstein et al. 2000). In
another small series, olanzapine was useful in mitigating cancer
pain and reducing opiate requirements among these patients (Khojainova et al. 2002). There is actually only one antipsychotic that
has demonstrated analgesic activity comparable to low-dose morphine: methotrimeprazine (Beaver et al. 1966). This agent is available in Canada and Europe but not in the United States. It appears
that the limited data on the efficacy of neuroleptics, the abundance
of other agents to choose from, and the side effects of the neuroleptics would warrant avoiding these agents. The risks of neuroleptic
use (e.g., extrapyramidal side effects) appear to far outweigh any
analgesic efficacy. Use of neuroleptics should probably be confined
to the patient who has delirium and psychosis.

■ MEXILETINE

Mexiletine is one of many antiarrhythmics that can be used for pain;
it has the advantage of being administered orally. The risk is that patients may experience untoward cardiac effects (i.e., the drug may
influence cardiac rhythms). Patients with heart block may be particularly vulnerable to adverse cardiac effects brought on by mexiletine. Mexiletine has been used to treat neuropathic pain. Doses are

initiated at 150 mg/day (given in divided doses) and increased gradually (approximately every 3–7 days) to a maximum of 1,200 mg/day, given in divided doses.

■ α2-ADRENERGIC AGONISTS

α2 Agonists (e.g., clonidine) are available for epidural administration for neuropathic pain (Eisenach et al. 1995). Hypotension and bradycardia can result from use of these agents, but the risk is reduced if low doses are used. Adverse effects include hemodynamic instability. There is a risk of rebound hypertension with acute withdrawal of therapy. Topical clonidine gel is being developed for use in neuropathic pain states. Tizanidine is also an α2 agonist, used for muscle relaxation.

■ N-METHYL-D-ASPARTATE ANTAGONISTS

Pharmacologic agents that interfere with the activity of the glutamate receptors, particularly NMDA, can mitigate pain. As discussed at the beginning of this chapter (see "Agents with Multiple Uses"), some changes are thought to occur within the CNS to promote long-term, chronic pain. These mechanisms are complex and have yet to be fully elucidated. Research implicates the excitatory neurotransmitter glutamate in the development and maintenance of chronic pain. Thus, pharmacologic agents interfering with glutamate binding at NMDA receptors have a role in pain relief.

Methadone

One isomer of methadone acts by blocking NMDA receptors (Shimoyama et al. 1997), which may contribute to the fact that methadone maintains analgesic efficacy as compared with other opioids and might not, therefore, require opiate rotations (Gorman et al. 1997; see sections "Agents with Multiple Uses" and "Tolerance, Dependence, and Pseudoaddiction").

Ketamine

Used primarily in veterinary settings, ketamine has been associated with very serious side effects in humans, including delirium, hallucinations, frightening nightmares, and dissociation. These side effects have limited its use among pain patients. Children appear to be less adversely affected by these side effects than are adults. Thus, ketamine has been used in pediatric analgesia. However, in subanesthetic doses, it may be possible to effect pain relief in adult patients without incurring these serious effects. Ketamine has been used in cases of postherpetic neuralgia, chronic phantom limb pain, fibromyalgia, and pain associated with spinal cord injury. It can be dosed orally at 50–60 mg four to six times daily (taken in juice or oral suspension). Ketamine's hallucinogenic properties have rendered it popular in the drug-abusing underground. Long-term use of ketamine is not currently advocated, partly because the long-term effects are unknown. It may result in long-term cognitive changes, hepatic dysfunction, and gastric ulcers.

Dextromethorphan

Widely available as an over-the-counter medication, dextromethorphan is notable for its antitussive effects. It is a low-affinity NMDA receptor antagonist that, when combined with opiate analgesics, can enhance opiate analgesia and reduce opiate tolerance (Elliott et al. 1994). Analgesic effects require dosing at rates substantially higher than those for antitussive effects. Dextromethorphan augments 5-HT in the CNS. Consequently, combination with serotonergic antidepressants (e.g., SSRIs) may predispose a person to serotonin syndrome.

■ CORTICOSTEROIDS

Corticosteroids have been used in pain states associated with chronic medical conditions (e.g., inflammatory pain, irritable bowel, spinal cord compression, and headache due to increased in-

tracranial pressure). The corticosteroids have also been used in cancer-related pain, especially when there are bone metastases, hepatic or biliary involvement from tumor, or epidural metastases with spinal cord compression. Side effects associated with corticosteroid use are summarized in Table 5–10. The benefits of steroid use must be weighed against the risks associated with long-term use. When administered intramuscularly, intrathecally, or epidurally, substantially lower doses can be used than when administered orally. The lower doses may help to reduce potential systemic adverse effects.

Corticosteroids inhibit the release of phospholipase A, necessary for the conversion of arachidonic acid to leukotrienes and prostaglandins. The latter are responsible for inflammatory pains; they also produce reduced ectopic firing of neurons (e.g., after amputation), producing phantom limb pain. Corticosteroids inhibit activity of C fibers, but not of other sensory fibers, (e.g., A-β fibers). Each of the corticosteroids produce equivalent analgesia (Bruera et al. 1985; Ettinger and Portenoy 1988). Selection of one over another can be based on the tolerability and the desire to avoid serious mineral-corticoid effects (e.g., dexamethasone). Patients in whom steroid use might be contraindicated include those with severe cardiac compromise, a predisposition to congestive heart failure, severe osteoporosis, diabetes mellitus, or electrolyte disturbances.

TABLE 5–10. **Side effects of corticosteroid use in pain**

Immune suppression (increased infection risk, *Candida* infection)

Myopathy

Sodium imbalance–electrolyte disturbance

Fluid overload (congestive heart failiure, peripheral edema, pulmonary edema)

Glucose intolerance (iatrogenic diabetes, worsening of preexisting diabetes mellitus)

Gastrointenstinal disturbances (bleeding, peritonitis)

Skin breakdown

Neuropsychiatric disturbances (mood, perceptual, and cognitive disturbances)

■ MUSCLE ANTISPASMODICS

Muscle antispasmodics include true muscle relaxants (e.g., baclofen and dantrolene) along with agents in which the mechanism of action is unclear (e.g., carisoprodol, cyclobenzaprine, methocarbamol, orphenadrine). Some of these agents may suppress polysynaptic reflexes and thereby may reduce pain, but they do not influence skeletal muscles per se.

Generally, antispasmodic agents are to be used for acute pain arising from muscle strain or injury (see Table 5–11). Baclofen might be indicated for more chronic pain arising from muscle spasticity (e.g., after stroke or severe spinal cord injury). The utility of these agents for long-term use is unclear. There may be abuse potential associated with carisoprodol and methocarbamol. Carisoprodol is metabolized to meprobamate; therefore, ongoing use might possibly lead to meprobamate dependence. Abrupt discontinuation of carisoprodol may produce mild withdrawal, including abdominal cramps, insomnia, nausea, headache, and anxiety. Carisoprodol is contraindicated in patients with acute intermittent porphyria. Severe psychiatric disturbances have been reported in association with baclofen use (psychotic depression), as well as with its abrupt discontinuation (mania) (Arnold et al. 1980; Sommer and Petrides 1992).

The side effects often associated with these agents include somnolence and anticholinergic effects. Patients should be advised that such agents can impede their ability to operate heavy machinery or to drive a vehicle. Combinations with other sedative agents (alcohol, sedative-hypnotics, benzodiazepines, and barbiturates) may produce additive sedative effects. Chlorzoxazone has been associated with cases of hepatotoxicity and might therefore be an unwise selection as a muscle relaxant for long-term use. This risk may be increased if it is combined with other agents with hepatotoxic effects (e.g., acetaminophen).

Baclofen is an agonist of GABA (B-type) receptors. It may also suppress the release of excitatory amino acids such as glutamate and inhibit substance P. It has been used primarily for

111

TABLE 5–11. **Dosing of muscle relaxants**

Baclofen: 5 mg tid up to 40–80 mg/day
Carisoprodol: 350 mg qid
Chlorzoxazone: 250–750 mg tid to qid
Cyclobenzaprine: 10 mg tid, up to maximum of 60 mg/day
Orphenadrine: 100 mg bid
Methocarbamol: 1,500 mg qid for 72 hours, then 1,000 mg qid
Diazepam: 2–10 mg tid to qid
Tizanidine: 2–8 mg tid to qid

---

spasticity, but it also may be helpful in reducing neuropathic pains (e.g., of trigeminal neuralgia) and other neuropathies. The routes of administration are oral and intrathecal.

Tizanidine is an α2 agonist (like clonidine) that may function to reduce muscle spasticity by decreasing the activity of excitatory spinal amino acid release, which can have an impact on muscle contractility.

Cyclobenzaprine is used in fibromyalgia; it has a tricyclic chemical structure and is accompanied by anticholinergic side effects. It is contraindicated in persons with ischemic heart disease, CHF, cardiac arrhythmias, or heart block. It is extremely lethal in overdose, and caution must be undertaken when prescribing this agent to persons with risk factors for suicide. Cyclobenzaprine must never be used in conjunction with MAOIs because of risks of toxic reactions including hyperthermia.

■ TOPICAL AGENTS

Topical agents allow for pain relief via direct application of analgesics to the skin, presumably at the direct source of pain, thereby bypassing significant systemic effects and the invoking of invasive procedures.

Capsaicin

Derived from red chili peppers, capsaicin has efficacy in reducing arthritic pain and some neuropathic pain states. The mechanism for

pain relief is thought to be derived from depletion of substance P at sites of pain. Alternatively, counterirritation mechanisms (see Chapter 2) may be involved. Some patients find the burning sensations at the site of application to be too uncomfortable, precluding use.

Lidocaine Patch

The lidocaine patch functions to ameliorate pain when applied to intact skin surfaces affected by pain (e.g., neuropathic pain). The local anesthetic is thought to mitigate pain by influencing voltage-sensitive sodium channels to stabilize neural membranes. The patch can provide approximately 12 hours of relief, requiring reapplication of additional patches for refractory and recurrent pain. The patch is generally well tolerated. However, irritation and erythema can occur at the site of application.

Eutectic Mixture of Local Anesthetics

A eutectic mixture of local anesthetics (EMLA) is a solution consisting of two local anesthetics (lidocaine and prilocaine). This topically applied anesthetic agent has marked analgesic properties (Kapelushnik et al. 1990). It is customarily employed in conditions involving skin surgery, such as curettage of skin lesions, split-thickness graft harvesting, collagen implants, removal of warts and port-wine stains, and so forth. Application of EMLA can cause localized vasoconstriction of skin. In addition, methemoglobinemia and hypoxia can also arise as a response to prilocaine contained in the EMLA solution. Edema and erythema can arise as well, particularly in application of EMLA to diseased tissues or skin.

■ PLACEBO EFFECTS

The physiological aspects of pain are inextricably linked with cognitive and emotional aspects. Thus, it is not uncommon to find that many patients with pain can derive relief from placebos (i.e., agents or interventions believed to be inefficacious). In experimen-

tal paradigms, placebo effects of pain relief were encountered in 15%–58% of patients (Turner et al. 1994). Factors mediating the placebo effect include patient expectations and hopes for relief. Placebo effects are expected to be enhanced by the conviction of the clinician of the expected relief as well as the costs of the intervention. It is possible that administration of a placebo may reduce patient anxiety and distress, thereby mitigating pain awareness. On the other hand, placebo administration has at times been associated with increases in endogenous opiate release within the CNS, thereby mitigating pain.

Caution is advised not to ascribe any influence to a treatment that is nothing more than the natural course and variability intrinsic to a disease state. Thus, experimental approaches assessing the efficacy of a treatment will naturally require a placebo arm and perhaps a wait-list control group to tease out those changes that occur over time. In addition, the clinician is cautioned about dismissing the complaints of a patient who appears to respond to a placebo. The response does not inherently imply that the allegations of pain are psychologically based.

■ REFERENCES

Abernethy DR, Greenblatt DJ, Steel K, et al: Impairment of hepatic drug oxidation by propoxyphene. Ann Intern Med 97:223–224, 1982

Ansari A: The efficacy of newer antidepressants in the treatment of chronic pain: a review of current literature. Harv Rev Psychatry 7:257–277, 2000

Arnold ES, Rudd SM, Kirshner H: Manic psychosis following rapid withdrawal from baclofen. Am J Psychiatry 137:1466–1467, 1980

Barkin RL, Fawcett J: The management challenges of chronic pain: the role of antidepressants. Am J Ther 7:31–47, 2000

Beaver WT, Wallenstein SL, Houde RW, et al: A comparison of the analgesic effects of methotrimeprazine and morphine in patients with cancer. Clin Pharmacol Ther 7:436–466, 1966

Bouckoms AJ, Litman RE: Clonazepam in the treatment of neuralgic pain syndrome. Psychosomatics 26:933–936, 1985

Brannon GE, Stone KD: The use of mirtazapine in a patient with chronic pain. J Pain Symptom Manage 18:382–385, 1999

Bruera E, Roca E, Cedaro L, et al: Action of oral methylprednisolone in terminal cancer patients: a prospective randomized double-blind study. Cancer Treat Rep 69:751–754, 1985

Buckley FP, Sizemore WA, Charlton JE: Medication management in patients with chronic nonmalignant pain: a review of the use of a drug withdrawal protocol. Pain 26:153–165, 1986

Chiarello RJ, Cole JO: The use of psychostimulants in general psychiatry: a reconsideration. Arch Gen Psychiatry 44:286–295, 1987

Diamond S, Freitag FG: The use of fluoxetine in the treatment of headache. Clin J Pain 5:200–201, 1989

Eisenach JC, DuPen SL, Dubois M, et al: Epidural clonidine analgesia for intractable cancer pain. Pain 61:391–399, 1995

Elliott K, Hynansky A, Inturrisi CE: Dextromethorphan attenuates and reverses analgesic tolerance to morphine. Pain 59:361–368, 1994

Ettinger AB, Portenoy RK: The use of corticosteroids in the treatment of symptoms associated with cancer. J Pain Symptom Manage 3:99–103, 1988

Finlayson RE, Maruta T, Morse RM, et al: Substance dependence and chronic pain: profile of 50 patients treated in an alcohol and drug dependence unit. Pain 26:167–174, 1986

Fishbain DA, Rosomoff HL, Rosomoff RS: Detoxification of nonopiate drugs in the chronic pain setting and clonidine opiate detoxification. Clin J Pain 8:191–203, 1992

Forrest WH, Brown BW, Brown CR, et al: Dextroamphetamine with morphine for the treatment of postoperative pain. N Engl J Med 296:712–715, 1977

Galer BS: Neuropathic pain of peripheral origin: advances in pharmacologic treatment. Neurology 45(suppl 9):17–25, 1995

Gomez-Perez FJ, Rull JA, Dies H, et al: Nortriptyline and fluphenazine in the symptomatic treatment of diabetic neuropathy: a double-blind crossover study. Pain 23:395–400, 1985

Goodnick PJ, Breakstone K, Khumar A, et al: Nefazodone in diabetic neuropathy: response and biology. Psychosom Med 62:599–600, 2000

Gorman AL, Elliott KJ, Inturrisi CE: The d- and l-isomers of methadone bind to the noncompetitive site on the N-methyl-D-aspartate (NMDA) receptor in rat forebrain and spinal cord. Neurosci Lett 223:5–8, 1997

Gratz SS, Simpson GM: MAOI-narcotic interactions (letter). J Clin Psychiatry 54:439, 1993

Inturrisi CE: Role of opioid analgesics. Am J Med 77(suppl):27–37, 1984

Kapelushnik J, Koren G, Solh H, et al: Evaluating the efficacy of EMLA in alleviating pain associated with lumbar puncture; comparison of open and double-blinded protocols in children. Pain 42:31–34, 1990

Keeri-Szanto M: The mode of action of promethazine in potentiating narcotic drugs. Br J Anaesth 46:918–924, 1974

Khojainova N, Santiago-Palma J, Kornick C, et al: Olanzapine in the management of cancer pain. J Pain Symptom Manage 23:346–350, 2002

Khurana RC: Treatment of painful diabetic neuropathy with trazodone (letter). JAMA 250:1392, 1983

King SA, Strain JJ: Benzodiazepine use by chronic pain patients. Clin J Pain 6:143–147, 1990

Kishore-Kumar R, Schafer SC, Lawlor BA, et al: Single doses of the serotonin agonists buspirone and m-chlorophenylpiperazine do not relieve neuropathic pain. Pain 37:223–227, 1989

Larson AA, Takemori AE: Effect of fluoxetine hydrochloride (Lilly 110140), a specific inhibitor of serotonin uptake, on morphine analgesia and the development of tolerance. Life Sci 21:1807–1812, 1977

Laska EM, Sunshine A, Mueller F, et al: Caffeine as an analgesic adjuvant. JAMA 251:1711–1718, 1984

Lee RL, Spencer PSJ: Effect of tricyclic antidepressants on analgesic activity in laboratory animals. Postgrad Med J, 56(suppl 1):19–24, 1980

Leo RJ, Narendran R: Anticonvulsant use in the treatment of bipolar disorder: a primer for primary care physicians. Primary Care Companion to the Journal of Clinical Psychiatry 1:74–84, 1999

Leo RJ, Narendran R, DeGuiseppe B: Methadone detoxification of tramadol dependence. J Subst Abuse Treat 19:297–299, 2000

Maciewicz R, Bouckoms A, Martin JB: Drug therapy of neuropathic pain. Clin J Pain 1:39–49, 1985

Maltbie AA, Cavenar JO, Sullivan JL, et al: Analgesia and haloperidol: a hypothesis. J Clin Psychiatry, 40:323–326, 1979

Maruta T: Prescription drug-induced organic brain syndrome. Am J Psychiatry 135:376–377, 1978

Max MB, Lynch SA, Muir J, et al: Effects of desipramine, amitriptyline, and fluoxetine on pain in diabetic neuropathy. N Engl J Med 326:1250–1256, 1992

McLean MJ: Clinical pharmacokinetics of gabapentin. Neurology 44(suppl 5):17–22, 1994

McNairy SL, Maruta T, Ivnik RJ, et al: Prescription medication dependence and neuropsychologic function. Pain 18:169–177, 1984

McQuay H, Carroll D, Jadad AR, et al: Anticonvulsant drugs for management of pain: a systematic review. Br Med J 311:1047–1052, 1995

Nehra A, Mullick F, Ishak KG, et al: Pemoline associated hepatic injury. Gastroenterology 99:1517–1519, 1990

Pick CG, Paul D, Eison MS, et al: Potentiation of opioid analgesia by the antidepressant nefazodone. Eur J Pharmacol 211: 375–381, 1992

Portenoy RK: Opioid therapy for chronic nonmalignant pain: a review of the critical issues. J Pain Symptom Manage 11:203–217, 1996

Portenoy RK, Hagen NA: Breakthrough pain: definition, prevalence and characteristics. Pain 41:273–281, 1990

Ragheb MA, Powell AL: Failure of sulindac to increase serum lithium levels. J Clin Psychiatry 47:33–34, 1986

Remillard G: Oxcarbazepine and intractable trigeminal neuralgia. Epilepsia 35:528–529, 1994

Rumore MM, Schlichting DA: Clinical efficacy of antihistamines as analgesics. Pain 25:7–22, 1986

Rundell JR, Wise MG: Pain and analgesics, in Concise Guide to Consultation Psychiatry, 3rd Edition. Washington, DC, American Psychiatric Publishing, 2000, p 213

Saper JR, Silberstein SD, Lake AE, et al: Double-blind trial of fluoxetine: chronic daily headache and migraine. Headache 34:497–502, 1994

Saper JR, Lake AE, Tepper SJ: Nefazodone for chronic daily headache prophylaxis: an open-label study. Headache 41:465–474, 2001

Schreiber S, Backer MM, Weizman R, et al: Augmentation of opioid induced antinociception by the atypical antipsychotic drug risperidone in mice. Neurosci Lett 228:25–28, 1997

Schreiber S, Getslev V, Backer MM, et al: The atypical neuroleptics clozapine and olanzapine differ regarding their antinociceptive mechanisms and potency. Pharmacol Biochem Behav 64:75–80, 1999

Shimoyama N, Shimoyama M, Elliott KJ, et al: D-methadone is antinociceptive in the rat formalin test. J Pharmacol Exp Ther 283:648–652, 1997

Silberstein SD, Young WB, Hopkins MM, et al: Olanzapine in the treatment of refractory migraine and chronic daily headache. Cephalalgia 20:382–383, 2000

Sindrup SH, Gram LF, Brosen K, et al: The selective serotonin reuptake inhibitor paroxetine is effective in the treatment of diabetic neuropathy symptoms. Pain 42:135–144, 1990

Sindrup SH, Grodum E, Gram LF, et al: Concentration-response relationship in paroxetine treatment of diabetic neuropathy symptoms: a patient-blinded dose-escalation study. Ther Drug Monit 13:408–414, 1991

Solaro C, Uccelli MM, Brichetto G, et al: Topiramate relieves idiopathic and symptomatic trigeminal neuralgia. J Pain Symptom Manage 21:367–368, 2001

Sommer BR, Petrides G: A case of baclofen-induced psychotic depression. J Clin Psychiatry 53:211–212, 1992

Stambaugh JE, Wainer IW: Drug interaction: meperidine and chlorpromazine, a toxic combination. J Clin Pharmacol 21:140–146, 1981

Sternbach H: The serotonin syndrome. Am J Psychiatry 148:705–713, 1991

Swerdlow M: Anticonvulsant drugs and chronic pain. Clin Neuropharmacol 7:51–82, 1984

Taiwo YO, Fabian A, Pazoles CJ, et al: Potentiation of morphine antinociception by monoamine reuptake inhibitors in the rat spinal cord. Pain 21:329–337, 1985

Turner JA, Deyo RA, Loeser JD, et al: The importance of placebo effects in pain treatment and research. JAMA 271:1609–1614, 1994

Ventafridda V, Caraceni A, Saita L, et al: Trazodone for deafferentation pain: comparison with amitriptyline. Psychopharmacology (Berl) 95(suppl):S44–S49, 1988

Weissman DE, Haddox JD: Opioid pseudoaddiction: an iatrogenic syndrome. Pain 36:363–366, 1989

Zakrzewska JM, Chaudhry Z, Nurmikko TJ, et al: Lamotrigine (Lamictal) in refractory trigeminal neuralgia: results from a double-blind placebo controlled crossover trial. Pain 73:223–230, 1997

6

PSYCHOTHERAPY

Given that pain is a multidimensional construct, a number of psychotherapeutic and adjunctive techniques can be employed to address the biologic, psychologic, and social features associated with and contributing to pain (Table 6–1). These are not mutually exclusive interventions but complement each other to effectively address a particular patient's needs and produce relief—that is, reducing sensory components of pain (e.g., by relaxation and hypnosis) or reducing the emotional and psychosocial distress that can accompany pain.

TABLE 6–1. **Components of pain and associated psychotherapeutic interventions**

Pain component	Psychotherapeutic intervention
Biologic	Relaxation training
	Biofeedback
Psychologic	
Cognitive	Cognitive-behavioral therapy
	Hypnosis
Affective	Dynamically oriented therapy
	Supportive psychotherapy
Social	Behavior therapy
	Marital, couples, and family therapies
	Vocational training

The psychotherapies differ with regard to their approach, perspectives, and goals. Behavioral therapy is based on learning principles and holds that the patient engages in behavior(s) maintained by environmental contingencies. To modify behavior, the proactive therapist, in conjunction with others in the patient's life, modifies those contingencies to facilitate desired behaviors or extinguish problematic ones.

By contrast, psychodynamically oriented therapies are based on the perspective that the patient's behaviors are grounded in earlier developmental experiences. To understand these, the therapist relies on exploration of defenses, transference, and resistance (Lakoff 1983). The patient is active, producing the material that makes up the focus of the therapeutic interventions. The therapist integrates and interprets the material brought forth in therapy, presenting it for the patient's assimilation and use. Ideally, the patient gains insight into the origins of these behaviors and then can make determinations of how to readjust current patterns of behavior to more satisfactorily meet his or her needs.

If behavioral therapy and psychodynamically oriented therapies are considered to be the extreme poles of a continuum of psychotherapeutic approaches, supportive psychotherapy and cognitive-behavioral therapy (CBT) would lie somewhere along the middle. With these, there is no attempt to relate current behavior patterns to early developmental experiences. In supportive therapy, positive transferences are encouraged, and attempts are made to bolster adaptive defenses. In contrast, CBT focuses on the patient's belief systems that are temporally related to problematic behaviors, and that, when modified, bring about behavior change.

Selection of therapeutic approach depends on the patient's needs and desired goals, the resources available, and the therapist's training, skills, and preferences. Thus, if a patient presents with excessive and incapacitating use of opiate analgesics, excess reclining, and deficiencies in self-care, the behavioral approach might be entertained. However, this approach would probably be abandoned if the therapist is unable to enlist the support of others with whom the patient resides to maintain the behavioral contin-

gencies that would result in modifications of maladaptive behaviors. Dynamically oriented therapies are designed to bring about fundamental personality changes and address relationship difficulties, but these therapies might well be abandoned if the patient is not psychologically minded or is in a terminal condition, in which life expectancy could prove to be prohibitive. CBT could be more desirable in such situations, but it would be abandoned if the patient cannot modify cognitive strategies encompassing his or her worldview and, similarly, coping strategies, due to intervening cognitive disorders.

■ RESISTANCE TO PSYCHOTHERAPY

Among patients with complex pain, there can be several challenges to the prospect of psychotherapy. Such patients have a history of medical disappointments and could well be frustrated with health care providers. As a consequence, these patients might believe there is no relief on the horizon; they could be angry, suspicious, and defensive; and they may possibly reject psychological interventions (Stieg et al. 1999).

To have the patient align with the therapist and learn the work of psychotherapy, the therapist needs to establish an atmosphere of safety. The therapist will need to facilitate an understanding of the processes involved in the therapy by educating the patient about the role of therapy and what the patient can come to expect from the work of therapy in addressing pain-related issues. A particular mechanism might involve emphasizing the empowerment that can be derived from therapy. Although all the variables in an individual's life—and in particular, pain—are not entirely under one's direct control, patients may be able to effect changes in their lives—within the range of their abilities—and take control of their lives. The therapist will be instrumental in forging the therapeutic alliance and a working relationship.

For some patients, being proactive in effecting life changes can be a stirring and stimulating prospect, empowering them to take

charge of their lives, pain, quality of life, and destinies. For others, this can be a frightening prospect and one that is to be avoided at all cost. The therapist will need to address such ambivalences in the context of the early work in therapy.

Some patients are more amenable to effecting changes in their lives than are others. Such changes can include making efforts to reduce medication use or misuse, increasing physical activity, increasing social participation, returning to productive activity, undertaking weight loss, or addressing nicotine, alcohol, or substance abuse cessation. Patient readiness for the rehabilitation changes required in chronic pain can be conceived of in several stages (Prochaska and DiClemente 1983). Some persons are not at all ready to effect life changes or see no need for lifestyle modifications (i.e., are in a stage of precontemplation). Others might be ambivalent about making such changes but feel that they lack insight into how to go about making them (contemplation). Patients in the contemplation phase can benefit from education and exploration of the impact of pain on current life patterns. Following this phase is the preparation phase, in which a patient begins to make efforts to effect change; then come the action and maintenance phases, in which the patient, with the assistance of the therapist and others in his or her life, employs strategies to effect changes and maintains the modifications in behavior while avoiding lapses to less effective coping and behavioral strategies.

Resistance to therapy can be overcome by engaging the chronic pain patient. First, the therapist must accept the pain at face value rather than trying to ascertain its validity or establishing its somatic origins. The therapist's focus should be on the patient's subjective *experience* of pain and the *impact* of that pain on the patient's life. Second, education of the patient about the bridge between psychological factors and pain might be required. Finally, the therapist can enlist the patient by emphasizing that the goals of therapy can empower the patient by facilitating growth, coping, adaptation, and so forth.

■ FACTORS TO BE ADDRESSED IN PSYCHOTHERAPY

Regardless of the psychotherapeutic approach undertaken, there are certain essential psychological components of the pain experience that are likely to be the focus of therapy. Some of these might be more central to a particular psychotherapeutic approach than are others.

Affect

Chronic pain is associated with a wide range of psychosocial problems, including strained relationships, alienation from others, problems with depression and anger, and loss experiences (e.g., bodily integrity, self-efficacy). The psychological experiences of chronic pain patients can include significant mood disturbances. These, in turn, can have an impact on thought patterns and belief systems, all of which can profoundly influence the pain experience and the extent to which patients adapt to their condition, adhere to treatment, and participate in the work of rehabilitation.

Little can be done to facilitate rehabilitation and restoration of functioning unless comorbid mood disorders are addressed and treated. Given that the neurophysiology and neuroanatomy of pain processing pathways overlap with those of affective processing and experience, pain perception and mood states (e.g., depression and anxiety) have mutually reciprocal relationships. Thus, affective states can influence pain perception, pain reporting, and pain-related behaviors. For example, the severity of depressive symptoms has been shown to predict the number and severity of pain complaints (Hawley and Wolfe 1988). Depression is a significant predictor of average daily pain (Affleck et al. 1991).

The experience and expression of anger can have an impact on chronic pain. Higher levels of anger (as well as depression and anxiety) are found among patients with chronic low back pain compared with asymptomatic control subjects (Feuerstein 1986). Poorly managed anger adversely affects pain levels. Similarly, patients with chronic tension headache differed from control subjects

in their experience and expression of anger (Hatch et al. 1991). Headache patients were prone to hostility (i.e., feelings of resentment, suspicion, and mistrust), anger arousal (i.e., perceiving situations as annoying or frustrating and aroused to anger frequently), and anger suppression (i.e., more likely to suppress angry feelings once aroused). However, once overtly angry, headache patients tended to expend less control over the expression of anger than control subjects. Taken together, these studies suggest that modulation of anger and hostility might be a major determinant of the experience of certain chronic pain conditions (Burns 1997).

In the context of psychotherapy, the presence of unpleasant emotions can be a focus so as to reduce distress. On the other hand, emotions—including anger—contain information value. The patient can become empowered by using the information gleaned from these emotions. So, for anger, the emotion might serve as a signal that one's rights have been violated, one's needs are not being met, an injustice has been done, or one is compromising oneself. Recognizing this, patients may possibly expend less energy suppressing anger and, instead, engage in measures such as figuring out how it is that their needs are not being met and what to do about it. The experience of anger is likely to contribute to physical discomfort when there is a conflict around the expression of anger and there are high levels of hostility.

Psychotherapy can be particularly useful in assisting patients with pain to manage unpleasant emotional states. The basic approach is outlined in Table 6–2. However, the approaches differ. Psychodynamically oriented approaches might consider how emotions were dealt with and managed earlier in development. The strategy invoked is to demonstrate how such approaches, when employed in adulthood, are ineffective in producing growth. CBT, on the other hand, is more focused on here-and-now experiences, problem solving, and development of effective coping strategies.

Factors that contribute to impairments in regulating emotions are outlined in Table 6–3. Certain disorders—for example, posttraumatic stress disorder (PTSD) and dissociative and somatoform disorders—are characterized by an inability to access emotions, leading

125

TABLE 6–2. **Psychotherapy interventions employed to facilitate access of emotions**

Help patients to:

Identify and label feelings

Recognize affect as a signal

Identify the precipitant for the feelings

Express feelings with words instead of actions (e.g., substance abuse, excess narcotic use, suicide gestures)

Reduce anhedonia

Take better care of themselves

Determine what can be done with unpleasant feelings (e.g., use judicious expression of emotions, take constructive action)

TABLE 6–3. **Reasons why emotions are poorly identified and regulated**

Patient fears that, if emotions are expressed:

She or he will be abandoned

The emotions (experienced as intense states) might lead to some catastrophic result (e.g., rage-filled reaction)

Patient has not learned that emotions can be expressed appropriately

Patient has not had good role models for the effective expression of emotion (e.g., had parent who had tantrums)

Patient is unable to access emotions

PTSD, dissociative disorders, personality disorders, substance abuse disorders

Defenses (e.g., isolation of affect, alexithymia)

Note. PTSD = posttraumatic stress disorder.

---

to affective blunting, somatic amplification, or both. Even among pain patients without comorbid Axis I disorders, there may be a propensity to employ defenses (e.g., isolation of affect and alexithymia) that shield one from intolerable emotions (Beutler et al. 1986).

Defenses

Early psychodynamic conceptualizations of pain emphasized that the symptoms of pain served a function (see Table 6–4), such as

126

TABLE 6–4.	Early psychodynamic conceptualizations of pain
Proponent	**Concept**
Freud (1893)	Psychological distress is expressed through somatic complaints
	Chronic pain is similar to mourning
Szasz (1957)	Pain serves a symbolic function for emotions that are difficult to tolerate and therefore remain unexpressed
	Pain diverts attention away from the emotion and underlying conflict
	Pain provides one with a basis for seeking assistance from others
Engel (1959)	Pain serves to
	Absolve one from guilt
	Distract one from aggressive impulses
	Rationalize failure and justify one's persistent perception of being defeated

allowing one to cope with unpleasant emotions, enlisting the support of others, or the expiation of guilt. Such conceptualizations have been difficult to corroborate empirically (Weisberg and Keefe 1999) but nonetheless illustrate that conflicts and defenses against those conflicts can have an impact on the experience of pain.

Defenses serve to reduce the access of intolerable affective states or impulses from awareness. For example, if a person cannot tolerate an unpleasant emotion (e.g., anger), he or she might project that emotion onto others (e.g., the therapist), leading to potential disruptions in relationships (e.g., the doctor–patient relationship). Primitive defenses might also include projective identification, whereby the patient enlists the object onto whom he or she has projected to act out the patient's aggressive impulses. Such strategies can potentially undermine relationships and exasperate available support systems. Additional defenses accompanying chronic pain include denial, reaction formation, and repression (Tauschke et al. 1990).

Chronic pain patients may have deficits in self-regulation brought on by difficulties in managing affect and behavior. For example, alexithymia, present among those who demonstrate asymbolic and concrete thinking, is characterized by the patient's inability to identify and communicate feeling states (Krystal 1982). Just as often, the person's feelings are vague, ill defined, and confusing. These factors can lead to impairments in self-regulation that could bring about generalized states of distress and "acting out" in ways that undermine treatment, disturb relationships, and exacerbate life problems. For example, intense feelings can be temporarily dissipated in several ways: by focusing on pain (instead of the unpleasant emotion), through use of analgesics that can produce changes in one's emotional states (e.g., opiates), and through abuse of substances.

In examining the therapist–patient relationship, the therapist can be aware of the defenses employed and can redirect the patient's attention to the problematic emotions that may be underlying the defense. Similar to addressing unpleasant emotional states, the goals of therapy may be to assist the patient with identifying the utility of his or her defenses, replacing destructive or primitive defenses, and substituting healthier defenses (e.g., humor, sublimation).

A number of higher-level defenses can be employed in the management of unpleasant emotional states. Of these, humor can be quite effective. Patients who are humorless are prone to being overwhelmed by the ordinary vicissitudes of life. Similarly, loss of humor among those enlisted to assist in the care of the patient might signal impending "burn-out." In experimental paradigms, individuals exposed to painful stimuli had greater pain tolerability when exposed to laughter-inducing tapes than persons who used distracting mental tasks (e.g., calculating mental arithmetic) or those who were not given any instruction about strategies to use with regard to tolerating pain (Cogan et al. 1987).

A question arises as to whether laughter is the same as humor. Laughter is really a reaction to a laughter-provoking event, whereas humor is a defense employed to diffuse the emotional valence of one's actions. Humor is a mechanism of distancing oneself from life

stressors, examining one's own actions, and so forth. Nonetheless, the utility of humor with regard to pain has been long advocated.

Belief Systems and Cognitive Distortions

One's beliefs can have an impact on pain, treatment, and response to treatment. Belief systems (or *schemata*) are of three major types. One type includes belief systems that are broad and encompass aspects and beliefs about one's life, world, relationships, and so forth. Second are those that are considered to be more stable, influencing one's relationships, work ethic, and manner of relating to others—these would be commensurate with personality characteristics. Third, there are beliefs that are more or less specific to the pain experience. The stable beliefs affecting personality style as well as those pertaining specifically to pain are likely to influence coping and adaptation to the entire pain experience. They can be evaluated by various assessment techniques (DeGood and Tait 2001) and might become some of the grist for the mill in psychotherapeutic interventions. These beliefs can affect coping strategies and are likely to be of relevance in interventions such as cognitive-behavioral, dynamic, and supportive therapies. A person with a grin-and-bear-it schema would approach pain brought on by physical therapy differently from the person who views pain as reflecting a serious pathological state. For the latter patient, activity might be construed as dangerous. A person who believes that pain is equivalent to disability may be more inclined to neglect usual responsibilities than one who does not.

Expectations and beliefs about treatment are likewise likely to have an impact on a person's response to pain and a patient's treatment adherence. Thus, one's perception of the patient's role (e.g., proactive, informed, and instrumental versus passive, uninformed, and dependent on the physician's interventions) will likely affect treatment adherence and willingness to explore possible treatment interventions. Similarly, the patient might have expectations about the role of the physician and others involved in the multidisciplinary treatment of pain. A patient's expectation might be that the

only effective treatment entirely alleviates pain and discomfort. In reality, however, a more plausible approach might be to expect some relief, along with improved adaptation and quality of life. For some patients, such improvements can fall short of expectations. Some patients see the role of treatment to be exclusively medically based, whereas others might be amenable to recognizing that psychological variables can, and often do, reduce pain and improve life quality. Similarly, expectations of treatment outcome are likely to have an impact on one's expectations of recovery, rehabilitation, and restoration of function.

Belief systems can arise from one's early developmental experiences, earlier life experiences, earlier experiences with the medical community (either direct or indirect through the medical encounters shared with others who had been ill), and relationships with others. Beliefs shape expectations, not only about recovery and rehabilitation but also what one can expect out of life in general (e.g., shaping one's sense of future hope versus helplessness). Such belief systems influence how one views oneself, shaping one's sense of self-efficacy, autonomy, and self-esteem (Seligman 1990).

In addition to belief systems, the patient's cognitive styles and propensity toward cognitive distortions (see Chapter 3) are likely to reduce self-efficacy, hamper development of effective coping, drain the patient's support systems, accentuate unpleasant emotional states (e.g., anger, anxiety, and depression), and exacerbate pain. For example, catastrophizing (i.e., the tendency to view and expect the worst in response to pain) has been seen as a cognitive approach that may predispose one to heightened pain (Sullivan et al. 1998). Cognitive distortions such as this can be determined, or at least influenced, by mood states (e.g., depression and anxiety). Because depression often coexists with unremitting pain, it becomes difficult to determine whether catastrophizing is a result of pain and predisposes one to depression, or whether pain and comorbid depression result in a tendency to catastrophize.

Catastrophizing may consist of three distinct cognitive distortions: rumination, magnification, and helplessness (Sullivan et al.

1995). The clinician's identification of these distortions, ascertained by careful clinical inquiry (see Chapter 3) and perhaps by use of assessment scales, could be pivotal to understanding the psychological, emotional, and other disabling aspects of pain. The goal of cognitive-behavioral strategies would be to address these distortions. Altering these, the patient may more effectively cope, may experience less emotional distress, and may overcome some of the disabling aspects of the pain.

■ BEHAVIOR THERAPY

The goal of behavior therapy is to mitigate excessive problematic pain-associated behaviors (e.g., excess medication usage, limping) and increase those adaptive behaviors occurring infrequently or not at all (e.g., walking, exercise, self-care, work). The steps involved in behavior therapy are outlined in Table 6–5. When originally described, behavior therapy was conducted with chronic pain patients on an inpatient basis (Fordyce et al. 1982). The therapy was highly structured by the therapist and treating staff. In outpatient settings, behavior therapy is obviously less well controlled. The assistance of others is needed to ensure that environmental contingencies are systematically applied at home or in other relevant settings.

Behavior therapy is predicated on the recognition that the events (consequences) following a behavior will influence the extent to which that behavior is likely to recur. Simply, behaviors that are followed by pleasant or desirable consequences are likely to be repeated in the future, whereas those followed by negative consequences are not likely to recur. Thus, behaviors followed by reinforcement will increase in occurrence in the future. There are two types of reinforcement: positive and negative. Positive reinforcement increases the likelihood of a target (i.e., desired) behavior by *providing a positive, pleasant, or desired consequence*. On the other hand, negative reinforcement increases the likelihood of a target (desired) behavior by *removing an unpleasant consequence*. Be-

131

TABLE 6–5.　**Steps of behavior therapy**

Step 1: Define problem behaviors (operants) that warrant attention (e.g., medication use, excess reclining, or avoidance of activities)

Step 2: Determine the relationship between operants and environmental consequences (i.e., identify reinforcers and the temporal contingencies that exist to maintain these)

Step 3: Assess whether the link between operants and reinforcers is modifiable (i.e., identify whether reinforcers can be modified so that these become contingent on desired [adaptive] behaviors, identify how frequently reinforcers should be applied after desired behaviors occur, identify what quotas might need to be established, identify those persons who should be involved in the contingency management process [e.g., spouse, significant other, etc.])

Step 4: Establish how the systematic disruption of problem behaviors and consequences can be conducted (i.e., how to extinguish undesired behaviors [which reinforcers should be withheld and when])

Step 5: Establish transferability to home and work (i.e., consider to what extent the contingencies can be translated into the home, work, or any setting in which it becomes necessary to maintain these desired behaviors; perform follow-up assessments; determine if contingencies need to be modified in other settings; determine if the newly learned behaviors have been extinguished and whether these can be reinstated)

Source.　Adapted from Fordyce 1985.

---

havior change is brought about by active modification of the consequences that follow the patient's behavior. Reinforcement can include something given to the person—for example, attention, praise, or the chance to do something the patient finds rewarding (e.g., rest, reading, watching a favorite TV program). A contingency might be established that if the patient walks 200 feet, the patient is rewarded with watching a favored 30-minute television program. Quotas might be set for greater distances, over time, upon which reinforcement would be contingent (Fordyce et al. 1985).

　　Undesirable behaviors are those interfering with adaptive functioning (e.g., excess medication use or avoidance of rehabilitative measures leading to generalized deconditioning). Undesirable behaviors can be extinguished by modifying the consequences.

When the reinforcers that normally follow these behaviors are withheld, the behavior is less likely to recur. Alternatively, aversive consequences (e.g., punishment) can be applied following the behavior and are likely to reduce the likelihood of recurrence. In behavior therapy, punishments are not employed to modify problematic pain-related behaviors. There are several drawbacks to the use of punishment (e.g., the patient engages in these behaviors when the "punisher" is not around to notice).

Alternative approaches in behavior therapy might make use of token economies. This system could be required when more sustained behavioral changes are needed. In such scenarios, tokens are administered to the patient to reinforce desired behaviors. Accumulation of a predetermined number of tokens can be exchanged for a highly desired reinforcer (e.g., a special dinner, a purchase, a trip). Tokens are given less frequently over time and paired with other secondary reinforcers (e.g., praise).

Another strategy employed to modify a patient's behavior involves storing or accumulating a reward that the patient might collect at the end of a predetermined period of time; the patient maintains the desired behavior to avoid the significant loss of the reward. This strategy is often used to facilitate extinction of undesirable behaviors such as smoking. Thus, every day a patient goes without smoking, the dollar amount of a pack of cigarettes is held or accumulated in a bank. If the patient avoids smoking for a predetermined period of time (e.g., 6 months), he or she keeps the accumulated money and can do with it as he or she wills (except to purchase cigarettes). If, on the other hand, the patient relapses in smoking, say after 2 months, the money accumulated in the bank is never awarded to the patient (e.g., is given to a charity).

Critics of behavior therapy argue that the behavioral modifications might not be sustained. Setbacks can occur once the desired outcome is achieved or the incentive is gone. Alternative reinforcers (e.g., praise, attention) may need to be set in place to maintain the behaviors. The behavioral changes can dissipate in settings (e.g., home or work) where reinforcement patterns are less systematic or consistent. In addition, despite the changes acquired in be-

havior therapy, the patient may nonetheless experience pain—what is modified is the overt behavior, not the perception of pain.

Critics also argue that the behavioral approach is simplistic—specifically that the person engages in behavior because they come to *expect* a particular outcome. Thus, it fails to factor in those qualities of being human that influence and dictate behavior. For example, expectation, anticipation, thinking, planning, and remembering can also influence behavior and mediate pain-related behavior and perception (Seligman 1990).

As an illustration, passivity and inactivity can be particularly problematic in a variety of pain states (e.g., low back pain and arthritis). This lack of activity can result in generalized deconditioning, muscle weakness, and reduced endurance—all of which can exacerbate pain once an effort is undertaken. From a behavioral perspective, such passivity might be reinforced by others (e.g., a spouse who engages in solicitous behaviors and tends to the patient's needs once the inactivity is noticed). An alternative explanation might attribute the inactivity or restricted activity to *expectations* the patient has that activity will exacerbate pain. Thus, the patient is avoiding the prospect of pain, a factor that may be more pivotal in determining the inactivity. Yet another explanation suggests that passivity arises from the patient's belief that what he or she does is pointless (i.e., learned helplessness), so why bother to walk, exercise, and so forth? Thus, the cognitive-behavioral approach has been invoked to address problematic behaviors by taking into account the cognitive aspects of the patient that might dictate such behaviors.

■ COGNITIVE-BEHAVIORAL THERAPY

Cognitive-behavioral therapy (CBT) has been applied to a number of different chronic pain problems, including low back pain, headache, fibromyalgia, osteoarthritis, rheumatoid arthritis, and temporomandibular joint disorders (Turner and Chapman 1982a). CBT addresses the correction of distorted thinking processes and the development of strategies (coping) with which to deal effectively with

pain, its effects, and psychosocial stressors. A number of meta-analyses have addressed the efficacy of CBT. The effectiveness of CBT has not always been clear (e.g., studies vary with regard to populations examined and the outcome measures employed). Chronic pain patients reportedly demonstrated improvements in psychological adjustment and had reductions in reported pain levels after CBT compared with patients in a standard medical treatment condition (Compas et al. 1998; Keefe et al. 1992). By contrast, when return to work was assessed among low back pain patients, CBT was not any more effective than control situations (Scheer et al. 1997).

Nonetheless, any person with a persistent pain problem potentially could benefit from CBT. CBT focuses on internal appraisals of pain and disability by examining and addressing the cognition, emotions, and behaviors associated with pain and pain-related activities. There is less reliance on outcome contingencies (as in behavioral approaches).

CBT is conducted in about 8–12 50-minute sessions. The therapy is structured, with clear agendas set by the patient and therapist focusing on prominent areas of concern for the patient. The therapist is directive, guiding the use of homework treatments, outlining exercises, and assessing the efficacy of the modalities employed, yet this role remains flexible, with the patient's input guiding any shifts undertaken in the therapy. CBT assumes a collaborative effort between the patient and therapist (Fishman and Loscalzo 1987).

The model for understanding the approach of CBT is illustrated in Figure 6–1. In this model, disturbed emotional and behavioral responses are a direct function of specific maladaptive cognitions (i.e., one's beliefs, expectations, and thought processes). These in turn lead to an array of physiologic changes that can precipitate or exacerbate pain. CBT emphasizes modification of maladaptive cognitions and beliefs (schemas) and the development of effective coping strategies. CBT provides patients with direction and instruction to reappraise thoughts and events occurring in their life experiences. Faulty appraisals and misattributions are reframed and replaced with those that are less irrational. The presumption, then, is that there will be less physiological arousal occurring within

135

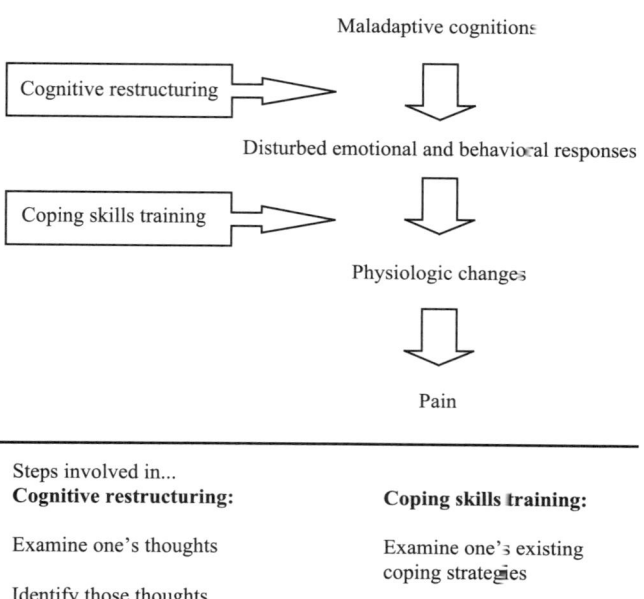

FIGURE 6–1. **Approach of cognitive-behavioral therapy.**

the patient. This diminished arousal, in turn, would be less apt to accentuate the individual's pain experiences.

In CBT, it is recognized that the patient often cannot control or avoid distressing life events. However, the patient can almost always exert some control over how much distress, suffering, and life

disruption those events produce. This control can be achieved by altering one's perceptions of these events, their significance, and their meaning and by altering one's coping. Unlike other psychotherapeutic approaches, external contingencies of reward, internal dispositions, and acquired developmental processes are de-emphasized.

Patients who use CBT skills taught to them in sessions are those with the best long-term results. Consequently, homework is required. This homework entails keeping a diary (much like the pain diary described in Chapter 3), in which the patient records his levels of pain in different situations, along with feelings and thoughts occurring at the time. Homework assignments, if completed properly, help the patient and therapist identify those situations, moods, feelings, and thought processes associated with pain. This then highlights the points of interventions to work on in therapy (i.e., which cognitions require restructuring and when to employ coping strategies).

Cognitive restructuring is used to teach patients to identify and modify maladaptive, negatively distorted thoughts that may lead to negative feelings, such as depression, anxiety and anger. For patients with pain, emotional reactions to pain can be greatly influenced by thoughts. Coping skills training is aimed at helping patients develop a repertoire of skills for managing pain and stress and providing patients with a general set of problem-solving or coping skills that can be used in a wide range of situations that induce pain.

Coping refers to the strategies used by the person to deal with the pain and life stressors (Weickgenant et al. 1993). The strategies employed are based on how the person appraises a given situation or life event. Components of appraisal include the value or significance the person assigns to the event, the perception of the impact of the event, and the assessment of the resources one believes him- or herself to have with which to deal with the event.

The diversity and range of coping strategies employed might signal that the patient's repertoire of dealing with pain and its effects on his or her life require modification. Ineffective coping may possibly be associated with psychiatric disturbances such as depression. For example, depressed low back pain patients were found to be restricted in the range and types of coping strategies they used,

compared with nondepressed low back pain patients (Weickgenant et al. 1993). The therapist helps the patient develop a broader range of effective coping strategies by examining existing coping strategies, determining their effectiveness, and facilitating the development of a broader range of strategies. Different strategies may need to be employed in different settings, and patients may need assistance in deciphering which strategies would be most effective.

Active coping can involve developing problem-solving strategies (e.g., problem-focused coping, social support seeking). By contrast, passive coping involves internal self-statements that the patient learns to say to himself or herself to facilitate coping. Passive coping strategies might include wishful thinking, self-blame, and avoidance. For example, depressed low back pain patients were inclined to be less productive and to employ passive coping strategies when dealing with life stressors, whereas nondepressed low back pain patients employed active coping strategies. However, the latter group did employ passive coping strategies when attempting to deal with the pain experience (Weickgenant et al. 1993). Coping can then be either problem focused or emotion focused.

To help patients modify coping strategies, identify currently employed strategies; assess the utility of the existing strategies (whether they facilitate the patient's relief); and point out, develop, and refine alternatives. Thus, the patient who tends to employ passive strategies, such as self-blame and avoidance, might be encouraged to develop strategies that are more active and self-soothing.

CBT has the advantage of broad applicability in a number of situations. It is a relatively low-cost intervention and appears to be cost-effective. On the other hand, CBT has the disadvantage of requiring sustained active patient participation. Therapists need to have specialized training in CBT in order to use it effectively.

■ SUPPORTIVE THERAPY

Much of what clinicians do can be considered under the auspices of supportive psychotherapy. For the patient with chronic or complex

pain, complete pain relief might not be possible; supportive therapy might then be a viable approach. A warm, reflective, and empathic approach is undertaken to reduce patient distress and reassure the patient that he or she is understood and that the magnitude of his or her plight is appreciated. Feedback is given, providing patients with the outcome and findings of physical and laboratory assessments, pain assessments, and psychometric testing. Rather than telling the patient that "nothing can be done," the therapist emphasizes that modification and improvement in functioning are essentially the patient's responsibility. This emphasis can enhance the patient's sense of personal control and self-efficacy, which is critical for overcoming the chronic pain patient's tendency to succumb to powerlessness and helplessness. Therapists can offer a menu of concrete advice for strategies to reduce discomfort, improve sleep, address medication use, and develop pain-modulating interventions (e.g., relaxation training). Such a menu fosters the notion of the patient's responsibility and autonomy by allowing the patient to select those aspects of treatment that are most appealing; thus, this approach might facilitate patient compliance (Miller and Sanchez 1994).

Ongoing follow-up is required. The interventions described above will be most successful when reexposure to the patient allows for repeated interventions. In addition, setbacks can be the basis for determining what modifications in medications and other treatment interventions might be required. Follow-up reinforces the notion that the patient and physician or clinician are working in concert to effectively mitigate pain and optimize adaptive functioning, while restoring pleasure and balance and bolstering relationships in the patient's life. With this reinforcement, the patient can avoid the potential pitfall of viewing him- or herself as passive and helpless in the treatment process.

■ MARITAL, COUPLES, AND FAMILY THERAPY

Pain is often myopically viewed as an individual patient's problem. Painful disorders have an impact on a broader spectrum of persons,

including the patient's partner and family, along with friendships and work relationships. Conversely, social factors can contribute to the onset, exacerbation, maintenance, and course of the pain disorder.

Significant changes in the functioning and activity of the family unit can arise as a result of having a member with pain. These changes can include alterations in the role responsibilities within the home in order to assume those that the pain patient is no longer able to perform. Such role modifications can be emotionally laden, with some members feeling burdened and the patient experiencing loss of self-efficacy or feeling as though he or she is viewed as incapable. There can be resulting shifts of influence and decision making within the home.

Several stressors may affect the patient's relationships. One such stressor may be related to financial issues, such as lost employment, treatment costs, and inadequate medical coverage. The patient and partner (along with other family members) may disagree about the feasibility of return to work or exploration of other vocational pursuits.

Another stressor may involve the reactions of others to the patient's pain. The reactions of persons within the home can be quite varied, including solicitous responses, withdrawal, and indifference. The solicitous spouse or significant other of the patient might inadvertently reinforce pain complaints and related pain behaviors (e.g., grimacing, limping, sighing) by eagerly accommodating the patient when such behaviors are expressed. Some studies have demonstrated that the degree of solicitous behavior on the part of one's partner is an important factor in determining or predicting pain reports (Block et al. 1980).

Patients also vary in their response to others' reactions. They may harbor expectations of how the partner (or others within the family) should respond to their pain complaints and pain-related behaviors. They may view such responses negatively (e.g., as demeaning or indicative of the patient's "invalid" status), or they may view them as supportive and helpful.

Strained communication patterns within the couple or family may be another stressor. Direct discussion of the patient's behavior

may be difficult. The pain may serve as a means of avoiding discussion about particular topics, which leads to unresolved conflicts and emotional difficulties. Sexual dysfunction and a decline in intimacy from pre-pain periods may add to the burden of the patient and his or her partner as well. Formal sex therapy may be indicated, especially when such difficulties foreshadow more deleterious effects on the relationship.

Normal interests (e.g., in outside hobbies and activities) might no longer be available to the patient, partner, or other family members. Social support networks that would normally be relied upon might be less accessible. The patient and his or her primary caregivers may have little emotional reserve remaining to support and care for others within the family.

As a result of any or all of these factors, the partner–patient dyad and family relationships as a whole can experience marked strain as a result of the pain disorder. Thus, marital and family therapy can be useful to address these issues, mitigating the strain experienced by the patient and others in the patient's life (Romano and Schmaling 2001). Cohesive family relationships and a supportive, mutual, and intimate relationship with a partner can be a buffer against depression for the pain patient. In addition, pain patients in such relationships tend to respond best to treatment and have lower levels of disability (Kerns and Haythornthwaite 1988; Kerns and Turk 1984).

Despite the difficulties that can afflict couples in which pain is prominent, such couples typically remain together for long periods of time. One possible explanation is that the pain serves the role of preserving homeostasis within a troubled relationship. External pressures (e.g., how others would interpret divorce or separation when one partner is so ill) may also influence why some couples remain together. Financial factors can prove to be prohibitive for one or both parties, especially when disability interferes with work functioning and financial support. Substantial financial gains could be hoped for through pending litigation, which might mean that the well partner would want to hold out for a piece of the expected financial gain. Interestingly, partners can also come to endorse sig-

nificant pain problems as well. Often, there is overlap of the pain in location and quality with those complaints of the pain patient (Shoevar and Perkel 1990).

Assessment scales and questionnaires can augment the information gleaned from clinical interview. For example, the West Haven–Yale Multidimensional Pain Inventory (WHYMPI), mentioned in Chapter 3, has a portion devoted to analyzing the partner's responses to pain. Other assessment instruments that assess relationship satisfaction and the family environment are available as well. These can be quite helpful when attempting to address issues arising in the social milieu of the pain patient (Romano and Schmaling 2001).

■ GROUP THERAPY

One of the most devastating effects of chronic pain can be the isolation it produces for the patient. Group therapy, including self-help groups, can serve to diffuse the sense of isolation experienced by the pain patient. These groups allow for the mutual sharing of experiences, provide an opportunity to learn from the experiences of others, foster education about treatment strategies, and foster coping strategies. The shared experiences of persons in the group can offer the patient a sense of being fully understood, often without the requirement of having to explain their experiences or their emotions to others who do not share the same level of physical pain.

Some groups are exclusive—that is, organized around particular disorders (e.g., groups for persons with fibromyalgia, arthritis, cancer pain). Others can be inclusive—broader and open to persons with recurrent or chronic pain of various sorts. Some groups are open to family members and significant others as well.

The purposes of group therapy include universalization (i.e., reduction of feelings of isolation) and providing a forum in which mutual support, information exchange, advice, modeling of effective coping, and abreaction of emotional experiences are possible. The structure of the group sets the stage for and dictates the focus

and perspective of the participants. To be effective, the "rules" of the group process need to be delineated early. If patients are allowed to ventilate distress and can respond to the support and advice offered by peers, attendance in therapy sessions can be a source of inspiration and empowerment. A special benefit arising from group process is abreaction, whereby repressed, emotionally laden experiences are brought to conscious awareness (i.e., reexperienced), and in the process, insight is gained. Some members of the group can inspire others with hope or the means to effectively address emotional-psychological consequences associated with the pain experience (Keefe et al. 1996).

Psychotherapeutic goals can be organized around exploring individual psychodynamics and bringing about personality change. Self-help groups, on the other hand, have vastly different goals—fostering emotional well-being—and focus on coping with specific life problems. Groups vary as to whether they are organized around a particular philosophy or approach. For example, some groups have actually adapted the 12-step program originated within Alcoholics Anonymous, substituting *pain* for *alcohol* (Back and Neck Injury 2002). The goals of such programs are to view pain as something one might not be able to fully control or remove. Thus, adaptations in a person's life might be required in order to overcome the many obstacles in life, relationships, and spiritual life.

■ ADJUNCTIVE INTERVENTIONS

Adjunctive interventions are not forms of therapy but are adjunctive techniques that can be undertaken with the pain patient. These techniques can complement other medical treatments and psychotherapies.

Biofeedback

Biofeedback refers to a procedure in which physical parameters (e.g., muscle tension) are continuously monitored and *fed back* to the patient, who attempts to alter the physical parameter. For exam-

ple, an individual attempting to regulate and modify the degree of muscle tension in forehead muscles would have electromyographic electrodes placed on the forehead. The electrical signals from these electrodes would be relayed to a monitor and presented in any of a number of formats (e.g., visual, auditory). The patient, attending to the signal, would use the information presented to develop strategies to reduce muscle tension. The principle relies on the idea that the patient uses the feedback signal as an indicator of the degree of physical activity that can be modified. In pain management, the idea is that the physical parameter measured and ideally altered is somehow linked to the genesis of pain (Turk et al. 1979; Turner and Chapman 1982b).

Various biofeedback procedures can be employed, focusing on selected physiological parameters for selected pain states. Thus, biofeedback from electromyography (EMG) assists the patient in learning to reduce muscle tension; the levels of measured muscle tension are signaled back to the patient for modification. This technique is useful in tension headache, temporomandibular joint disorders, fibromyalgia, and other myofascial pain disorders. Thermal biofeedback monitors skin temperature to give the patient an indicator of the degree of peripheral vasodilation. The cooler the skin, the greater the vascular constriction, reflecting the amount of prevailing sympathetic activity. By increasing the skin temperature, one is able to suppress the extent of sympathetic activity. This approach has been used in the treatment of migraine and sympathetically maintained pain. Electroencephalography (EEG) has also been linked with biofeedback. Brain electrical activity is fed back to the patient and is subject to modification by the patient. The goal is to achieve states of alpha rhythm brain activity that reflect a state of relaxation. Customarily, EEG biofeedback is quite cumbersome and is not regularly used in pain treatment settings.

The technology involved in biofeedback has enhanced the opportunities and approaches available in pain management. Eventually, with practice, the patient learns to attend to physical cues signaling that relaxation, deep breathing, and changes in cognitive

strategies are required (e.g., sensing one's own heightened muscle tension). The patient is then able to invoke those strategies to reduce the tension without the use of the biofeedback equipment. However, some practitioners question the utility of biofeedback and the necessity of all the cumbersome technology, arguing that other strategies (e.g., relaxation training) are equally efficacious (Silver and Blanchard 1978).

Relaxation and Imagery Training

Relaxation and imagery (R&I) has been employed in both acute and chronic pain and successfully implemented in the treatment of tension headache, migraine headache, temporomandibular joint pain, chronic back pain, and myofascial pain syndrome (Turner and Chapman 1982a). Progressive muscle relaxation (PMR) is the most common approach used. In PMR, the patient is instructed to tense muscles in a region of the body or a limb and then subsequently relax those muscles. The tension and subsequent relaxation of muscle groups is conducted in a logical and sequential manner, generally from head to foot or the reverse. For some patients (e.g., those with myofascial pain and fibromyalgia), the process of tensing sequential muscle groups could prove to be too difficult or fatiguing. Consequently, alternative measures can be employed (e.g., guided imagery or deep breathing exercises).

Autogenic training is similar to PMR in that the patient focuses on sequential and progressive relaxation of parts of the body, but the step of tensing muscles in those regions is not required. Instead, the patient is asked to focus on sensations of heaviness and warmth extending throughout the body.

Guided imagery involves talking the patient through vivid images that are particularly comforting and relaxing. The patient is asked to imagine a place that he or she finds most relaxing in order to set the stage for being in an emotional state that would be inconsistent with anxiety or tension. The patient is then guided to vividly recapture as much of the imagined place as possible—the sights, the sounds, smells, tastes, and physical sensations and feelings.

Deep breathing exercises involve the direction of deep breathing in a manner that potentiates a deepened relaxation. A script for deep breathing exercises is provided in Table 6–6. The patient is instructed in deep breathing so that the technique can be used at home. The technique can be employed in a matter of few seconds or over a span of several minutes (McCaffery and Beebe 1999).

R&I offers several clinical advantages. It is easy to for clinicians to learn how to implement R&I and it is easily learned by patients as well. Lack of patient practice at home limits its usefulness. Unlike biofeedback, R&I requires no specialized equipment. At most, patients might require a tape player or compact disc (CD) player in order to practice R&I. Thus it is a low-cost intervention. Patients may be more receptive to R&I compared with other interventions, such as hypnosis, about which there may be misconceptions.

As far as disadvantages are concerned, R&I is not a sufficient treatment for pain states. Adverse effects may arise, including muscle cramping and fatigue, particularly with the use of PMR. In addition, certain patients might find it difficult to gain any benefit from R&I. Highly distressed or distractible patients might have marked difficulty concentrating on the techniques required. In addition, patients distracted by intense, severe pain might find that they are unable to benefit from R&I. Some religious patients and those who are rigid or concrete in their thinking might be resistant to R&I, fearing that it invokes practices contrary to their spiritual experiences or cognitive styles. (This resistance can generally be overcome with thoughtful patient education and reassurances.) Skeptical patients might not construe any benefit to the technique. In some cases, the approach of biofeedback might be more convincing, because the patient receives feedback about biological parameters that improve in response to relaxation techniques.

In a review of nine studies examining the use of R&I alone in pain reduction, only four studies showed a significant difference among pain outcome measures between pre- and posttreatment (Carroll and Seers 1998). In only three studies was a significant improvement found with R&I as compared with a wait-list control condition. This analysis suggests that whereas R&I can have some

TABLE 6–6.	**Script for breathing exercise**

Have the patient assume a comfortable position in a quiet place where there will be no interruptions. Ask the patient to imagine that he or she is doing this exercise in a place that is calming and relaxing. Then, instruct the patient as follows:

1. Breathe in slowly and deeply.
2. As you breathe out slowly, feel yourself beginning to relax as tension begins to leave your body.
3. Now, breathe in and out regularly and slowly. Constrict your abdominal muscles, feel your chest wall expand as your abdomen compresses inward. Feel your ribs expand, hold this, then slowly release. As you release the air, feel your body relax more and more. Imagine tension leaving your body with each exhalation.
4. As you breathe in, slowly count to three. As you breathe out, slowly count to three. Each time you breathe out, repeat a word to yourself— a word such as "peace" or "relax."
5. Repeat steps 3 and 4 as needed, for up to about 20 minutes.
6. End with a slow deep breath. As you breathe out, say to yourself "I feel relaxed."

efficacy in mitigating pain experiences, it probably is not sufficient as a sole intervention. When compared with alternate treatments, behavior therapy was found to be more effective than R&I, and in another study, biofeedback was found to yield better long-term results when followed up at 6 months, as compared to R&I.

Hypnosis

Hypnosis emerged in the late 1400s from a belief in the healing power of magnets and a belief in the influences of cosmic magnetism, which maintained that magnetic waves emerging from stars and the moon affected behavior. (As farfetched as it sounds, some people still adhere to this belief—for example, thinking that emergency departments are busier during and as a result of a full moon.) Misattributions were erroneously made about the healing power of magnets. For example, magnets were placed in plaster casts to heal broken bones. In fact, healing occurred due to the nat-

ural healing of the bone within the cast but not to any influences of the magnet.

Mesmer, known as the Father of Hypnosis, likewise employed magnets, in the form of a magnetic rod, in order to heal. (This rod probably became the prototype of the magician's wand some time later). He waved the rod along the patient's body to "heal." His practice, needless to say, fell into ill repute. Much later, Esdaile, a surgeon in Bengal, India, employed hypnosis for surgical procedures and child delivery. In his reports, hypnosis was effective in anesthetizing patients during these procedures.

Current conceptualizations view hypnosis as a form of focused attention, useful in acute and chronic pain states including headache, fibromyalgia, back pain, trigeminal neuralgia, arthritis, phantom limb pain, and cancer pain. It is a self-induced state brought on by the patient with the assistance of the hypnotist.

Hypnotic responsiveness varies considerably from person to person but appears to be a stable trait. A number of scales are used to assess responsiveness to hypnosis (Kurtz and Strube 1996). These test the patient's ability to respond to a variety of hypnotic suggestions. The most important factor determining response appears to be the patient's imaginative absorption, which the skillful hypnotist is able to capitalize on (Smyser and Baron 1993). Pain reduction is predicted by imaginative absorption.

The mechanism of pain relief brought on by hypnosis is unclear. Questions arise as to whether pain (unpleasant sensations) is removed or reactions to normally painful stimuli are removed. For example, Esdaile reported success in using hypnosis for patients in surgery but admitted that many patients were not entirely pain free. For example, some patients "moved and moaned' or awoke in the midst of the operation and "cried out." Afterward, however, they appeared to be amnestic for the surgery and the pain. In the acute pain setting, patients reacted as if they had pain, but subsequently could not recall the painful experience (Barber 1963; Orne 1976).

Analgesia produced through hypnosis is an active process involving the patient's full cooperation. Imaging technology has supported that the process of hypnosis produces signal changes in areas

of the brain concerned with sensation and perception (i.e., the sensory cortex, thalamus) and areas of the brain where sensory information is integrated (Raz and Shapiro 2002).

Various hypnotic techniques, summarized in Table 6–7, offer a noninvasive intervention to mitigate pain. Some patients are more susceptible to hypnosis than are others. Thus, hypnosis might not be a suitable intervention for every patient with complex pain. Hypnosis requires active psychological engagement with the patient in order to be effective; thus, barriers previously mentioned for R&I can likewise interfere with hypnosis.

■ VOCATIONAL REHABILITATION

Patients with pain can experience significant losses, including the loss of work. Beyond the obvious resultant loss of income, and perhaps medical coverage, the loss of work can imply several other losses for the patient depending on the meaning of work for that person. For many persons, work is a source of self-identity, power, influence, and a social network. Loss of work, therefore, can mean the feared loss of control and a feared loss of usefulness.

Psychiatrists can be helpful in facilitating pursuit of vocational training. Vocational rehabilitation may be helpful in facilitating the patient's transition back to the workplace. If the patient is not returning to his or her prior work, vocational rehabilitation can serve an instructional role, helping the patient develop skills that will be suitable for other kinds of work. Vocational rehabilitation can be helpful in fostering the patient's independence, autonomy, and self-efficacy. In addition, vocational rehabilitation can assist the patient particularly when there is financial need, ineligibility for disability or compensation, and the need for insurance and medical coverage. Vocational rehabilitation can help the patient go beyond the boundaries of his or her illness. Many state agencies provide vocational and educational services for persons with disabilities that can help patients adapt to a work setting. Within such programs, the patient's interests, skills, aptitudes, limitations imposed by physical and psychiatric conditions, and employ-

TABLE 6–7.	Techniques of hypnosis

Dissociation: The patient is taught to experience another state, place, or time, such as in a vivid daydream, so as to dissociate from the awareness of pain.

Time disorientation: The patient is taught to distort the perception of time (e.g., experiencing a recurrent painful sensation as rapidly passing).

Substitution of sensations: The patient is taught to substitute the unpleasant sensation with another that is more tolerable or less incapacitating. The technique is most effective if the substituted sensation is not entirely pleasant (e.g., substituting a stabbing pain for a pinching pain).

Displacement: The patient is taught to move the painful sensation to another area of the body. For example, if a pain is experienced in the patient's dominant hand, interfering with work, the patient can learn to displace the pain to the small finger on the left hand—and thereby be less adversely affected by it.

Reinterpretation: The patient is taught to alter the meaning of the pain to an interpretation that is better tolerated. The pain encountered after a burn, for example, can be reinterpreted as the efforts of the body to restore healing, to channel soothing fluids to bathe and clean up damaged cells.

ment needs might be assessed. Based on these assessments, work training and supervision is provided, with eventual job placement.

■ REFERENCES

Affleck G, Tennen H, Urrows S, et al: Individual differences in the day-to-day experience of chronic pain: a prospective daily study of rheumatoid arthritis patients. Health Psychol 10:419–426, 1991

Back and Neck Injury/Chronic Pain: Chronic Pain Anonymous. Available at: http://www.backandneck.miningco.com/library/blchair.html. Accessed June 1, 2002

Barber TX: The effects of "hypnosis" on pain. Psychosom Med 25:303–333, 1963

Beutler LE, Engle D, Oro-Beutler ME, et al: Inability to express intense affect: a common link between depression and pain? J Consult Clin Psychol 54:752–759, 1986

Block A, Kremer E, Gaylor M: Behavioral treatment of chronic pain: the spouse as a discriminative cue for pain behavior. Pain 9:243–252, 1980

Burns JW: Anger management style and hostility: predicting symptom-specific physiological reactivity among chronic low back pain patients. J Behav Med 20:505–522, 1997

Carroll D, Seers K: Relaxation for the relief of chronic pain: a systematic review. J Adv Nurs 27:476–487, 1998

Cogan R, Cogan D, Waltz W, et al: Effects of laughter and relaxation on discomfort thresholds. J Behav Med 10:139–144, 1987

Compas BE, Haaga DAF, Keefe FJ, et al: Sampling of empirically supported psychological treatments from health psychology: smoking, chronic pain, cancer, and bulimia nervosa. J Consult Clin Psychol 66:89–112, 1998

DeGood DE, Tait RC: Assessment of pain beliefs and pain coping, in Handbook of Pain Assessment, 2nd Edition. Edited by Turk DC, Melzack R. New York, Guilford, 2001, pp 320–345

Feuerstein M: Ambulatory monitoring of paraspinal skeletal muscle, autonomic and mood-pain interaction in chronic low back pain. Paper presented at the 7th annual meeting of the Society of Behavioral Medicine, San Francisco, CA, March 5–8, 1986

Fishman B, Loscalzo M: Cognitive-behavioral interventions in management of cancer pain: principles and applications. Med Clin North Am 71:271–287, 1987

Fordyce WE, Shelton JL, Dundore DE: The modification of avoidance learning pain behaviors. J Behav Med 5:405–414, 1982

Fordyce WE, Roberts AH, Sternbach RA: The behavioral management of chronic pain: a response to critics. Pain 22:113–125, 1985

Hatch JP, Schoenfeld LS, Boutros NN, et al: Anger and hostility in tension-type headache. Headache 31:302–304, 1991

Hawley DJ, Wolfe F: Anxiety and depression in patients with rheumatoid arthritis: a prospective study of 400 patients. J Rheumatol 15:932–941, 1988

Keefe FJ, Dunsmore J, Burnett R: Behavioral and cognitive-behavioral approaches to chronic pain: recent advances and future directions. J Consult Clin Psychol 60:528–536, 1992

Keefe FJ, Baupre PM, Gil KM: Group therapy for patients with chronic pain, in Psychosocial Approaches to Pain Management: A Practitioner's Handbook. Edited by Gatchel RJ, Turk DC, New York, Guilford, 1996, pp 259–282

Kerns RD, Haythornthwaite J: Depression among chronic pain patients: cognitive-behavioral analysis and effects on rehabilitation outcome. J Consult Clin Psychol 56:870–876, 1988

Kerns RD, Turk DC: Depression and chronic pain: the mediating role of the spouse. J Marriage Fam 46:845–852, 1984

Krystal H: Alexithymia and the effectiveness of psychoanalytic treatment. Int J Psychoanal Psychother 9:353–388, 1982

Kurtz RM, Strube MJ: Multiple susceptibility testing: is it helpful? Am J Clin Hypn 38:172–184, 1996

Lakoff R: Interpretive psychotherapy with chronic pain patients. Can J Psychiatry 28:650–653, 1983

McCaffery M, Beebe A: Pain: Clinical Manual for Nursing Practice, 2nd Edition. St. Louis, MO, CV Mosby, 1999

Miller WR, Sanchez VC: Motivating young adults for treatment and lifestyle change, in Alcohol Use and Misuse by Young Adults. Edited by Howard G, Nathan PE. Notre Dame, IN, University of Notre Dame Press, 1994, pp 55–82

Orne MT: Mechanisms of hypnotic pain control, in Advances in Pain Research and Therapy, Vol 1. Edited by Bonica JJ, Albe-Fessard D. New York, Raven, 1976, pp 717–726

Prochaska JO, DiClemente CC: Stages and processes of self-change of smoking: toward an integrative model of change. J Consult Clin Psychol 51:390–395, 1983

Raz A, Shapiro T: Hypnosis and neuroscience: a cross talk between clinical and cognitive research. Arch Gen Psychiatry 59:85–90, 2002

Romano JM, Schmaling KB: Assessment of couples and families with chronic pain, in Handbook of Pain Assessment, 2nd Edition. Edited by Turk DC, Melzack R. New York, Guilford, 2001, pp 346–361

Scheer SJ, Watanabe TK, Radack KL: Randomized controlled trials in industrial low back pain. Part 3. Subacute/chronic pain interventions. Arch Phys Med Rehabil 78:414–423, 1997

Seligman MEP: Learned Optimism. New York, Pocket Books, 1990

Sholevar GP, Perkel R: Family systems intervention and physical illness. Gen Hosp Psychiatry 12:363–372, 1990

Silver BV, Blanchard EB: Biofeedback and relaxation training in the treatment of psychophysiological disorders: or are the machines really necessary? J Behav Med 1:217–239, 1978

Smyser CH, Baron DA: Hypnotizability, absorption, and subscales of the Dissociative Experiences Scale in a nonclincal population. Dissociation: Progress in the Dissociative Disorders 6:42–46, 1993

Stieg RL, Lippe P, Shepard TA: Roadblocks to effective pain treatment. Med Clin North Am 83:809–821, 1999

Sullivan MJL, Bishop S, Pivik J: The pain catastrophizing scale: development and validation. Psychol Assess 7:524–532, 1995

Sullivan MJL, Stanish W, Waite H, et al: Catastrophizing, pain, and disability in patients with soft-tissue injuries. Pain 77:253–260, 1998

Tauschke E, Merskey H, Helmes E: Psychological defence mechanisms in patients with pain. Pain 40:161–170, 1990

Turk DC, Meichenbaum DH, Berman WH: Application of biofeedback for the regulation of pain: a critical review. Psychol Bull 86:1322–1338, 1979

Turner JA, Chapman CR: Psychological interventions for chronic pain: a critical review, II: operant conditioning, hypnosis, and cognitive-behavioral therapy. Pain 12:23–46, 1982a

Turner JA, Chapman CR: Psychological interventions for chronic pain: a critical review, I: relaxation training and biofeedback. Pain 12:1–21, 1982b

Weickgenant AL, Slater MA, Patterson TL, et al: Coping activities in chronic low back pain: relationship with depression. Pain 53:95–103, 1993

Weisberg JN, Keefe FJ: Personality, individual differences, and psychopathology in chronic pain, in Psychosocial Factors in Pain. Edited by Gatchel RJ, Turk DC. New York, Guilford, 1999, pp 56–73

7

SPECIAL TECHNIQUES IN PAIN MANAGEMENT

■ ACUPUNCTURE

Acupuncture is among the oldest forms of pain interventions, dating as far back as 2600 B.C. Its use has been applied to patients with acute and chronic pain, but the mechanism of action remains unclear. Acupuncture has been a source of marked controversy in Western medicine because of the lack of clear understanding of its physiologic effects. One reason for this lack of understanding is that the points of stimulation in acupuncture are derived from ancient Chinese beliefs about disease processes and are not related to known nervous system pathways.

Nonetheless, anecdotal evidence does support that the technique of acupuncture, if performed properly, can produce significant physiological changes, some of which have pain-mitigating effects (Brown et al. 1974; Han and Terenius 1982; Mayer et al. 1977). These changes can include the following:

- Increased endorphin levels within the central nervous system (CNS) (naloxone antagonizes the effectiveness of acupuncture)
- Augmenting of other neurotransmitters, including dopamine, serotonin, and norepinephrine (use of serotonin-blocking agents can reduce analgesic effects produced by acupuncture, whereas agents such as clomipramine may possibly augment acupuncture-induced analgesia)

154

- Altered electroencephalogram (EEG) and cortical evoked potentials
- Other physiologic effects (e.g., vasodilation) that arise from the technique

The efficacy of acupuncture may have more to do with the therapeutic relationship between the patient and the acupuncturist than with any direct physiologic effects of the needle insertions. The trust and confidence in the procedure engendered by that relationship might be key to the perceived efficacy of acupuncture.

Technique

Needles (20–100 gauge) are inserted at varying angles through the skin, corresponding to the areas that can mediate pain in various parts of the body. Needles can be disposable or reusable; sterilization is required between applications in the case of reusable needles. Once inserted, the needles are manipulated (e.g., rotated in place, oscillated, or raised up and down with a twirling motion). More recently, electrical stimulation by way of the needles has been employed. Electrical stimulation is less labor intensive and allows for more homogenous and consistent stimulation than manual manipulation techniques.

Indications

Acupuncture has been employed in a number of pain states, including headache, musculoskeletal pains, arthritis, bursitis, and synovitis.

Complications

Fainting, seizures, infection, and pneumothorax (if needles are inserted into the trunk) are some of the complications that can arise from acupuncture. Needles can break after insertion, requiring surgical excision. When electrical currents are applied to the needle, localized skin burns can result.

Contraindications

Patients receiving anticoagulants may be prone to bleeding and hemorrhage. Patients with rheumatic heart disease can develop bacterial endocarditis as a complication of acupuncture. Because of the changes in the vasculature arising from acupuncture, hypovolemic patients might be particularly prone to syncope. Acupuncture has led to spontaneous abortion in the first 3 months of pregnancy and thus should be avoided in the first trimester.

■ TRANSCUTANEOUS ELECTRICAL NERVE STIMULATION

Transcutaneous electrical nerve stimulation (TENS) is a modality employed to reduce pain in an array of acute and chronic pain states, including labor pain, postoperative pain, neuropathic pain, and musculoskeletal pain. When TENS is used in such settings, patients require less in the way of analgesics (e.g., opiates) and, depending on the circumstances, report increased activity, less interference with work, and improved functional abilities. A TENS unit consists of a battery and electrodes. The electrodes are placed along the surface of the skin overlying painful areas. The battery generates electrical currents of approximately 100 milliamperes (mA); the pulses' rate and width are modifiable by the patient. The efficacy of TENS has been supported by evidence of counterirritation techniques, whereby stimulation of A-β fibers inhibits the pain-promoting activities within the substantia gelatinosa. The efficacy of TENS units has been called into question (Loeser et al. 1975; Tyler et al. 1982).

■ REGIONAL NEURAL BLOCKADE

Regional neural blockade (RNB) encompasses a number of techniques whereby nociceptive inputs of nerve fibers are interrupted. The activity of thin and unmyelinated nerve fibers (e.g.,

A-δ and C fibers) is particularly prone to inhibition, requiring minimal doses of anesthetic agents. If higher doses are used, it is possible to inhibit larger myelinated fibers, such as motor neurons.

The purpose of RNB is multifaceted. RNB interventions can serve a diagnostic function, helping to clarify the source of pain (e.g., deciphering peripheral nerve pain from sympathetically mediated pain). Some procedures may be invoked to provide prophylaxis of future pain after surgical procedures (e.g., to minimize phantom limb pain post-amputation). In addition, RNB techniques may be invoked to provide therapeutic pain relief in selected disorders, especially in those chronic pain disorders involving sympathetically mediated pain and complex regional pain syndrome. At times, RNB is employed to determine the suitability of other, more permanent interventions (e.g., neural destruction techniques). The types of RNB techniques and how these are employed, complications, and indications are summarized extensively elsewhere (Barash et al. 2001).

Anesthesia at the Level of the Spinal Cord

Anesthesia at the level of the spinal cord involves application of anesthetics to influence spinal or sympathetic nerves, or both, to produce pain relief. Subarachnoid application of anesthetics involves insertion of a needle through the dura mater, applying the anesthetic into the cerebrospinal fluid. Epidural anesthesia involves application of the anesthetic outside the dura mater—the dura mater is not punctured (at least not intentionally).

The subarachnoid administration of anesthetics allows for more direct access of anesthetics to pain-relaying and sympathetic nerves. On the other hand, the epidural space contains areolar (fat) tissue, epidural veins, and lymphatic tissue, into which the anesthetic will diffuse and be absorbed. Thus, epidural administration is an indirect means of providing blockade of pain-sensitive nerves entering the spinal cord. Because of the distance traveled by the anesthetic agent and absorption of the agent by the fat layer

surrounding the dura, anesthetics introduced in this manner take a longer time to exert a full effect. In addition, less intense sensory (and motor) blockade results from epidural injection compared with subarachnoid injection. Consequently, to achieve anesthesia through the epidural technique, generally more anesthetic is required than is the case for subarachnoid injections. The dura mater is not penetrated or broken through, so post–spinal-injection headache and meningitis are less likely to occur with epidural injection. Epidural anesthesia is also less likely to produce cardiovascular effects that are observed with subarachnoid injections.

After the anesthetic is introduced, sympathetic blockade is achieved first. The sympathetic nerve fibers are small and unmyelinated and are more susceptible to the effects of the anesthetic agents than are the larger myelinated fibers. Next, the sensory fibers are affected. Motor fibers tend to be deeper in the nerves, and because of this, greater diffusion of the anesthetic is required to influence motor blockade. To test the sensory level of anesthesia achieved, the clinician first checks the patient's ability to detect temperature at various dermatomal skin levels. The sensory level of anesthesia can also be clarified by testing the sensitivity of various dermatomes to mild pinprick sensation (see Table 7–1). The extent of motor blockade should likewise be assessed.

TABLE 7–1. **Dermatomal levels for spinal anesthesia**

Anesthesia intended for	Dermatomal level
Lower extremities	T12
Hip	T10
Vagina, uterus	T10
Bladder, prostate	T10
Testes, ovaries	T8
Lower intra-abdominal area	T6
Other intra-abdominal areas	T4

Note. Dermatome T10 is located at the level of the umbilicus, and T4 is located at the level of the nipples. However, these locations are not absolute; sensory dermatomes may overlap considerably.

158

TABLE 7–2.	Complications and contraindications of subarachnoid and epidural analgesia

Complications	Contraindications
Subarachnoid	**Absolute**
Hypotension	Lack of patient consent
Post–spinal-injection headache	Allergy or sensitivies to local
High spinal	anesthetics
Nausea, vomiting	Increased intracranial pressure
Urinary retention	Infection at the potential puncture
Backache	site
Epidural	**Relative**
Unintentional injection of	Hypovolemia
anesthetic	Coagulopathy
Into subarachnoid space	Sepsis
Into vascular space	Progressive neurologic diseases
Wet tap	Chronic back pain
Local anesthetic overdose	
Hypotension	
Spinal cord trauma	
Epidural hematoma	

Complications associated with subarachnoid and epidural injections are summarized in Table 7–2. Puncture of the dura mater during an intended epidural injection, referred to as *wet tap*, can produce significant headache. After subarachnoid injection, analgesia and paralysis may be produced at levels higher than intended (i.e., *high spinal*). In this way, sympathetic innervation to vital organs arising from thoracic spinal segments can be inadvertently suppressed, resulting in compromised cardiac output and ventilatory mechanics. Contraindications for both techniques are also outlined in Table 7–2 (Barash et al. 2001).

Multiple agents can be administered using the subarachnoid and epidural techniques, including opiates, steroids, α2 adrenergic agonists (e.g., clonidine), and muscle relaxants (e.g., ba-

159

TABLE 7–3.	Risks of continuous epidural or subarachnoid anesthetic infusions

Catheter problems
    Moving
    Kinking
    Breaking
    Disconnection
    Occlusion (by fibrosis in epidural placement site)
Infection
    Local infection
    Epidural abscess
    Meningitis

clofen). Continuous opiate analgesia can be applied through implantable drug delivery systems inserted through the epidural or subarachnoid route. These systems are often employed in cancer pain and are being increasingly explored in chronic, nonmalignant pain. Risks associated with continuous implantable infusions are summarized in Table 7–3.

Peripheral Nerve Blockade

In cases in which pain is refractory to pharmacologic treatment, peripheral nerve block can be an option (Raj 1996) Somatic nerve blocks are used in patients with intractable pain, generally from cancerous invasion of parts of the body, including the nervous system. At times, these blocks are employed in peripheral nerve pain, sciatica, and carpel tunnel syndrome. In addition, peripheral nerve blocks are employed to provide analgesia during localized surgery so that the patient can avoid general anesthesia.

    Nerve blocks involve the application of local anesthetic agents or neurolytic agents to precipitate neural blockade. Nerve blocks can be destructive or nondestructive. In the case of nondestructive blockade, a local anesthetic agent (lidocaine or bupivacaine) is applied to a nerve. This is a temporary procedure, but it can

be quite effective in mitigating pain. The blockage might be of sufficient duration to allow the patient to become more proactive with physical therapy, which in turn might set the stage for further health improvements and rehabilitation. Nerve destruction, a permanent procedure, is brought on by application of ethanol, phenol, or other agents that result in destruction of the nerve. Neural destruction is never attempted unless local application of anesthetics has first been tried. If local anesthetics fail to produce pain relief, it is unlikely that neural destruction will be effective in mitigating pain.

Anesthetic infusions can produce untoward effects (e.g., hypotension, localized numbness, muscle weakness, infection, and bleeding). Such measures should never be attempted unless resuscitation equipment is readily available.

Sympathetic Nerve Blockade

As with peripheral nerve blockade, a number of comparable measures can be undertaken to reduce pain that is sympathetically mediated. Complex pain syndromes involving the arm, head, and neck might benefit from stellate ganglion blockade. Similarly, diffuse pain in the lower extremities can benefit from lumbar sympathetic blockade. Visceral pain syndromes (e.g., pain arising from the pancreas and other upper abdominal organs) can be mitigated by celiac plexus block; pain originating from pelvic organs can be reduced with hypogastric plexus block (Eisenberg et al. 1995). Such measures may not provide complete pain relief. However, even if only partial relief is achieved, this may be sufficient to allow the patient to lower the amount of opiate analgesics required, thereby reducing the risks of untoward effects.

Sympathetic nerve blockades are employed in conditions of unremitting pain arising from the viscera, generally induced by cancer. In some cases, the use of opiate analgesics and adjuvants proves to be unsatisfactory or intolerable. Uses for and types of autonomic nerve blocks are summarized in Table 7–4.

161

TABLE 7–4. Uses of autonomic nerve blocks

Type of nerve block	Uses
Sphenopalatine ganglion block	Frontal headache
	Cluster headache
	Migraine headache
Stellate ganglion block	Complex regional pain syndrome
	Postherpetic neuralgia
	Intractable angina pectoris
	Vascular insufficiency (e.g., Raynaud disease, scleroderma)
Celiac ganglion block	Pain arising from viscera, secondary to cancer
	Pancreas
	Alimentary tract (esophagus through transverse colon)
Superior mesenteric ganglion block	Pain arising from viscera, secondary to cancer
	Bladder, kidney, ureters
	Distal colon, rectum
	Prostate, testicle
	Uterus
Hypogastric plexus block	Pelvic, vaginal, scrotal pain
	Buttock, inguinal pain

■ NEUROSURGICAL TECHNIQUES: TREATMENT OF LAST RESORT

Neurosurgical techniques consist of ablative and neural stimulation techniques. In general, these techniques are invoked for severe, refractory pain conditions, particularly in cancer-related pain.

Ablative Techniques

Ablative techniques involve removal or destruction of nerve centers or other components of pain pathways. In trigeminal neuralgia, for example, efforts have been directed at ablation of the trigeminal

ganglion. Ablation is achieved by injection of lytic agents (e.g., glycerol, phenol) into the ganglion by means of the foramen ovale at the base of the skull or by direct destruction of the ganglion (e.g., by radiofrequency coagulation). On the other hand, pain that appears to be sympathetically mediated may respond to destruction of a sympathetic ganglion. However, ablative techniques are not effective in spinal cord injury–related pain.

Cordotomy is another technique whereby spinothalamic tracts are disrupted as they ascend to higher CNS structures (Frazier et al. 1937; Garber and Hassenbusch 2001). Needles are inserted between cervical disks, at or below the level of C4, and directed at the anterolateral aspects of the spinal cord. In this way, the spinothalamic tracts are disrupted, thereby interrupting the pain transmission. The cordotomy procedure is cumbersome and is weighted with a number of untoward effects. As a consequence, cordotomy is rarely employed, and then only employed in patients with severe, unilateral pain who have short life expectancies. The procedure is generally avoided, and preference is given to other interventions for pain (including analgesic and adjuvant medication use).

Commissurotomy involves destruction of the spinothalamic tracts as they cross from the dorsal horn through the ventral commissure to the contralateral side of the spinal column (Garber and Hassenbusch 2001). The destruction of the commissure will involve spinothalamic tracts that are crossing from either side of the spinal cord. Thus, commissurotomy is employed in cancer patients in whom there is persistent, refractory pain that is present bilaterally in both flanks or in the midline (e.g., pelvic or rectal regions). There can be destruction of motor fibers, however, and some patients experience ataxia and paresis as a result.

Neural Stimulation Techniques

Stimulation techniques are employed to suppress the activity of nerves relaying painful information. Inhibition is rather dramatic, such that when high-frequency, low-amplitude stimulation is applied, dorsal horn cell activity is inhibited (Leak and Ansel 1996).

Stimulation techniques have been used in chronic, intractable pain affecting the limbs or the trunk (this can include conditions such as phantom limb pain, arachnoiditis, neuropathy, and complex regional pain syndrome).

Neural stimulation techniques can be employed within the CNS (i.e., through implantable devices inserted within the spinal column to stimulate the dorsal horn) or peripherally. The peripheral technique is employed to treat neurogenic pain in the limbs; a generator and stimulation electrodes are placed beneath the skin, and the electrodes are placed in proximity of the peripheral nerve.

Because spinal cord stimulation is such a complex procedure, this approach is reserved for those patients whose pain has been refractory to other interventions or for whom other interventions prove intolerable. Stimulation is not allowable in patients who have a demand cardiac pacemaker, who require magnetic resonance imaging (MRI) in the immediate future, or who have ongoing substance dependence. In addition, because of the invasiveness of this procedure, there must be a clearly identified basis for the nature of the pain. Ambiguous conditions in which the precipitant or cause remains unclear are not likely to have successful results with such interventions.

Psychiatric consultation is likely to be requested to evaluate prospective candidates for neurosurgical interventions (Nelson et al. 1996). The presence of major psychiatric disturbances (e.g., psychosis, major mood disorders, somatoform disorders, or suicidality) is likely to predict poor response to surgical interventions. Significant cognitive deficits contraindicate such interventions as well, because the patient with a cognitive deficit might not have the capability to adhere to treatment and to mobilize surgical assistance if problems from the procedure were to arise. Because ongoing litigation can adversely affect a patient's response to treatment and potentiate claims of pain, it too may contraindicate the undertaking of invasive neurosurgical procedures. All these factors should be weighed against potential benefits and considered in light of the prognosis and course of the underlying medical condition. Among patients with chronic nonmalignant pain, these factors might be

more of an issue in deciding who is a candidate for surgery compared with patients who have terminal conditions and limited life expectancies. Psychiatric treatment might be invoked to address psychological contraindications that, if treated successfully, could render the patient a candidate for surgical interventions.

■ REFERENCES

Barash PG, Cullen BF, Stoelting RK (eds): Clinical Anesthesia, 4th Edition. Philadelphia, PA, Lippincott, Williams & Wilkins, 2001

Brown ML, Ulett GA, Stern JA: Acupuncture loci: techniques for location. Am J Chin Med 2:67–74, 1974

Eisenberg E, Carr DB, Chalmers TC: Neurolytic celiac plexus block for treatment of cancer pain: a meta-analysis. Anesth Analg 80:290–295, 1995

Frazier CH, Lewy FH, Lowe SN: The origin and mechanism of paroxysmal neuralgic pain and the surgical treatment of central pain. Brain 60:44–51, 1937

Garber JE, Hassenbusch SJ: Neurosurgical operations on the spinal cord, in Bonica's Management of Pain, 4th Edition. Edited by Loeser JD, Butler SH, Chapman CR, et al. Philadelphia, PA, Lippincott, Williams & Wilkins, 2001, pp 2023–2037

Han JS, Terenius L: Neurochemical basis of acupuncture analgesia. Annu Rev Pharmacol Toxicol 22:193–220, 1982

Leak WD, Ansel AE: Neural stimulation: spinal cord and peripheral nerve stimulation, in Pain Management: A Comprehensive Review. Edited by Raj PP. St. Louis, MO, Mosby, 1996, pp 327–334

Loeser JD, Black RG, Christman A: Relief of pain by transcutaneous stimulation. J Neurosurg 42:308–314, 1975

Mayer DJ, Price DD, Rafii A: Antagonism of acupuncture analgesia in man by the narcotic antagonist naloxone. Brain Res 121:368–372, 1977

Nelson DV, Kennington M, Novy DM, et al: Psychological selection criteria for implantable spinal cord stimulators. Pain Forum 5:93–103, 1996

Raj PP: Peripheral nerve blocks, in Pain Management: A Comprehensive Review. Edited by Raj PP. St. Louis, MO, Mosby, 1996, pp 200–226

Tyler E, Caldwell C, Ghia JN: Transcutaneous electrical nerve stimulation: an alternative approach to the management of postoperative pain. Anesth Analg 61:449–456, 1982

8

COMMON PAIN DISORDERS

■ HEADACHE

The most common pain complaint prompting medical evaluation is headache, estimated to account for 10 million office visits annually in the United States (Collins 1986).

Tension Headache

Tension headache (TH) is very common, affecting as much as 70% of men and 85% of women annually. TH can also occur among persons with migraine headache (MH)—often confounding diagnostic features—but is not any more prevalent among persons with MH. Classically, the features of TH involve a pressing and tightening quality that is bilateral and often described as band-like or surrounding the head (Welch 2001). The intensity of TH can vary from mild to moderate in severity. Although TH can inhibit activities, it does not prohibit them. TH is rarely aggravated by routine activities such as walking and climbing stairs. Generally, TH is not accompanied by nausea, vomiting, or photo- or phonophobia.

TH is thought to arise from peripheral changes (i.e., myofascial pain sensitivity and increased pericranial muscle activity). TH can be brought on by physical and psychological stress as well as poor posture and ergonomic conditions. Emotional factors can contribute to the frequency and severity of headache. It is speculated that limbic system activity invoked during emotional distress might both contribute to muscle contraction and inhibit

endogenous antinociceptive pathways; however, the exact process remains unclear (Holm et al. 1986).

Treatment of acute episodes of TH includes use of nonsteroidal anti-inflammatory drugs (NSAIDs) such as ibuprofen, ketorolac, ketoprofen, and naproxen (see Table 8–1). There does not appear to be any indication for muscle relaxants or analgesics containing opiates. Prophylaxis of TH is probably facilitated most by tricyclic antidepressants (TCAs). A TCA can be used for 4 months. If the frequency of headache is reduced significantly, the TCA can be tapered and discontinued. There might be a need to reinstate the TCA for longer-term use if the headaches recur.

In a recent study, nefazodone was effective in treating patients with chronic daily headache. However, patients with comorbid depression had better results from nefazodone than those who were not depressed (Saper et al. 2001). Other researchers have reported that patients with chronic daily headache had reduced symptoms with amitriptyline, nortriptyline, or stress management. No information was provided about which patients with headache were more apt to benefit from these measures (Holroyd et al. 2001). Serotonin-selective antidepressants and venlafaxine might also be efficacious in chronic headache (Ansari 2000; Diamond 1995).

Effective psychotherapeutic modalities include biofeedback training and relaxation training. Stress management therapy and cognitive-behavioral therapy (CBT) can also be helpful in reducing stress levels, but they are probably most effective when combined with relaxation or biofeedback training (Holroyd et al. 1977). Characteristics of patients who are likely to improve with the use of psychotherapeutic treatment are summarized in Table 8–2. Of these factors, the most striking is that those patients in relaxation training who show positive responses by the fourth session (as measured by muscle level reactivity on electromyogram [EMG]) are likely to have an excellent response to relaxation or biofeedback training (Bogaards and ter Kuile 1994). Uncontrolled studies have revealed that dental complications may predispose some persons to TH, and these persons

167

TABLE 8–1.	Treatment of headache
Abortive	**Prophylactic**

Abortive	Prophylactic
Tension headache	
NSAIDs	Antidepressants
Acetaminophen	Tricyclic antidepressants
Aspirin	SSRIs (e.g., fluoxetine)
	Nefazodone
Migraine headache	
Triptans (e.g., sumatriptan, zolmitriptan, naratriptan)	β-blockers
	Calcium-channel blockers
Ergotamines	Methysergide
NSAIDs	Ergotamines
Butorphanol	Tricyclic antidepressants
Opiates	Valproate
Caffeine	Clonidine
Antiemetics	
Cluster headache	
Oxygen inhalation	Lithium
Ergotamines	Verapamil
Sumatriptan	Ergotamines
	Methysergide
	Steroids

Note. NSAIDs = nonsteroidal anti-inflammatory drugs; SSRIs = selective serotonin reuptake inhibitors.

TABLE 8–2.	Factors influencing likelihood of response to psychotherapeutic measures in patients with tension headache

Young age of patient

Shorter duration of headache, compared with chronic headache

Relaxation training that produces at least 50% reduction of activity as shown on EMG by the fourth session (predictive of an excellent response)

Lower scores on psychometric measures of depression, compared with higher scores

Patient's requiring minimal analgesia

Note. EMG = electromyogram

may respond favorably to occlusal adjustments and splints and therapeutic masticatory exercises.

Migraine Headache

MH occurs less frequently than TH, affecting approximately 6% of men and 15%–18% of women. Hormonal influences might account for these gender differences, because the rates of migraine among prepubescent boys and girls are equal (Silberstein 1992). Classically, MH can last approximately 4–72 hours. Generally, these headaches are unilateral, with a pulsating quality. Intensity of MH is moderate to severe (i.e., inhibits and prohibits activities). MH is often aggravated by routine activities (e.g., walking, climbing stairs). MH is often accompanied by photo- or phonophobia, nausea, and vomiting (Welch 2001).

MH can be preceded by an aura. MH without aura is approximately twice as frequent as MH with aura. However, both can occur in the same patient. The variability in the features of MH, even in the same person among different episodes, can complicate the diagnosis. Aura precedes MH and develops gradually over several minutes, but it generally does not last beyond 60 minutes. The aura is followed by the headache, generally within 60 minutes. By definition, *aura* suggests a neurologic symptom emanating from central nervous system (CNS) influences but are fully reversible. At times, MH can be preceded by more than one aura, occurring in succession. Aurae must be distinguished from other neurologic symptoms that can signal other disorders (e.g., seizure or transient ischemic attacks). The commonly encountered aurae are listed in Table 8–3. Given that these symptoms can mimic symptoms of other disorders and can trigger marked patient and physician distress, psychiatric evaluation of the patient might be requested. Careful assessment of the patient is warranted to differentiate symptoms of migraine (e.g., visual or auditory hallucinations) from those of psychiatric disorders such as schizophrenia or delirium. Differentiating these features from functional psychiatric disorders is possible based on the patient's longitudinal history,

169

TABLE 8–3.	Common aurae associated with migraine headache

Visual
    Flashing lights
    Fortification spectra
    Scotomata
    Hemianopsia
    Visual hallucinations
Auditory
    Abnormal auditory sensations (e.g., tinnitus)
    Auditory hallucinations
    Decreased hearing
Olfactory
    Abnormal olfactory sensations
    Olfactory hallucinations
Sensory
    Paresthesia
    Vertigo
Motor
    Weakness

family history, and presence of cognitive and other neurologic symptoms. The transience of aurae and their temporal relationship to headache and other migraine features suggest MH instead of functional psychiatric disorders. The clinician is cautioned against hastily initiating antipsychotic medications, thus failing to appropriately evaluate and treat the migraine condition. Of most concern is that other serious conditions (e.g., transient ischemic attacks) may be dismissed as reflecting functional psychiatric disturbances, and work-up and appropriate treatment (e.g., with clopidogrel) might be overlooked.

Common precipitants of MH include alcohol use, emotional distress, and menstruation. It is interesting to note that MH frequency appears to decline during pregnancy and menopause, supporting the notion that hormonal factors have an impact on MH. However, hormone therapy during menopause can prolong the migraine condition

even after menopause (Epstein et al. 1975). Certain psychiatric disorders (e.g., childhood somnambulism) may possibly predict adulthood MH.

Treatment of MH depends on the frequency and severity of the headaches, the presence of neurologic symptoms, and the impact of potential interventions on the patient's lifestyle. Headaches occurring once per month or less might require only abortive therapies, whereas those of greater frequency may possibly require prophylactic interventions (see Table 8–1). Agents customarily employed for abortive therapy include isometheptene mucate (a sympathomimetic amine used to constrict dilated cranial and cerebral arterioles), ergotamines, sumatriptan and other "triptans," NSAIDs, and in refractory cases, intravenous lidocaine. Isometheptene is fairly well tolerated, avoiding gastrointestinal side effects that often accompanying other interventions. NSAIDs might be poorly tolerated, because they can aggravate the nausea and vomiting that often accompany migraine. Sumatriptan has high efficacy and quick onset when administered subcutaneously but works more slowly when administered by intranasal or oral routes. The triptans ought to be avoided in patients with cardiovascular and cerebrovascular disorders (Matchar et al. 2002).

Prophylactic treatment strategies are listed in Table 8–1. The pharmacologic agents listed are intended to reduce the morbidity and disability associated with recurrent MH. Those agents with moderate to high efficacy with minimal side effects include amitriptyline, valproate, propranolol, timolol, and lisuride (not available in the United States) (Ramadan et al. 2002).

Among psychotherapeutic interventions, relaxation training, biofeedback, and CBT are all somewhat effective in the prophylaxis of MH (Campbell et al. 2002). However, no one modality has been demonstrated to be any more efficacious in MH than any other. Certainly, integrated or combination modalities might prove to be effective for some patients. Additional improvements can be achieved when psychotherapeutic interventions are combined with judicious use of pharmacologic interventions.

Cluster Headache

Cluster headache (CH) is significantly less common than either TH or MH. Gender is a factor in CH, with a marked prevalence among males. CH begins in one's 30s or 40s. The pain occurs in a series of attacks spanning weeks to months, with pain-free intervals of months to years. During the active period, headache can occur daily or every other day. Typically, the pain is unilateral, located in the ocular, frontal, and/or temporal areas (Welch 2001). The headache can last anywhere from 15 minutes to 2 hours. Associated features include conjunctival injection, lacrimation, stuffiness of the nose on the affected side, rhinorrhea, and ipsilateral ptosis and miosis.

Alcohol can precipitate CH during active periods. Another precipitant might be increased altitude. Treatment (see Table 8–1) includes oxygen as the primary abortive agent, applied at 10 L/minute via nasal cannula. Prophylactic interventions can include ergot alkaloids, sumatriptan, methysergide, and lithium carbonate. (The latter is generally used in more chronic forms of CH.) Clearly, avoidance of alcohol can constitute a prophylactic intervention. Note that the combination of lithium with NSAIDs would be deleterious, raising the risk of severe lithium toxicity.

■ BACK PAIN

The second most common pain complaint prompting medical evaluation is low back pain. Estimates suggest that United States health care costs expended for low back pain approximate $50 billion annually. Back pain has become one of the most common and, simultaneously, one of the most elusive of chronic pain disorders. Without a doubt, back pain results in significant morbidity and constitutes the leading cause of long-term disability in the United States (Atlas and Deyo 2001).

Clinicians dealing with complaints of back pain are often confronted with a perplexing differential diagnosis. Common

172

TABLE 8–4. **Common causes of back pain**

Intervertebral disc rupture or herniation
Meningeal irritation
   Infection
   Tumor
   Bleeding
Arachnoiditis
Trauma
Prior back surgery
Facet injury
Lumbar ligament injury
Neoplasm
Spinal cord involvement (extremely dangerous)
Cauda equina syndrome (extremely dangerous)

---

causes of back pain include those listed in Table 8–4. Back pain can emanate from injury in a number of body areas (e.g., the vertebrae, facet joints, nerve roots, muscle, and connective tissue). In 60% of back pain patients, there is often no direct relationship between physical findings discovered on physical examination or diagnostic testing and the patient's perceived level of pain, disability, and psychological distress (Reesor and Craig 1988). Patients whose back pain appears disproportionate to the level of pathology noted on examination have a marked propensity toward depression and maladaptive cognitive patterns, compared with those with clear pathology for their pain. Such patients are particularly prone to catastrophizing as a maladaptive cognitive approach.

The negative attitudes and beliefs that chronic back pain patients have that might contribute to affective associations with the pain include a sense of loss over aspects of one's life resulting from the pain. The medical system becomes a fundamental aspect of one's life, which can be perplexing and troubling to patients who often become frustrated with ineffective treatment strategies and extensive diagnostic testing. At times, physicians can be struggling

with the lack of clear identifiable causes of the pain or with frustration at the inability to arrive at a reasonable treatment strategy. This struggle may possibly be communicated to the patient, who might perceive the physician's approach as an endorsement of not taking the patient seriously. Patients often feel frustrated by their lack of relief and may feel helpless and sometimes hopeless (Walker et al. 1999).

Patients with back pain have demonstrated marked back muscle tension on electromyography (EMG) when discussing situations that were personally distressing, compared with other chronic pain patients or healthy control subjects. Additionally, back pain patients have demonstrated a protracted latency to recover or resume normal back muscle tone on EMG after cessation of the discussion (Flor et al. 1985). Distress caused or exacerbated by such discussions contributes to physiological changes that potentially aggravate back pain.

Exercise is a fundamental aspect of treatment. When physicians are successful at encouraging patients to remain active and resume their usual activity levels, the patients will have reduced disability and will return to work rapidly (Waddell et al. 1997). The longer patients are out of work, the harder it is for them to return (McGill 1968). Surgical intervention might be required for structural and mechanical causes (e.g., disk herniation, spinal nerve encroachment). Nerve blocks, epidural anesthetics, or spinal anesthetics might also provide relief, particularly if back pain is accompanied by radicular pain.

Medications to consider for treatment are summarized in Table 8–5. Antidepressants do not appear to have any analgesic effect greater than placebo in patients with chronic back pain (Turner and Denny 1993). However, they could be useful for patients with comorbid depression or anxiety disorders that complicate the patient's coping, adaptation, and rehabilitation process (Deyo and Weinstein 2001). Brief courses of CBT have been efficacious in reducing perceived disability and facilitating return to work in chronic low back pain patients (Turner 1996).

174

TABLE 8–5.	**Treatment options for back pain**

Exercise
   Flexibility exercises
   Range-of-motion exercises
   Aerobic exercises
   Muscle strengthening exercises (e.g., of abdominal muscles)
Return to activity
Medications
   Nonsteroidal anti-inflammatory drugs, acetaminophen
   Tramadol, opioid analgesics
   Antidepressants (primarily for mood disturbances)
Other interventions
   Surgery
   Spinal cord stimulation

■ NONARTICULAR PAIN DISORDERS

Myofascial Pain

Myofascial pain refers to a syndrome in which the patient complains of pain in nonarticular regions of the body, originating from muscle and precipitated by muscle trigger points. The nature of the pain can simulate other disorders (e.g., trigger points in trapezius and cervical muscles can produce headache pain, and those in the paravertebral muscles can produce low back pain). Identification of trigger points is essential in order to diagnose myofascial pain.

Trigger points are taut bands, palpable in muscles, that are approximately 1 cm or more across and that can roll beneath or between the fingers. Taut bands of this kind can be present in both symptomatic pain-generating muscles and in nonpainful muscles. The bands are tender, producing severe radiating pain on palpation. When stimulated, these taut bands contract briskly, producing a twitch. There may be commensurate restriction in range of motion of the limb containing the affected muscles. Pathological investigations have not consistently demonstrated specific pathologic changes associated with trigger points.

Treatment of trigger points is possible with physiotherapy, specifically stretching and passive manipulation. Heat therapy or cryotherapy (i.e., application of cold) or application of transcutaneous electrical nerve stimulation (TENS) may also be useful adjuncts to treatment.

Fibromyalgia

Fibromyalgia, by contrast, requires the presence of multiple tender points for diagnosis. These points are located on both sides of the body above and below the waist. Failure to meet the requisite number and distribution of tender points required for fibromyalgia leads to a diagnosis of myofascial pain syndrome. The American College of Rheumatology (ACR) criteria for the diagnosis of fibromyalgia (Wolfe et al. 1990) are listed in Table 8–6. Some researchers and clinicians consider the diagnostic criteria to be too restrictive, requiring identification of a specific number and location of tender points to establish the diagnosis. Yet there can be tender points in other regions of the body that are not included in the "acceptable" locations defined by the ACR.

TABLE 8–6.   **Diagnostic criteria for fibromyalgia**

Widespread pain of 3 months' duration

Pain consists of axial pain, on both the right and left sides of the body, and above and below the waist. Pain must be present in at least three segments of the body.

There must be at least 11 tender points (of the critical 18) on digital examination:

Insertion of the nuchal muscles into the occiput

Upper border of the midportion of the trapezius

Muscle attachments to the medial scapular border

Anterior C5 and C7 intertransverse spaces

Second rib space (approximately 3 cm from the sternal border)

Muscle insertions at the lateral epicondyle

Upper outer quadrant of the gluteal muscle

Muscle attachments posterior to the greater trochanter

Medial fat pad of the knee proximal to the joint

Source.   Adapted from Wolfe et al. 1990.

Fibromyalgia is a controversial disorder. Some physicians have considered it no more than a rheumatologic rubric for somatoform disorders (Hadler 1997). The prevalence of fibromyalgia varies depending on the populations under study. In general medical clinics, the rate of fibromyalgia is approximately 5%–10%, whereas in rheumatology practices, the rate is approximately 15%. Estimates of fibromyalgia in the general population are approximately 2%, with prevalence rates higher among women (3%) than men (0.5%). The rate of diagnosis is higher among females than males and appears to increase with age. Higher rates of fibromyalgia are noted among women age 50 and older.

Patients with fibromyalgia suffer immensely; additional features of the disorder are summarized in Table 8–7. In addition to muscle pain, some patients can experience joint pain and stiffness. Fatigue is prominent, due to the deconditioning that results from chronic pain and the patient's attempts to reduce pain by rest. Other factors causing or contributing to fatigue include poor sleep, depression, and accompanying endocrine abnormalities (i.e., abnormalities in the hypothalamic-pituitary axis).

Sleep disturbances are characterized by disordered, poorly restorative sleep. Fibromyalgia patients can be characteristically light sleepers, with a propensity to frequent arousals precipitated by noise, disruptions in the environment, or psychological distress. Some patients with fibromyalgia have alpha rhythm intrusions into Stage 3 and Stage 4 sleep (Cohen et al. 2000). During these stages, there are normally slow wave patterns (on electroencephalogram [EEG]), and it is a time when restorative functions within the body are undertaken. Alpha rhythms signal a heightened arousal and suggest easy arousability and a diminution of normal restorative functions. Alpha rhythm intrusions are not exclusive to fibromyalgia but can occur in a number of other chronic pain disorders.

Sleep disturbances can also arise from restless legs syndrome (i.e., unusual sensations such as tingling, itching, or cramping that occur in the lower extremities with reclining but are alleviated with leg movement, stretching, or walking). Although movement provides relief, it interferes with sleep. Restless leg disturbances can occur in as many as 30% of fibromyalgia patients.

TABLE 8–7.	Features associated with fibromyalgia

Pain
Fatigue
Disordered sleep
Cognitive dysfunction
Dizziness
Psychological distress
Restless legs syndrome
Irritable bowel syndrome
Irritable bladder
Cold intolerance
Neurally mediated hypotension

Irritable bowel symptoms (constipation, diarrhea, or alternating constipation and diarrhea) along with abdominal pain and distention can occur in fibromyalgia. Similarly, irritable bladder (dysuria, urgency, frequency in the absence of urinary tract infection or cystitis) can occur.

Paradoxical hypotensive reactions can arise resulting from catecholamine surges. Venous pooling reduces ventricular filling, resulting in lowered blood pressure. The heart rate is normally increased to compensate for the reduced pressure. During catecholamine surges, ventricular contractions increase so much that the ventricles have insufficient time to fill. Vagal reflexes are initiated, precipitated by ventricular mechanoreceptors, leading to syncope or near-syncope experiences.

Psychological distress commonly occurring with fibromyalgia includes depression and anxiety. Depression is common in patients with fibromyalgia, but the rate of fibromyalgia is not necessarily higher among depressed patients. Other common disorders accompanying fibromyalgia include somatization disorders and pain disorders. High rates of childhood sexual abuse are seen in patients with fibromyalgia. Such experiences might contribute to disturbances in coping strategies commonly encountered in these patients.

There are few controlled studies assessing the efficacy of various treatment measures (see Table 8–8 for a summary of these treatment strategies). Exercise is probably most effective. A variety of

178

exercises can be undertaken to enhance muscle tone and reduce deconditioning, and aerobic activity can improve sleep and reduce cold intolerance. High-impact activities (e.g., jogging) may possibly exacerbate pain. Certain exercises (e.g., ski machines) might be better tolerated, because they involve less impact loading for patients. Treatment of pain can be attempted with the use of antidepressants, and antidepressants can also reduce comorbid depression. Low doses are generally required for pain, whereas the usual antidepressant doses might be required for comorbid mood or anxiety disorders. Some clinicians advocate the use of tramadol, and opiate analgesics might be required, at least temporarily. Other agents for associated features of FM (e.g., restless legs syndrome) are listed in Table 8–8.

TABLE 8–8. **Treatment strategies for fibromyalgia**

Patient education
Psychiatric treatment
Sleep hygiene
Exercise
Massage
Pharmacologic treatment
   Anxiolytics (for anxiety)
   Antidepressants (for pain, comorbid depression)
   Tramadol, opiate analgesics (for pain)
   Muscle relaxants (to reduce discomfort of muscle cramping)
   Dopamine agonists (e.g., ropinirole, pramipexole, or carbidopa-
      levodopa 10/100 at bedtime [first choice for restless legs syndrome]);
      clonazepam 0.5 mg–1.0 mg at bedtime is an alternative for restless
      legs syndrome
   Serotonin agonists (e.g., tegaserod [for constipation-type irritable
      bowel])
   Serotonin antagonists (e.g., alosetron [for diarrhea-type irritable
      bowel])
   Antispasmodics (e.g., donnatal or dicyclomine [for irritable bowel
      syndrome] or oxybutynin [for irritable bladder])
   Fludrocortisone (for neurally mediated hypotension)
   Sedative-hypnotics

A multidisciplinary approach to pain management is advocated for patients with fibromyalgia. Involvement of psychiatrists, rheumatologists, and physiatrists might best lead to a comprehensive treatment approach. Group therapy can be very helpful for these patients. The context of such groups can reduce the sense of isolation that can occur in patients with a debilitating disorder, can foster group problem solving, and allows for the sharing of effective treatment strategies among peers. Demands on medical resources could be reduced by patients' participation in such groups.

■ OSTEOARTHRITIS AND RHEUMATOID ARTHRITIS

In addition to the nonarticular rheumatologic conditions discussed previously, a number of articular disorders warrant the attention of the pain specialist. Among these, osteoarthritis (OA) and rheumatoid arthritis (RA) are among the most common. In the United States, as many as 40 million persons are affected by arthritis and musculoskeletal conditions.

OA is the most common form of arthritis and is the most prevalent articular disease affecting elderly persons. It is also known as degenerative joint disease and affects multiple joints, including the distal interphalangeal joints, the proximal interphalangeal joints, and knees but rarely wrist, shoulder, or metacarpal-phalangeal joints. Weight-bearing joints are most apt to be affected. Because of joint degeneration, OA causes significant morbidity, accounting for substantial work disability in persons over age 50 years. The condition results from destruction of joint cartilage by chondrocytes.

OA can arise from primary joint dysfunction, involving the synovial capsule, or it can arise from secondary processes (e.g., prior injury or joint trauma). Symptoms of OA can be very distressing and can include pain, joint stiffness (especially after inactivity), swelling, deformity, and ultimate loss of function.

Treatment endeavors should include weight loss, exercise (especially of the knee joints), and analgesics. Weight loss becomes

TABLE 8–9.	**Treatment of osteoarthritis**

COX-2 inhibitors
Nonsteroidal anti-inflammatory drugs
Steroids
Topical agents
   Capsaicin
   Methyl salicylate creams
Intra-articular injections
   Glucocorticoids
   Hyaluronate
Nonpharmacologic interventions
   Weight loss
   Surgical management
     Arthroplasty
     Arthroscopic removal of loose bodies
Emerging trends
   Exogenous growth factors (to stimulate chondrocyte proliferation)
   Transplantation of healthy chondrocytes, engineered to maximally
     produce growth factors

Note. COX=cyclooxygenase.

difficult for many patients, particularly because patients tend to minimize activity levels so as to avoid pain. Thus, they run the risk of becoming deconditioned and less capable of sustaining aerobic activity and physical fitness. Pain relief can be brought forth by any of the NSAIDs. COX-2 inhibitors might be better tolerated because of their reduced propensity to interfere with gastric and renal functioning. These and other medications to employ in the treatment of OA are summarized in Table 8–9.

RA, on the other hand, is an inflammatory process affecting the synovium of articular joints and producing a number of systemic manifestations. RA affects approximately 1%–2% of the population, with about two to three times as many as women affected as men. The joints affected by RA include the hands, wrists, elbows, ankles, feet, and cervical spine. The joints can be swollen and tender. Over time, significant deformities of the hands occur, including

181

TABLE 8–10.   **Treatment of rheumatoid arthritis**

Anti-inflammatory agents
    Nonsteroidal anti-inflammatory drugs
    COX-2 inhibitors
    Corticosteroids
Antirheumatic drugs
    Leflunomide
    Soluble interleukin-1 receptor therapy
        Anakinra
    Tumor necrosis factor inhibitors
        Etanercept
        Infliximab
    Methotrexate
    Hydroxychloroquine
    Sulfasalazine
    Intramuscular gold
    Cytotoxic agents
        Cyclosporine A
        Azathioprine
        Cyclophosphamide

Note.   COX = cyclooxygenase.

---

ulnar deviation and the swan-neck and boutonniere deformities of
the fingers. Patients with RA experience a number of systemic problems arising from the inflammatory processes of the disease. These
problems can include subcutaneous nodules, anemia, vasculitic processes, entrapment neuropathy, interstitial nephritis, and effusions
(pericardial and pleural). Treatment endeavors directed at RA include those listed in Table 8–10.

    Because there is so much loss, disability, and discomfort ac-
companying arthritic conditions, it is not surprising that significant
mood disturbances can accompany the disorder. Depression appears to be the most prevalent psychological disturbance accompanying OA and RA. Pain severity among patients with arthritis was
found to be correlated with the presence of depression—higher
among those who are depressed, compared with nondepressed

patients or those with only a remote history of depression (Frank et al. 1988). The relationship between pain severity and mood disturbances is not exclusive to depression, however. Ratings of pain severity have also been associated with other unpleasant emotional states such as anger and anxiety (Huyser and Parker 1999). In addition, functional impairments and perceived disability associated with arthritic conditions are likewise related to these emotional states. Depression and anxiety can interfere with treatment (e.g., participation in an exercise program and weight loss). Mood disturbances can also impede appropriate adherence to other aspects of treatment. Consequently, psychopharmacologic agents, although not directly analgesic in arthritic conditions, can indirectly reduce emotional distress and perceived functional impairments and thereby reduce perceived pain severity and facilitate treatment.

Psychological variables can mediate levels of pain and disability as well. Cognitive approaches—including a propensity to catastrophize, overgeneralize, or selectively abstract—appear to be related to levels of distress and disability associated with arthritic conditions (Smith et al. 1988). Those patients with passive coping strategies (e.g., wishful thinking, self-blame) have poorer functional abilities than those with more active, problem-solving approaches (Young 1992). Thus, psychotherapies (e.g., CBT) might be particularly advantageous in improving functional adaptations in patients with arthritic conditions by addressing cognitive distortions and fostering improved coping strategies.

■ NEUROPATHIC PAIN

Neuropathic pain is often confusing, owing in part to the fact that the causes of neuropathic pain are often unclear. In addition, treatment of neuropathic pain can be difficult to achieve, and the pain can progress to the point of causing complete disability. Consequently, patients and physicians alike can be frustrated with neuropathic pain, being overwhelmed by its effects and disgruntled with its relatively refractory quality.

Neuropathic pain is associated with features of unusual sensations in an area of the body that worsen over the course of the day and over time. Typically, patients describe the pain as constant burning or electric in quality in a body area that had been previously injured but that demonstrates no ongoing damage (Rowbotham 1995). The pain often emanates from areas of the body that on physical examination demonstrate sensory loss. The pain is characterized by allodynia (i.e., pain produced by normally nonnoxious stimulation) and hyperpathia (i.e., exaggerated pain response to a noxious stimulus). At times, physical signs commensurate with sympathetic nervous system involvement are present.

Neuropathic pain can arise from a number of sources (see Table 8–11). A-δ and C fibers are neurons responsible for mediation of pain. Processes that aggravate the pain-relaying A-δ and C fibers can include nerve impingement (e.g., carpel tunnel syndrome, tumor impingement on brachial or lumbar plexus, and disk herniation compressing adjacent nerve roots). Trigeminal neuralgia is attributed to localized compression of the trigeminal nerve by neighboring vascular structures. For these conditions, nerve conduction studies might reveal delays in the conduction velocities between the affected (painful) side and the unaffected side. EMG might also reveal concomitant weakness when the motor components of the nerve are adversely affected. Investigations such as computed tomography (CT) or magnetic resonance imaging (MRI) can allow visualization of the affected nerves. Treatment is directed at relieving the underlying compression or nerve irritation (e.g., decompression of the median nerve, use of anticancer drugs, radiation therapy, splinting the affected limb, corticosteroids). Nerves that are damaged by illness or trauma can lead to firing of neurons at ectopic sites in a way that relays pain. For example, large-diameter fibers (A fibers) are damaged in disease states such as diabetes mellitus. When this happens, C fibers fire unabatedly, relaying chronic pain in the distribution of the affected nerve.

Peripheral nociceptors relay information from the skin, joints, muscles, bone, organs, and so forth. The fibers synapse on second-order neurons within the spinal cord. These, in turn,

184

TABLE 8–11. **Types of painful neuropathies**

Anatomic conditions causing neuropathy
  Entrapment neuropathy (carpal tunnel syndrome, ulnar entrapment, others)
  Trigeminal neuralgia
Medical conditions causing neuropathy
  Diabetic neuropathy
  HIV-related neuropathy
  Malignancy
  Postherpetic neuralgia
  Rheumatologic conditions producing neuropathy (rheumatoid arthritis, Sjögren syndrome, systemic lupus erythematosus)
Toxin-induced neuropathy
  Alcohol
  Arsenic
  Cisplatin
  Dideoxynucleoside
  Paclitaxel
  Vincristine
Guillain-Barré syndrome
Fabry disease
Vasculitic neuropathy
Amyloid neuropathy
Idiopathic distal small-fiber neuropathy

---

relay information to third-order neurons within the thalamus. Damage to peripheral fibers can actually lead to spontaneous firing in second- or third-order neurons in the pain-mediating process. This firing can be perceived as painful. CNS lesions (e.g., stroke, arteriovascular malformations) can also produce pain in the pain transmission pathway.

Treatment strategies employed for neuropathic states are summarized in Table 8–12. The mainstay of treatment includes TCAs, anticonvulsants, antiarrhythmics, and topical agents (Galer 1995). Other treatment interventions that can mitigate the pain experience include transcutaneous electrical nerve stimulation (TENS), biofeedback, relaxation training, and hypnosis.

185

TABLE 8–12.	Treatment strategies for neuropathic pain
Anticonvulsants	Gabapentin 900–3,600 mg/day
	Carbamazepine 600–1,200 mg/day
	Valproic acid 750–2,500 mg/day
	Clonazepam 0.5–3 mg/day
Opiates	Methadone 5–100 mg/day
	Tramadol 50–400 mg/day
Antidepressants	Amitriptyline 25–200 mg/day
	Nortriptyline 25–150 mg/day
	Desipramine 25–200 mg/day
Other medications	Mexiletine 450–900 mg/day
	Dexamethasone 6–100 mg/day
	Topical capsaicin
Other interventions	Transcutaneous electrical nerve stimulation
	Sympathetic nerve blocks
	Epidural and intrathecal nerve blocks
	Nerve ablation
	Cordotomy, rhizotomy
	Spinal stimulation
	Hypnosis, biofeedback, relaxation training

■ SYMPATHETICALLY MEDIATED PAIN: COMPLEX REGIONAL PAIN SYNDROMES

Two types of disorders make up the complex regional pain syndromes (CRPS). These are designated CRPS I (previously referred to as reflex sympathetic dystrophy) and CRPS II (previously referred to as causalgia). CRPS I results from some inciting event, often a traumatic, infectious, or vascular event within soft tissue, whereas CRPS II arises from direct nerve injury (Bonica 1973). In either case, the inciting event induces a series of responses that are mediated by the sympathetic nervous system. If these conditions are untreated or unabated, the sympathetic nervous system responses produce marked trophic changes in a limb.

Characteristics of Complex
Regional Pain Syndromes

CRPS is characterized by a number of symptoms and signs. The most prominent feature is pain, often throbbing (for CRPS I) or burning (for CRPS II). The pain is usually constant, but paroxysms of pain can occur, ranging from mild to severe. Initially, the pain is often located at the site of injury, but it can extend through the entire affected limb. Over time, there can be extension of pain to other limbs unaffected by the initial trauma or injury. The affected limb is often exquisitely sensitive to ambient temperature, touch, or stimulation associated with movement. Thus, the patient will tend to guard the painful limb and withdraw from physical examination that could raise the risk of pain from touch or direct manipulation. In addition, there are a number of changes in temperature, skin, muscle tone, vascular, and bone that occur as the course of the disorder progresses. Classic features of CRPS include changes in blood flow over the limb, with resultant temperature changes in the affected limb as compared with other limbs; edema; and trophic skin changes, along with changes in the musculature and changes in bone scan activity and density. The rate of progression of the changes associated with CRPS is variable from person to person.

Several investigations can be employed to assess the features and staging of CRPS. For example, skin temperature depends on the extent of cutaneous blood flow, which is under the direct influence of sympathetic activity. In early stages of CRPS, thermography can reveal increased temperature in the affected limb compared with the contralateral limb or other limbs of the body. In later stages, skin blood flow and temperature will be reduced. Bone scanning by scintigraphy can reveal increased activity throughout the bones of the affected limb. Bone density measurements can reveal progressive changes in the bone of the affected limb over time.

Treatment

Treatment approaches for CRPS include pharmacologic approaches (see Table 8–13). A number of invasive techniques are employed as

TABLE 8–13.	Treatment of complex regional pain syndrome

Medications
    α-Adrenergic agents
        Clonidine
        Propranolol
        Prazosin
        Phenoxybenzamine
    Calcium channel blockers
    Opioids
    Anticonvulsants
    Antidepressants
Local nerve block
Regional sympathetic block
Sympathectomy
Physical therapy

well, given the relatively refractory nature of such syndromes to pharmacologic approaches. Nerve blocks are employed to disrupt ongoing sympathetic nervous system activity in the affected limb. For patients who are unable to sustain extended relief from repeated blocks, surgical interventions to disrupt sympathetic nervous system activity are employed (sympathectomy).

Affective disorders are common among patients with CRPS—for example, more than 60% of patients meet criteria for major depression (Galer et al. 2001). In addition, substance abuse disorders are common among this population. There is controversy about whether premorbid psychological disturbances predispose one to CRPS. In any event, psychiatric treatment for these conditions is warranted. Biofeedback and relaxation training can reduce distress and foster adaptive strategies with which to deal with pain (Barowsky et al. 1987).

■ PHANTOM LIMB PAIN

After amputation, it is common for patients to experience sensations of the removed limb, just as though it were present (phantom

sensations). In some cases, these sensations progress to painful sensations perceived to be emanating from the amputated limb. This phantom limb pain can be disabling.

Although phantom limb sensations are almost universal following amputation, approximately 85%–97% of amputees experience some form of pain. Sensations are almost immediate, whereas pain might not emerge for some time after amputation (e.g., 1 month to 1 year). Pain is often characterized as burning, cramping, or aching. Other features (e.g., crushing, squeezing, twisting, pins-and-needles, and grinding) are also described (Jensen et al. 1985). Pain can be exacerbated by physical stimulation and emotional factors (e.g., depression). The characteristics of phantom limb pain can vary widely in terms of the quality of sensory experiences and impact on quality of life. Thus, in mildest forms of phantom limb pain, patients can experience mild, intermittent paresthesias that do not interfere with normal activity or sleep; in its extreme form, paresthesias can be constant and very uncomfortable, interfering with activity and sleep.

The course of phantom limb pain is variable, with up to 56% of patients reporting resolution or improvement in symptoms over time. Pain emerging over time warrants investigation of possible causes producing pain (e.g., infection at the site of amputation, scar tissue, neuroma formation). The cause of phantom pain is unclear. Peripheral processes (i.e., spontaneous discharges emanating from severed nerves containing A-δ and C fibers) brought on by scar tissue in the amputated limb were thought to be the basis of this pain. Spontaneous discharges such as these can be inhibited by infusions of lidocaine but could be exacerbated by irritation of the stump (e.g., tapping) or cold exposure. Alternatively, central processes (i.e., reverberating neural circuits within the CNS) have also been implicated as the basis for phantom limb pain.

Specific psychological correlates of persons experiencing phantom limb pain are lacking. However, some data tend to suggest that among those experiencing this form of pain, there is a tendency to be rigid, inflexible, and self-reliant; to suppress emotions (thus depriving one of the propensity to grieve the lost limb); and to cope

by using denial as a primary defense. It is theorized that phantom limb pain may possibly arise from psychopathologic interpretations of phantom limb sensations (Parkes 1973).

Treatment can include antidepressants and anticonvulsants (Hord 1996). However, controlled studies on the efficacy of such agents are generally lacking; efficacy has been based mostly on anecdotal reports. Another group of agents, β-blockers, can also reduce phantom limb pain and can be considered as alternatives to, or used in conjunction with, antidepressants and anticonvulsants. Opiates tend not to be effective for long-term use in phantom limb pain.

Surgical interventions have been employed in the past for phantom limb pain, but because of limited utility, have been largely abandoned (e.g., thalamotomy, sympathectomy, cordotomy). Neurolytic and sympathetic blocks might be useful in selected cases. Epidural anesthesia administered for 3 days prior to the amputation can reduce the severity of postoperative phantom limb pain (Bach et al. 1988). Psychological therapies (e.g., relaxation training) may possibly help to reduce the distress associated with the pain and help to reduce the pain sensations. Psychotherapy might be required to help the patient mourn the loss of the limb, address concerns over physical appearance or disfigurement, and facilitate adaptation to the use of prostheses and making the changes necessary to modify one's usual activities.

■ CANCER AND HIV

Pain complicates the clinical picture of approximately 50% of patients with metastatic cancer (Ahles et al. 1983). The nature of the pain—its location, intensity, radiation, quality, and other characteristics—can vary depending on the type of cancer, its progression, and the treatment measures undertaken to treat it.

Among patients with HIV/AIDS, prevalence rates for pain vary from 30% to 97%. The variability in prevalence rates of pain associated with HIV is in part attributable to the progression of the disease and the clinical settings in which patient evaluations were conducted (Breitbart and Patt 1994). Common pain-related disorders

associated with HIV/AIDS (Lebovits et al. 1989) are summarized in Table 8–14.

Pain ratings for patients with cancer are higher among those with comorbid psychiatric conditions compared with those without such conditions (Massie and Holland 1987). Common psychiatric comorbidity includes adjustment disorders, depression, anxiety, and delirium.

TABLE 8–14. **Common pain states associated with HIV/AIDS**

Nociceptive
Cutaneous
   Kaposi's sarcoma
   Oral cavity pain
      Candidiasis
      Aphthous ulcers
      Herpes simplex virus and cytomegalovirus infection
Visceral
   Ulcerative esophagitis
   Gastritis
   Pancreatitis and biliary tract disorders
   Tumor
   Infection
Deep somatic
   Arthralgias
   Back pain
   Myopathies
Headache
   Meningitis
   Encephalitis
   Iatrogenic causes (e.g., zidovudine)
Neuropathic
Mononeuropathy
Guillain-Barré syndrome
Mononeuropathy multiplex
Polyneuropathy
Herpes simplex (postherpetic neuralgia)
Antiretroviral toxicity associated neuropathy

Effective pain treatment is obviously contingent on the nature and source of pain (Benedetti et al. 2000). Thus, opioids might be required for severe bone pain due to metastases, fractures, or both; antidepressants, anticonvulsants, or both may be employed in neuropathic types of pains. Pharmacologic approaches to pain management (see Table 8–15) need to be customized to the patient's needs, factoring pain severity, impact on functioning, and tolerability of side effects. Anti-inflammatory agents are required for mild pain, but opioids might be required for moderate to severe pain states. Dosing schedules should be simple, to maximize adherence, and should be administered in the least invasive manner. Persistent pain requires around-the-clock dosing of analgesics. Certainly psychiatric interventions, including pharmacotherapy and psychotherapy, are prudent in conditions in which there is psychiatric comorbidity. Adjunctive techniques (e.g., hypnosis, relaxation training, biofeedback, or deep breathing exercises) might facilitate mitigation of pain and accompanying psychological distress. However, the presence of an underlying delirium would certainly limit the ability of the patient to yield any benefit from psychotherapeutic interventions. In such cases, resolution of the underlying medical condition, the addition of antipsychotics, or both, might be required to reduce the interference of any psychological interventions by a delirium.

The attributions assigned to the pain by the cancer patient can be the basis for a great deal of psychological distress. It is not uncommon for the patient to ascribe ominous interpretations to the presence of the pain, which in turn could exacerbate the pain experience. However, such attributions that pain could signal disease progression might not be entirely unrealistic (Ahles et al. 1983). Other sources of distress can include immediate concrete needs (e.g., financial needs, housing, transportation), family or interpersonal concerns, changes in one's autonomy and independence, need for assistance with activities of daily living, and spiritual concerns (e.g., after-life issues, making amends, mending interpersonal conflicts). Such issues, once identified, might require the joint efforts of the psychiatrist, psychologist, social worker, and pastoral counselor for effective management (Holland 1999).

TABLE 8–15.   **Management of cancer pain and pain associated with HIV and AIDS, based on pain ratings**

Mild (1–3)
  Consider nonsteroidal anti-inflammatory drug, acetaminophen
  If ineffective, augment with opiate
  If ineffective, administer short-acting opiate
Moderate (4–6)
  Consider short-acting opiate
  Consider augmentation of opiates with psychotropics
  Address side effects of opiates (gastrointestinal side effects, sedation, delirium)
Severe (7–10)
  Consider rapid dose increases of short-acting opiate
    5–10 mg morphine (or equivalent)
    Reassess after 1 hour
      Double the dose if pain is unchanged, reassess after 1 hour
      Repeat dose if pain level is halved, reassess after 1 hour
      If improved (pain is less than 50% of original level), reassess after 1 hour
  Administer the effective dose administered after 4 hours, then give this dose every 4 hours around the clock
  Consider augmentation of opiates with psychotropics
  Address side effects of opiates (gastrointestinal side effects, sedation, delirium)

Note. Pain ratings are based on scale 1–10.

■ REFERENCES

Ahles TA, Blanchard EB, Ruckdeschel JC: The multidimensional nature of cancer-related pain. Pain 17:277–288, 1983

Ansari A: The efficacy of newer antidepressants in the treatment of chronic pain: a review of current literature. Harv Rev Psychiatry 7:257–277, 2000

Atlas SJ, Deyo RA: Evaluating and managing acute low back pain in the primary care setting. J Gen Intern Med 16:120–131, 2001

Bach S, Noreng MF, Tjellden NU: Phantom limb pain in amputees during the first 12 months following limb amputation, after preoperative lumbar epidural blockade. Pain 33:297–301, 1988

Barowsky EI, Zweig JB, Moskowitz J: Thermal biofeedback in the treatment of symptoms associated with reflex sympathetic dystrophy. J Child Neurol 2:229–232, 1987

Benedetti C, Brock C, Cleeland C, et al: NCCN practice guidelines for cancer pain. Oncology 14:135–150, 2000

Bogaards MC, ter Kuile MM: Treatment of recurrent tension headache: a meta-analytic review. Clin J Pain 10:174–190, 1994

Bonica JJ: Causalgia and other reflex sympathetic dystrophies. Postgrad Med 53:143–148, 1973

Breitbart W, Patt RB: Pain management in the patient with AIDS. Hem/Onc Annals: The Journal of Continuing Education in Hematology and Oncology 2:391–399, 1994

Campbell JK, Penzien DB, Wall EM: Evidenced-based guidelines for migraine headache: behavioral and physical treatments. The US Headache Consortium. Available at: http://www.aoa-net.org/guidelines.php, accessed June 2002

Cohen MJM, Menefee LA, Doghramji K, et al: Sleep in chronic pain: problems and treatments. Int Rev Psychiatry 12:115–127, 2000

Collins JG: Prevalence of selected chronic conditions, United States, 1979–1981. Data from the National Health Survey. Vital Health Statistics 10:1–66, 1986

Deyo RA, Weinstein JN: Low back pain. N Engl J Med 344:363–370, 2001

Diamond S: Efficacy and safety profile of venlafaxine in chronic headache. Headache Quarterly, Current Treatment and Research 6:212–214, 1995

Epstein MT, Hockaday JM, Hockaday TDR: Migraine and reproductive hormones throughout the menstrual cycle. Lancet 1:543–548, 1975

Flor H, Turk DC, Birbaumer N: Assessment of stress-related psychophysiological reactions in chronic back pain patients. J Consult Clin Psychol 53:354–364, 1985

Frank RG, Beck NC, Parker JC, et al: Depression in rheumatoid arthritis. J Rheumatol 15:920–925, 1988

Galer BS: Neuropathic pain of peripheral origin: advances in pharmacologic treatment. Neurology 45(suppl 9):17–25, 1995

Galer BS, Schwartz L, Allen RJ: Complex regional pain syndromes, type I: reflex sympathetic dystrophy, and type II: causalgia, in Bonica's Management of Pain, 3rd Edition. Edited by Loeser JD, Butler SH, Chapman CR, et al. Philadelphia, PA, Lippincott Williams & Wilkins, 2001, pp 388–411

Hadler NM: Fibromyalgia, chronic fatigue, and other iatrogenic diagnostic algorithms. Postgrad Med 102:161–177, 1997

Holland JC: Update: NCCN practice guidelines for the management of psychosocial distress. Oncology 13:459–507, 1999

Holm JE, Holroyd KA, Hursey KG, et al: The role of stress in recurrent tension headache. Headache 26:160–167, 1986

Holroyd KA, Andrasik F, Westbrook T: Cognitive control of tension headache. Cognit Ther Res 1:121–133, 1977

Holroyd KA, O'Donnell FJ, Stensland M, et al: Management of chronic tension-type headache with tricyclic antidepressant medication, stress management therapy, and their combination. JAMA 285:2208–2215, 2001

Hord AH: Phantom pain, in Pain Management: A Comprehensive Review. Edited by Raj PP. St. Louis, MO, Mosby, 1996, pp 483–491

Huyser BA, Parker JC: Negative affect and pain in arthritis. Rheum Dis Clin North Am 25:105–121, 1999

Jensen TS, Krebs B, Nielsen J, et al: Immediate and long-term phantom limb pain in amputees: incidence, clinical characteristics and relationship to pre-amputation limb pain. Pain 21:267–278, 1985

Lebovits AH, Lefkowitz M, McCarthy D, et al: The prevalence and management of pain in patients with AIDS: a review of 134 cases. Clin J Pain 5:245–248, 1989

Massie MJ, Holland JC: The cancer patient with pain: psychiatric complications and their management. Med Clin North Am 71:243–258, 1987

Matchar DB, Young WB, Rosenberg JH, et al: Evidence-based guidelines for migraine headache in the primary care setting: pharmacologic management of acute attacks. The US Headache Consortium. Available at: http://www.aoa-net.org/guidelines.php, accessed June 2002

McGill CM: Industrial back programs: a control program. J Occup Med 10:174–178, 1968

Parkes CM: Factors determining the persistence of phantom pain in the amputee. J Psychosom Res 17:97–108, 1973

Ramadan NM, Silberstein SD, Freitag FG, et al: Evidence-based guidelines for migraine headache in the primary care setting: pharmacologic management for prevention of migraine. The US Headache Consortium. Available at: http://www.aoa-net.org/guidelines.php, accessed June 2002

Reesor KA, Craig KD: Medically incongruent chronic back pain: physical limitations, suffering, and ineffective coping. Pain 32:35–45, 1988

Rowbotham MC: Chronic pain: from theory to practical management. Neurology 45(suppl 9):5–10, 1995

Saper JR, Lake AE, Tepper SJ: Nefazodone for chronic daily headache prophylaxis: an open-label study. Headache 41:465–474, 2001

Silberstein SD: The role of sex hormones in headache. Neurology 42(suppl 2):37–42, 1992

Smith TW, Peck JR, Milano RA, et al: Cognitive distortion in rheumatoid arthritis: relation to depression and disability. J Consult Clin Psychol 56:412–416, 1988

Turner JA: Educational and behavioral interventions for back pain in primary care. Spine 21:2851–2857, 1996

Turner JA, Denny MC: Do antidepressant medications relieve chronic low back pain? J Fam Pract 37:545–553, 1993

Waddell G, Feder G, Lewis M: Systematic reviews of bed rest and advice to stay active for acute low back pain. Br J Gen Pract 47:647–652, 1997

Walker J, Holloway I, Sofaer B: In the system: the lived experience of chronic back pain from the perspectives of those seeking help from pain clinics. Pain 80:621–628, 1999

Welch KMA: Headache, in Bonica's Management of Pain, 3rd Edition. Edited by Loeser JD, Butler SH, Chapman CR, et al. Philadelphia, PA, Lippincott Williams & Wilkins, 2001, pp 867–894

Wolfe F, Smythe HA, Yunus MB, et al: The American College of Rheumatology 1990 criteria for the classification of fibromyalgia: report of the Multicenter Criteria Committee. Arthritis Rheum 33:160–172, 1990

Young LD: Psychological factors in rheumatoid arthritis. J Consult Clin Psychol 60:619–627, 1992

9

SPECIAL POPULATIONS

The recognition and treatment of pain in the very young and the very old has been poor. There are fears, misconceptions, and stereotypes that have an impact on pain management among pregnant patients, culturally distinct groups, and persons with substance abuse histories. Unique issues also arise among patients with terminal conditions and their families.

■ GERIATRICS

Elderly persons are prone to multiple medical conditions predisposing them to pain. Estimates suggest that rates of chronic pain among elderly persons are twice those of younger individuals (Crook et al. 1984). The elderly are also likely to experience pain from terminal medical conditions (Cleeland 1998). Among community samples, 20%–50% of older persons endorsed chronic pain (Crook et al. 1984), whereas among those in long-term-care settings, estimates of chronic pain are substantially higher, approaching 45%–80% (Ferrell 1990; Roy and Thomas 1986; Won et al. 1999). Untreated pain interferes with adaptive functioning, with interpersonal functioning, and with maintaining quality of life. Common disorders contributing to chronic pain include arthritis, cancer, diabetic neuropathy, herpes zoster, and osteoporosis (Ferrell 1991; Gallagher et al. 2000).

Underrecognition of Pain in Elderly Patients

Unfortunately, pain is often poorly recognized and poorly treated among the elderly (Sengstaken and King 1993). Reasons include poor recognition of symptoms, inadequate time spent evaluating patients, and failure to inquire into pain symptoms. Appetite and sleep disturbances, social withdrawal, reduced inclination to engage in activities, and distress resulting from pain can be mislabeled as an emotional disturbance (e.g., depression or anxiety). Ascertaining pain can be further hindered by dementia. Inadequate trials of medications to relieve pain, concerns regarding medication's adverse effects, and addiction fears interfere with effective treatment.

Unusually painless presentation of elderly patients with common illnesses might have contributed to misconceptions that pain sensitivity is reduced among the elderly. Much has yet to be learned about age-related physiologic changes within the nociceptive pathway system. Although transmission via A-δ and C neurons might be altered with age, the role such changes have in interfering with the recognition or perception of pain remains unclear. Physiologic changes in the nociceptive system occurring with age might not bear much clinical significance (Gagliese et al. 1999).

On the other hand, there might be alterations in the affective (limbic) and cognitive (cortical) processes that are factors in the processing and appreciation of pain. Still, elderly patients could have a reduced inclination to communicate or report pain, which might emanate from belief systems held by some elderly people (e.g., that pain is to be expected as one ages and therefore does not warrant clinical attention). Further investigation is warranted to assess to what extent such factors influence the perception and reporting of pain among the elderly population.

Nonetheless, careful assessment of the older patient is necessary to effectively address and treat pain. Some education of the patient might be required to circumvent the problems of erroneous expectations interfering with the reporting of pain. Some elderly patients could be concerned that notifying physicians of their pain might invoke treatments that are invasive and painful, that could

complicate other health conditions, or that might involve hospital-
ization and, therefore, separation from family and other usual supports.

Standard assessment scales can be employed in an attempt to
quantify the degree of discomfort experienced (see Chapter 3).
Some of these might be easier for the elderly to use than are others.
Thus, for example, a visual analog scale is harder for elderly patients to comprehend and reliably use, compared with other assessment devices (e.g., numeric rating scales, faces scale, or verbal
scales) (Herr and Mobily 1993).

From a biopsychosocial perspective, it becomes imperative to
understand the psychological and social factors contributing to the
patient's plight and pain. Among the elderly, the psychological issues that prevail include concerns over life review and the need to
have fulfilled life goals and made contributions to the world.

Treatment Strategies

Older patients are often excluded from studies assessing various
medication effects in pain reduction. Often, an attempt is made in
clinical trials to avoid the influences of other medical conditions or
drug interactions with coadministered medications. Thus, for example, most of the literature on employing psychotropic agents in pain
mitigation has largely focused on diverse patient populations, not
exclusively on the elderly.

The pharmacologic approaches discussed in Chapter 5 are applicable to the geriatric patient with chronic pain. Opiates might be
indicated in acute pain, in chronic malignant pain, and in cases of
chronic nonmalignant pain. The elderly can be particularly sensitive to the adverse effects of analgesic agents (e.g., sedation, confusion, and constipation associated with opiates and gastrointestinal
effects associated with nonsteroidal anti-inflammatory drugs
[NSAIDs]) (AGS Panel on Chronic Pain in Older Persons 1998). In
some cases, particularly in patients with neuropathic pain and those
with psychological factors contributing significantly to pain, a variety of psychotropics might be available for use (Leo and Singh

2002). In general, the approach with the elderly patient is that initial doses should be low and incremental increases should proceed slowly, guided by the diminution of pain, improvement in function, and tolerability of side effects.

Some effects of pain (e.g., sleep disturbances and appetite suppression) arising from ongoing pain might require attention. Hence, efforts should be directed at the development of sleep hygiene strategies and the selective use of sedating agents (e.g., zolpidem, trazodone, antihistamines, and possibly benzodiazepines). Cyproheptadine and megestrol acetate have been employed in situations in which a pharmacologic intervention is selected to increase appetite.

Nonpharmacologic approaches ought to be considered in the treatment of the elderly patient with pain (AGS Panel on Chronic Pain in Older Persons 1998). These endeavors—including exercise, transcutaneous electrical nerve stimulation (TENS), acupuncture, massage, relaxation training, and psychotherapy, among others—can supplement pharmacologic and other invasive treatment strategies.

■ PEDIATRICS

As in the case of the elderly, pain management among children has been abysmally poor. For example, the level of analgesics provided to children postoperatively was markedly low compared with adults in comparable surgical interventions (Beyer et al. 1983). Part of this poor pain management has been due to misconceptions about pediatric pain, to inadequate pain assessments and scales for use in young children, and to fears about the use of powerful analgesics (e.g., opiates) among young patients.

The neonatal nervous system is well equipped to process nociceptive input (Goldschneider et al. 2001). However, the communication of painful states is limited. Common chronic pain states in children include headache, recurrent abdominal and chest pain, and those pain states associated with chronic illnesses (e.g., diabetes,

sickle cell anemia, hemophilia, juvenile rheumatoid arthritis, and cancer).

Pain and Childhood Developmental Phases

Any pain management approach needs to include the psychological, cognitive, and emotional factors present at varying developmental phases appropriate to children. Among infants, pain is responded to reflexively, with expression of discomfort conveyed through crying. The nature of facial expressions and crying patterns appear to be distinct for pain, as compared with other unpleasant states (e.g., hunger) (Sifford 1997). Among toddlers, words might be expressed for pain (e.g., "ouch" and "boo-boo"). However, such children are likely to view pain in terms of punishment (i.e., as an indicator of being "bad"). It is imperative that provision of pain relief be undertaken in a way that avoids fostering such misconceptions. At school age, in concrete operational ways, the child can assign emotional terms to pain. Pain is no longer viewed as punishment, and the child can assimilate cause-and-effect understanding of the pain. Differentiation among varying pain intensities becomes possible at approximately ages 5–7. Later, among young adults, there is a sense of invulnerability (which could account in part for the reckless behaviors that precipitate injuries warranting pain treatment). Body image, peer relations, and school attendance are central to their experiences. Thus, the presence of pain can threaten the adolescent's invulnerability, separate him or her from peers, and lead to concerns about self-image and self-esteem.

Pain Assessment Scales

Pain assessments need to be appropriate to developmental stage, and suitable assessment scales can be helpful. In infants and preverbal children, the emphasis of assessment scales is on observational methods—including assessments of crying patterns, facial expressions, and physiologic parameters (blood pressure, diaphoresis, heart rate, and respiratory rate). Among verbal young children, one

can add quantifiable pain assessments (e.g., the "poker chip" tool, "oucher" scale, and faces scale). Some instruments (e.g., the visual analog scale and pain diaries) are appropriate for older children and adolescents (Stevens 1997).

The poker chip tool involves use of concrete objects, poker chips, to quantify or approximate pain ratings. The child is asked to rate the pain intensity by choosing up to four poker chips, depicting "pieces" of hurt. This method can be a particularly useful assessment index for younger children (i.e., ages 4–8 years). One problem with this assessment tool is that the child is unlikely to tease out how much "hurt" is related to pain per se and how much is ascribable to the affective components (e.g., fear associated with the pain).

The "oucher" scale is a variant of the faces scale, with six photographs of children's expressions in varying degrees of distress organized vertically alongside a numeric scale ranging from 0 to 100. The ratings, however, can vary depending on which anchors are employed. For example, if the lowest pain rating is depicted with a smiling face as opposed to a photograph with a neutral facial expression, different pain ratings might be endorsed. Thus, the examiner is cautioned to use the same scale consistently when comparing pain ratings of a young child over time. There might be differences in pain ratings, depending upon the ethnic backgrounds and genders depicted in the photographs in the scale as well.

The faces scale (see Chapter 3) can be used with children to rate pain severity. It is fairly easily understood at about age 6 and thereafter. It allows one to bypass the potential gender and ethnic biases that can confound pain ratings encountered with the oucher scale.

Pain diaries can be useful for adolescents with pain. They can also be useful for parents of younger children who are unable to complete the diary. In the diary, pain ratings are ranked, and descriptions can be noted of ongoing environmental factors, extenuating circumstances, prevailing mood states, thought patterns, and other factors. The diary can reveal temporal patterns between pain states and mood, thought processes, and extenuating circumstances

surrounding the adolescent's pain. Diaries can be useful to encourage young adults to develop self-management strategies and could foster increased mastery over one's pain.

Analgesics, as outlined in Chapter 5, need to be applied judiciously and dosed according to weight (Leith and Weisman 1997) as well as the tolerability of side effects. Routes of administration need to be selected to provide the least invasiveness and distress in application of the analgesic. Very painful conditions (e.g., sickle cell crisis and moderate to severe postoperative pain) can require opiate analgesics. These should not be withheld because of fears of addiction.

Specialized analgesic techniques used with children include local anesthetics and eutectic mixture of local anesthetics (see Chapter 5). Patient-controlled anesthesia (PCA) or anesthesia controlled by the parent can be employed for severe pain states. PCA might be best employed with children who are at least age 6 (Berde and Masek 1999). The advantage of PCA is that the patient can control the amount of analgesic administered. Parent-controlled analgesia raises the risk that misinterpretation of the child's behaviors can result in too little or too much of an analgesic administered. Certainly, other interventions might include physical therapy, occupational therapy, and psychotherapeutic interventions.

■ PREGNANCY

Due to concerns about fetal effects, the use of analgesics during pregnancy has been restricted. Opioid treatment during pregnancy has been documented in cases of women treated with methadone for opiate dependence and with brief opioid requirements during labor. In such cases, the risks to the fetus far outweigh the potential risks arising from either continued heroin use or complications arising in the delivery process. Nonetheless, concerns still arise with regard to the use of analgesics for pregnant women who experience malignant or nonmalignant pain in the course of pregnancy. Long-term exposure of the fetus to opiates is likely to produce the following

204

effects in the newborn: opiate dependence, acute withdrawal after delivery, and growth retardation. Some patients might still be capable of achieving long-term relief of pain with spinal or intrathecal administration of opiates while minimizing the infant's exposure to the opiate (Wen et al. 1996).

Among other analgesics, NSAIDs administered during pregnancy can prolong labor, result in constriction of the ductus arteriosus in the fetus, and produce renal and hematologic abnormalities in the newborn (Ostensen 1998). Other agents (e.g., aspirin) have been invoked to treat complications in late pregnancy (e.g., pre-eclampsia), although the risks to fetal growth and development have been a concern.

Use of adjuvant agents (e.g., antidepressants and anticonvulsants) carries with it the risks of fetal complications (e.g., neural tube defects), increased spontaneous abortion rates, and anticholinergic effects in the newborn.

For women who are breast-feeding, acetaminophen and ibuprofen appear to be safest among the nonopioid analgesics due to their high protein binding (Ebert 1997). Most opioids are safe for use during lactation without harm to the breast-feeding infant. The infant's methadone exposure is determined by the maternal dose and time of breast-feeding in relation to when peak drug effects are obtained. Breast-feeding is permitted for women taking methadone in doses less than 20 mg/day and should occur at least 6–10 hours after the methadone dose was received (Renehan 1989).

■ CULTURAL ISSUES

With clichés such as "no pain, no gain" and slogans such as "tough it out," one can only be impressed with popular notions about pain. Societal attitudes toward pain may evoke reluctance to report pain and fear of stigma associated with pain complaints.

Although there are no racial or ethnic differences in the ability to discriminate pain (Zatzick and Dimsdale 1990), culture influences what meanings persons derive from illness, suffering, and pain. The psychiatrist addressing pain patients must consider the impact cultural influences might have on the pain experience. Thus,

in some black communities, Christian religious beliefs have a profound impact on the understanding of pain. In such communities, suffering has a redeeming function and efforts to avoid pain might constitute a "failure of faith" (Crawley et al. 2000).

Cultural biases and stereotypes might impede effective pain treatment. For example, in one study, Hispanic persons in the United States were less likely to receive analgesics for fractures than were nonminorities (Todd et al. 1993). A recent multicenter study assessing the adequacy of pain management in cancer found that nonwhite patients with metastatic cancer pain were more likely to have inadequate pain treatment as compared with white cancer patients (Cleeland et al. 1994). Several factors have been identified that may contribute to disparities in the treatment of pain among nonwhite patients (see Table 9–1).

The tendency to be expressive or unemotional about pain can be dictated by a person's ethnic, religious, and familial background. Language and cultural impediments to pain treatment might be overcome through the use of culturally sanctioned pain assessments. Some assessment instruments (e.g., McGill Pain Questionnaire) have been translated into various languages for such purposes.

TABLE 9–1. **Barriers to pain management in minority patients**

Language
Less frequent follow-up care
   Loss to follow-up
   Poor arrangement of follow-up services
   Poor access to follow-up services
Addiction concerns
Analgesics unavailable in pharmacies in areas in which minorities live
  (e.g., pharmacies may not stock opiates for fear of theft and violence)
Economic disadvantages (e.g., limited resources result in decisions based
  on paying for analgesics versus paying for other necessities)
Inadequate assessment
   Culturally inappropriate pain rating scales
   Basing of pain assessments on the clinician's perception of overt pain
     behaviors

Economic disparities affecting certain subcultures might preclude medical follow-up with pain management. Those patients living in financially disadvantaged areas might not have access to prescribed analgesics; pharmacies in such areas might not stock analgesics because of fears regarding theft.

Although the prevailing cultural norm within the United States and that of the legal system emphasize the importance of a person's autonomy and the primacy of the individual in decision making, this is not shared by many other cultural communities. Thus, among other cultures, the primacy of the family may be emphasized in the decision-making process (Kagawa-Singer and Blackhall 2001). While exploring treatment interventions, the clinician may have to consider varying approaches to decision making, factoring in the need to include others in the patient's life in the proposal of potential treatment options.

■ SUBSTANCE-DEPENDENT AND SUBSTANCE-ABUSING PATIENTS

The patient presenting with pain complaints who simultaneously has ongoing substance abuse or dependence (or a prior history of either) can pose significant challenges in terms of treatment options. Although effective pain management should never be withheld because of an abuse or addiction history, effective treatment might require an array of pain-reducing approaches (e.g., use of adjunctive agents, agents with low abuse potential, and physical and psychological therapies, as well as patient participation in a concurrent substance abuse treatment program). The patient's detoxification from the substance(s) on which he or she is dependent might be required before the initiation of treatment.

Detoxification is required for the patient who is alcohol dependent. In some cases, the substances abused might have appeal as a means of controlling one's psychological distress (e.g., cannabis and benzodiazepine abuse to address underlying anxiety or ineffective coping). Hence, psychological interventions, along with pru-

dent psychopharmacologic interventions for underlying psychiatric disorders, might also be required to effect optimal pain control.

Patients who receive long-term opiates for treatment of pain can become addicted to the opiates. This issue is one that raises controversy. Some authors suggest that opiate dependence does not accompany appropriate dosing in pain patients (Portenoy and Foley 1986). Nonetheless, the issue can and does arise—that patients who have been treated with analgesics can become dependent upon pain medications.

Iatrogenic Drug Dependence

As mentioned, persons may become addicted to medications prescribed by physicians to treat pain (e.g., opioids, benzodiazepines, stimulants). The patient might seek out multiple physicians for the provision of such medications, or a single physician may be involved. Patients might offer somatic complaints in order to acquire medications. The prescription of medications might be construed as a sign of caring and nurturance. The well-meaning physician might be highly esteemed and valued by the patient and as a consequence might placate the patient's requests for additional medications.

The clinician might not anticipate the patient's risk of dependence on the medications. Often, clinicians are so preoccupied with the patient's allegations of pain that they fail to recognize that increasing levels of medications are being requested or that, despite the use of these medications, the patient's functioning does not appear to improve in adaptive areas. This should signal that the medications are not effective or might be inappropriately consumed by the patient such that the misused medications interfere with the patient's adaptive function and rehabilitation.

In cases of iatrogenic drug dependence, the patient may require careful systematic detoxification from the medications on which he or she has become dependent. The patient's functioning might then improve. Behavioral measures could be required to deemphasize the focus on somatic complaints. Cognitive-behavioral interventions might be required to address ineffective coping,

troublesome cognitive appraisals, and adverse emotions arising as a consequence of these. It is these emotions the patient has been trying to "treat" with the medications prescribed.

There are concerns that long-term use of opiates might actually interfere with pain mitigating processes. A number of cellular mechanisms are being explored to assess mechanisms underlying tolerance to analgesic efficacy (Fishbain et al. 1992; Streltzer 2001). It should be borne in mind that the opiate-dependent patient requires substantially higher opiate doses to effectively manage severe pain conditions.

General Guidelines for Detoxification From Opiates

Although opiate withdrawal can be physically uncomfortable, it is not life threatening. Opiate withdrawal can be conducted with any opiate. However, use of long-acting opiates allows for more rapid taper of the opiate without incurring significant physical discomfort. Toward this end, methadone, levorphanol, and more recently buprenorphine have been employed for this purpose. The tapering of opiates should proceed gradually. Strategies for detoxifying patients should be based on dose equivalencies of opiates (see Chapter 5). In general, the dose of the opiate required to prevent significant withdrawal symptoms is approximately 25% of the previous day's dose. Although rates of tapering opiates can vary substantially, the taper should be gradual enough so as not to create marked distress for the patient. Clinicians often rely on objective parameters of definitive withdrawal to decide when supplemental doses of opiates are required or when more gradual tapering should be employed. Subjective experiences of opiate withdrawal, brought on by a dramatic taper, are difficult to quantify but can nonetheless be particularly distressing for patients. These subjective variables should be taken into account when decisions are made regarding the rate of opiate taper. Otherwise, the patient might be inclined to abandon detoxification treatment. Conversely, discomfort is inevitable when patients withdraw from opiates. If one attempts too gradual a taper of opiates to avoid any possible discomfort, the pro-

cess of detoxification would be inordinately protracted. Clonidine could be a useful adjunct in mitigating some of the symptoms of autonomic nervous system activation associated with opiate withdrawal (Fishbain et al. 1992). During the course of detoxification, it could be imperative to undertake simultaneous measures to mitigate pain; otherwise, the distress to which the patient is subjected might be too great. Administering methadone in divided doses may help toward this end, until other strategies have been effectively put in place.

Detoxification From Other Agents

Agents other than opiates require detoxification as well. Ergot alkaloids are customarily applied in cases of migraine headache. When these agents are used chronically, however, patients can become dependent on them, and abrupt discontinuation results in precipitation of rebound vascular-type headache. Patients can become accustomed to maintaining their use of these agents so as to avoid precipitation of rebound headache. At times, detoxification might be required to reduce the excess use of these agents (Fishbain et al. 1992).

Ongoing or recent cocaine dependence contraindicates psychostimulant use in the management of pain or side effects induced by treatment (e.g., sedation associated with opioid treatment). Detoxification from cocaine, amphetamine, or other stimulants may be critical to the rehabilitation and reclamation of the pain patient who simultaneously has been dependent on these agents. Detoxification from stimulants might be required in patients who have become dependent on the use of these agents in the course of long-term treatment. Antidepressants (e.g., bupropion) and anticonvulsants (e.g., carbamazepine) have been invoked for detoxification from stimulants and might also serve a pain-mitigating function.

Withdrawal from sedatives or hypnotics can be physically uncomfortable and potentially life threatening if not managed properly. Benzodiazepine dependence can emerge from long-term use of benzodiazepines. Detoxification must be undertaken carefully to

avoid significant withdrawal symptoms. Severity of withdrawal might be related to the potency of the benzodiazepine used. High potency agents, such as lorazepam and alprazolam, are more likely to produce severe withdrawal symptoms than are less potent agents, such as diazepam and chlordiazepoxide (Lader 1987). Another factor determining the severity of withdrawal symptoms is the rapidity with which the benzodiazepine is discontinued. Abrupt discontinuation is more likely to precipitate severe withdrawal symptoms, whereas more gradual discontinuation is more apt to produce less severe withdrawal symptoms. However, gradual dose reductions of benzodiazepines might not suppress all of the signs and symptoms of withdrawal (Schwerzer et al. 1990).

During the taper, the benzodiazepine dose should be reduced approximately 25% per week. A more gradual taper might need to be undertaken if symptoms of withdrawal are too distressing or significant. If patients are abusing short-acting agents, benzodiazepine detoxification is best accomplished by switching to longer-acting agents (e.g., diazepam). The taper of long-acting agents can be conducted much more rapidly than that of shorter-acting agents. One concern that arises is whether symptom rebound can occur after successful benzodiazepine detoxification. This rebound can include reoccurrence of prior sleep disturbances or anxiety at levels higher than had been previously experienced.

Smoking cessation is part of a comprehensive rehabilitative program. Cessation produces significant improvements in a patient's overall health, along with improving physical endurance to maintain increased activity. Bupropion has been employed in the early course of nicotine withdrawal to reduce craving. Hypnosis and acupuncture have also been invoked to facilitate cessation.

■ PATIENTS WITH TERMINAL CONDITIONS

Patients with terminal medical conditions who have pain require compassionate care. In addition to pain management, sensitivity to the patient's perceptions of and concerns regarding death are required. Patients with terminal conditions require regular visitation,

a fact frequently ignored by physicians, who often focus on correctable disease or might subconsciously view a patient's death as their failure. Visiting, even when a patient avoids discussions about their health or prognosis, conveys that the clinician is reliable, dependable, and available should the occasion (and need) arise to more openly discuss important issues that surround a terminal condition.

Patients may require physical contact, appropriate to the context of the situation, to convey support and attentiveness. Attention to the content of what the patient says is necessary, as is answering the patient's questions in an honest and respectful manner. Patients may inquire about the nature of their illnesses and whether they are at terminal stages. By basing their responses on what s known about the nature and course of the illnesses, physicians can be honest without eradicating hope. Building false hopes is discouraged.

Some patients can find such disclosures to be overwhelming, which the physician may assume is a form of "denial." However, this assumption can be insulting to the patient and perhaps intrusive, especially if a psychiatric consultant is asked to evaluate the patient about this presumed denial. Respect for the patient's defenses, even denial, may well be required at such times. Aggressively attempting to eradicate this defensive stance may serve only to distance the patient, causing him or her to become more resistant to the clinician's efforts and care. On the other hand, patients may have fears about asking questions or may not know how to begin making inquiries. The physician might inquire of the patient how much it is he or she wishes to know about the current illness, thus facilitating dialogue on the matter.

Physicians also need to be sensitive about the extent to which the patient, family, significant others, and medical staff are aware of the terminal nature of the patient's illness. Every effort should be made to facilitate communication between the patient and family (and significant others) about the prospect of death—but, again, the issue should be gently and respectfully broached, not forced. Reluctance on the part of the physician to openly discuss such matters may come from fear that the family and patient will think the physician has given up on effective care of the patient or fears of discouraging or upsetting the patient and family. Opening discussion among family and

the patient could help reduce the isolation, loneliness, and even the dehumanizing features that surround death for the patient. Family conflicts can emerge around the time of death. Opening dialogue between family members at such times can relieve their stress and help them begin the work of bereavement. Family meetings can provide an opportunity for refocusing on the issues that matter.

Physicians can be the target of anger from the patient, the family, or both. Taking a defensive stance in such situations should be avoided. The patient and family might need to ventilate their feelings about death and about the meaning of the patient's illness for them. The best strategy might be to articulate the feelings and emotions underlying the anger. For example, "This has been such a long illness and a long struggle for everyone. It is impossible to imagine what it feels like to be challenged with the prospect that our life activities are interrupted prematurely, that our dreams will go unfulfilled." Or, "It probably feels as though I let you down." Such approaches are likely to diffuse the tension of the impending death and are less likely to escalate into a conflict, as could be the case if the physician took a defensive stance. The doctor may be the "safest" target of anger, especially if unresolved matters in the patient's relationships are too overwhelming to address directly in the final days.

The family and patient may need reassurance that pain will be maximally controlled. The patient and others may be concerned that pain control will make the patient unaware of his or her surroundings or otherwise incapacitated. Modifying the patient's pain-relief regimen according to his or her wishes is desirable, whereas withholding effective pain treatment to appease the family's need to keep the patient alert is not. Family members may need to be reminded that severe pain will likely mitigate the sedating properties of opiates and other analgesics. They could also need reassurance the analgesics will not result in or hasten the patient's death.

Hospice Care

Hospice care is a system of care for patients with terminal conditions and their families. The goals of therapy within hospice care

are to provide palliation (i.e., pain management) but not cure and to ensure dignity of care without the encumbrances of life support measures and invasive procedures.

Care for patients is often arranged in the home, an environment that is familiar and often more comfortable for the patient. Access to the patient by family, friends, and customary supports are more feasible when the patient remains at home. Service to the patient is coordinated among family, other members of the patient's usual support system, medical and mental health personnel, clergy, and volunteers.

Generally, the cost of hospice care is far less than that for hospital care. However, higher costs are incurred when hospice care is provided in nursing homes or hospitals or when patients are furnished with care in an established hospice setting. Medicare coverage is provided for hospice care; however, there are limitations to the coverage provided (Table 9–2). Medicare provides a flat fee for hospice services. Thus, funding provided for a patient living 6 months is quite low, but if the patient lives beyond 6 months, the provision of hospice services continues without reimbursement and the hospice agency incurs a financial loss. As a result, hospice agencies may be reluctant to accept patients whose illnesses are not inclined to result in death within 6 months. Physicians may be inclined to erroneously withhold an offer of hospice care to patients and their families, fearing that the anticipated time until death might exceed 6 months. Therefore, physicians may be offering hospice care to patients too late in the course of the illness.

TABLE 9–2.   **Medicare requirements for hospice care**

Physician must certify that the patient's condition is terminal (i.e., the
    patient's life expectancy is expected to be 6 months or less)

Patient must consent to hospice care in lieu of traditional hospital care

Hospice care agency must be certified by Medicare in order to accept
    benefits from the federal government

As more patients require hospice services, psychiatric involvement will be ever increasing in hospice care. Many patients develop psychiatric symptoms either as a consequence of the illnesses that prompted their admission or as effects of treatment. Common psychiatric disturbances likely to be encountered include mood disturbances, anxiety, delirium, and dementia. A number of psychiatric interventions and medications can be employed to reduce the deleterious effects of these psychiatric disturbances. Psychiatrists can be particularly influential in ensuring that pain is adequately addressed in hospice patients.

Family members and friends may have emotional difficulties associated with hospice care. These can include a sense of futility, anticipatory bereavement, guilt (i.e., viewing hospice as a "giving up" on the patient or a withholding of necessary care), and despair. Psychiatrists can be helpful in facilitating the family's adjustment to the hospice care transition and in preventing emotional difficulties from impeding connections with the patient that might be required in the time they have remaining. Psychiatrists can help the family recognize that the focus has become one of ensuring improved quality of life for the patient and can help them maximize the time they have available. Issues concerning death and dying may need to be a focus of care for the patient as well as his or her family and other loved ones.

Religious Issues and Spirituality

Issues of spirituality may be encountered when caring for the patient who has a terminal condition. There may be uncertainties and confusion about treatment decisions (e.g., advanced directives), particularly if the patient has fears about the moral implications of a particular treatment. Sometimes religious inquiries can arise when there is a conflict with the physician about prognosis, a distrust of the medical system, and/or a rejection of the clinician's expertise. Some patients are distressed about the prognosis, therefore hoping that miracles might occur to intervene on their behalf. After all, when the prognosis is grim, who would not want to hope for a miracle? In situations in which there is persistent pain or severe unto-

ward effects of treatment, some patients may be concerned about punishment, guilt, and prior transgressions.

Many physicians feel unskilled or uncomfortable addressing religious or spiritual issues, often bypassing them to focus on somatic concerns, treatment issues, or even the psychological underpinnings of the discussion (Lo et al. 2002). Yet avoidance of these topics can further increase the patient's isolation as he or she struggles with issues pertaining to such matters. This avoidance may inadvertently jeopardize the therapeutic alliance.

Because of the diversity of concerns that can prompt issues of spirituality, careful inquiry by the physician may expose the patient's underlying concerns or fears (Table 9–3). While respecting the patient's spiritual issues and dilemmas, the clinician should attempt to reflect religious issues back onto the patient—for example, by inquiring "Why do you ask?" or "I wonder if you have concerns about what to do next?" Open-ended inquiry can lead to discussions of matters that have an impact on treatment and on the doctor–patient relationship. The clinician is cautioned against being drawn into the potential pitfalls of religious and theological arguments, scriptural interpretations, and so forth that can bypass the patient's underlying concerns. It might be also be prudent to elicit the support of others (e.g., clergy and pastoral counselors) when confronted with moral issues.

TABLE 9–3.   **Approaches to dealing with spiritual issues**

Use open-ended inquiry

Acknowledge the patient's spiritual concerns

Empathize with the patient

Refocus spiritual questions back onto the patient

Attempt to clarify whether the patient's spiritual dilemmas are about

  Decisions about further treatment interventions

  Decisions about advance directives

  The doctor–patient relationship

  Questions about the validity and utility of medical interventions

Avoid reassuring the patient prematurely

Avoid trying to solve the patient's spiritual dilemmas for him or her

---

■ REFERENCES

AGS (American Geriatrics Society) Panel on Chronic Pain in Older Persons: The management of chronic pain in older persons. J Am Geriatr Soc 46:635–651, 1998

Berde CB, Masek B: Pain in children, in Textbook of Pain, 4th edition. Edited by Wall PD, Melzack R. London, England, Churchill Livingstone, 1999, pp 1463–1477

Beyer J, DeGood DE, Ashley LC, et al: Patterns of postoperative analgesic use with adults and children following cardiac surgery. Pain 17:71–81, 1983

Cleeland CS: Undertreatment of cancer pain in elderly patients. JAMA 279:1914–1915, 1998

Cleeland CS, Gonin R, Hatfield AK, et al: Pain and its treatment in outpatients with metastatic cancer. N Engl J Med 330:592–596, 1994

Crawley L, Payne R, Bolden J, et al: Palliative and end-of-life care in the African American community. JAMA 284:2518–2521, 2000

Crook J, Rideout E, Browne G: The prevalence of pain complaints in a general population. Pain 18:299–314, 1984

Ebert AM: Use of nonnarcotic analgesics during breastfeeding. J Hum Lact 13:61–64, 1997

Ferrell BA: Pain in the nursing home. J Am Geriatr Soc 38:409–414, 1990

Ferrell BA: Pain management in elderly people. J Am Geriatr Soc 39:64–73, 1991

Fishbain DA, Rosomoff HL, Rosomoff RS: Drug abuse, dependence, and addiction in chronic pain patients. Clin J Pain 8:77–85, 1992

Gagliese L, Katz J, Melzack R: Pain in the elderly, in Textbook of Pain, 4th Edition. Edited by Wall PD, Melzack R. London, England, Churchill Livingstone, 1999, pp 991–1006

Gallagher RM, Verma S, Mossey J: Chronic pain: sources of late-life pain and risk factors for disability. Geriatrics 55:40–47, 2000

Goldschneider KR, Mancuso TJ, Berde CB: Pain and its management in children, in Bonica's Management of Pain, 3rd edition. Edited by Loeser JD, Butler SH, Chapman CR, et al. Philadelphia, PA, Lippincott Williams & Wilkins, 2001, pp 797–812

Herr KA, Mobily PR: Comparison of selected pain assessment tools for use with the elderly. Appl Nurs Res 6:39–46, 1993

Kagawa-Singer M, Blackhall LJ: Negotiating cross-cultural issues at the end of life: "You got to go where he lives." JAMA 286:2993–3001, 2001

Lader M: Long-term anxiolytic therapy: the issue of drug withdrawal. J Clin Psychiatry 48:12–16, 1987

Leith PJ, Weisman SJ: Pharmacologic interventions for pain management in children. Child Adolesc Psychiatr Clin N Am 6:797–815, 1997

Leo RJ, Singh A: Pain management in the elderly: use of psychopharmacologic agents. Annals of Long-Term Care: Clinical Care and Aging 10:37–45, 2002

Lo B, Ruston D, Kates LW, et al: Discussing religious and spiritual issues at the end of life. JAMA 287:749–754, 2002

Ostensen M: Nonsteroidal anti-inflammatory drugs during pregnancy. Scand J Rheumatol 107:128–132, 1998

Portenoy RK, Foley KM: Chronic use of opioid analgesics in non-malignant pain: report of 38 cases. Pain 25:171–186, 1986

Renehan BW: The galactopharmacopedia. Narcotic analgesics: use in the breastfeeding woman. J Hum Lact 5:135–137, 1989

Roy R, Thomas M: A survey of chronic pain in an elderly population. Can Fam Physician 32:513–516, 1986

Schwerzer E, Rickels K, Case WG, et al: Long-term therapeutic use of benzodiazepines, II: effects of gradual taper. Arch Gen Psychiatry 47:908–915, 1990

Sengstaken EA, King SA: The problems of pain and its detection among geriatric nursing home residents. J Am Geriatr Soc 41:541–544, 1993

Sifford LA: Psychiatric assessment of the child with pain. Child Adolesc Psychiatr Clin N Am 6:745–781, 1997

Stevens B: Pain assessment in children: birth through adolescence. Child Adolesc Psychiatr Clin N Am 6:725–743, 1997

Streltzer J: Pain management in the opioid-dependent patient. Curr Psychiatry Rep 3:489–496, 2001

Todd KH, Samaroo N, Hoffman JR: Ethnicity as a risk factor for inadequate emergency department analgesia. JAMA 269:1537–1539, 1993

Wen YR, Hou WY, Chen YA, et al: Intrathecal morphine for neuropathic pain in a pregnant cancer patient. J Formos Med Assoc 95:252–254, 1996

Won A, Lapane K, Gambassi G, et al: Correlates and management of nonmalignant pain in the nursing home. J Am Geriatr Soc 47:936–942, 1999

Zatzick DF, Dimsdale JE: Cultural variations in response to painful stimuli. Psychosom Med 52:544–557, 1990

FORENSIC ISSUES
PERTAINING TO PAIN

■ MEDICATION DIVERSION

The issues around medication diversion have acquired increasing media, public, and legal attention, especially as related to pain medications. *Diversion* refers to the misappropriation of prescribed medications, either by physicians or by other persons who acquire medications from treating sources. Opiate analgesics of all sorts and varieties can be diverted for their abuse appeal. In the past, agents such as butorphanol had abuse appeal; lately, concerns about diversion have focused on oxycodone. The controlled release formulation, when crushed and taken into the body intranasally or intravenously, produces a sensation of euphoria; in some communities its popularity has exceeded that of crack cocaine and heroin (Tough 2001).

From a drug regulatory standpoint, medication diversion has been difficult to control, because medications are produced by a legitimate pharmaceutical company, prescribed by doctors, and dispensed, presumably, to legitimate patients. There are neither drug lords to contend with nor border patrol issues. Instead, the culprits can include physicians (who, for example, acquire illicit drugs in exchange for prescribing medications with diversion appeal), patients, and others associated with legitimate patients who surreptitiously divert the medications meant for the patient. The Internet has become an increasingly popular source of acquisition of controlled

substances as well. For a nominal fee, one's claims are reviewed by an on-line "physician" who then arranges for delivery of controlled substances to the individual through the mail. Again, from a drug regulatory standpoint, these Internet sources have been difficult to monitor and control.

Many psychoactive medications can be diverted. Clearly, the opiates are particularly appealing for their euphoric effects, allowing the abuser to avoid the encumbrances and risks associated with intravenous heroin abuse. On the other hand, benzodiazepines, barbiturates, and psychostimulants have also been diverted because of their appeal "on the street."

Physicians may possibly be colluding with patients in the diversion process. Physicians might be swept away by patient insinuations that if the physician really "cared about" him or her, the medications would be prescribed. Idealization of the physician who complies with the patient's demands and the physician's need for such idealizations can result in the blurring of boundaries that traps the physician into prescribing medications with diversion appeal. Overidentification with the patient and the propensity to assume the mantle of power and authority to alleviate the patient's distress can lead to inappropriate prescription of such medications. In addition, the physician's inward denial regarding reasonable treatment alternatives can interfere with stopping such endeavors. Thus, for example, despite the ongoing pain and distress reported by the patient, the physician ignores alternative strategies to address pain, instead increasing the doses of the opiates (or other requested medications) to appease the patient. The physician can have difficulty managing the hostile, demanding patient, could be unable to set therapeutic limits, and might fear the patient's threats to stop treatment—all of which can perpetuate inappropriate prescribing practices and potential drug diversion.

If diversion is suspected, the physician is entitled to shore up reasonable precautionary practices. Thus, the use of a patient treatment contract (as described in Chapter 5, Table 5–4) might be required. The details of the contract can specify that the patient

will have to comply with random checks of pill counts in order to continue in treatment. Exhausting one's prescribed medications shortly after receiving them could suggest that the medications are being diverted to others. The patient might need to be approached to clarify the reasons for the significantly lower than expected pill counts and the whereabouts of that medication. If insufficiently accounted for, a decision can be made to terminate the treatment plan.

Undertaking legal measures once diversion is substantiated is a consideration, but the clinician faces a risk of confidentiality breach under such circumstances. Legal consultation should be sought before any law enforcement reports are filed. Consultation with colleagues and use of alternative treatment strategies (e.g., use of medications with less abuse or diversion appeal, acupuncture, transcutaneous electrical nerve stimulation [TENS] units, physical or occupational therapies, massage) could be considered in managing any ongoing pain.

■ CONFIDENTIALITY

Patient information can be released only with the authorization of the patient or under proper legal compulsion. For the release authorization to be valid, the patient must be informed of the purposes of the release and the recipient(s) to whom the information would be sent. At times, the patient must be informed of the extent of the information released and its contents. Of course, to authorize release of information, the patient must be competent (as described later) to give consent for the release (American Psychiatric Association 1987).

Clinicians must always ensure that the contents of the patient's medical record are kept confidential. In the era of managed care and the sweeping demands of insurance companies, reimbursement is often tied to the review of the medical record (Hartmann 2001). Physicians often find that their business interests (e.g., reimbursement) are at odds with patient protection. Patients need to be apprised that the contents of the medical

record might be requested in order for reimbursement to be possible. If refused, the insurance company might not make payments for the cost of the services provided. It may be possible in some cases to withhold, without adversely influencing reimbursement, selected aspects of the record that the patient finds too difficult to divulge.

In addition, relevant, easily identifiable information pertaining to a specific patient's case cannot be divulged for educational, training, or publication purposes. If the content of a patient's history, presentation, or similar information is to be used for such purposes, every effort should be made to remove any identifying information that would allow the intended audience to identify the source.

The courts might require that physicians divulge the confidential information contained in a medical record. Legal consultation might be required to assist the clinician in determining the extent of the information that needs to be disclosed. At times, the full content of the record is not required, and particularly personal matters might be best avoided in the legal forum to protect the patient's privacy.

To protect a patient (or another person) from imminent danger, it might be required that the clinician reveal confidential information (*Tarasoff v. Regents of the University of California* 1976). Thus, if a patient threatens self-harm, has a realistic plan, is at risk for lethality, and is not working with the clinician in any way to ensure his or her safety, the clinician might have no recourse but to divulge aspects of the history to potential sources of help who might be able to mobilize the patient's safety (e.g., family, friends, police, crisis services). The clinician must have good cause to suspect that the patient (or another person) is at risk of imminent danger and that other alternatives are not available to remediate the situation. Again, the extent of the information revealed could be limited to only those aspects that will affect the decision making at hand and ensure the safety of the patient and others. Clinicians must be familiar with state laws that regulate such disclosures and with limitations of the confidentiality regulations.

■ INFORMED CONSENT, COMPETENCY, AND CAPACITY

The first 10 amendments of the United States Constitution, known as the Bill of Rights, were created to protect citizens from the infringement of basic freedoms (e.g., speech, press, religion). A corollary of the basic foundation established by the Bill of Rights is the common-law principle of self-determination that guarantees the individual a right to privacy and protection against the actions of others that might threaten bodily integrity. An extension of self-determination includes the right to exercise control over one's body (e.g., the right to accept or refuse treatment).

Informed Consent

Informed consent is required of patients in order to authorize any medical assessment, diagnostic test, or treatment intervention. For a patient to give informed consent, the courts have established that three elements must be present. First is disclosure (i.e., the patient must be told about the nature, purpose, risks, and benefits of the proposed assessment, test, or intervention). Second, the patient must assent or refuse voluntarily, without coercion. Third, the patient must be competent to give consent. Often, when the patient refuses the interventions proposed by the physician, there is a question about the decision-making abilities of the patient. One of the most vexing issues facing physicians is the management of medical treatment when an individual's rational decision making is questionable (Roth et al. 1977). Psychiatrists might, therefore, be enlisted to assess the mental and cognitive abilities of the patient to give consent.

Competency

Competency is a legal term referring to a person's requisite natural or legal qualifications to engage in an endeavor. It is a broad term, spanning a range of activities including entering into a contract, preparing

a will, and making medical decisions. When a person's competency is called into question, the judiciary must decide whether the person possesses those requisite qualifications. Failing that, the patient is deemed incompetent. The cumbersome and potentially expensive efforts involved in such a legal proceeding are often prohibitive. The delays involved in arranging for and undergoing a formal court proceeding can add substantially to the cost of hospital care and may incur risks to the patient's health (President's Commission 1982).

Capacity

The term *capacity* is frequently mistaken for *competency*. Capacity is determined by the physician (often, although not exclusively, by a psychiatrist), not by the judiciary. *Capacity* refers to an assessment of the person's psychological abilities to understand, appreciate, and form rational decisions (Leo 1999). A capacity assessment essentially determines the validity of a patient's decision to undergo or forego a particular proposed treatment. Table 10–1 summarizes a reasonable guide for the physician assessing a patient's decision-making capacity (Leo 1999). Inquiries should be directed to the patient, according to the guidelines, and the patient's responses should be systematically recorded in the medical record, preferably as quotations. Failure at any component of this line of inquiry would mean that the patient does not have the capacity to make reasoned decisions regarding the proposed medical treatment.

TABLE 10–1. **Guide for assessing capacity**

The patient must demonstrate an understanding of each of the following:
1. Current medical condition
2. Natural course of his or her current medical condition
3. Proposed treatment intervention
4. Potential risks and benefits of the proposed treatment intervention
5. Consequences of refusing the proposed treatment intervention
6. Presence of any viable alternatives to the proposed treatment intervention
7. Potential risks and benefits of alternative treatments

If a person lacks the capacity to make treatment decisions, it may be incumbent on the consulting psychiatrist to remedy barriers to capacity. In some cases, disturbances in the doctor–patient relationship (i.e., ineffective communication) might be the sole basis for the lack of capacity. The psychiatrist may be enlisted to clarify and rectify such communication difficulties. In other cases, a psychiatric disturbance (e.g., delirium, psychosis, or a mood disorder) may be impeding the patient's capacity to give informed consent, but once rectified (e.g., through use of medication, therapy), can enable them to do so.

If the patient lacks capacity and the problem is not remediable, the treating clinician (other than a psychiatrist) may need to invoke substituted consent. Although states vary as to who may be appointed as a substitute, this role often falls to spouses, relatives, ethics boards, and so forth. In some situations, a judicial decision of incompetence is required. If so deemed, the patient would have a court-appointed guardian assigned to make medical decisions on his or her behalf.

■ LITIGATION AND PAIN

Concerns naturally arise about the potential role of ongoing litigation and its effect on the experience of pain, the rehabilitation process, and allegations of disability. It is conceivable that the pursuit of litigation could have an impact on treatment and rehabilitation (Gatchel et al. 1995). People with whiplash injuries who were in the midst of litigation reported more pain than those who were no longer involved in litigation (i.e., whose cases were settled or resolved) (Swartzman et al. 1996). However, there was no statistically significant difference between those who were in the midst of litigation and those who were not as regards employment status, return to work, and functional adaptation. The clinician is cautioned against making causal assumptions about the role of the litigation in influencing the patient's agenda (Schwartzman et al. 1996). Three possible interpretations need to be entertained:

1. Pain is exaggerated so as to increase the magnitude of the monetary gain of a litigation claim

2. The stress of the litigation process has led to marked muscle tension, resulting in accentuation and exaggeration of pain complaints
3. A third factor (e.g., fears of disability, long-term effects of pain, fears of future limitations in work capacity, fears of unemployment and financial hardship) has led to the accentuation of pain complaints as well as the pursuit of litigation

Careful attention to the types of concerns the patient has could be highly informative in determining which of these interpretations is operating. Attentive listening can lead to those interventions that allay the patient's fears. One of the biggest concerns that patients have is that their pain complaints might not be well received or might be misinterpreted as a ploy to achieve secondary gains. Reassurance that the clinician is working with the patient to address his or her pain, improve functional adaptation, and reduce disability while improving quality of life can help to alleviate such fears. The clinician may need to openly discuss the issues and concerns that beset the patient so that they no longer concern the patient and so they do not adversely affect the doctor–patient relationship.

In addition, pain management has received increasing legal attention. A physician was found guilty of elder abuse based on the premise that he inadequately treated a patient's pain before the patient's death (Albert 2001). In a similar action, a physician was sanctioned by the Oregon Board of Medical Examiners for negligence (i.e., the failure to meet the standard of care as it related to inadequate pain management) (Charatan 1999). As these cases illustrate, external pressures are increasing to ensure that physicians are knowledgeable about effective pain management. Consultation with pain management specialists would be warranted in particularly difficult cases.

■ DISABILITY COMPENSATION

Disability Versus Impairment

A *disability* is a putative deficit in functioning, implying a lack of ability to perform activities required for work. It is rather subjective (i.e.,

is a perception of restriction of function). On the other hand, an *impairment* is an abnormality in psychological or physiologic functioning, verifiable by a clinician, based on observable findings (e.g., physical and mental status examination, laboratory findings). The determination of eligibility for disability awards can be quite complex, and the standards vary depending on the agency from which the award is sought. The basis for the claim involves a review of evidence gathered from a number of medical and, in some cases, nonmedical sources.

Workers' Compensation

Workers' compensation is a system of laws ensuring that compensation awards are provided for persons who sustain injuries during the course of work; it does not litigate fault or negligence (Crook 1994). The goal of workers' compensation is to provide the injured employee with money to cover the costs of medical expenses and provide some portion of lost wages. A person who is injured while on duty is not entitled to intangible compensation (e.g., for pain and suffering). Critical to the award is the nature of the alleged injury and its relationship to the work setting. A compensable physical or mental injury must be reasonably connected to the work. The injury cannot arise solely from the worker's own health risks (e.g., coronary artery disease brought on by years of cigarette smoking). Similarly, preexisting illnesses are not compensable. However, preexisting illnesses can predispose a person to complications arising from work injuries. In such cases, the injury and its treatment are compensable. To qualify as compensable, the injury must be accidental and cannot be deliberately self-inflicted.

Critical to workers' compensation is the establishment that the impairment interferes with the performance of prior work. Prior work includes those jobs that are suitable to, or related to, one's training and qualifications. Determinations of awards are contingent upon the anticipated prognosis and the impact of the injury on one's functional capacity. *Functional capacity* refers to one's abilities to perform activities of daily living (ADL), manage one's finances, maintain relationships, and so forth.

TABLE 10–2.	Limitations considered by Social Security Administration adjudicators
Physical limitations	**Mental limitations**
Exertional	Understanding and memory deficits
Postural	Concentration deficits
Manipulative	Deficits in social interaction
Visual	Deficits in adaptation
Communicative	Severe emotional disturbances
Environmental	Psychosis

Social Security Disability

Unlike workers' compensation awards, Social Security disability awards are based on the finding that one's physical or mental impairment interferes with the ability to perform *any* job in the national economy, not just one's former job (see Table 10–2). The impairment cannot be transient but must be present for a continuous period of at least 12 months (Social Security Administration 2001). According to the Social Security Administration (SSA), in order to be eligible for disability the impairment must preclude working to meet a minimum standard of financial income. Essential to the assessment of claims of pain disabilities is the assessment of one's functional capacity (Enelow and Leo 2002) (including ADLs, ability to lift, carry, push, pull, sit, stand, walk, manipulate, see, hear, understand, remember, concentrate, follow simple instructions). In addition to financial compensation, recipients can become eligible for medical insurance (i.e., Medicaid or Medicare) (Institute of Medicine 1987; Leo and Del Regno 2002).

Veterans Administration Benefits

The Veterans Administration (VA) offers a disability program for disabled American veterans. Unlike the SSA, no means test is required. Unlike the SSA and worker's compensation systems, there is no requirement that the individual demonstrate an inability to

work. Compensation through the VA is of two types: service-connected benefits (i.e., for disabilities acquired in the course of military service) and non-service-connected benefits (i.e., for disabilities acquired after military service and precluding ability to work at a substantial level) (Institute of Medicine 1987). In order to be compensable, the alleged mental and/or physical disability must be validated by medical sources and must be expected to last indefinitely. For a person to qualify for benefits, a clinician must provide medical documentation that substantiates the allegation of a disorder that is grounded in anatomic or physiologic evidence and appropriate clinical signs and symptoms. In addition to financial awards, beneficiaries are eligible to receive medical care provided through the VA health system, including physical rehabilitation, prosthetic devices (if required), and vocational rehabilitation services.

Disability and the Doctor–Patient Relationship

Several issues need to be addressed with the patient who intends to file a claim for disability benefits (Mischoulon 2002), because the outcome of the disability determination can have an impact on the doctor–patient relationship. Ambivalence can arise in response to a favorable decision. Although allowance of a disability award means access to resources of financial support and medical insurance, it might also stir feelings of dependency, inadequacy, and loss of self-sufficiency in the patient. On the other hand, an unfavorable decision might be interpreted negatively (e.g., a withholding of needed resources). Such feelings can be directed at the treating physician. Discussions between the physician and patient before the claim is submitted could possibly diffuse these potential reactions and prevent them from impeding the treatment alliance.

It would be prudent for the physician to review with the patient the process by which disability determinations are made, emphasizing that the physician does not make the decision about disability eligibility but that the decision rests with adjudicators (and possibly judges and courts if appeals are undertaken). In addition, patients should be apprised that the physician is but one source contacted by

disability adjudicators for clinical information, and clinical information is considered in light of information provided from other sources.

It is imperative that a signed release of information be obtained *before* any information is disclosed to any agency determining disability eligibility. The limits of confidentiality need to be disclosed to the patient (American Psychiatric Association 1987). Addressing this matter directly avoids the potential for confrontations regarding disclosure of sensitive information after it has been provided to disability or compensation reviewers.

The nature of the disability program intrinsically creates incentives for claimants to maximize monetary gains by emphasizing functional limitations and overstating the severity of illnesses (Fontana and Rosenheck 1998). The person with mild symptoms who dramatizes the severity of his or her disability can trigger marked countertransference reactions in the clinician (Heiman and Shanfield 1978). Physicians might harbor resentment and other feelings at being pulled into the position of rewarding idleness, inactivity, and dependency. Inattention to countertransference reactions can lead the physician to underestimate the severity of the claimant's symptoms, distance him- or herself from the patient, and thereby undermine any attempts at rehabilitation.

Clinicians could have concerns about the unstructured time patients have once disability benefits are awarded. There could be concerns that treatment endeavors (e.g., development of autonomy and self-sufficiency) might be undermined. Among the factors that adversely influence return to work after a disabling injury is the length of time spent on disability compensation (Chatfield 1998). Other factors include current litigation, significant depression and psychiatric comorbidity, substance abuse, and lack of personal satisfaction with work (Chatfield 1998).

Directly addressing such concerns with the patient could be meaningful and therapeutic (i.e., laying the foundation for vocational rehabilitation and work preparatory skills). In addition, the time available off work might allow for pursuit of more intensive treatment, including psychotherapy, group therapy, and day treatment. In

this way, the pursuit of disability benefits does not become an end in itself but a means to improve the rehabilitation of the patient.

■ REFERENCES

Albert T: Doctor guilty of elder abuse for undertreating pain. Am Med News, July 23, 2001, pp 1, 4

American Psychiatric Association Committee on Confidentiality: Guidelines on confidentiality. Am J Psychiatry 144:1522–1526, 1987

Charatan F: Doctor disciplined for "grossly undertreating" pain. Br Med J 319:728, 1999

Chatfield JW: Symptom magnification: an overview from clinical practice, in Pain Management: A Practical Guide For Clinicians, 5th Edition, Vol 2. Edited by Weiner RS. Boca Raton, FL, St. Lucie Press, 1998, pp 737–742

Crook PL: Worker's compensation, in Handbook of Pain Management, 2nd Edition. Edited by Tollison CD, Satterthwaite JR, Tollison JW. Baltimore, MD, Williams & Wilkins, 1994, pp 722–731

Enelow AJ, Leo RJ: Evaluation of the vocational factors impacting on psychiatric disability. Psychiatr Ann 32:293–297, 2002

Fontana A, Rosenheck R: Effects of compensation-seeking on treatment outcomes among veterans with posttraumatic stress disorder. J Nerv Ment Dis 186:223–230, 1998

Gatchel RJ, Polatin PB, Mayer TG: The dominant role of psychosocial risk factors in the development of chronic low back pain disability. Spine 20:2702–2709, 1995

Hartmann L: Confidentiality, in Ethics Primer of the American Psychiatric Association. Edited by American Psychiatric Association Ethics Committee. Washington, DC, American Psychiatric Association, 2001, pp 39–44

Heiman EM, Shanfield SB: Psychiatric disability assessment: clarification of problems. Compr Psychiatry 19:449–454, 1978

Institute of Medicine Committee on Pain, Disability, and Chronic Illness Behavior: Disability determination and the role of pain, in Pain and Disability: Clinical, Behavioral, and Public Policy Perspectives. Edited by Osterweis M, Kleinman A, Mechanic D. Washington, DC, National Academy Press, 1987, pp 37–65

Leo RJ: Competency and the capacity to make treatment decisions: a primer for primary care physicians. Prim Care Companion J Clin Psychiatry 1:131–141, 1999

Leo RJ, Del Regno P: Social Security claims of psychiatric disability: elements of case adjudication and the role of primary care physicians. Prim Care Companion J Clin Psychiatry 3:255–262, 2002

Mischoulon D: Potential pitfalls to the therapeutic relationship arising from disability claims. Psychiatr Ann 32:299–302, 2002

President's Commission for the Study of Ethical Problems in Medicine and Biomedical and Behavioral Research: Making Health Care Decisions: A Report on the Ethical and Legal Implications of Informed Consent in the Patient–Practitioner Relationship. Washington, DC, Government Printing Office, 1982

Roth LH, Meisel A, Lidz CW: Tests of competency to consent to treatment. Am J Psychiatry 134:279–284, 1977

Social Security Administration: Disability evaluation under Social Security. SSA Publication No. 64-039. Baltimore, MD, Social Security Administration, January, 2001

Swartzman LC, Teasell RW, Shapiro AP, et al: The effect of litigation status on adjustment to whiplash injury. Spine 21:53–58, 1996

Tarasoff v Regents of the University of California, 17 Cal 3d 425, 551 P2d 334, 131 Cal Rptr. 14 (1976)

Tough P: The oxycontin underground. The New York Times, July 29, 2001, pp 50–63

INDEX

*Page numbers printed in **boldface** type refer to tables or figures.*

AA. *See* Alcoholics Anonymous
ABA. *See* American Board of
    Anesthesiology
ABPMR. *See* American Board of
    Physical Medicine and
    Rehabilitation
ABPN. *See* American Board of
    Psychiatry and Neurology
Accreditation Council for Graduate
    Medical Education (ACGME),
    3–4
ACDs. *See* Anticonvulsant drugs
Acetaminophen, 93
    for management of cancer pain,
      192
Acetylcholine, in pain processing,
    22
ACGME. *See* Accreditation
    Council for Graduate Medical
    Education
ACR. *See* American College of
    Rheumatology
Activities of daily living (ADL),
    227
Acupuncture, 153–155
    complications, 154
    contraindications, 155
    indications, 154

for pain in the elderly, 200
    technique, 154
ADL. *See* Activities of daily living
Affect
    in evaluation of the pain patient,
      39–41
    psychotherapy and, 123–125,
      125
Affective-motivational pathway, **17**
Alcoholics Anonymous (AA), 142
α2-adrenergic agonists, 107. *See
    also individual drug names*
American Board of Anesthesiology
    (ABA), 3
American Board of Physical
    Medicine and Rehabilitation
    (ABPMR), 3
American Board of Psychiatry and
    Neurology (ABPN), 3
American College of
    Rheumatology (ACR), 175
Amitriptyline
    for migraine headache, 170
    for neuropathic pain, **185**
Analgesics. *See also individual
    drug names*
    nonopioid, 92–94
    opiate, 79–91

Analgesics *(continued)*
  on the spinal level, 24
  through hypnosis, 147–148
Anesthesia
  dermatomal levels for spinal,
    157
  at the level of the spinal cord,
    156–159, **157, 158, 159**
  patient-controlled, 203
Anger, 41
  Antiarrhythmic drugs for
    neuropathic pain, 184. *See
    also individual drug names*
Anticonvulsant drugs (ACDs),
    100–102. *See also individual
    drug names*
  for neuropathic pain, 184, **185**
  side effects, **103**
Antidepressants, 94–99. *See also
    individual drug names*
  monoamine oxidase inhibitors, 97
  for neuropathic pain, **185**
  selective serotonin reuptake
    inhibitors, 98
  tricyclic, 95–97, **96**
  uses, 94–95
Antihistamines, 102–103. *See also
    individual drug names*
Antispasmodics, 110–111. *See also
    individual drug names*
Anxiety disorders, **40,** 41, 70–72, **71**
Anxiolytics, 103–104. *See also
    individual drug names*
Appetite suppression, 200
Aspirin, 92–93
Autogenic training, 144
Autonomic nerve blocks, **161**
Autonomic nervous system, role in
    pain, 18–19

Back pain, 171–174
  common causes, **172**
  treatment options, **174**
Baclofen, 110–111
  dosing, **111**
Behavior therapy, 130–133, **131**
  steps of, **131**
Belief systems and cognitive
    distortions, 128–130
Benzodiazepines, 103–104. *See
    also individual drug names*
  controversies with use in chronic
    pain, **105**
  detoxification from opiates and,
    209–210
Bill of Rights, 223
Biofeedback, 142–144
  for migraine headache, 170
  for neuropathic pain, 184, **185**
  for tension headache, 166
Biopsychosocial paradigms, 4–7, **6**
  dimensions of pain and model
    of, 11–12, **11**
Bradykinin, in pain processing, 22
Buprenorphine, **80**
  multiple uses of, 88
Bupropion, **96,** 98–99
Buspirone, 104
Butorphanol, **80**

Cancer, 189–191
Capacity, 224–225, **224**
  functional, 227
Capsaicin, 111–112
  for neuropathic pain, **185**
Carbamazepine, 101
  for neuropathic pain, **185**
  side effects, **103**
Carisoprodol, 110, **111**

Catastrophizing, **43,** 129–130

CBT. *See* Cognitive-behavior therapy

Celiac ganglion block, **161**

Cell death. *N*-methyl-D-aspartate and, 21

Central nervous system (CNS)
 neurochemicals in pain processing, 22–24
 nonopiate endogenous inhibitory neurotransmitters, 23–24
 pain-augmenting neurotransmitters, 22–23
 pain-modulating processes within, 19–24

CH. *See* Cluster headache

Chlorzoxazone, 110, **111**

Chronic pain
 acute vs., 25–32
 categories, 27–29, **28**
 causes, **21**
 classification, 26–27, **27**
 multi-axial classification, 31–32
 patient with simple vs., 29–31, **30, 31**
 simple vs. complex, 29, **31**

Clonazepam, for neuropathic pain, **185**

Clozapine, 106

Cluster headache (CH), 172
 treatment, **167**

CNS. *See* Central nervous system

Codeine, **80**

Cognitive-behavior therapy (CBT), 133–137, **135**
 approach, **135**
 for migraine headache, 170

Cognitive patterns, 41–44, **43**

Commissurotomy, 162

Compassion in Dying Federation, 1–2

Competency, 223–224

Complex regional pain syndromes (CRPS), 185–187
 characteristics, 186
 treatment, 186–187, **187**

Confidentiality, 221–222

Conversion disorder, 40

Coping strategies, 44–45, 136–137

Coping Strategies Questionnaire (CSQ), 58, **50**

Cordotomy, 162
 for neuropathic pain, **185**

Corticosteroids, 108–109, **109**. *See also individual drug names*
 side effects, **109**

Couples therapy, 138–141

COX-2. *See* Cyclooxygenase-2 inhibitors

CRPS. *See* Complex regional pain syndromes

CSQ. *See* Coping Strategies Questionnaire

Culture
 barriers to pain management in minority patients, **205**
 economic disparities, 206
 pain and, 204–206

Cyclobenzaprine, **111**

Cyclooxygenase-2 (COX-2) inhibitors, 94. *See also individual drug names*
 for osteoarthritis, 180

Death, 72

Deep breathing exercises, 145
 script, **146**

Defenses, psychotherapy and, 125–128, **126**

Dejerine-Roussy syndrome, pain perception and, 25

Delirium, **40**

Depression, **40**, 69–70

Desipramine, for neuropathic pain, **185**

Dexamethasone, for neuropathic pain, **185**

Dextroamphetamine, 104

Dextromethorphan, 108

Dezocine, **80**

Diazepam, **111**

Disability compensation, 226–231
  disability and doctor–patient relationship, 229–231
  disability vs. impairment, 226–227
  Social Security disability, 228, **228**
  Veterans Administration (VA) benefits, 228–229
  workers' compensation, 227

Disease conviction, 42

Displacement, **149**

Dissociation, **149**

Dorsal horn, anatomy, 14–16

DSM-IV-TR, diagnostic criteria for pain disorder, **65–66**

Electroencephalography (EEG), 143

Electromyography (EMG), 143, 173

EMLA. *See* Eutectic mixture of local anesthetics

Emotions
  psychotherapy interventions to facilitate access of, **125**

reasons for poor identification and regulation, **125**

Endogenous opiates, in pain processing, 23

Epidural analgesia
  complications and contraindications, **158**
  risks of continuous anesthetic infusions, **159**

Ergotamines, for migraine headache, 170

Eutectic mixture of local anesthetics (EMLA), 112

Exercise
  for back pain, 173
  for pain in the elderly, 200

FABQ. *See* Fear Avoidance Beliefs Questionnaire

Face pain, 14

Faces scale, **52**, 53, 202

Family therapy, 138–141
  with terminal patient, 212

Fear Avoidance Beliefs Questionnaire (FABQ), **50**, 58

Fentanyl, **80**

Fibromyalgia, 175–179
  diagnostic criteria, **175**
  features, **177**
  treatment strategies, **178**

5-HT, 99. *See also* Serotonin

Fluphenazine, 106

Forensic issues, 219–232
  capacity, 224–225, **224**
  competency, 223–224
  confidentiality, 221–222
  disability compensation, 226–231. *See also* Disability compensation

informed consent, 223
litigation and pain, 225–226
medication diversion, 219–221
Frontal cortex, role in pain, 18
Functional capacity, 227

Gabapentin, 100–101
for neuropathic pain, **185**
side effects, **103**
Geriatrics, 197–200
side effects of pain, 200
treatment strategies, 199–200
underrecognition of pain in
elderly patients, 198–199
Glutamate, in pain processing, 23
Group therapy, 141–142
Guided imagery, 144

Hansen disease (leprosy), pain
perception and, 25
Headaches, 165–171
cluster, 172
migraine, 168–170
tension, 165–168
treatment, **167**
Helplessness, **43**
Help-rejecting, **43**
Histamine, in pain processing,
22
HIV/AIDS, 189–192
common pain states, **190**
treatment, 191, **192**
Hospice care, 212–214, **213**
Hydromorphone, **80**
Hypnosis, 146–148, **149**
for neuropathic pain, 184, 185
techniques, **149**
Hypochondriasis, **40**
Hypogastric plexus block, **161**

Impairment, vs. disability, 226–227
Informed consent, 223
Instruments
for assessment of acute and
chronic pain, **50**
behavioral measures, 53–55
for evaluation of the pain
patient 48–60
factors that suggest poor surgical
outcome for pain disorders,
49
multidimensional pain scales,
55–57
psychological assessments,
57–60
psychometric pain scales, **50**
single dimension scales, 51–53,
52
International Association for the
Study of Pain, 31–32
Interviews, for evaluation of the
pain patient, 35–37, **36**
Isometheptene mucate, for migraine
headache, 170

Joint Commission on Accreditation
of Healthcare Organizations
(JCAHO), 2

Ketamine, 108

Labeling, **43**
Lamotrigine 101–102
side effects, **103**
Leprosy (Hansen disease), pain
perception and, 25
Levorphanol, **80**
Lidocaine patch, 112
Lisuride, for migraine headache, 170

Magnification, **43**
Malingering, **69**
MAOIs. *See* Monoamine oxidase inhibitors
Marital therapy, 138–141
Massage, for pain in the elderly, 200
McGill Pain Questionnaire (MPQ), 55, **50, 56**
Medical condition, with pain disorder, 64
Medications
    diversion, 219–221
    as indicator of pain experience and severity, 54
    interdisciplinary, 3–4
Medicine. *See* Medications
Meperidine, **80**
Methadone, 107
    dosing and use, **80**
    multiple uses of, 87–88
    for neuropathic pain, **185**
Methocarbamol, **111**
Methotrimeprazine, 106
Methylphenidate, 104
Mexiletine, 106–107
    for neuropathic pain, **185**
Migraine headache, 168–170
    common aurae associated with, **169**
    treatment, **167,** 170
Minnesota Multiphasic Personality Inventory (MMPI), **50,** 58–60, **60**
Mirtazapine, **96**
MMPI. *See* Minnesota Multiphasic Personality Inventory
Monoamine oxidase inhibitors (MAOIs), 97

Mood, in evaluation of the pain patient, 39–41
Morphine, **80**
    for management of cancer pain, **192**
MPQ. *See* McGill Pain Questionnaire
Multi-axial pain, classification, 31–32
Muscle antispasmodics, 110–111. *See also individual drug names*
    side effects, 110
Muscle relaxants, dosing, **111**. *See also individual drug names*
Mycobacterium leprae, pain perception and, 25
Myofascial pain, 174–175

Nalbuphine, **80**
Nefazodone, **96**
    for tension headache, 166
Nerve ablation, for neuropathic pain, **185**
Neurochemicals, in pain processing, 22–24
Neuroleptics, 106. *See also individual drug names*
Neurons
    first order, 12–14, **14**
    second-order, 15, **17**
    sensory neural fiber types, **14**
    third-order, 16–18
Neuropathic pain, 182–185
    categorization, 27–29, **28**
    origins, 183, **184**
    treatment strategies, 184, **185**
    types, **184**

Neurosurgery. *See also* individual
techniques; Surgery
ablative techniques,
161–162
neural stimulation techniques,
162–164
techniques, 161–164
Neurotensin, in pain processing,
24
Neurotransmitters
inhibitory, 23
nonopiate endogenous
inhibitory, 23–24
in pain processing, 23–24
pain-augmenting, 22–23
N-methyl-D-aspartate (NMDA)
antagonists
dextromethorphan, 108
ketamine, 108
methadone, 107
role in pain, 21, 107–108
Nociceptive pain
categorization, 27–29, **28**
definition, 11
Nonopioid analgesics, 92–94.
*See also individual drug
names*
Nonsteroidal anti-inflammatory
drugs (NSAIDs), 92–94
for migraine headache, 170
for osteoarthritis, 180
for tension headache, 166
Norepinephrine, in pain processing,
24
Nortriptyline, for neuropathic pain,
185
NRS. *See* Numeric rating scale
NSAIDs. *See* Nonsteroidal anti-
inflammatory drugs

Numeric rating scale (NRS), 51,
52, 53

OA. *See* Osteoarthritis
Olanzapine, 106
Opiate analgesics, 79–91. *See also
individual drug names*
abuse, 90
concurrent medical conditions
and, 84
dependence, 89–90
dosing guidelines, **86**
drug interactions, 83–84
guidelines for detoxification
from, 208–209
guidelines for use, 79, 82, **83**
for management of cancer pain,
192
with multiple uses, 87–88
for neuropathic pain, **185**
patient contracts, 90–91, **92**
pseudoaddiction, 89–90
route of administration, 85–87
side effects, 82–83
tolerance, 89–90
Opiate receptors
descending inhibition of
pain pathways and,
24–25
endogenous
in pain processing, 23
physical effects, 24
Orphenadrine, **111**
Osteoarthritis (OA), 179–182
treatment, 179–180, **180**
"Oucher" scale, 202
Overgeneralization, **43**
Oxcarbazepine, 101–102
Oxycodone, **80**

Pain
 acute vs. chronic, 25–32
  categories of chronic, 27–29, **28**
  classifications, 26–27, **27**
  features distinguishing, **27**
  multi-axial pain classification, 31–32
  patient with simple vs. chronic pain, 29–31, **30, 31**
 after healing, 22
 among children, 200–203
 common disorders, 165–195
  back pain, 171–174
  cancer, 189–191
  complex regional pain syndromes, 185–187
  fibromyalgia, 175–179
  headache, 165–171
  HIV/AIDS, 189–192
  myofascial pain, 174–175
  neuropathic pain, 182–185
  osteoarthritis, 179–182
  phantom limb pain, 187–189
  rheumatoid arthritis, 179–182
 common pain states associated with HIV/AIDS, **190**
 control during pregnancy, 203–204
 culture and, 203–204
 dimensions and the biopsychosocial model, 11–12, **11**
 in the elderly, 197–200
 evaluation of the patient, 35–62
 facial, 14
 forensic issues, 219–232
 interdisciplinary pain medicine, 3–4
 litigation and, 225–226
 management, 2–3
  special techniques, 153–164
 medications as indicator of pain experience and severity, 54
 multi-axial classification, 31–32
 nociception, 11
 organic vs. psychogenic causes, 4–5
 pharmacology, 79–117. *See also individual drug names*
 psychiatric comorbidities, 63–77
 psychiatric differential diagnosis and, 63–77
 psychotherapeutic interventions and components of, **119**
 psychotherapy and, 119–151
 relationship between anxiety and, **71**
 role of psychiatrists in multidisciplinary pain medicine, 7–9, **8**
 sensory pathways of, 11–25
 side effects in the elderly, 200
 traditional medical models vs. biopsychosocial paradigms, 4–7, **6**
Pain diary, 54–55, 202–203
Pain disorder, **40**, 63–69
 DSM-IV-TR diagnostic criteria, **65–66**
 with a general medical condition, 64
 other somatoform disorders vs., 64–66
 pain and deceit, 68–69, **69**

psychogenic, 63–64
somatic amplification and its
function, 67–68
somatoform disorders vs., 66
Pain history, 37–48
Pain medicine
certifying examination in, 3
as subspecialty, 3–4
Patient
capacity, 224–225, **224**
competency, 223–224
confidentiality, 221–222
drug contract with opiate
analgesics, 91, **92**
evaluation, 35–62
conducting an interview,
35–37, **36**
coping strategies, 44–45
longitudinal approach, 46–48
pain history, 37–48
components, **36**
obtaining, **38**
problematic cognitive
patterns in pain, **43**
psychological component,
39–45
somatic component,
37–38
social and adaptational
component, 45–46
of treatment suitability, 48
informed consent, 223
pain assessment instruments,
48–60
for acute and chronic pain, **50**
behavioral measures, 53–55
factors that suggest poor
surgical outcome for
pain disorders, **49**

multidimensional pain scales,
55–57
psychological assessments,
57–60
psychometric pain scales, **50**
single dimension scales,
51–53, **52**
with simple vs. complex chronic
pain, 29–31, **30, 31**
social history, 45–46
terminal status, 72
with terminal conditions,
210–215
anger and, 212
family and, 212
hospice care, 212–214, **213**
religious issues and
spirituality, 214–215,
215
–therapist relationship, 127,
221–222, 229–231
Patient-controlled anesthesia
(PCA), 203
Pediatrics, 200–203
pain and childhood
developmental phases,
201
pain assessment scales, 201–203
treatment, 203
Pemoline, 105–106
Pentazocine, **80**
role in pain, 19–20
Peripheral nerve blockade,
159–160
Personality disorders, 74
Personalization **43**
Phantom limb pain, 187–189
surgical interventions, 189
treatment, 189

Pharmacology, of pain, 79–117.
*See also individual drug
names*
α2-adrenergic agonists, 107
anticonvulsant drugs, 100–102
antidepressants, 94–99
antihistamines, 102–103
anxiolytics, 103–104
benzodiazepines, 103–104
corticosteroids, 108–109, **109**
cyclooxygenase-2 (COX-2)
inhibitors, 94
mexiletine, 106–107
muscle antispasmodics, 110–111
neuroleptics, 106
N-methyl-D-aspartate (NMDA)
antagonists, 107–108
dextromethorphan, 108
ketamine, 108
methadone, 107
nonopioid analgesics, 92–94
opiate analgesics, 79–91
placebo effects, 112–113
stimulants, 104–106
topical agents, 111–112
tramadol, 91–92
Phenytoin, side effects, **103**
Placebo effects, 112–113
PMR. *See* Progressive muscle
relaxation
"Poker chip" tool, 202
Posttraumatic stress disorder
(PTSD), 72
Potassium ion, in pain processing,
22
Pregnancy, pain control during,
203–204
Progressive muscle relaxation
(PMR), 144

Propranolol, for migraine headache,
170
Prostaglandins, in pain processing, 22
Pseudoaddiction, 73–74. *See also*
Substance abuse/dependence
of opiate analgesics, 89–90
Psychiatric disorders
accompanying acute and chronic
pain, **40**
pain as a prominent complaint
with, **67**
Psychiatrists, role in
multidisciplinary pain
medicine, 7–9, **8**
Psychogenic pain, categorization,
27–29, **28**
Psychotherapy, 119–151
affect and, 123–125, **125**
behavior therapy, 130–133, **131**
belief systems and cognitive
distortions, 128–130
biofeedback, 142–144
cognitive-behavioral therapy,
133–137, **135**
components of pain and
associated
psychotherapeutic
interventions, **119**
couples therapy, 138–141
defenses and, 125–128, **126**
to facilitate access of emotions,
125
family therapy, 138–141
group therapy, 141–142
hypnosis, 146–148, **149**
marital therapy, 138–141
for pain in the elderly, 200
reasons why emotions are poorly
identified and regulated, **125**

relaxation and imagery training, 144–146, **146**

resistance to, 121–123

supportive therapy, 137–138

vocational rehabilitation, 148–149

Psychotropic drugs, for management of cancer pain, **192**

PTSD. *See* Posttraumatic stress disorder

Quality of life indices, **50**, 56–57

Questionnaires, **50**

RA. *See* Rheumatoid arthritis

R&I. *See* Relaxation and imagery training

Reflex sympathetic dystrophy. *See* Complex regional pain syndromes

Regional neural blockade (RNB), 155–161

anesthesia at the level of the spinal cord, 156–159, **157, 158, 159**

autonomic nerve blocks, **161**

dermatomal levels for spinal anesthesia, **157**

peripheral nerve blockade, 159–160

purpose, 156

subarachnoid and epidural analgesia

complications and contraindications, **158**

risks of continuous anesthetic infusions, **159**

sympathetic nerve blockade, 160, **161**

Reinterpretation, **149**

Relaxation and imagery (R&I) training, 144–146, **146**

for migraine headache, 170

for neuropathic pain, 184, **185**

for pain in the elderly, 200

for tension headache, 166

Religious issues, with terminal patient, 214–215, **215**

Restless legs syndrome, 176

Rexed layers, role in pain, 14–15

Rheumatoid arthritis (RA), 179–182

treatment, **181**

Rhizotomy, for neuropathic pain, **185**

Risperidone, 106

RNB. *See* Regional neural blockade

Rostroventral medulla (RVM), role in pain, 19–20

RVM. *See* Rostroventral medulla

Schemata, 128–130

Schizophrenia, 74–75

Selective abstraction, **43**

Selective serotonin reuptake inhibitors (SSRIs), **96**, 98

Self-fulfilling prophecies, **43**

Sensations, substitution, **149**

Sensory-discriminative pathway, **17**

Sensory pathways, 11–25

assessment, 11, **11**

autonomic nervous system's role in pain, 18–19

opiate receptors and descending inhibition of pain pathways, 24–25

Sensory pathways *(continued)*
pain-modulating processes
within the central nervous
system, 19–24
neurochemicals in pain
processing, 22–24
endogenous opiates, 23
inhibitory
neurotransmitters, 23
nonopiate endogenous
inhibitory
neurotransmitters,
23–24
pain-augmenting
neurotransmitters,
22–23
pain-augmenting mechanisms
and emergence of
chronic pain, 20–22, **21**
pain-reducing pathways,
19–20
pain-relaying pathways and
mechanisms, 12–18
dorsal horn anatomy,
14–16
first-order neurons, 12–14, **14**
second-order neurons, 16, **17**
third-order neurons, 16–18
Serotonin, in pain processing, 22,
23–24
Sexual abuse, 47–48
Sexual dysfunction, **40**
Sleep disorders, **40**
in the elderly, 200
Social Security disability, 228,
228
Somatization disorder, **40**
Somatoform disorders, **40**
pain disorder vs., 66

Sphenopalatine ganglion block,
161
Spinal stimulation, for neuropathic
pain, **185**
Spinothalamic tract, 16, **17**
SSRIs. *See* Selective serotonin
reuptake inhibitors
Stellate ganglion block, **161**
Stimulants, 104–106. *See also*
individual drug names
Subarachnoid analgesia
complications and
contraindications, **158**
risks of continuous anesthetic
infusions, **159**
Substance abuse/dependence, **40,**
73–74, 206–210. *See also*
pseudoaddiction
detoxification, 206–207, 209
guidelines for detoxification
from opiates, 208–209
iatrogenic drug dependence,
207–208
of opiate analgesics, 89–90
Substance P, in pain processing,
22–23
Substantia gelatinosa, role in pain, 15
Sumatriptan, for migraine
headache, 170
Superior mesenteric ganglion
block, **161**
Supportive therapy, 137–138
Surgery. *See also* individual
techniques; Neurosurgery
factors that suggest poor surgical
outcome for pain disorders,
49
intervention for phantom limb
pain, 189

neurosurgical techniques for
pain management, 161–164
postoperative pain, 49
Sympathetic nerve blockade, 160,
161
for neuropathic pain, **185**
Sympathetic nervous system,
ongoing pain and, 21–22

*Tarasoff v. Regents of the University
of California,* 222
TENS. *See* Transcutaneous
electrical nerve stimulation
Tension headache (TH), 165–168
factors influencing likelihood of
response to
psychotherapeutic
measures, **167**
treatment, 166–168, **167**
Time disorientation, **149**
Timolol, for migraine headache, 170
Tizanidine, **111**
Topical agents, 111–112. *See also
individual drug names*
for neuropathic pain, 184, **185**
Topiramate, 101–102
Tramadol, 91–92
for neuropathic pain, **185**
Transcutaneous electrical nerve
stimulation (TENS), 15, 155
for neuropathic pain, 184, **185**
for pain in the elderly, 200
Transducers, role in pain, 12–13
Trazodone, 99, **96**

Tricyclic antidepressants, 95–97,
96, 97
side effects, **97**
for tension headache, 166

U.S. Constitution, 223

VA. *See* Veterans Administration
benefits
Valproate
for migraine headache, 170
side effects, **103**
Valproic acid
for neuropathic pain, **185**
VAS. *See* Visual analog scale
VDS. *See* Verbal descriptor scales
Venlafaxine, **96**, 98–99
Ventral posterior nucleus (VPN),
role in pain, 16
Verbal descriptor scales (VDS), 51,
52
Veterans Administration (VA)
benefits, 228–229
Visual analog scale (VAS), 51, **52,**
53
Vocational rehabilitation, 148–149
VPN. *See* Ventral posterior nucleus

West Haven–Yale
Multidimensional Pain
Inventory (WHYMPI), **50,**
57–58
Wind up, 21
Workers' compensation, 227

Types of painful neuropathies 184
Treatment strategies for neuropathic pain 185
Treatment of complex regional pain syndrome. 187
Common pain states associated with HIV/AIDS 190
Management of cancer pain and pain associated
  with HIV and AIDS, based on pain ratings 192

9 Special Populations

Barriers to pain management in minority patients 205
Medicare requirements for hospice care 213
Approaches to dealing with spiritual issues 215

10 Forensic Issues Pertaining to Pain

Guide for assessing capacity 224
Limitations considered by Social Security
  Administration adjudicators 228

6 Psychotherapy

Components of pain and associated psychotherapeutic
interventions. 119
Psychotherapy interventions employed to facilitate
access of emotions 125
Reasons why emotions are poorly identified
and regulated 125
Early psychodynamic conceptualizations of pain. 126
Steps of behavior therapy 131
Script for breathing exercise. 146
Techniques of hypnosis 149

7 Special Techniques in Pain Management

Dermatomal levels for spinal anesthesia 157
Complications and contraindications of subarachnoid
and epidural analgesia 158
Risks of continuous epidural or subarachnoid anesthetic
infusions. 159
Uses of autonomic nerve blocks. 161

8 Common Pain Disorders

Treatment of headache 167
Factors influencing likelihood of response to
psychotherapeutic measures in patients
with tension headache 167
Common aurae associated with migraine headache 169
Common causes of back pain 172
Treatment options for back pain 174
Diagnostic criteria for fibromyalgia 175
Features associated with fibromyalgia 177
Treatment strategies for fibromyalgia. 178
Treatment of osteoarthritis 180
Treatment of rheumatoid arthritis. 181

Factors that suggest poor surgical outcome for
  pain disorders 49
Psychometric pain scales used in assessing
  chronic pain. 50
Pain assessment instruments for acute and
  chronic pain. 50
Short form of the McGill Pain Questionnaire 56

---

4 Common Psychiatric Comorbidities and Psychiatric Differential Diagnosis of the Pain Patient

DSM-IV-TR diagnostic criteria for pain
  disorder. 65
Psychiatric disorders in which pain can be a prominent
  complaint 67
Factors that raise suspicion of malingering. 69

---

5 Pharmacology of Pain

Opiate dosing and use 80
Opioid therapy guidelines for chronic nonmalignant
  pain 83
Dosing guidelines 86
Items to be factored into patient contract for use with
  controlled substances 92
Antidepressant use in chronic pain 96
Tricyclic antidepressant side effects 97
Uses of anticonvulsants in various pain conditions. 101
Side effects of anticonvulsants 103
Controversies associated with benzodiazepine use
  in chronic pain 105
Side effects of corticosteroid use in pain. 109
Dosing of muscle relaxants 111

LIST OF TABLES

1 Introduction

Traditional versus biopsychosocial models
of pain. 6

Role of psychiatrists in pain management
(biopsychosocial approach) 8

2 Sensory Pathways of Pain and Acute Versus Chronic Pain

Dimensions of pain and the biopsychosocial model. 11

Sensory neural fiber types. 14

Causes of chronic pain 21

Features distinguishing acute and chronic pain 27

Categories of chronic pain 28

Common problems encountered by patients with
chronic pain 30

Simple versus complex chronic pain 31

3 Evaluation of the Pain Patient

Obtaining a pain history 38

Psychiatric disorders accompanying acute and
chronic pain 40

Problematic cognitive patterns in pain 43

Patients With Terminal Conditions	210
Hospice Care	212
Religious Issues and Spirituality	214
References	216

10 Forensic Issues Pertaining to Pain 219

Medication Diversion	219
Confidentiality	221
Informed Consent, Competency, and Capacity	223
Informed Consent	223
Competency	223
Capacity	224
Litigation and Pain	225
Disability Compensation	226
Disability Versus Impairment	226
Workers' Compensation	227
Social Security Disability	228
Veterans Administration Benefits	228
Disability and the Doctor–Patient Relationship	229
References	231

Index 233

8 Common Pain Disorders 165

Headache. 165
   Tension Headache 165
   Migraine Headache 168
   Cluster Headache. 171
Back Pain 171
Nonarticular Pain Disorders 174
   Myofascial Pain. 174
   Fibromyalgia 175
Osteoarthritis and Rheumatoid Arthritis. 179
Neuropathic Pain. 182
Sympathetically Mediated Pain: Complex Regional Pain
   Syndromes 185
   Characteristics of Complex
      Regional Pain Syndromes. 186
   Treatment. 186
Phantom Limb Pain 187
Cancer and HIV 189
References. 192

9 Special Populations. 197

Geriatrics. 197
   Underrecognition of Pain in Elderly Patients 198
   Treatment Strategies 199
Pediatrics. 200
   Pain and Childhood Developmental Phases 201
   Pain Assessment Scales. 201
Pregnancy 203
Cultural Issues. 204
Substance-Dependent and
   Substance-Abusing Patients. 206
   Iatrogenic Drug Dependence. 207
   General Guidelines for Detoxification
      From Opiates. 208
   Detoxification From Other Agents 209

6	**Psychotherapy**	**119**

Resistance to Psychotherapy 121
Factors to Be Addressed in Psychotherapy 123
    Affect 123
    Defenses 125
    Belief Systems and Cognitive Distortions 128
Behavior Therapy 130
Cognitive-Behavioral Therapy 133
Supportive Therapy 137
Marital, Couples, and Family Therapy 138
Group Therapy 141
Adjunctive Interventions 142
    Biofeedback 142
    Relaxation and Imagery Training 144
    Hypnosis 146
Vocational Rehabilitation 148
References 149

7	**Special Techniques in Pain Management**	**153**

Acupuncture 153
    Technique 154
    Indications 154
    Complications 154
    Contraindications 155
Transcutaneous Electrical Nerve Stimulation 155
Regional Neural Blockade 155
    Anesthesia at the Level of the Spinal Cord 156
    Peripheral Nerve Blockade 159
    Sympathetic Nerve Blockade 160
Neurosurgical Techniques: Treatment of Last Resort 161
    Ablative Techniques 161
    Neural Stimulation Techniques 162
    References 164

5	**Pharmacology of Pain**	**79**

Opiate Analgesics 79
    Guidelines for Use 79
    Tolerance, Dependence, and Pseudoaddiction 89
    Opiate Abuse 90
    Patient Contracts 90
Tramadol 91
Nonopioid Analgesics 92
    Cyclooxygenase-2 Inhibitors 94
Antidepressants 94
    Tricyclic Antidepressants 95
    Monoamine Oxidase Inhibitors 97
    Selective Serotonin Reuptake Inhibitors 98
    Other Antidepressants 98
Anticonvulsant Drugs 100
Antihistamines 102
Benzodiazepines and Anxiolytics 103
Stimulants 104
Neuroleptics 106
Mexiletine 106
α2-Adrenergic Agonists 107
N-Methyl-D-Aspartate Antagonists 107
    Methadone 107
    Ketamine 108
    Dextromethorphan 108
Corticosteroids 108
Muscle Antispasmodics 110
Topical Agents 111
    Capsaicin 111
    Lidocaine Patch 112
    Eutectic Mixture of Local Anesthetics 112
Placebo Effects 112
References 113

"Patienthood" as a Psychosocial State:
   The Patient With Simple Versus Chronic Pain 29
   Multi-Axial Pain Classification 31
References 32

3 Evaluation of the Pain Patient. 35

Conducting an Interview 35
Obtaining the Pain History 37
   Somatic Component. 37
   Psychological Component 39
   Social and Adaptational Component 45
   Longitudinal Approach 46
   Evaluation of Treatment Suitability 48
Pain Assessment Instruments 48
   Single Dimension Scales 51
   Behavioral Measures 53
   Multidimensional Pain Scales 55
   Psychological Assessments 57
References 60

4 Common Psychiatric Comorbidities and Psychiatric Differential Diagnosis of the Pain Patient. 63

Pain Disorder. 63
   Pain Disorder Versus Other Somatoform Disorders . . . 64
   Somatic Amplification and Its Function 67
   Pain and Deceit 68
Depression. 69
Anxiety 70
Substance-Related Disorders. 73
Personality Disorders. 74
Schizophrenia 74
References 75

CONTENTS

Introduction to the Concise Guides Series. . . . . **xix**

---

1 Introduction 1

Pain Management 2
Interdisciplinary Pain Medicine 3
Traditional Medical Models of Pain Versus
    Biopsychosocial Paradigms 4
The Role of Psychiatrists in Multidisciplinary
    Pain Medicine. 7
References. 9

---

2 Sensory Pathways of Pain and Acute Versus Chronic Pain. 11

Sensory Pathways 12
    Pain-Relaying Pathways and Mechanisms 12
    The Autonomic Nervous System's Role in Pain. 18
    Pain-Modulating Processes Within the Central
        Nervous System 19
    Opiate Receptors and Descending Inhibition of
        Pain Pathways. 24
Acute Versus Chronic Pain. 25
    Classifications of Acute and Chronic Pain 26
    Categories of Chronic Pain 27

To my parents, Carmela and Olivio,
and my close friends, John Brink and James Serapiglia,
for their support and encouragement

Note: The authors have worked to ensure that all information in this book is accurate at the time of publication and consistent with general psychiatric and medical standards, and that information concerning drug dosages, schedules, and routes of administration is accurate at the time of publication and consistent with standards set by the U. S. Food and Drug Administration and the general medical community. As medical research and practice continue to advance, however, therapeutic standards may change. Moreover, specific situations may require a specific therapeutic response not included in this book. For these reasons and because human and mechanical errors sometimes occur, we recommend that readers follow the advice of physicians directly involved in their care or the care of a member of their family.

Books published by American Psychiatric Publishing, Inc., represent the views and opinions of the individual authors and do not necessarily represent the policies and opinions of APPI or the American Psychiatric Association.

Copyright © 2003 American Psychiatric Publishing, Inc.
ALL RIGHTS RESERVED

Typeset in Adobe's Times and Helvetica.

Manufactured in the United States of America on acid-free paper
07 06 05 04 03   5 4 3 2 1
First Edition

American Psychiatric Publishing, Inc.
1000 Wilson Boulevard
Arlington, VA 22209
www.appi.org

Library of Congress Cataloging-in-Publication Data
Leo, Raphael J., 1962-
    Concise guide to pain management for psychiatrists / Raphael J. Leo.– 1st ed.
        p. ; cm — (Concise guides)
    Includes bibliographical references and index.
    ISBN 158562103X (alk. paper)
    1. Pain–Treatment–Handbooks, manuals, etc. 2. Pain–Psychological aspects–Handbooks, manuals, etc. 3. Psychotherapy–Handbooks, manuals, etc. 4. Chronic pain–Handbooks, manuals, etc. I. Title. II. Concise guides (American Psychiatric Publishing)
    [DNLM: 1. Pain–therapy. 2. Pain–psychology. WL 704 L576c 2003]
    RB127.L397 2003
    616'.0472–dc21

    2002043676

British Library Cataloguing in Publication Data
A CIP record is available from the British Library.

CONCISE GUIDE TO
Pain Management for Psychiatrists

Raphael J. Leo, M.D.
Medical Director, University Consultation-Liaison Services
Department of Psychiatry
State University of New York at Buffalo
School of Medicine and Biomedical Sciences
Buffalo, New York

Washington, DC
London, England

CONCISE GUIDES

Robert E. Hales, M.D.
Series Editor

CONCISE GUIDE TO
Pain Management for Psychiatrists

In memory of my father and
to my mother

Acknowledgments

Writing this acknowledgment is a pleasure, for it gives me a chance to give public thanks to the many individuals and institutions who have helped me in the writing of this book.

The starting point for any researcher into the rights of ex-offenders is the Special Project "The Collateral Consequences of a Criminal Conviction" [23 VANDERBILT LAW REVIEW 929 (1970)]. It is a distinguished, comprehensive effort, and its imprint can be found throughout this book.

Noel Dennis, Bobbi Bonfeld, and Karen Goldstein did prodigious research. Noel Dennis's research formed the basis for chapters IX and XI; he also assisted with checking sources in other chapters. Bobbi Bonfeld's research formed the basis for Appendix A. Karen Goldstein's research formed the basis of Chapter X.

The Commission on Correctional Facilities and Services sponsored by the American Bar Association was very generous in sharing with me its research into the problems of ex-offenders. I profited considerably from interviews with Melvin T. Axilbund, Donald Cook, Robert Horowitz, and James Hunt of the commission. I was also helped by Gary Weissman and William R. Thruckmorton, Sr., of the United States Department of Labor; Polly Feingold; Robert Plotkin of the Mental Health Law Project; and the staffs of the ACLU National Prison Project and the Legal Action Center.

Special thanks are due to my colleagues at the New

York Civil Liberties Union and to the Union itself. I would also like to acknowledge the financial assistance of The Fund for the City of New York and the Florence V. Burden Foundation; both have supported my work in criminal justice over the years.

I owe a large debt to Kathy Durkin, my indefatigable secretary. Her superb skills, high sense of responsibility, and patience were and are greatly appreciated.

I'm very grateful to the warmhearted folks who worked on the second floor of Larsen Hall at the Harvard Graduate School of Education during 1977. They cheerfully shared with me their already crowded office space and made me feel quite at home.

Lastly, my deepest thanks to Zina Steinberg. Although her sacrifices nearly equaled my own in the writing of this book, she robustly supported it to the last.

Contents

	Preface	11
	Introduction	13
I.	An Overview of Civil Disabilities	15
II.	The Right to Retain Citizenship	24
III.	The Right to Become a Citizen	29
IV.	The Right to Hold Public Office	34
V.	The Right to Vote	42
VI.	Domestic Rights	50
	A. Divorce	50
	B. The Right to Marry and Procreate	55
	C. Sterilization	56
	D. Parental Rights	60
	E. The Right to Change Your Name	65
VII.	The Right to Employment	71
	A. Employers and Their Practices	74
	The Government as Employer	74
	Private Employers	77
	Occupational Licensing	80
	B. The Right to Employment	88
	The Right to Public Employment and Occupational Licensing	88
	The Right to Private Employment	96
VIII.	Property, Insurance, Pensions, Contracts, Miscellaneous	104
IX.	The Right to Be a Juror	119
X.	The Right to Be a Witness	126
XI.	Criminal-Registration Statutes	133

XII.	The Restoration of Lost Rights	140
XIII.	Changing the Law	154
	Appendices	
	A. Voting Rights	159
	B. Licensing Restrictions	171
	C. Legal Assistance	196
	D. Organizations Providing Job Assistance to Ex-Offenders	201
	E. Legal Standards	234

Preface

This guide sets forth your rights under present law and offers suggestions on how you can protect your rights. It is one of a continuing series of handbooks published in cooperation with the American Civil Liberties Union.

The hope surrounding these publications is that Americans informed of their rights will be encouraged to exercise them. Through their exercise, rights are given life. If they are rarely used, they may be forgotten and violations may become routine.

This guide offers no assurances that your rights will be respected. The laws may change and, in some of the subjects covered in these pages, they change quite rapidly. An effort has been made to note those parts of the law where movement is taking place but it is not always possible to predict accurately when the law *will* change.

Even if the laws remain the same, interpretations of them by courts and administrative officials often vary. In a federal system such as ours, there is a built-in problem of the differences between state and federal law, not to speak of the confusion of the differences from state to state. In addition, there are wide variations in the ways in which particular courts and administrative officials will interpret the same law at any given moment.

If you encounter what you consider to be a specific abuse of your rights you should seek legal assistance. There are a number of agencies that may help you, among them ACLU affiliate offices, but bear in mind that the

ACLU is a limited-purpose organization. In many communities, there are federally funded legal service offices which provide assistance to poor persons who cannot afford the costs of legal representation. In general, the rights that the ACLU defends are freedom of inquiry and expression; due process of law; equal protection of the laws; and privacy. The authors in this series have discussed other rights in these books (even though they sometimes fall outside the ACLU's usual concern) in order to provide as much guidance as possible.

These books have been planned as guides for the people directly affected: therefore the question and answer format. In some of these areas there are more detailed works available for "experts." These guides seek to raise the largest issues and inform the nonspecialist of the basic law on the subject. The authors of the books are themselves specialists who understand the need for information at "street level."

No attorney can be an expert in every part of the law. If you encounter a specific legal problem in an area discussed in one of these handbooks, show the book to your attorney. Of course, he will not be able to rely *exclusively* on the handbook to provide you with adequate representation. But if he hasn't had a great deal of experience in the specific area, the handbook can provide helpful suggestions on how to proceed.

Norman Dorsen, Chairperson
American Civil Liberties Union

Aryeh Neier, Executive Director
American Civil Liberties Union

The principal purpose of these handbooks is to inform individuals of their rights. The authors from time to time suggest what the law should be. When this is done, the views expressed are not necessarily those of the American Civil Liberties Union.

Introduction

Apart from punishment imposed because of a conviction, a convicted person loses many important civil and constitutional rights and many commonly accepted privileges of citizenship. For years after a person has been discharged from probation or parole or has completed a prison term, paid a fine, or complied with a restitution order, a conviction may curtail his* right to vote, hold political office, obtain an occupational or professional license, or serve as a juror. These and other severe consequences result from a conviction and are imposed automatically by law and remain effective throughout a person's life.

These consequences are collateral to a conviction and are commonly called "civil disabilities." They are rooted in history and are out of place in today's society. Despite severe criticism by scholars, study commissions, judges, lawyers, corrections officials, prisoners, and ex-convicts that they are unfair, harsh, and counterproductive, civil disabilities are remarkably resistant to change. Although the unquestionable trend is to reduce civil disabilities in number and scope, the collateral consequences of a conviction are a severe problem for the ex-offender.

This book is about the rights of ex-offenders—that is, people convicted of crimes who have served their entire

* Because the overwhelming portion of ex-offenders are men, male pronouns are generally used in this book except for one section of Chapter VI.

sentences and are no longer under jurisdiction of the state as a result of the convictions. It discusses questions such as: May they vote? Must they register with the local police when they go to a new town? May they be licensed as barbers, chauffeurs, private guards, ambulance attendants, or accountants? May they work as high government officials in a government drug or rehabilitation program? May they sit on a school board, work for a law enforcement agency, run for mayor? Will a conviction automatically dissolve their marriages? Will an innocent spouse be able to terminate a convicted person's rights as a parent? May they get a passport to travel abroad? May the rights lost because of a conviction be restored?

As will be quickly clear, only a few of these questions may be answered easily and with certainty. Often the answer varies from state to state; occasionally the answer varies within a state. In few cases, it is not possible to give a definitive answer for any jurisdiction.

The question of collateral consequences of a conviction has been largely ignored—that is, ignored by everyone except ex-offenders. Only recently have bar associations, scholars, and social reformers focused on the problems of ex-convicts and the way in which civil disabilities create and compound these problems. But this attention to the ex-offender has begun to have an impact. Legislatures and the courts are displaying a new sensitivity to the rights of convicted persons. The abominable "civil-death" statutes are slowly being repealed, statutes restoring rights are being adopted, and courts seem less hesitant than in the past to invalidate a civil disability as unconstitutional. Although these developments suggest that ex-offenders may look forward to fairer treatment in the future, they have not yet wrought the changes fairness requires.

Current law continues to disparage the ex-offender and struggles to escape the irrationalities of its own history. It must be changed if the legal status of the ex-offender is to comport with simple dignity and equality.

I
An Overview of Civil Disabilities

What is a civil disability?
A civil disability is the loss of a civil or constitutional right such as the right to vote, hold public office or serve on a jury upon conviction of a crime. This loss, which is usually automatic and often permanent, is different from any sanction such as a fine or imprisonment that may be imposed following a conviction. Civil disabilities, which have usually been thought of as a collateral consequence to a conviction, are harsh and have been criticized in many quarters.

What is a disabling law?
A disabling law imposes a civil disability.

Who is affected by disabling laws?
Anyone convicted of a serious crime may lose some of his civil or constitutional rights.

How many living Americans have been convicted of a crime at one time or another?
No one knows how many living adult Americans have conviction records. We know how many violent crimes are committed annually, how many Americans are arrested annually, and how many Americans are in prison on any given day. But we do not know how many living Americans

have at one time or another been determined guilty of a crime. By all accounts, however, it is several million.

How many kinds of disabling laws are there?

Basically two. There are laws which withdraw specific rights from a person, such as the right to vote or to serve on a jury. There are also "civil-death" statutes, which deem a person civilly dead in the eyes of the law. The intent of a civil-death statute is to withdraw all legal rights from a person.

What is a civil-death statute?

A civil-death statute is a blanket provision that deprives a criminal of all rights while imprisoned. These rights are not restored until a person is released from prison, and then only partially. Although civil death is an antiquated concept, it has had a profound impact in shaping the law pertinent to the ex-offender.

A typical civil-death statute provides: "A person sentenced to imprisonment in the state prison for life is thereafter deemed civilly dead" and a "sentence of imprisonment in a state prison for any time less than for life suspends all the civil rights of the person so sentenced, and forfeits all public offices and all private trusts, authority and power during such imprisonment."[1]

Courts in this country hold that the doctrine of civil death does not apply unless it is provided for by statute, and then it is strictly construed.

Is the doctrine of civil death in disfavor?

Yes. About five states now have civil-death statutes and the number is diminishing.[2]

Is the doctrine of civil death constitutional?

As a general matter, the constitutionality of civil death has not often been questioned. As applied to specific rights such as the right of access to the courts, however, the doctrine has not only been questioned but invalidated.[3]

What are some of the rights a person may lose because of specific civil-disability statutes?

The more common method for withdrawing rights as a

result of a conviction is through the adoption of specific disabilities which take effect upon conviction and remain effective unless removed by statute. The range of specific disabilities is enormous, including such traditional rights as the right to vote, hold public office, serve as juror, and obtain professional and occupational licenses.

How common are civil-disability laws?

Very. Every state, the federal government, the District of Columbia, every major city, and most towns, villages, and hamlets have disabling laws.

Are civil disabilities the same in every state?

No. There is tremendous variation in disabling laws from one state to another and between the states and the federal government.

Most civil disabilities are embodied in state law, and usually these restrictions are embodied in statutes, although some state constitutions contain disabling provisions. The United States Constitution does not impose any civil disabilities.

Because courts have hesitated to invalidate civil disabilities on federal constitutional grounds, the collateral consequences of a conviction are peculiarly a matter of state and local government prerogative.

What is the extent of disabling laws?

We don't know exactly. There is no complete index of these laws. And one could not be compiled without being outdated by the time it was completed.

The most thorough recent review of disabling laws is the 1970 Special Project by the staff of the *Vanderbilt Law Review* entitled "The Collateral Consequences of a Criminal Conviction."[4] This exceptional study is the most important reference in the field. Even it, however, does not pretend to have identified all disabling laws.

Two of the more important specialized reports are Herbert S. Miller's *The Closed Door: The Effect of a Criminal Record on Employment with State and Local Public Agencies*[5]; and George A. Pownall's *Employment Problems of Released Prisoners*.[6] These two excellent reports review employment discrimination against ex-convicts.

What types of crimes result in civil disabilities?

There are three general categories of disabling crimes: (1) felonies, (2) infamous crimes, and (3) crimes involving moral turpitude. These categories overlap, but they are not coterminous. States use one, two, or all three of these categories of crimes in determining when civil disabilities are imposed.

A crime categorized as a *felony* presents little interpretative problem. Both the common law and current statutory law have developed simple, objective standards of determining whether a crime is a felony. Generally, this standard reflects the degree of punishment that may be imposed upon the convicted defendant. Thus, in New York, a felony is statutorily defined as any crime for which the minimum period of imprisonment is at least one year.[7] While the definition of a felony may vary from one jurisdiction to another, it is defined with similar certainty in nearly all jurisdictions.

The category of *infamous crimes* is much more difficult to define. Although the phrase "infamous crime" is rooted in history, that history tends to cloud rather than clarify its meaning. Historically, the phrase "infamous crime" was applied to the commission of a fraudulent or untrustworthy act. That relatively narrow focus, however, has been generally replaced by two themes, both expanding substantially the definition of the term. An infamous crime is now defined as a crime involving an infamous punishment, defined as death or imprisonment,[8] or as any crime that breaches the moral principles of the community.[9] Under the latter standard, crimes categorized as felonies or misdemeanors have been held to be infamous crimes.[10] Because the concept of "a community's moral principles" is elastic and ambiguous, it is often uncertain what crimes are infamous crimes within a particular jurisdiction. Obviously states differ in their interpretation of this term.

Some states impose a civil disability upon a person convicted of a crime involving *moral turpitude,* a vague term which is broadly defined and includes misdemeanors and felonies. The meaning of the term "moral turpitude" varies from state to state and over time, but the definition always depends on the nature of the act committed, not on the severity of the punishment imposed.[11]

A misdemeanor which is not categorized as an infamous

crime or crime involving moral turpitude does not usually spawn a civil disability.

Will a person who pleads *nolo contendere* be subjected to civil disabilities?

Probably.[12] The literal meaning of *nolo contendere* is "I do not wish to contend." The term has been subjected to many interpretations, including that it is a confession, an implied confession, a plea of guilty, a compromise between the government and the accused, and an agreement on the part of the accused that the facts charged may be considered as true for the purposes of the particular case. In deciding whether a person is subject to civil disabilities, a plea of *nolo contendere* is generally considered the same as a plea of guilty.

Will a mere arrest result in the imposition of civil disabilities?

No. Statutes that automatically impose civil disabilities are triggered by convictions. However, an arrest may influence an administrative agency, especially one responsible for licensing occupations. The statutes guiding licensing agencies are usually vague and authorize the rejection of an application not only because of a conviction but because of "disgraceful conduct" or a similar category. A licensing agency may view an arrest or the circumstances surrounding an arrest as relevant to these provisions.

When are civil disabilities imposed?

There are three distinct moments within the criminal process at which civil disabilities may be imposed. Because legislatures have tended not to specify when particular disabilities become effective, courts must usually decide the issue. As a result, the rule varies from one state to another, and, at times, within a state depending on the particular disability in question.

The three moments are as follows:

> First, a few states impose civil disabilities, especially the right to hold public office, upon the determination of guilt. Thus, in these states, disabilities will affect a defendant upon the plea of guilty, a verdict of guilty

by a jury after trial, or the finding of guilt by a court when a jury trial has been waived.[13]

Second, some states impose civil disabilities only after a determination of guilt and the imposition of judgment and sentence, but before the completion of any appeal.[14] Civil disabilities in these states apply to a convicted defendant whether the sentence be imprisonment, the suspension of the sentence, or probation. In these states, however, a convicted defendant will not be subject to civil disabilities if a court suspends the imposition of the judgment *and* sentence.

Third, other states impose civil disabilities upon the completion of appeals.[15] The one broad exception to this rule is the right to hold public office. Here it is usually argued that because a guilty officeholder has lost the public trust necessary to perform the duties of public office, removal should occur either upon the determination of guilt or the imposition of a sentence.[16] Because this rule yields a harsh result if a conviction is reversed, some states will not remove a public officeholder until appeals are completed.[17]

Will one state's civil disabilities be imposed upon a person because of a conviction in another state?

Most states will impose their civil disabilities upon a person who has been convicted of a crime in another state. Civil-disability statutes are supposedly designed to protect the public's interest rather than punish the offender. Because the public's interest is unchanged regardless of the state in which the person was convicted, courts conclude that the legislation setting forth specific disabilities were intended to apply to foreign convictions.[18]

What are the dominant qualities of civil disabilities?

Civil disabilities are imposed upon convicted individuals automatically. Normally a statute barring a person from voting, holding public office, serving as a juror, or obtaining an occupational license expressly provides that it is effective upon conviction. No other action by the state or the individual is required prior to the imposition of the disability. Thus, variations in individual circumstances make no difference; in fact, there is no process by which they may be considered prior to the imposition of a civil disability.

Civil-disability laws are overly broad. The laws of most jurisdictions provide for a blanket imposition of disabilities upon offenders convicted of serious crimes. These laws do not differentiate among offenders on the basis of individual background. A first offender convicted of a less serious felony is treated the same as a multiple offender convicted of a more serious felony. Nor do these laws correlate particular disabilities with related crimes. The pattern in all jurisdictions is to impose the same or a similar set of disabilities on all offenders regardless of the nature of the underlying crime.

The pattern of civil disabilities within a jurisdiction or among jurisdictions is inconsistent. For example, within a particular state, conviction of a crime may disqualify employees in certain occupations, but not others, from receiving pension benefits. Similarly, a conviction may bar an offender from some licensed occupations but not from other related ones.

Moreover, the specific disabilities imposed as a result of a conviction vary widely among states. Hence some states allow convicted felons to vote and serve as jurors, others do not. These variations are enhanced by differing judicial interpretations of such important terms as "infamous crime" or "crime involving moral turpitude." States also differ in the definition of the term "conviction" and in the respect they accord a foreign conviction or the restoration of civil rights by a foreign jurisdiction. These enormous variations among jurisdictions cast doubt on the substantiality and soundness of the reasons most often professed to support disabilities.

Some civil disabilities, especially occupational and professional licenses, are often applied in accordance with vague and ambiguous standards. The most common of these requirements is that a person have "good moral character" in order to secure a particular license. The phrase "good moral character" is not defined, but is often used to deny a license to an otherwise eligible ex-convict. Surely not all ex-convicts are without good moral character, but licensing agencies regularly assume that they are. Even when a licensing agency is more flexible toward ex-convicts, it does not define the vague term "good moral character."

Most civil disabilities last forever. All states have one or more procedures for restoring an individual's civil rights, but these procedures are not automatic and none remove all disabilities. Consequently, most ex-convicts will suffer the loss of rights for an exceedingly long time if not for life.

In sum, the dominant qualities of civil disabilities are that they are automatically imposed, overly broad, inconsistent, vague, and interminable.

NOTES

1. IDAHO CODE ANN. §§ 18–311, 18–310 (1948).
2. *See, e.g.,* ARIZ. REV. STAT. § 13–1653 (1956); IDAHO CODE §§ 18–310, 18–311 (1948); Mo. ANN. STAT. § 222.010 (1959); R.I. GEN. LAWS §§ 13–6–1 to –2 (1956); S.D. COMPILED LAWS ANN. § 23–48–35 (1967).
3. Thompson v. Bond, 421 F. Supp. 878 (W.D. Mo. 1926) (three-judge court); Bush v. Reid, 516 P. 2d 1215 (Alaska 1973); Delorme v. Pierce Freightlines Co., 353 F. Supp. 258 (D. Or. 1973). *See also* Note, *Civil Death Statutes and the Convict's Right to Bring Civil Suit,* 4 CAP. U.L. REV. 123 (1975).
4. Special Project, *The Collateral Consequences of a Conviction,* 23 VANDERBILT L. REV. 929 (1970). For other surveys *see:* Note, *The Effect of State Statutes on the Civil Rights of Convicts,* 47 MINN. L. REV. 835 (1963). Note, *Criminals' Loss of Civil Rights,* XVI U. of FLA. L. REV. 328 (1963); Note *Civil Disabilities of Felons,* 53 VA. L. REV. 403 (1967); Damaska, *Adverse Legal Consequences of Conviction and Their Removal: A Comparative Study,* 59 J. CRIM. L.C. & P.S. 347 (1968); Portnoy, *Employment of Former Offenders,* 55 CORNELL L. REV. 306 (1970); Note, *Reducing Civil Disabilities for Convicted Felons in North Dakota: A Step in the Right Direction,* 50 N.D.L. REV. 61 (1973); Note, *New Approaches to the Civil Disabilities of Ex-Offenders,* 64 KENT L. REV. 382 (1975).
5. Published in 1972 and distributed by National Technical Information Service, Springfield, Va. 22151.
6. Published in 1969 and distributed by National Technical Information Service, Springfield, Va. 22151.
7. N.Y. PENAL LAW § 10.00(5) (McKinney 1975).

AN OVERVIEW OF CIVIL DISABILITIES 23

8. *Ex parte* Wilson, 114 U.S. 417, 422–29 (1885); Mackin v. United States, 117 U.S. 348, 351–52 (1886).
9. *See* Johnson v. State, 4 Md. App. 648, 244 A. 2d 632 (1968).
10. State *ex rel.* Stinger v. Krueger, 280 Mo. 293, 305–06, 217 S.W. 310, 313 (1919); State v. O'Shields, 163 S.C. 408, 161 S.E. 692 (1931).
11. Courts have rejected challenges that the term is unconstitutionally vague. *See, e.g.,* Jordan v. De George, 341 U.S. 223 (1951).
12. *But see* State v. Thrower, 272 Ala. 344, 131 So. 2d 420 (1961).
13. *See, e.g.,* GA. CODE ANN. § 26–401(d) (Revision 1969); ILL. ANN. STAT. ch. 38, § 2–5 (Smith Hurd 1964); LA. CODE CRIM. PRO. ANN. art. 934(3) (West 1967); MONT. REV. CODES ANN. § 94–4809 (1969).
14. *See, e.g.,* Prewitt v. Wilson, 242 Ky. 231, 46 S.W. 2d 90 (1932); Donnell v. Board of Registration of Medicine, 128 Me. 523, 149 A. 153 (1930); Hunter v. State, 193 Md. 596, 606–07, 69 A.2d 505, 509–10 (1949).
15. *See, e.g., In re* Riccardi, 182 Cal. 675, 189 P. 964 (1920); Vinsant v. Vinsant, 49 Iowa 639 (1878); Woodmen of the World v. Dodd, 134 S.W. 254 (Tex. Civ. App. 1911).
16. *See, e.g.,* State *ex rel.* Blake v. Levi, 109 W. Va. 277, 153 S.E. 587 (1930); Bell v. Treasurer of Cambridge, 310 Mass. 484, 38 N.E. 2d 660 (1941).
17. *See e.g.,* City of Pineville v. Collet, 294 Ky. 853, 172 S.W. 2d 640 (1943); State *ex rel.* Heartsill v. County Election Bd., 326 P.2d 782 (Okla. 1958).
18. *See, e.g., In re* Minner, 133 Kan. 789, 3 P. 2d 473 (1931); Attorney Gen. *ex rel.* O'Hara v. Montgomery, 275 Mich. 504, 267 N.W. 550 (1936).

II

The Right to Retain Citizenship

May a U.S. citizen convicted of a crime be punished by being stripped of his citizenship?

No, because of theories based on two distinct provisions of the U.S. Constitution. The Eighth Amendment ban against cruel and unusual punishment[1] bars the denationalization of a U.S. citizen as a penalty for the conviction of a crime. In invalidating a statute providing for the denationalization of citizens dishonorably discharged from the armed forces after a court-martial conviction for desertion in time of war, the U.S. Supreme Court in 1958 stated in *Trop v Dulles:*

> . . . the use of denationalization as a punishment is barred by the Eighth Amendment. There may be involved no physical mistreatment, no primitive torture. There is instead the total destruction of the individual's status in organized society. It is a form of punishment more primitive than torture, for it destroys for the individual the political existence that was centuries in the development. The punishment strips the citizen of his status in the national and international political community. His very existence is at the suffrance of the country in which he happens to find himself. While any one country may accord him some rights, and presumably as long as he remained in this country he would enjoy the limited rights of an alien, no country need do so because he is state-

THE RIGHT TO RETAIN CITIZENSHIP

less. Furthermore, his enjoyment of even the limited rights of an alien might be subject to termination at any time by reason of deportation. In short, the expatriot has lost the right to have rights.[2]

The second theory also rests on the U.S. Constitution. The first sentence of the Fourteenth Amendment provides that "All persons born or naturalized in the United States, and subject to the jurisdiction thereof, are citizens of the United States and of the State wherein they reside."[3] The Supreme Court relied on this statement in 1967 when it invalidated a statute providing that a U.S. citizen shall lose his citizenship if he votes in an election in a foreign state.[4] In *Afroyim v. Rusk*, the Court argued that the opening statement of the Fourteenth Amendment denied Congress the power to take away a person's citizenship unless it was voluntarily surrendered.

> We hold that the Fourteenth Amendment was designed to, and does, protect every citizen of this Nation against a congressional forcible destruction of his citizenship, whatever his creed, color or race. Our holding does no more than to give to this citizen that which is his own, a constitutional right to remain a citizen in a free country unless he voluntarily relinquishes that citizenship.[5]

Thus, a citizen convicted of a crime retains his citizenship even if the crime is of the most serious and heinous nature. Of course, a convicted citizen may lose many of the rights and privileges of citizenship—such as the right to vote, hold public office, or serve on a jury—but he does not lose his status as a citizen unless he voluntarily relinquishes it.

Does this mean that a federal statute providing for denationalization upon conviction of treason, of advocating the overthrow of the United States government by force or violence, is unconstitutional?

Probably. A federal statute provides for the expatriation of citizens convicted of rebellion or insurrection against the United States; advocating the overthrow of the United States government by force or violence; preventing or delaying execution of any law of the United States by force; or taking, seizing, or possessing any property of the United States by force.[6]

Although this statute has not been declared unconstitutional, the Supreme Court's decisions in *Trop* and *Afroyim* place its validity in doubt.[7] *Trop* specifically held that the Eighth Amendment prohibits denationalization as a punishment. *Afroyim* stands for the proposition that Congress lacks the power to strip a person born or naturalized in the United States of his citizenship. The statute would appear invalid under either rule.

Does the Supreme Court's decision in Rogers v. Bellei alter these conclusions?

Probably not. The Supreme Court judgment in *Rogers v. Bellei* broke the rule that *Trop v. Dulles* and *Afroyim v. Rusk* had established.[8] Taken together, *Trop* and *Afroyim* seemed to stand for the proposition that Congress lacked the power to denationalize a person because of Eighth and Fourteenth Amendment principles; a person could cease to be a citizen only if he voluntarily surrendered his citizenship. But in 1971, a closely divided Court held in *Rogers* that Congress had the power to place reasonable conditions on a person's U.S. citizenship if such citizenship was granted by statute.

Bellei was born in Italy of an alien father and a mother who was a U.S citizen. Under Italian law, he was an Italian citizen, and under a 1934 statute he was a U.S. citizen. U.S. law required that a person who became a citizen by virtue of being born abroad of parents, one of whom was an alien and the other a U.S. citizen, must be physically present in the United States continuously for five years between the ages of fourteen and twenty-eight or lose his citizenship.[9] Bellei failed to meet this requirement and was denationalized.

If the Supreme Court had followed the *Trop* and *Afroyim* rule, the 1934 statute, which stripped Bellei of his citizenship because of his failure to satisfy the residency requirement, would have been invalidated. But the Court distinguished those cases and argued that Bellei was not within the scope of the Fourteenth Amendment's definition of citizenship because he was neither born nor naturalized within the United States. Because Bellei's citizenship arose solely from a statutory basis, the Court contended, Congress had the authority to condition the citizenship so long as it did so reasonably. In this case, the residency requirement was reasonable.

Although the *Rogers* decision weakens the holdings in *Trop* and *Afroyim*, it is unlikely to cause a change in the rule that a person may not be stripped of his citizenship as a penalty for a conviction. The Eighth Amendment's ban against cruel and unusual punishment as interpreted in *Trop* would appear to bar denationalization regardless of whether a person's citizenship rested on the Fourteenth Amendment or a statute.[10]

Does a conviction affect a person's right to obtain a passport?

Generally not. The current rules adopted by the Secretary of State pertinent to the issuance of passports do not deny passports to citizens on the basis of a criminal conviction. Under existing rules, however, a passport shall not be issued to a person subject to an outstanding federal warrant of arrest for a felony, a court order or parole or probation conditions forbidding his departure from the United States, or a subpoena in a matter involving a federal prosecution or grand jury investigation of a felony.[11]

Although passport authorities do not initiate investigations to determine if an applicant has a criminal record, an applicant must swear on the passport application that he has not "been convicted by a court or court martial of competent jurisdiction of committing any act of treason against, or attempting by force to overthrow, or bearing arms against, the United States, or conspiring to overthrow, put down or to destroy by force, the Government of the United States."[12] A person convicted of one of the enumerated acts must submit an explanatory statement under oath. Apparently this inquiry is made on the assumption that citizens convicted of such crimes lose their citizenship.[13]

Would a rule denying passports to convicted persons be constitutional?

No. Because a person may not leave or enter the United States without a passport, such a rule would substantially interfere with a person's fundamental right to travel. As a result, the rule would be valid only if the government could offer a compelling interest as justification. It is unlikely the government could do so. Nevertheless, it is important to note that passports were regularly denied to "habitual criminals" during the 1950s.[14] That practice, however, was not reviewed by the Supreme Court, and if it arose today it probably would not be upheld.

NOTES

1. U.S. CONST. amend. VIII.
2. Trop v. Dulles, 356 U.S. 86, 101–2 (1958).
3. U.S. CONST. amend. XIV.
4. Afroyim v Rusk, 387 U.S. 253 (1967).
5. *Ibid*. at 263.
6. 8 U.S.C. § 1481 (a)(9).
7. Trop v. Dulles, *supra* note 2; Afroyim v. Rusk, *supra* note 4.
8. Rogers v. Bellei 401 U.S. 815 (1971); Trop v. Dulles, *supra* note 2; Afroyim v. Rusk, *supra* note 4.
9. 8 U.S.C. § 1401 (b).
10. Trop v. Dulles, *supra* note 2.
11. 22 C.F.R. § 51.70(a)(1), (2), (5).
12. Passport Application, § G, Dept. of State, Form DSP–11 (1–77).
13. 8 U.S.C. § 1481 (a)(9).
14. Ehrlich, T., *passports*, 19 STAN. L. REV. 129, 137 (1966).

III

The Right to Become a Citizen

Unlike a citizen whose citizenship does not appear to be affected by a criminal conviction, a criminal conviction has serious consequences for a person wishing to enter the United States or become a U.S. citizen.

Generally, the government has broad power over aliens and has woven a very complex set of rules and procedures affecting their rights to enter or remain in the United States. A criminal conviction is just one of several grounds justifying the exclusion or deportation of an alien. Therefore a person without a criminal conviction may be excluded or deported from the United States.[1]

On the other hand, not all convictions will bar a person from entering the United States or from becoming a naturalized citizen, or cause a person to be deported. And those that would be a bar vary depending on whether a person is seeking to enter the United States, to become a citizen, or to keep from being deported. Moreover, even if a person has been convicted of a crime which would normally be a bar, there may be an exception to the prohibition.

What kind of criminal convictions will prevent a person from entering the United States?

Under federal immigration law, there are three basic rules relating to criminal convictions and affecting eligibility.

First, a person convicted of a nonpolitical crime involving moral turpitude is prohibited from entering the United States. This prohibition, however, does not apply to a person who is convicted of such a crime under the age of eighteen, provided at least five years have elapsed from the date of conviction or the last day of imprisonment resulting from such conviction.[2]

Second, a person convicted of two or more nonpolitical offenses for which the combined imprisonment term imposed was five years or more is prohibited from entering the United States. This prohibition applies even though the offenses did not involve moral turpitude or if the convictions arose from a single scheme of misconduct or were obtained in a single trial.[3]

Third, a person is denied entrance into the United States if convicted of any law or regulation relating to the illicit possession of or traffic in narcotics.[4]

Although a person may be covered by the first or second rule cited above, he may nevertheless be permitted to enter the United States if he is a spouse, child, or parent of an American citizen or of an alien who has been lawfully admitted to the United States as a permanent alien.[5] This exception does not cover a person convicted of a drug-related offense, and as a general rule drug-related offenses are treated harshly by the laws affecting the rights of aliens.

As an aside it is worth noting that besides convictions, federal law establishes numerous categories which bar a person from entering the United States. For example, narcotic-drug addicts, chronic alcoholics, polygamists, and anarchists are prohibited from entering the United States. Likewise, a prostitute, a person likely to become a public charge, or a person who has engaged in immoral sexual acts is prohibited from entering the United States.[6]

Might a conviction bar an alien from becoming a naturalized citizen?

Possibly. Federal law provides that an applicant for naturalization must have "good moral character" for at least five years preceding the date of the application.[7] A conviction may result in a finding that a person lacks good moral character.

What does "good moral character" mean in this context?

Although the phrase "good moral character" is vague at best, federal law offers some concrete rules. Federal law prescribes that a person lacks good moral character if convicted of (i) any offense during the pertinent time period which could have barred his admission to the United States in the first place, (ii) murder, (iii) two or more gambling offenses, or (iv) any other offense which resulted in imprisonment for at least one hundred and eighty days, regardless of whether the underlying offense or offenses occurred within the five years preceding the application.[8] Even in the absence of a conviction, federal law prescribes that an application for naturalization shall be denied if the applicant is a habitual drunk, has committed adultery, or has earned his income principally from illegal gambling.[9]

Apart from these concrete rules, courts may find that a person lacks good moral character after considering several factors including arrests, traffic violations, and convictions committed prior to the five-year period.[10]

Might a conviction cause an alien to be deported?

Possibly. Currently, three types of crimes may cause a person to be deported.

1. A person convicted of possessing or carrying a weapon designed to shoot automatically or a weapon commonly known as a sawed-off shotgun will be deported.[11]
2. A person who is or has been any time after entry a narcotic-drug addict or who is convicted of violating any law or regulation relating to the illicit traffic in narcotics will be deported. For a drug-related offense, there is no requirement that a sentence be imposed for the conviction to lead to deportation.[12]
3. A person convicted of a crime involving moral turpitude committed within five years after entry who is sentenced to imprisonment or imprisoned for one year or longer will be deported. Also a person convicted of two crimes involving moral turpitude not arising out of a single scheme of criminal misconduct regardless of the sentence or whether the two convictions were in a single trial will be deported.[13]

Despite the apparent inflexibility of these rules, a person could be spared their harshness in some circumstances. Generally an alien convicted of a crime other than a drug-related offense cannot be deported if he has been given a full and unconditional pardon by the President of the United States or a state governor or if the court imposing his sentence makes a recommendation to the Attorney General that he not be deported.[14] Also, the Attorney General is authorized to suspend a deportation order if an alien has been in the United States for a continuous period of ten years following the act constituting a ground for deportation, he proves he has been a person of good moral character, and he establishes that his deportation would result in unusual hardship to himself or family or another alien.[15]

Is it constitutional to deport a person because of a conviction?

Yes. The Supreme Court has consistently upheld statutes authorizing the deportation of convicted aliens as part of the government's power to determine on what conditions aliens may remain within the country.[16] In upholding these statutes, courts refuse to characterize deportation as punishment which might implicate constitutional doctrines, but they are willing to construe them strictly. Thus in one case, the Supreme Court prohibited an attempt to deport a person convicted of an offense involving moral turpitude when he was a citizen even though he was subsequently denaturalized.[17]

NOTES

1. *See, e.g.*, 8 U.S.C. § 1251(a)(3) and 8 U.S.C. §§ 1182 (a)(1), (2), (25).
2. 8 U.S.C. § 1182(a)(9).
3. 8 U.S.C. § 1182(a)(10).
4. 8 U.S.C. § 1182(a)(23).
5. 8 U.S.C. § 1182(g), (h), (i).
6. 8 U.S.C. § 1182(a) (5), (11), (12), (13), (15), (28) (A); 8 U.S.C. § 1251(a) (6) (A), (11).
7. 8 U.S.C. § 1427(a); 8 U.S.C. § 1101(f).
8. 8 U.S.C. § 1101(f)(5), (6), (8).
9. 8 U.S.C. § 1101(f)(1), (2), (4).

THE RIGHT TO BECOME A CITIZEN 33

10. *See, e.g.,* Marcantonio v. United States, 185 F. 2d 934 (4th Cir. 1950); In re Siacco's Petition, 184 F. Supp. 803 (D. Md. 1960).
11. 8 U.S.C. § 1251 (a)(14).
12. 8 U.S.C. §1251 (a)(11).
13. 8 U.S.C. § 1251 (a)(4).
14. 8 U.S.C. § 1251 (b).
15. 8 U.S.C. § 1254 (a)(2).
16. Mahler v. Eby, 264 U.S. 32 (1924).
17. Costello v. Immigration and Naturalization Service, 376 U.S. 120 (1964).

IV
The Right to Hold Public Office

A person convicted of a crime will be barred from holding most important governmental positions. These prohibitions remain effective unless the restoration of an ex-convict's rights removes the prohibition. The arguments most often offered in support of this prohibition boil down to trying to minimize corruption in government.

Public office is not public employment. The term "public office" generally refers to high government office, regardless of whether it is elective or appointive, at the federal, state, and local level. While the term has been defined to include government positions of varying levels of responsibility, it does not include essentially clerical or low-level administrative jobs.[1]

As a practical matter, however, the barriers encountered by ex-convicts in securing public employment are more critical to the average offender than those barring ex-convicts from holding public office. Few ex-convicts are qualified for high public office; many more jobs are available under the rubric of public employment.

Nevertheless, the rigid application of this rule is unfair and wasteful. This prohibition, combined with disfranchisement (discussed in Chapter V), unnecessarily alienates ex-convicts from the political life of the country. It also deprives the government of many talented individuals who might make special contributions to the corrections field and treatment of drug addicts.

The prohibition also deprives the electorate of their

right to elect the individual of their choice. A better approach would be to trust the electorate's judgment to choose public officeholders. As the President's Commission on Law Enforcement and Administration of Justice stated over a decade ago:

> Although certain offenses are clearly related to fitness to hold such positions, it is rarely necessary to provide for automatic disqualification in order to protect society. Instead, where there is someone with authority to appoint or remove, or where the public has such authority through its power to elect, it seems generally preferable to rely on their judgment. The relevance of particular convictions or terms of imprisonment to fitness for the particular position can then be considered.[2]

If flat prohibitions against ex-convicts holding public office are to continue, they should be restricted in accordance with the following guidelines:
1. There should be a direct and reasonable relationship between the crime committed and the duties of the public office.
2. The term "public office" should be narrowly construed so that fewer governmental positions are encompassed by the term than presently.
3. The crimes resulting in disqualification should be narrowly defined.
4. An automatic disqualification resulting from a conviction should be effective for a short and specific period of time.

What is a public office?

Constitutional or statutory provisions ordinarily bar ex-convicts from "holding any office of trust, honor or profit under this [s]tate"[3] or more simply from holding any "office."[4] These terms, which mean the same thing, apply to state and local public offices and to appointive and elective positions.

While these terms are imprecise, courts have generally defined these terms so that a minimal number of positions come within their reach. One court, for example, has stated that five elements would seem "indispensable" to make a public office.

(1) It must be created by the Constitution or the Legislature, or by a municipality or other body with authority conferred by the Legislature. (2) There must be a delegation of a portion of the sovereign powers of government to be exercised for the benefit of the public. (3) The powers conferred and the duties to be discharged must be defined either directly or indirectly by the Legislature or through Legislative Authority. (4) The duties must be performed independently and without control of a superior power other than the law. (5) The office must have some permanency and continuity and the officer must take an official oath.[5]

Under this and other tests, courts have held the positions of city manager,[6] postmaster,[7] school-board member,[8] and county treasurer[9] to be public offices. Courts have also held the positions of deputy sheriff,[10] deputy clerk of court,[11] and assistant city attorney[12] not to be public offices.

Does the U.S. Constitution restrict ex-convicts from holding federal public office?
With the limited exception of section 3 of the Fourteenth Amendment,[13] the United States Constitution does not bar offenders from holding any positions in the federal government.

May Congress or a state add qualifications to public offices created by the United States Constitution?
No. Neither Congress nor the states may add qualifications to constitutionally created positions. Thus an ex-convict may be elected President, Vice-President, or to either house of Congress because they are constitutionally created offices and the Constitution does not bar offenders from holding them.

May Congress establish qualifications for nonconstitutionally created public offices in the federal government?
Yes. Congress has passed statutes that exclude persons

convicted of specified offenses from holding any nonconstitutionally created federal office. Hence, for example, a person convicted of (1) falsifying, destroying, or removing public records or document,[14] (2) receiving compensation in matters affecting the government,[15] or (3) rebellion[16] or treason[17] are disqualified.

The most notable federal statute barring ex-offenders from federal employment is the Omnibus Crime Control and Safe Streets Act of 1968. This provision applies to anyone convicted of a felony (defined as an offense for which imprisonment is authorized for a term exceeding one year)[18] in a federal, state or local court of

(1) inciting a riot or civil disorder; (2) organizing, promoting, encouraging, or participating in a riot or civil disorder; (3) aiding or abetting any person in committing any offense specified in clause (1) or (2); or (4) any offense determined by the head of the employing agency to have been committed in furtherance of, or while participating in, a riot or civil disorder.[19]

Besides the discretion vested in hiring officials provided for in section 4 of the statute, two points deserve emphasis. An offender covered by this statute is not just barred from public office; he is barred from holding any position in the federal government or the government of the District of Columbia. This prohibition lasts for five years from the date of conviction, at which time it lapses.[20]

May a state add qualifications to a nonconstitutionally created federal public office?
No.

Do states bar ex-convicts from holding state public office?
Yes. Most states prohibit persons convicted of serious crimes from holding elected or appointed public office in state and local government by state statute, constitutional provisions, or both.

Although a state constitution may not expressly bar offenders from public office, a state legislature may have the authority to do so. In one case, the Indiana Supreme Court held that a constitutional provision authorizing the legislature to deny the right to vote to persons convicted of an infamous crime also gives the legislature the authority to bar such persons from holding public office.[21]

State prohibitions barring ex-convicts from holding public office take two forms. First, provisions expressly bar persons convicted of felonies, infamous offenses, or specified offenses from holding office.[22] Second, states indirectly bar offenders from public office by requiring that a holder of a public office be a qualified voter. Most ex-convicts are disqualified as voters, and are therefore precluded from holding public office.[23]

Does a public officeholder lose his office upon conviction of a crime?

Yes. The federal government[24] and most state governments have laws which require the forfeiture of a public office held at the time of conviction. As with qualifications for holding office, however, these forfeiture provisions vary considerably. For example, a person may be forced to forfeit his office if he is convicted of a felony,[25] an infamous crime,[26] a crime of moral turpitude,[27] violations of the official oath of office,[28] or malfeasance in office.[29] In addition to forfeiture provisions, most states possess impeachment procedures, modeled after the one contained in the United States Constitution, which may be used to remove a convicted officeholder.[30]

A federal officeholder may be removed from office in the absence of explicit forfeiture provisions if convicted of a crime which would have made him ineligible for the office in the first place.[31]

Will a public officeholder convicted of a crime be forced to forfeit his office prior to the completion of appeals?

Generally yes. In such cases, courts usually reason that removal from office does not constitute part of the judgment of conviction, but is a consequence imposed in the interest of the public and of sound government, and that it would be against this public interest to retain in office a person convicted and hence presumed guilty, pending appeal.[32]

Will an ousted public officeholder be permitted to regain his office if the conviction is reversed on appeal?

Normally not. In upholding this rule, courts argue that the public interest demands that public affairs be administered by officers whose character is not clouded by a conviction and that efficient government requires a constancy and continuity of service which precludes the changing of officers during a specified term.[33]

Does the U.S. Constitution limit the power of Congress or a state to bar ex-convicts from public office?

Theoretically yes, but practically no. While the U.S. Constitution prohibits arbitrary employment qualifications, courts are very inclined to find prohibitions barring ex-convicts from holding public office reasonable and valid.[34] In fact, the reasonableness of the prohibition is seldom the issue presented to the courts. More commonly, courts assume the reasonableness of the prohibition and focus on whether there is a conviction, whether the conviction is one which bars an offender from holding public office or whether a pardon or other restorative device permits an otherwise barred person from holding public office.[35]

The closest the Supreme Court has come to this issue in recent years was in *De Veau v. Braisted*.[36] The New York Waterfront Commission Act of 1953, whose purpose was to "keep criminals away from the waterfront," barred any union employing a felon from collecting dues or contributions from pier superintendents, hiring agents, longshoremen, and port watchmen. The Court found the waterfront an "appalling situation" requiring "drastic action." It upheld the challenged statute stating that "barring convicted felons from certain employments is a familiar legislative device to insure against corruption in a specified vital area."[37]

NOTES

1. *See Civil Disabilities*, 23 VAND. L. REV. 929, 987 (1970).
2. PRESIDENT'S COMMISSION ON LAW ENFORCEMENT AND THE ADMINISTRATION OF JUSTICE, TASK FORCE REPORT: CORRECTIONS 90 (1967).
3. *See, e.g.*, DEL. CONST. art. 2, § 21.

4. *See, e.g.,* KY. CONST. § 150; N.M. STAT. ANN. § 5–1–2 (1968).
5. Pope v. Commissioner of Internal Revenue, 138 F. 2d 1006, 1009 (6th Cir. 1943). The Supreme Court of Arizona stated in Stapleton v. Frohmiller, 85 P. 2d 49, 52 (1938), that a position of public office must have three characteristics: "(a) the specific position must be created by law; (b) there must be certain definite duties imposed by law on the incumbent; and (c) they must involve the exercise of some portion of the sovereign power."
6. State v. Shelden 213 P. 92 (1923).
7. State *ex rel.* Wimberly v. Barham 137 So. 862, 864 (1931).
8. *Ibid.*, at 864.
9. State *ex rel.* Good v. March 249 N.W. 295, 298 (1933).
10. Kemp v. Wilson 84 So. 636, 637–38 (1919).
11. Jeffries v. Harrington 17 P. 505, 506 (1888).
12. State *ex rel.* Glenn v. Wilkinson 124 So. 211, 212 (1929).
13. "No person shall be a Senator or Representative in Congress, or elector of President and Vice President, or hold any office, civil or military, under the United States, or under any State, who, having previously taken an oath, as a member of Congress, or as an officer of the United States, or as a member of any State legislature, or as an executive or judicial officer of any State, to support the Constitution of the United States, shall have engaged in insurrection or rebellion against the same, or given aid or comfort to the enemies thereof. But Congress may by a vote of two-thirds of each House, remove such disability." U.S. CONST. amend. XIV. §3.
14. 18 U.S.C. § 2071 (1964).
15. 18 U.S.C. §203 (1964).
16. 18 U.S.C. §2383 (1964).
17. 18 U.S.C. § 2331 (1964).
18. 5 U.S.C. §7313(b)(Supp. 1977).
19. 5 U.S.C. §7313(a)(Supp. 1977).
20. *Ibid.*
21. Lucas v. McAfee, 29 N.E. 2d 403, *petition for rehearing denied*, 29 N.E. 2d 588 (1940).
22. *See, e.g.,* KAN. CONST. art. 5, §2 (felony); LA. REV. STAT. ANN. § 15:572.1(A)(Supp. 1970)(felony); WIS. CONST. art. 13, § 3 (infamous crime); GA. CODE ANN. §89–101 (1963)(moral turpitude); ARK. CONST. art. 5, § 9 (perjury, bribery, embezzlement).
23. *See e.g.,* Mitchell v. Kinney, 5 So. 2d 788 (1942).
24. Congress has enacted several statutes which require the forfeiture of public office by persons convicted of specified crimes: *See e.g.,* 18 U.S.C. §1907 (farm credit examiner

convicted of improperly disclosing the names of Federal land bank borrowers must forfeit the office); 18 U.S.C. §655 (bank examiner who is convicted of stealing money from a bank which is a member of the Federal Reserve System or insured by the Federal Deposit Insurance Company must forfeit the office).

25. *See, e.g.,* Iowa Code Ann., 66.1 (1949); Va. Code §2.1–36 (1950).
26. *See, e.g.,* Del. Const. art. 15, § 6; Mich. Stat. Ann. § 6.693 (1956).
27. *See e.g.,* Tenn. Code Ann. §§ 8–2701–2801 (1955).
28. *See, e.g.,* N.Y. Pub. Off. Law § 30 (Mckinney, Supp. 1977).
29. *See, e.g.,* Nev. Rev. Stat. § 197.230 (1967).
30. Article II, Section 4 of the United States Constituion provides, "The President, Vice President and all civil officers of the United States, shall be removed from Office on Impeachment for, and Conviction of, Treason, Bribery, or other high Crimes and Misdemeanors." This rarely used provision is ambiguous in two respects. It is unclear what positions are included in the phrase "all civil officers." Although a United States Attorney General ruled that members of Congress are not included [17 Op. Att'y Gen. 419 (1882)]. The meaning of the phrase "high Crimes and Misdemeanors" is uncertain, as was made clear by the congressional debates prior to resignation of Richard Nixon from the presidency.
31. *See* notes 14–20, *supra,* and accompanying text.
32. *See generally* 71 A.L.R. 2d 593 (1960).
33. *See generally* 106 A.L.R. 644 (1937).
34. *See* Hawker v. New York, 170 U.S. 189 (1898)(upholding provision excluding felons from practicing medicine).
35. Authority diverges on this last issue. *See, e.g.,* People *ex rel.* Symonds v. Gualano, 260 N.E. 2d 284 (Ill. App. Ct. 1970)(governor's certificate of restoration removed disqualification); *contra,* Ridgeway v. Catlett, 379 S.W. 2d 277 (1964)(disqualification irrespective of pardon).
36. 363 U.S. 144 (1960).
37. *Ibid.* at 158–59.

V

The Right to Vote

The right to vote is fundamental. The Supreme Court has characterized it as the "essence of a democratic society"[1] and a "preservative of other basic civil and political rights."[2] Voting is also an important symbol of citizenship, representing the right to participate in the political life of the country. Nevertheless, ex-convicts are today denied the right to vote in about half the states.[3]

Three reasons are generally offered to justify this disfranchisement. None of them are satisfactory.[4]

First, it is argued that ex-convicts have significantly less interest in the democratic process than other citizens. This seems hardly true. Like everyone else, the daily lives of ex-offenders are deeply affected by government.

Second, it is contended that disfranchisement of ex-convicts is necessary to prevent voting frauds. The prevention of electoral fraud is important, but disfranchising all ex-felons protects this value only haphazardly. Blanket provisions deny the franchise to many who are no more likely to abuse the ballot than persons never convicted. Simultaneously they grant the franchise to many who have been convicted of a misdemeanor even though the underlying offense was a violation of the election laws. The state has many means to protect the integrity of the elective process that are more effective and less drastic than disfranchising all ex-felons.

Third, is is argued that granting the franchise to former felons might result in a voting pattern subversive to the interests of an orderly society.[5] This is an unsupported claim. There is no evidence that former felons could or would use the franchise to subvert the societal order. Certainly states which allow ex-convicts to vote have not been subverted. Moreover, it is certainly contrary to democratic principles, if not the Constitution, to decide who may vote on the basis of how they will vote. No one would countenance the denial of the ballot to a person because of religious or ethnic identities or because of political belief. Similarly there is little to justify the denial of the ballot to ex-offenders.

The franchise is the individual's fundamental means of participation in the political life of the nation. It forms an important part of the modern conception of citizenship, and the denial of the franchise may well impede an ex-convict's identification with the larger society. The current trend to repeal laws barring ex-convicts from voting should continue and be accelerated.

Do states disfranchise ex-convicts?
Yes. About half the states bar ex-convicts from voting in state or federal elections.[6]

For what types of crimes will a person currently be disfranchised by a state?
Although the question cannot be answered precisely, most states disfranchise ex-convicts because of crimes totally unrelated to the electoral process.[7] Some states disfranchise anyone convicted of a "felony," an "infamous crime," a "crime involving moral turpitude," or a "crime punishable by imprisonment in state penitentiaries." Definitions of these terms differ from state to state and may vary within a state, but they are broad terms hardly limited to election-law offenses.

Other states have established particular lists of disqualifying crimes, most of which have no reasonable relationship to voting. For example, the South Carolina constitution disqualifies persons from voting who have been convicted of burglary, arson, obtaining goods or money under false pretenses, perjury, forgery, robbery, bribery, adultery, bigamy, wife-beating, housebreaking, receiving stolen goods, breach of the trust with fraudulent intent, fornication, sodomy, incest, assault with intent to ravish, miscegenation, larceny, or crimes against the election laws.[8] And according to one study, disfranchisement extends to those convicted of vagrancy in Alabama, breaking a water pipe in North Dakota, horse-stealing in Ohio, and stealing "any wool, mohair or edible meats" in Texas.[9]

May an ex-convict disfranchised under state law vote in federal elections?

No. The U.S. Constitution provides that the voting qualifications established by the states for state elections shall also apply to the elections for the U.S. House of Representatives and Senate[10] and in presidential elections.[11]

Has the Supreme Court decided whether the disfranchisement of ex-convicts is consistent with the U.S. Constitution?

Yes. In *Richardson v. Ramirez*,[12] the Supreme Court was recently confronted with an important appeal from the California Supreme Court.[13] The California court held that the state's disfranchisement of felons violated the Equal Protection clause of the Fourteenth Amendment to the United States Constitution. Relying upon recent Supreme Court decisions, the California court said that the right to vote was fundamental and that as a result the state must show that disfranchisement was justified by a compelling state interest, the class of people disfranchised was not too large or too small in terms of the interest being advanced, and that no alternative ways were available to protect the state interest that were less burdensome to the right to vote. The California court ruled that disfranchisement was unnecessary to prevent voting fraud and that the state had ample, less burdensome methods for preventing election fraud.

The U.S. Supreme Court overruled the California court, but in an unexpected way. The Court held that section 2 of the Fourteenth Amendment explicitly permitted states to deny the franchise to felons.[14] It did not say that a state *must* deny the franchise to felons; it said that a state could *choose* to deny the franchise to felons. The result: the United States Constitution permits each state to decide whether felons shall be permitted to vote.

Under the *Ramirez* decision, are ex-convicts disfranchised under federal or state law?

State law. Federal law permits states to disfranchise ex-convicts; it does not force the disfranchisement. Thus, an ex-convict who is not permitted to vote is disfranchised under state law.

For what types of crimes may a person be disfranchised under *Ramirez*?

It is not clear. Although the Supreme Court stated that section 2 of the Fourteenth Amendment authorized the disfranchisement of felons, section 2 actually refers to "participation in rebellion, or other crime." It does not refer to felonies, crimes involving moral turpitude, infamous crimes, or crimes resulting in imprisonment—the phrases normally used by states to identify those ex-convicts who are disfranchised. Thus it is uncertain whether the Supreme Court intended to include under section 2 the broad range of offenders normally disfranchised under state law.

Does *Ramirez* leave open the possibility that a state's disfranchisement provision may be invalidated under the U.S. Constitution?

Yes. The crime categories resulting in disfranchisement might be too vague to result in evenhanded enforcement of voting requirements. For example, many states disfranchise persons convicted of an infamous crime or a crime involving moral turpitude. These terms are vague and are seldom given a definitive interpretation by a state court or state's attorney general. As a result, voting registrars throughout a state might interpret the terms differently. This unequal application of voting requirements would give rise to a claim under the equal-protection clause of the Fourteen Amendment to the United States Constitution.[15]

Does *Ramirez* preclude the possibility that disfranchisement provisions may be unconstitutional on state constitutional grounds?

No. Under our federal system of government, a particular statute may be inconsistent with a state constitution as well as the U.S. Constitution. The U.S. Supreme Court will not review a state-court decision which rests on independent state-law grounds. Hence if a state court declares the disfranchisement of ex-convicts unconstitutional on state-law grounds, the U.S. Supreme Court will not review the decision.

Is it worth challenging disfranchisement provisions in state court on state-law grounds?

Absolutely. State courts are showing a more vigorous respect for individual rights than in the recent past and a willingness to break rank with the U.S. Supreme Court on specific issues.

The claims asserted in state court would be similar to those traditionally made in federal court, since most state constitutions embody clauses which give rise to claims similar to federal constitutional ones.

On what theories might a disfranchisement provision be challenged in state court?

Assuming a state constitution has the necessary clause, three theories should be used to challenge the constitutionality of disfranchisement provisions:

First, disfranchisement provisions of ex-convicts violate an ex-convict's rights under the equal-protection clause. Most states which have an equal-protection clause in their constitution will follow the two-tier equal-protection analysis developed by the U.S. Supreme Court. Under this analysis, voting would be a fundamental right requiring that the discrimination be justified by a compelling state interest, that the classifications not be overinclusive or underinclusive in terms of the interest being advanced, and that there be no less drastic available alternative to disfranchisement which would protect the state's interest. This is a difficult standard for any state to satisfy.

Second, disfranchisement should be challenged as violating an individual's right to participate in the political process. This right rests on the First Amendment to the U.S. Constitution, which guarantees free speech, a free press, freedom of assembly, and the right of an individual to petition the government for redress of grievances. Although the Supreme Court has occasionally acknowledged this theory, none of its decisions has firmly endorsed it.[16] Nevertheless, the doctrine is strong enough to be presented to the state courts for evaluation.

Third, disfranchisement provisions should be challenged as a violation of the prohibition against cruel and unusual punishment.[17] This theory argues that disfranchisement is an excessive and disproportionate punishment and fails to comport with human dignity. This is a difficult argument, for it requires that a court find that disfranchisement serves no legitimate nonpenal state interest. Although that appears to be true, no court has ever so held.

Is it a crime for a disfranchised ex-convict to vote?

Possibly. As a practical matter, many ex-convicts are unaware that they are barred from voting in a particular state. They therefore seek to register to vote and are permitted to do so because of administrative oversights. Many states try to discourage this practice by making it a misdemeanor or a felony for a disfranchised person to register or to vote. In states with such prohibitions, it may be a defense that the person did not know he was disfranchised.[18]

Does the disfranchisement of ex-convicts disproportionately affect nonwhites?

Yes. Blacks and other minority-group Americans are convicted of serious crimes at rates disproportionate to their representation in the nation's total population. Thus, the use of serious crimes unrelated to the electoral process to disqualify voters in effect discriminates against minority citizens.

Moreover, there is at least some evidence that in some jurisdictions the intent behind the disfranchisement of ex-convicts was to discriminate against blacks. For example, prior to 1968, the Mississippi Constitution did not disqualify murderers or rapists from voting, even though it disqualified persons convicted of bribery, theft, arson, obtaining money or goods under false pretense, perjury, forgery, embezzlement, or bigamy. The intent behind the former disfranchising provisions was described by the Mississippi Supreme Court in an 1896 opinion as follows:

> By reason of its previous condition of servitude and dependence, this [the Negro] race had acquired or accentuated certain peculiarities of habit, of temperament, and of character which clearly distinguished it as a race from that of the whites—a patient docile people—but careless, landless, and migratory within limits, without forethought, and its criminal members given rather to furtive offenses than to robust crimes of the whites. Restrained by the federal constitution from discriminating against the Negro race, the convention discriminated against its characteristics and the offenses to which its weaker members were prone.[19]

Do states that disfranchise ex-convicts ever restore the right to vote?

Yes. Many states restore the right to vote either automatically, by pardon, or by other procedures. (See Chapter XII "The Restoration of Lost Rights," and Appendix A.)

NOTES

1. Reynolds v. Sims, 377 U.S. 533, 555 (1964).
2. *Ibid.* at 562.
3. See Appendix A; Note, *Disfranchisement of Ex-felons: A Cruelly Excessive Punishment*, 7 Sw. L. Rev. 124, 126, n. 15 (1975)
4. *See generally*, Note, *The Need for Reform of Ex-felon Disenfranchisement Laws*, 83 YALE L.J. 580 (1974); Note, *Disenfranchisement of Ex-felons: A Reassessment*, 25 STAN. L. REV. 845 (1973).
5. *See, e.g.,* Green v. Board of Elections of City of New York, 380 F. 2d 445, 451–52 (2nd Cir. 1967).
6. *See supra* note 3.
7. Only Maine, Massachussetts, Pennsylvania, and Vermont disfranchise because of election-law offenses. See Appendix A, Table I.

8. S.C. CONST., art. 2, § 6.
9. Note, *Disenfranchisement of Ex-felons: A Reassessment,* 25 STAN. L. REV. 845–46 (1973).
10. U.S. CONST., art. I, § 2 and amend. XVII.
11. U.S. CONST., art II, § 1.
12. 418 U.S. 24 (1974)
13. Ramirez v. Brown, 9 Cal. 3d 199, 507 P. 2d 1345 (1973); *rev'd sub nom.* Richardson v. Ramirez, 418 U.S. 24 (1974).
14. Section 2 of the Fourteenth Amendment reads in its entirety:

    "Representatives shall be apportioned among the several states according to their respective numbers, counting the whole number of persons in each state, excluding Indians not taxed. But when the right to vote at any election for the choice of electors for President and Vice-President of the United States, Representatives in Congress, the Executive and Judicial officers of a State, or the members of the Legislature thereof, is denied to any of the male inhabitants of such State, being twenty-one years of age [changed by section 1 of the Twenty-Sixth Amendment], and citizens of the Unites States, or in any way abridged, except for participation in rebellion, or other crime, the basis of representation therein shall be reduced in the proportion which the number of such male citizens shall bear to the whole number of male citizens twenty-one years of age in such State."

15. *See, e.g.,* Richardson v. Ramirez, *supra* note 13, at 56; Thiess v. State Administrative Board of Elections, 387 F. Supp. 1038 (D. Maryland 1974).
16. Williams v. Rhodes, 393 U.S. 23, 31 (1968) (Justice Harlan, concurring); Kusper v. Pontikes, 414 U.S. 51 (1973).
17. *See, e.g.,* Note *Disfranchisement of Ex-felons: A Cruelly Excessive Punishment,* 7 Sw. L. Rev. 124 (1975).
18. *See, e.g.,* Lambert v. California, 355 U.S. 225 (1957), where a conviction for failing to register under a criminal-registration statute was dismissed because of the lack of notice.
19. Ratliff v. Beale, 74 Miss. 247, 266; 20 So. 965, 968 (1896).

VI

Domestic Rights

When the wind blows in a dust bowl, the fine sand pierces the most carefully placed protective covers, lodging itself in the most unexpected nooks and corners. The impact of a conviction is not dissimilar, and its impact on a person's domestic rights is perhaps the best example of a conviction's surprising reach.

By piling one consequence on top of another, it is possible that a person convicted of crime could be divorced, not only lose custody of his children but have them adopted over his objection, and be involuntarily sterilized. It is unlikely that one person would experience all three of these consequences, but it is not impossible.

Preserving family ties during imprisonment may reduce criminal recidivism. Thus, recent studies have consistently found a strong positive correlation between the maintenance of strong family ties and parole success.[1] Also, a person whose marriage survives his imprisonment is less likely to return to prison than his counterpart who confronts the post-prison experience alone.[2] Imprisonment, of course, presents a formidable challenge to family ties and tends more than any other consequence flowing from a conviction to cause their decay.

A. DIVORCE

May a conviction be grounds for a divorce?
Yes. In over half of the states, a spouse of a person who

is convicted after the marriage may obtain a divorce on the grounds of the conviction.[3] A divorce on such grounds was not acknowledged in the common law, however, and may be obtained only if it is specifically provided for in a statute.[4] In those states that have not made a conviction or imprisonment a separate ground for divorce, the innocent spouse may be able to use the conviction as evidence to prove other statutory grounds authorizing a divorce.[5]

The statutes permitting a divorce because of a conviction vary enormously. At minimum, all states require a conviction; commission of a crime or an indictment is not sufficient.

The states granting divorce to an innocent spouse fall roughly into three groups:

First, some states grant a divorce to an innocent spouse of a person convicted of a felony[6] or an infamous crime,[7] regardless of the sentence. Thus, an innocent spouse of a convicted felon placed on probation may obtain a divorce because of the conviction.

Second, some states authorize divorce when the guilty spouse is sentenced to prison, without requiring that the convicted spouse actually serve the sentence.[8] Because the divorce ground in these statutes is limited to felony convictions or sentences to the state penitentiary, the statutes probably contemplate a lengthy term of imprisonment.

Third, some states actually require that the guilty spouse be imprisoned as a result of the conviction. Many of these states require that the imprisonment period be for a minimum period.[9]

The rationales underlying these laws vary. In states which authorize divorce because of a conviction, regardless of the sentence, there is an assumption that the offender's character is so deficient as to render him an unsuitable spouse. In states which require a period of imprisonment before authorizing a divorce, deference is paid to the deprivation of a spouse's right to consortium, companionship, and financial interdependence.

What type of crimes constitutes grounds for a divorce?

It depends on the state statute. Some state statutes provide that a conviction for a felony,[10] or infamous crime,[11] or a crime involving moral turpitude,[12] or a crime leading to imprisonment in a state penitentiary[13] constitutes grounds for divorce.

The terms "felony" and "crime leading to imprisonment in a state penitentiary," although they vary from state to state, normally are clearly interpreted. However, the terms "infamous crime" and "crime involving moral turpitude" present substantial interpretational problems. What these terms mean when used in a statute setting forth a ground for divorce may differ from what they mean when they are used in other disabling laws, such as laws setting forth requirements for voting or public office. Also, the meanings of these terms differ from one state to another. Nevertheless serious crimes such as homicide, manslaughter, and rape would most definitely be included as part of their meaning.[14] It is not so clear, however, whether less serious crimes such as larceny or burglary are infamous crimes within the meaning of a divorce statute.

Will a conviction in one jurisdiction be grounds for divorce in another jurisdiction?

In other words, may an innocent spouse suing for divorce in one state use a conviction obtained in another state as grounds for divorce? This question obviously recurs for every kind of civil disability. But with divorce, there is a clear and somewhat new general rule.

Not long ago, a conviction or imprisonment outside the divorce state could not be used as grounds for a divorce unless it was specifically authorized by statute. But that is no longer the general rule. Some state statutes now specifically authorize divorce when conviction or imprisonment occurs in other jurisdictions,[15] even in foreign countries.[16] Moreover, in the absence of specific authorization, most courts now grant a divorce regardless of where the conviction or imprisonment occurs. There is even some authority for granting a divorce on the basis of a court-martial conviction.[17]

What are the matrimonial consequences for a convicted spouse who is sentenced to life imprisonment in a state that retains a civil-death statute?

The result in civil-death states varies. In at least one civil-death state, a marriage is terminated automatically once a defendant is sentenced to life imprisonment.[18] In other states, the innocent spouse must obtain a court decree dissolving the marriage or obtain a judgment of divorce.[19]

These statutes are based on the erroneous assumption that a defendant sentenced to life imprisonment will never be released from prison. In every jurisdiction today, a person sentenced to life imprisonment may be released from prison on parole or by pardon. Accordingly, the marriage consequences flowing from a life prison term in a civil-death state may create a set of circumstances not originally contemplated by the civil-death statutes.

When may a convicted spouse be sued for divorce on the grounds of the conviction?

It depends on what the statute setting forth the divorce grounds states. If the statute states that a conviction or sentence is grounds for divorce, then the innocent spouse may initiate a divorce action upon conviction or the imposition of sentence. When the statutory ground is imprisonment, it is likely that the convicted spouse must be imprisoned before the action is begun. If the statute specifies a minimum imprisonment period, the divorce action may not be instituted prior to the completion of the specified period. If, as is true in a few civil-death states, a marriage is dissolved automatically upon the imposition of a life sentence, no legal action or proceeding is needed to dissolve the marriage.

May an innocent spouse sue a convicted spouse for divorce while an appeal from the conviction is pending?

In most states, no. Few statutes provide that a conviction must be final before it may serve as a ground for divorce. But the little case law on this question requires that a conviction be final before a divorce will be granted.[20] If the ground for divorce, however, is a specified imprisonment period, and the convicted spouse has served that time, a reversal of the conviction will not bar a divorce based on the imprisonment.[21] Also, a marriage dissolved upon conviction in accordance with the terms of a statute will not be restored by a subsequent reversal of the conviction.[22]

Does a convicted spouse have any defenses to a divorce action?

Few. Divorce actions based on these grounds are difficult to defend successfully. For example, a pardon—whether granted before the divorce action was initiated, while it is pending, or after it is completed—is no defense in most states Traditional divorce defenses such as connivance, recrimination, and condemnation are not available to a convicted spouse as a practical matter even though they would appear to be appropriate.

Some states recognize one of two limited defense grounds. A few states require that the divorce proceeding be initiated within a specified period of time. For example, Idaho requires that a divorce action be initiated within one year after a pardon or termination of sentence.[23]

Second, at least one state[24] has authorized an unusual defense for a convicted spouse being sued for divorce. In Texas, a divorce will not be granted when the conviction of the defendant in the matrimonial action was based on testimony of the innocent spouse.

Should a divorce be granted solely because of a conviction?

This is a complicated question. Certainly the welfare of the spouse and child will often be best served by permitting a spouse to obtain a divorce. On the other hand, the preservation of family ties are of critical importance to many prisoners and often make the difference to a released prisoner between returning to crime and going straight.

A state's domestic-relations law is incapable of resolving the conflicting goals of terminating an unsuccessful marriage and preserving a prisoner's family ties. Certainly innocent spouses should be permitted to divorce, but not solely because of the nature of the crime or length of sentence. Such wooden rules are unfair, for they do not make divorce available in many circumstances when it would be justified.

In keeping with the current trend, all jurisdictions should make divorce available on grounds such as incompatibility or irreconcilable differences. These grounds should be defined to permit any innocent spouse to obtain a divorce when the nature of either the offense or the sentence gives rise to a reasonable desire in the spouse to end the marriage.

In addition to changing domestic-relations laws, reforms seeking to preserve family ties during imprisonment are necessary. For example, steps must be taken to ease a family's economic hardship during the period of incarceration and to permit the minimum consortium necessary to keep alive a wife's and husband's affection for one another during their separation.

B. THE RIGHT TO MARRY AND PROCREATE

Are there any restrictions on an ex-offender's right to marry?

Yes. But the restrictions are limited.

There are two kinds of restrictions on the right to marry. A few states declare a marriage void if the unconvicted spouse did not have knowledge of the past conviction for an infamous offense prior to the marriage.[25] Courts in these states analogize the marriage relationship to a civil contract and the failure to disclose the past conviction as constituting a fraud justifying a rescission or, in this situation, an annulment of the contract.[26] This is true even though misrepresentations of character do not ordinarily constitute fraud sufficient for an annulment. Under the rule of these cases, however, an innocent spouse will not be entitled to an annulment if he knew of the past conviction at the time of the marriage or if he continued in the marital relationship after discovery of the fraud. Because the basis of the annulment in these cases is fraud, they do not support the lessening of an offender's right to marry solely because of a conviction.

Second, the few states that retain civil-death statutes do not permit prisoners serving life sentences to marry on the ground that such prisoners are deemed civilly dead and thus are incapable of entering into a marriage contract. Such statutes, although termed a "medieval relic" and criticized as unnecessarily barring potentially important emotional ties,[27] have been held constitutional.[28]

May a conviction endanger a person's right to marry and have children?

Possibly. At least one state has a statute that prohibits a "habitual criminal" from marrying. This statute assumes that a habitual criminal is unfit to have a child and that a marriage prohibition is equivalent to a procreation prohibition. Hence, a Washington statute prohibits marriage by a "habitual criminal" unless it is established that procreation is not possible by the couple intending to marry.[29]

Are laws seeking to prohibit procreation by barring marriage constitutional?

Not likely. They wrongly assume that an unwedded couple will not procreate and that a wedded couple will. That assumption seems unfounded. Today an increasing number of married couples have no children and the number of unmarried parents is increasing. Moreover, these statutes fail to take account of an offender's crimes and background and the nature of his life since his last offense. It is likely that these statutes would be invalidated on any one of several legal theories.

C. STERILIZATION

About half the states have statutes providing for the involuntary sterilization of certain classes of people, even though the right to procreate is considered a basic civil right. For the most part, courts have held these statutes to be a valid exercise of the state's police power in accordance with the tone of Justice Holmes's famous statement in the landmark case of *Buck v. Bell*.[30] In holding valid an attempt by Virginia to sterilize involuntarily an institutionalized mentally retarded woman whose mother and daughter were also institutionalized and retarded, Justice Holmes stated, "the principle that sustains compulsory vaccination is broad enough to cover cutting the Fallopian tubes. Three generations of imbeciles are enough."[31]

The major focus of these statutes is on classes of people who are confined in public mental hospitals and are often denominated as "feeble-minded," "mentally retarded," "mentally deficient," or "mentally ill." But about a half dozen states have statutes providing for involuntary sterilization which seek to reach certain classes of offenders usually characterized as "habitual criminals."[32] And while the number of states providing for involuntary sterilization continues to decline and the number of sterilizations of offenders is not large, involuntary sterilization is a possibility.

Are statutes authorizing the sterilization of offenders vague?

Yes. For example, the Iowa statute seeks to cover persons who "would produce a child or children having an inherited tendency to . . . criminality, or degeneracy, or who would probably become a social menace. . . ."[33] Connecticut's statute authorizes involuntary sterilization of "persons by whom procreation would be inadvisable."[34] Wisconsin's statute is similar.[35] The Delaware and Oklahoma statutes apply to "habitual criminals" and define that term as applying to anyone convicted of at least three felonies.[36]

In no state is sterilization automatically required. State officials are vested with authority to decide whether or not to order involuntary sterilization. A statute that failed to vest state officials with this discretion would be unconstitutional.[37] Yet this discretion could result in arbitrary enforcement.

Must an offender be imprisoned in order to be vulnerable to involuntary sterilization?

A few statutes appear to limit involuntary sterilization only to imprisoned offenders.[38] Practically speaking, a state would try to sterilize only the imprisoned even if the statute authorized the sterilization of the unimprisoned.

Do statutes which seek to prohibit procreation of a certain class of offenders specify a means of sterilization?

With the exception of the Iowa statute, which specifically permits neither "castration nor removal of sound organs from the body,"[39] statutes prohibiting procreation of certain classes of offenders fail to specify a means of sterilization.

Do statutes which authorize sterilization for offenders apply to both men and women?

Yes. The statutes authorizing sterilization for a narrow class of offenders do not distinguish between men and women.

What is the purpose of the sterilization laws, and are they justified?

The often stated purpose of sterilization laws aimed at offenders is to reduce criminality. The effort assumes that criminal inclinations are transferred genetically from generation to generation. Sterilization thus becomes a crime-control device.

This rationale is not supported by scientific research. Science has not documented that criminality is genetically transferred.[4] Our limited knowledge of the causations of crime suggests that it is very complex and is strongly tied to environmental factors—that is social, economic, physical, and family factors. Accordingly, current sterilization laws aimed at controlling crime would seem unsupportable.

Sterilization threatens a basic civil right and should be countenanced, if at all, only if it is supported by a compelling interest. The unsupported rationale now offered to support sterilization hardly rises to the level of a compelling state interest.

Involuntary-sterilization laws aimed at offenders are not justified by corrections officials as punishment. If they were, they would violate the Eighth Amendment to the U.S. Constitution.

Has the Supreme Court ever decided the constitutionality of an involuntary-sterilization statute directed toward offenders?

Yes. And it held it unconstitutional. In *Skinner v. Oklahoma*,[41] the state, in accordance with its Criminal Sterilization Act, intended to perform a vasectomy on an offender convicted once of stealing chickens and twice of armed robbery. After losing in the Oklahoma Supreme Court, the offender appealed to the U.S. Supreme Court, arguing that the state statute violated the Eighth Amendment and the due-process and equal-protection clauses of the Fourteenth Amendment. Justice Douglas, writing the majority opinion in 1942, addressed only the equal-protection claim and found for the offender. He reasoned that because "marriage and procreation are fundamental to the very existence and survival of the race" and are "one of the basic civil rights of man," the habitual-offender statute had to be justified by a compelling state interest. After examining the types of crimes which would and would not subject an offender to sterilization and concluding that the "same quality of offense . . . sterilizes one and not the other," he held the statute unconstitutional.[42]

In *Skinner,* the Court did not decide whether the state's procedures were constitutional or whether involuntary sterilization violated the Eighth Amendment. It's analysis, applicable to every jurisdiction with a habitual-offender statute, turned on whether there was a substantial difference between the crimes which did and did not lead to sterilization. Finding that the crimes were intrinsically the same, the court held that the statute ran afoul of the equal-protection clause.

Can a person threatened with involuntary sterilization obtain a court order enjoining the sterilization?

Probably. A person threatened with involuntary sterilization has several excellent statutory and constitutional arguments to make.

For example, he can argue on statutory grounds (1) that he is not a member of the class defined in the statute (i.e. a "habitual criminal," or a person for whom "procreation would be inadvisable"; (2) that his condition might change so that sterilization is unnecessary; (3) that the preliminary procedures required in the statute were not followed; or (4) that criminality is not inheritable.

Moreover, statutes authorizing involuntary sterilization are vulnerable on constitutional grounds. For example, a statute may be unconstitutional because (1) it fails to comply with the procedural requirements of the due-process clause of the Fourteenth Amendment to the U.S. Constitution;[43] (2) it creates arbitrary classes of persons who are and are not subject to the involuntary-sterilization statutes and thus violates the equal-protection clause of the Fourteenth Amendment;[44] (3) it is unconstitutionally vague;[45] and (4) it violates the Bill-of-Attainder clause[46] and the Eighth Amendment.

What should a person do if threatened with involuntary sterilization?

Get a good lawyer. A court order will be required to stop state officials intent on involuntarily sterilizing a person. The legal arguments necessary to win such a case may be difficult and the procedures complex. A lawyer will be necessary.

D. PARENTAL RIGHTS

The collateral consequences of a conviction may seriously threaten a convicted person's parental rights. It is possible, for example, that an unmarried woman offender serving a long prison term would lose custody of her children. Or a married male offender who was divorced because of the conviction might have his child adopted over his objection.

These are extreme and infrequent consequences of a conviction. But they occasionally happen. And when they do, the female rather than the male offender is more likely to be affected for she is more likely to have a continuing interest in her child. For example, according to a Pennsylvania study, over 60 percent of the female prisoners surveyed were unmarried and 80 percent of these unmarried women had one or more children.[47]

The parental rights of convicted persons is an unsettled area. Traditionally courts assume that a child's best interests are served by remaining in the care and custody of a natural parent. This is a rebuttal presumption and is placed in question when a parent is convicted and imprisoned. The closer the underlying crime bears on parental responsibilities and the longer the imprisonment period, the weaker the presumption that a child's best interests are served by remaining in the natural parent's custody. In some situations a child's best interests may require the care and custody of another.

The resolution of these competing interests cannot be predicted in a particular case. Not only are a parent's substantive rights very substantial but the constitutionally required procedures with which a state must comply if it chooses to interfere with those rights are stringent. A natural parent with an able lawyer would probably be able to protect her rights.[48]

Is the parent-child relationship constitutionally protected?

Yes. The U.S. Supreme Court has often declared that the cluster of relationships arising out of a family are fundamental rights protected against governmental intrusions.[49] Governmental interference with these fundamental domestic relationships must be justified by a compelling state interest and be consistent with basic due-process rights.

The grounds justifying such intervention may generally be summarized as neglect,[50] abuse,[51] abandonment,[52] and failure to provide proper care and support.[53] There are other grounds, varying from state to state, but taken together the intent of these statutes is to remove a child from an environment created by the parents which is substantially injurious to the child.

How might a conviction or imprisonment affect a parent's rights?

There are two basic ways a conviction or imprisonment might be used to threaten a parent's rights: neglect and adoption proceedings. These are different legal proceedings which will be dealt with separately.

What constitutes a neglectful parent?

Every state has statutes providing for the care and protection of children, which authorize the state, after notice and a hearing, to remove a child from the custody of his parents and place the child in foster care or an institution. Typically these statutes authorize a finding of neglect if a court finds that the child has been abandoned, the parents are unfit, the home environment is detrimental to a child's morals, or the child lacks the proper food and shelter.[54]

A natural parent retains considerable legal interest in a child after a neglect finding, and may eventually be able to regain custody of the child. A parent found to be neglectful faces the danger, however, that the state may follow a neglect finding with a proceeding aimed at permanently terminating a person's parental rights.[55] In this case, the state must prove its case thoroughly, and there are many safeguards of the parents' rights.

Is conviction grounds for a finding of neglect?

No state equates a conviction with neglect. But at least one state, California, has a statute authorizing the initiation of a neglect proceeding when a child's parent has been "convicted of a felony" which proves the "unfitness" of a parent to have future custody.[56] By the terms of this statute, not every felony conviction would threaten a person's rights as a parent. The underlying crime must prove a parent's "unfitness" for future custody.[57]

Would it be constitutional for a state to terminate a parent's custody rights solely on the basis of a conviction?

No. A parent's rights to custody are constitutionally protected and may be terminated only on limited grounds that bear a direct relationship to a child's best interest and after a full judicial hearing subject to all due-process safeguards. Unless the underlying criminal behavior bore a direct relationship to a child's health and well-being, the conviction should not prejudice a convicted person's parental rights.

Does imprisonment constitute abandonment for the purpose of a neglect statute?

No, according to most courts. Courts usually resist viewing a parent's imprisonment as abandonment of a child.[58] They seem persuaded that forfeiture of parental rights on this ground would constitute an additional punishment in violation of constitutional rights.

This result would certainly seem the correct one, for a contrary conclusion would appear based on the unrealistic assumption that the convicted defendant committed the crime with the intention of being apprehended and imprisoned. Obviously any parent wanting to abandon a child could do so with less drama and risk.

Do some states permit the child of a convicted or imprisoned parent to be adopted without the voluntary consent of the parent?

Yes. All states have statutes providing for the legal

adoption of children. A natural parent's voluntary consent to the adoption is normally a prerequisite if a child is to be legally adopted. In a few circumstances, including the conviction or imprisonment of a natural parent, a natural parent's consent may be unnecessary for a child to be legally adopted.

A few states have statutes which expressly provide for the adoption of children without the consent of a natural parent who has been convicted or imprisoned.[59] In order for consent not to be required under these statutes, the conviction must lead to a minimum prison term. The length of the term varies from state to state; in South Dakota, for example, it must be at least one year; in Oregon and Rhode Island, three years.[60]

A few states key the elimination of the consent requirement to the loss of civil rights and not to a prison term of a specified length or a crime of a particular nature.[61] Thus the New York statute provides that a natural parent's consent shall not be required of a parent who has been deprived of civil rights and whose civil rights have not been restored. The Washington statute, which is less sweeping than the New York statute, does not automatically dispense with the consent requirement in every case. Rather, it dispenses with the requirement of parental consent where the crime leading to the loss of civil rights was of "such a nature that the welfare of the child would be best served by a permanent deprivation of parental rights."[62]

Will a court authorize adoption without the consent of a convicted or imprisoned parent when the pertinent statute does not expressly authorize it?

Not likely. Courts are reluctant to authorize adoption without the consent of a convicted or imprisoned parent unless it is expressly authorized by statute. Such decisions pay great deference to the rights of parents as well as the best interests of a child and do not equate imprisonment with abandonment or desertion or unfitness.

The only possible exception to this rule is when the parent's offense is directly related to parental fitness, as in the case of a parent convicted of child abuse,[63] or when the imprisonment period is very lengthy.[64]

Is a parent entitled to notice of the adoption proceedings?

Yes. A natural parent has a constitutional right to notice of adoption proceedings, and most statutes so require.[65] This rule does not apply if the natural parent's right to custody has been terminated by judicial decree.

Are statutes authorizing the adoption of a child without the consent of a convicted or imprisoned parent constitutional?

The few courts that have considered this question have not hesitated to permit adoption over the objection of a convicted or imprisoned parent when a statute expressly authorizes it.[66]

However, this is not a settled issue. While it may be constitutional for a state to authorize the adoption of a child over a parent's objection in some circumstances, those circumstances are not precisely defined. A convicted or imprisoned parent who appears to fall within the general limits of a statute should not assume that her child may be adopted without her consent. The law is unclear; a parent who opposes the adoption of her child should not allow important parental rights to be disposed of without a vigorous challenge in the courts.

May a conviction indirectly affect a convicted person's right to bar the adoption of her child?

Yes. Although a state's statute may not expressly authorize the adoption of a child without parental consent when the parent has been convicted or imprisoned, the conviction or imprisonment of a parent may be relevant to other grounds which authorize adoption without consent. For example, some states provide that the consent of a parent judicially deprived of custody is unnecessary.[67] This will be true whether or not custody has been terminated because of parental unfitness or because of a divorce action. Thus a person divorced on the ground of a conviction who fails to retain custody or visitation rights may have her child adopted without her consent.

Is an ex-convict permitted to adopt a child?

An ex-convict will probably find it very difficult to adopt a child. While the statutes that define who may adopt a child do not specifically exclude ex-convicts, the character requirements set forth in the statutes would probably be interpreted to preclude ex-convicts from adoption. Typical statutes, for example, require the adopting parent to be of "good moral" character, or be a "proper" or "suitable" person.

Few cases address the question of whether an ex-convict may adopt a child. One reported case facing this issue, however, suggests the difficulty an ex-convict seeking to adopt a child will face. In the *Petition of Berkowitz*,[68] an intermediate state appellate court affirmed a lower-court ruling denying the adoption petition because there was evidence that the petitioner had been discharged from his employment for forging his employer's checks and depositing them in his personal account. He was not convicted of any crime, and from the brief report of the case it does not appear that he admitted the allegations. Nevertheless, the court found that this justified a finding that he was not a person of reputable character.

E. THE RIGHT TO CHANGE NAMES

May an ex-convict change his name?

Yes. It is easy to imagine many prisoners who wish to put some distance between themselves and their past upon release from prison on parole by changing their names.

At common law, a person could change his name without having to obtain any approval from a court or any governmental body as long as the purpose of the name change was not to defraud someone. All that was necessary to exercise this right was to change the name and use it consistently. This easy method for changing a name is available today in many states.

Furthermore, all states have now enacted statutes which set forth a legal process for the formal changing of a name. In a few states, this formal process is exclusive, which means that the informal method recognized by the common law cannot be used in these states. The judicial process is usually simple and inexpensive.

Three general points are worth making:

First, an individual seeking a name change through the courts must file a petition which in some states require the petitioner to specify whether he has been convicted of a crime, and if so to give the details surrounding the conviction.[69] These statutes do not state that a conviction will bar an individual from obtaining a name change; they only require the petitioner to state whether he has been convicted. Thus, from the face of the statutes, it appears that an ex-convict's right to change his name through the courts is equal to that of anyone else.

Second, a court has discretion to grant or deny an individual's petition for a change of name. This discretion must be exercised reasonably and reflect the purposes of the statutes. A court may not deny an ex-convict's petition for a name change for punitive or arbitrary reasons.

Third, an ex-convict seeking a name change will have to satisfy a court that the reason for the name change is not for purposes of fraud. A court would make this inquiry even though the petitioner had not been convicted of a crime, but its inquiry will probably be more intense if the petitioner is an ex-convict.

Regardless of whether an ex-convict changes his name informally or formally, there will probably be some resistance from department stores, credit unions, banks, or government agencies that normally require evidence of identification.

May an innocent spouse of an ex-convict change the name of their child?

This situation arises when the ex-convict is a father of a child now in the custody of his former wife. By custom—and by law—a child of divorced parents usually retains the surname of the father even though the mother has custody of the child and uses her maiden name. When a child's father has been convicted of a crime, a mother occasionally seeks to change the child's surname to her maiden name. A mother may not do this informally in the tradition of the common law; she must make a formal application to the courts for a change of name.

Courts grant a father a protectible interest in having his child bear his name, regardless of the child's sex, and deny such petitions unless a mother has a compelling reason and the name change is in the best interests of the child.

The few reported cases on this subject suggest that the father's behavior will have to be very serious for the court to grant a name change petition for a child. In one reported case, a father had killed the child's maternal grandfather,[70] and in another the father was serving a life sentence for murder and under the law of that state was deemed civilly dead.[71]

A father is normally entitled to notice of an application to change his child's name. If a father is imprisoned in a state that has a civil-death statute, however, notice may not be required. In such a case, a court may require as a matter of discretion that the father be given notice of the application, and that certainly would be the better practice, but it is uncertain that a "civilly dead" father has a constitutional right to receive notice of the name-change application.

NOTES

1. HOLT AND MILLER, EXPLORATIONS IN INMATE-FAMILY RELATIONSHIPS, 61 (Research Division, Department of Corrections, Calif.) (1972); GLASER, EFFECTIVENESS OF A PRISON AND PAROLE SYSTEM, 379 (1964); OHLIN, THE STABILITY AND VALIDITY OF PAROLE EXPERIENCE TABLES (1954).
2. GLASER, *Supra* note 1, at 379.
3. *See generally Am. Jur.* 2d, Desk Book at 211.
4. *See generally* 24 AM. JUR. 2d, *Divorce and Separation*, §26.
5. *See, e.g.*, Brady v. Brady, 238 A. 2d 201 (1968).
6. *See, e.g.*, ARK. STAT. ANN. § 34–1202 (Supp. 1975).
7. *See, e.g.*, ARK. STAT. ANN. § 34–1202 (Supp. 1975); IND. CODE. ANN. § 31–1–11.53 (Supp. 1977).
8. *See, e.g.*, CONN. GEN. STAT. ANN. § 46–13 (Supp. 1967); MINN. STAT. A. § 518.06 (Supp. 1978).
9. *See, e.g.*, KAN. STAT. § 60–1601 (Supp. 1977) imprisonment resulting from felony conviction); N.H. REV. STAT. ANN. § 458.7 (1975) (one year or more); WASH. REV. CODE ANN. § 26.08.020 (Supp. 1977) (person must be imprisoned when divorce action is brought).
10. *See* note 6, *supra*.
11. *See* note 7, *supra*.
12. *See, e.g.*, GA. CODE ANN. § 30–102 (8).

13. *See* notes 8 and, *supra*.
14. *See, e.g.*, Holloway v. Holloway 55 S.E. 197 (1906; Sutherlin v. Sutherlin 61 N.E. 206 (1901).
15. *See, e.g.*, MD. ANN. CODE art. 16, § 24 (Supp. 1977).
16. *See, e.g.*, VT. STAT. ANN. tit. 15, § 551 (Supp. 1977).
17. Clark v. Clark, 94 N.H. 398, A.2d 162 (1947) (conviction for "absence from station and duty after leave had expired" comes within meaning of statute authorizing divorce based on conviction of a crime punishable by imprisonment of one year or more). For a different result, *see* Getz v. Getz, 332 Ill. App. 364, 75 N.E. 2d 530 (1947) (desertion in wartime held to be neither a felony nor infamous crime).
18. N.Y. DOM. REL. LAW § 6(2) McKinney, Supp. 1977).
19. *See generally* 139 A.L.R. 1308 (1942).
20. *See* Read v. Read, 119 Colo. 278, 202 P.2d 953 (1949).
21. *See, e.g.*, Cone v. Cone, 58 N. Y. 152 (1877); Colascione v. Colascione, 57 Misc. 2d 199, 291 N.Y.S. 2d 559 (Sup. Ct. 1968).
22. *See, e.g.*, State v. Duket, 90 Wis. 272, 63 N.W. 83 (1875).
23. IDAHO CODE § 32–615 (1963).
24. TEX. FAM. CODE ANN. tit. 1 § 3.04(b) (1975).
25. *See, e.g.*, W. VA. CODE § 48–2–1 (Supp. 1977).
26. *See* Douglass v. Douglass, 148 Cal. App. 2d 867, 307 P.2d 674 (2d Dist. Ct. App. 1957).
27. Johnson v. Rockefeller, 365 F. Supp. 377, 383 (S.D.N.Y. 1973) (three-judge court) (Lasker, J., dissenting).
28. *Ibid.*
29. WASH. REV. CODE ANN. § 26.04.030
30. Buck v. Bell 274 U.S. 200 (1927).
31. *Ibid.* at 207.
32. *See, e.g.*, CONN. GEN. STAT. ANN. § 19–569g (Supp. 1977); DEL. CODE tit. 16, § 5703 (1975); OKLA. STAT. tit. 43A, § 341 (1954); IOWA CODE ANN. § 145.9 (1972); WIS. STAT. ANN. § 46.12 (1957).
33. IOWA CODE ANN. § 145.9 (1972).
34. CONN. GEN. STAT. § 19–569g (Supp. 1977).
35. WIS. STAT. ANN. § 46.12 (1957).
36. DEL. CODE tit. 16 § 5703 (a) (1975); OKLA. STAT. tit. 43A, § 341 (1954).
37. *See, e.g.*, Davis v. Berry, 216 F. 413 (D.C. Iowa 1914), *rev'd on other grounds*, 242 U.S. 468 (1917).
38. *See e.g.*, CONN. GEN. STAT. ANN. § 19–569g (Supp. 1977); OKLA. STAT. tit. 43A, § 341 (1954); WIS. STAT. ANN. § 46.12 (1957).
39. IOWA CODE ANN. § 145.9 (1972).
40. *See, e.g.*, WILLIAMS, THE SANCTITY OF LIFE AND THE CRIMINAL LAW (1957).

41. 316 U.S. 365 (1942).
42. *Ibid.* at 541.
43. *See, e.g.,* Davis v. Berry, *supra* note 37; *In re* Opinion of Justices, 162 So. 123 (1935); Williams v. Smith, 131 N.E. 2 (1921); Brewer v. Valk, 167 S.E. 638 (1933); *In re* Hendrickson, 123 P. 2d 322 (1942).
44. *See, e.g.,* Skinner v. Okla., *supra* note 41; Haynes v. Lapeer Circuit Court, 166 N.W. 938 (1918); Smith v. Command, 204 N.W. 140 (1925); *In re* Thomson, 169 N.Y.S. 638, *aff'd.* 171 N.Y.S. 1094 (1918).
45. For a discussion of the vagueness doctrine in a related field, *see* Cicero v. Olgiati 410 F. Supp. 1080 (S.D.N.Y. 1976).
46. Davis v. Berry, *supra* note 37.
47. Note, *Civil Death Statutes and the Convict's Right to Bring Civil Suit,* 4 Cap. U. L. Rev. 123, 127 (1975).
48. Because the problems of parental rights appear to arise more often for the female offender than the male offender, the pronouns "she" and "her" will be used in this section.
49. Stanley v. Illinois, 405 U.S. 645 (1972); Griswold v. Connecticut, 381 U.S. 479 (1965); Prince v. Massachusetts, 321 U.S. 158 (1944); Pierce v. Society of Sisters, 268 U.S. 510 (1925); Meyer v. Nebraska, 262 U.S. 390 (1923).
50. *See, e.g.,* Del. Code, tit. 31 § 301 (1975).
51. *See, e.g.,* Conn. Gen. Stat. Ann., § 17–53 (1976).
52. *See, e.g.,* Mass. Gen. Laws Ann., ch. 273, § 1 (Supp. 1978).
53. *See, e.g.,* Colo. Rev. Stat. § 14–6–101 (1974).
54. *See* notes 50–53, *supra.*
55. *See, e.g.,* Cal. Civ. Code § 232 (West, Supp. 1977); Conn. Gen. Stat. Ann. § 17–43a (Supp. 1978).
56. Cal. Civ. Code § 232 (a) (4) (West, Supp. 1977)
57. *See In re* Melkonian, 313 P.2d 52, 152 C.A. 2d 250 (1957).
58. *See, e.g.,* Diernfeld v. People, 137 Colo. 238, 323 P.2d 628 (1958); State v. Grady, 231 Ore. 65, 371 P.2d 68 (1962); Fronk v. State, 7 Utah 2d 245, 322 P.2d 397 (1958); *In re* Jameson, 20 Utah 2d 53, 432 P.2d 881 (1967). *Contra, see* Jaques, 48 N.J. Super. 523, 138 A. 2d 581 (1958).
59. *See, e.g.,* Or. Rev. Stat. § 109.322 (1975); R.I. Gen. Laws § 15–7–7 (Supp. 1976); S.D. Compiled Laws Ann. § 25–6–4 (1976).
60. *Ibid.*
61. *See, e.g.,* N.Y. Dom. Rel. Law § 111 (McKinney Supp. 1976-77); Wash. Rev. Code Ann. § 26.32.040 (Supp. 1976).
62. *Ibid.*

63. *See, e.g.*, Petition of Kelly Minors, 6 Ariz., App. 299, 432 P.2d 158 (1967).
64. *See, e.g.*, Casper v. Huber, 85 Nev. 474, 456 P.2d 436 (1969).
65. *See, e.g.*, Armstrong v. Manzo, 380 U.S. 545 (1965); *In re* Estate of Hampton, 55 Cal. App. 2d 545, 131 P.2d 565 (1962).
66. *See, e.g.*, *In re* Anonymous, 17 Misc. 2d 691, 197 N.Y.S. 2d 870 (Sup. Ct. 1959); *In re* Adoption of O'Daniels, 128 N.Y.S. 2d 351 (Sup. Ct. 1953).
67. *See, e.g.*, CAL. CIV. CODE § 224 (West Supp. 1970); IOWA CODE ANN. § 600.3 (Supp. 1970); ME. REV. STAT. tit. 19, § 532 (Supp. 1970); MINN. STAT. ANN. § 259.24 (Supp. 1970).
68. 88 Ill. App. 2d 1, 232 N.E. 2d 72 (App. Ct. 1967).
69. *See, e.g.*, N.Y. CIV. RIGHTS LAW, § 61 (McKinney 1976).
70. Application of Yessner, 61 Misc. 2d 174, 304 N.Y.S. 2d 901 (Supp. Ct. 1969).
71. Application of Fein, 274 N.Y.S. 2d 547 (Civ. Ct., N.Y. County, 1966).

VII

The Right to Employment

Is employment important to an ex-convict?
Of course. Just as it is to anyone else. A job is a source of income, a setting to make friends, and a part of a person's concept of self. It helps to determine where one lives and how one uses spare time; it is an important influence on family life.

Do employers discriminate against ex-convicts?
Yes. Ex-convicts experience great difficulty in securing employment at all levels of government and in the private sector. One of the best studies of the problem, *Employment Problems of Released Prisoners*, by George A. Pownall, focused on the employment problems of released federal prisoners.[1] The major conclusions of that study were:

- Unemployment was very high among released prisoners. For example, in the mid-1960s, only 63.9 percent of the offenders in the sample were employed full-time compared to 82 percent of the national civilian labor force, and 17% of the offenders were unemployed—more than three times the national unemployment rate at the time.
- Many employed ex-convicts were underemployed, working in low-paid and dead-end jobs, often characterized by employment instability.

- Former offenders having the most difficulty in the job market were the poorly educated, the unmarried, the very young, older men, and blacks.
- The most difficult period for an ex-offender is the first six months after release, in employment as well as other important areas of life.
- The extent of the criminal record affected employment propects; the larger the number of incarcerations, the greater the obstacles facing a jobseeker. This meant that minorities faced more difficulty in securing employment than whites.

Pownall's findings were dramatic but probably understated the problem. Federal prisoners are probably more employable than prisoners convicted under the law of particular states. Because of the nature of federal crimes, federal prisoners tend to be older and better educated, and have had more consistent pre-arrest employment records, than state prisoners. Perhaps more significantly, federal prisoners tend to have a smaller portion of minority-group members than state prisoners.

Does employment discrimination against ex-offenders have a special impact on minorities?

Yes. As a general rule, employment discrimination based on criminal record has a disproportionate impact on minorities. As one study put it:

> What is clear is that employment decisions based on arrest and conviction records have a disproportionate effect on members of minority groups. And although all ex-offenders fare poorly in the job market, there is evidence that minority ex-offenders suffer even more than their white counterparts.[2]

Are ex-convicts qualified for the jobs not normally available to them because of employment barriers?

Yes. It is occasionally argued that the debate over employment discrimination against ex-convicts is academic, because most ex-convicts have poor skills and work habits and thus are unqualified for most jobs. Although there is some truth to this view, employment discrimination nevertheless bars many ex-convicts from obtaining jobs for which they are qualified.

Many, if not most, ex-offenders have some skills and have some employment record, and many jobs not available to ex-offenders do not require high job skills. For these, the artificial employment barriers are a critical stumbling block.

Ex-convicts are as good if not better workers than persons with comparable skills who do not have conviction records.[3] In one study, employers of ex-offenders were asked to evaluate their employees' punctuality, attendance, honesty, judgment, initiative, cooperativeness, accuracy, and industriousness; the opinion of the employers was that ex-offenders were no worse than other employees and possibly slightly better.[4] This conclusion is buttressed by the relatively low default rate of ex-offenders under the bonding program developed by the U.S. Department of Labor.[5]

In addition, ex-offenders who have low skills and poor work habits may not be that different from others who are disadvantaged. And yet there is a national policy, albeit often criticized as unimplemented, in favor of aiding the unconvicted disadvantaged in obtaining employment. It seems unfair for ex-offenders, who are in other respects similar to that population, to face sweeping employment barriers.

What are the major consequences of employment discrimination?

Although there is no conclusive evidence establishing a causal relationship between crime and unemployment for all offenders, many observers believe there is a close relationship between these two factors for most offenders.[6] For example, the RCA Institute, in a 1972 study entitled, *The Invisible Prison: An Analysis of Barriers to Inmate Training of Post-Release Employment in New York and Maine*, stated, "Employment . . . is more than simply a fringe benefit to freedom for the inmate; it can be a critical factor in his ability to break out of the syndrome of criminal activity. . . ."[7]

Daniel Glaser, in his widely respected study, *The Effectiveness of a Prison and Parole System*, concludes:

More than 90% of the felony arrests reported in the United States and an even higher percentage of recidivist felonies involve the taking of someone else's money or property. This fact, in conjunction with the strong association between recidivism and unemployment, suggests that the criminal activity which sends men back to prison in the United States is undertaken primarily as an alternative to legitimate gainful employment. Of course, we encounter some recidivism among ostensibly well-employed releasees and some nonrecidivism among long destitute ex-prisoners. But releasees who do not return to crime seem generally to be distinguished by the achievement of economic self-sufficiency, and by satisfaction in primary group relationships not requiring or encouraging disorderly or criminal activity.[8]

Employment is also important for reasons other than the financial contributions it makes to a person's life. Employment influences how a person chooses to use his leisure time, the choice of his friends, and his conception of himself. Glaser summed it up this way: "Employment is usually a major factor making possible an integrated 'style of life' which includes nonrecidivism, successful marriage, and satisfaction in other social relationships."[9]

Furthermore, an unemployed ex-offender may well be a public charge and may well cause his family to become a public charge. Long-term unemployment may cause an ex-offender to withdraw permanently from the nation's work force, thus limiting any social and economic contribution that he might make.

EMPLOYERS AND THEIR PRACTICES

The Government as Employer

Are public employment and public office the same thing?

No. The term "public office" is special and refers to elected and appointed governmental positions of special trust and honor.[10] Thus people in public office would include high state officials such as governor, attorney general, or agency commissioners and local officials such as mayor, school-board members, or police commissioners. In contrast, public employment refers to governmental jobs such as secretary, public works employees, firemen, policemen, park employees, receptionists and office clerks. The distinction between a public office and public employment may be difficult to make on occasion, and of course will vary from state to state, but the vast majority of governmental jobs fall within the category of public employment.

Does public employment represent a significant source of employment for ex-convicts?

Yes. Government employment at the federal, state, and local level is a large and growing source of jobs. The pertinent statistics were summarized in one study:

> State and local governments presently employ thirteen million persons, approximately fifteen percent of the nation's labor force. All trends indicate a rapid expansion of employment possibilities. In New York, state and local governments employed 941,700 persons in 1968. By 1980, 1,392,000 persons are expected to be employed, an increase of almost fifty percent. In 1968, New York City employed 381,900 people, and by 1980, this figure should reach 549,500, an increase of 43.9 percent.[11]

Many jobs in the public sector are not beyond the employment skills of many ex-convicts. The fact that many governments impose across-the-board barriers to exclude ex-convicts from jobs for which they would otherwise be suitable makes notable the conclusion reached by the President's Task Force on Prisoner Rehabilitation: "When it comes to providing jobs . . . those very entities that are responsible for rehabilitating prisoners—the states and the federal government—set a most unedifying example."[12]

Does the federal government discriminate against ex-convicts?

Yes. Although the U.S. Constitution does not require exclusion of convicted criminals from federal employment, federal statutes bar certain types of offenders from many federal positions. For example, under the Omnibus Crime Control and Safe Streets Act of 1968, a person convicted of inciting a riot or civil disorder and sentenced to at least one year in prison is ineligible for federal employment for five years after conviction.[13]

Ex-convicts may also be barred from employment regulated by the federal government. Felons, for example, may not serve as officers or directors of any labor organization under the Labor-Management Reporting and Disclosure Act of 1959 [14] Ex-convicts may be unable to obtain a security clearance and thus not be employable by the federal government or defense-related industry.

Even without explicit bars to hiring ex-convicts, governmental agencies retain broad discretion in deciding whether to hire an ex-convict. Although the U.S. Civil Service Commission accepts applications from ex-convicts at any time, it retains the right to review an applicant's suitability by reviewing such variables as the nature and seriousness of the offense, the age of offender at the time of conviction, the length of time between conviction and application, and evidence of individual adjustment to prison and community life.[15] This broad discretion may result in many ex-convicts being arbitrarily rejected for jobs.

May an ex-convict enlist in the armed forces?

The air force, navy, and marines do not bar persons convicted of crimes from enlisting. The army, however, bars anyone "convicted of a felon" from enlisting.[16] The Secretary of the Army may waive this barrier in "meritorious cases."[17]

Do state and local governments discriminate against ex-convicts?

Yes. By means of state constitutional and statutory, and local ordinances, many state and local governments bar ex-convicts from public employment. Some bars are permanent, while others lapse at a specified time after conviction. Generally, ex-convicts are barred from all jobs in police and correctional departments.

Across-the-board employment discrimination by states against ex-convicts is widespread. According to a 1972 study, sixteen states have statutory provisions restricting or excluding persons convicted of a crime, or of "notorious" or "disgraceful" conduct, from government employment.[18] In twelve of these sixteen states, such persons "may" be refused employment; in the other four states, such refusals are mandatory.

This same study also found that twenty-one states have statutory provisions which condition public employment on such vague factors as "character" and "reputation." Consequently, government agencies reject ex-convicts regularly because they do not satisfy the "character" or "reputation" requirements. As one commentator concluded, "Where the statutes do not prevent public employment entirely, the decision on hiring is regularly left to an administrative agency. Here, practical politics dictates that few ex-criminals actually be employed."[19] Thus, short of an outright rejection, an agency's "practical politics" may cause unreasonable delay in reviewing an ex-convict's application.

Private Employers

Do private employers discriminate against ex-convicts?

Yes. The great bulk of jobs are in the private sector, and while no law prohibits a private employer from hiring an ex-offender, most private employers refuse to hire ex-offenders.

Numerous studies have found substantial discrimination against ex-convicts by private employers. These employers reject ex-convicts if other labor supplies are available, hire ex-convicts only for the lowest level dead-end jobs, or underpay them. As one student reported his representative findings: "Of 475 potential employers interviewed in New York City, 312 stated unequivocally that they would never hire a released offender; 311 of the 312 said they would fire such a man if they inadvertently hired him and later learned of his past."[20]

What is bonding and why is it important?

Many jobs for which ex-offenders are suited are not available to them because of fidelity-bonding requirements.

A fidelity bond is a contract by which an employer is insured by the bonding company against any loss resulting from a dishonest employee covered by the bond. Fidelity bonding is generally considered good financial management, and fidelity-bonding companies seek to minimize their risk by establishing hiring guidelines which an employer must follow.

Under the restraint of these guidelines, a private employer will not hire an ex-offender for a job that is bonded. And since an employer usually obtains blanket bonding to cover all jobs, the number of jobs unavailable to ex-offenders because of bonding requirements far and away exceeds the number of jobs in which potential loss might legitimately bar ex-convicts.

The bonding requirement is a substantial impediment to employment for ex-offenders, for it encompasses many jobs for which many ex-offenders would otherwise be suitable. For example, as a general rule, bonding is required for hotel jobs, maids, babysitters, credit clerks, sales clerks, or collection agents. Moreover, the trend is that the number of jobs which require bonding is increasing. Accordingly, because most fidelity-insurance companies refuse to bond ex-convicts, a substantial and growing number of jobs are unavailable to ex-offenders.

There is some reason to believe that employers often use the contract with fidelity companies as a convenient excuse to deny employment to ex-offenders. For example there is some evidence that bonding companies have agreed to bond ex-offenders when pressed by employers. Also, according to one study, employers in the Los Angeles area conceded that although they lacked the capacity to assess the potential risk of individual employees, they had no plans to try to develop any. This passive stance by employers at least suggests that the requirements of bonding companies are consistent with a broadly held assumption that ex-convicts will be a poor employment risk.

Are ex-offenders poorer risks than the average employee?

The limited, inconclusive evidence pertinent to this important question suggests that ex-offenders are better risks than some company employees. The evidence derived by the Federal Bonding Program, explained more fully below, indicates that ex-offenders who did not qualify for normal fidelity bonding, and who were bonded under a special federal program, defaulted at a rate with a loss ratio—the ratio of dollars paid in claims to premiums collected—

somewhat lower than that reported for comparable activities in the fidelity-bonding industry as a whole.[21]

Should fidelity-bonding companies be prohibited from having a blanket exclusion against all ex-offenders?

There are strong reasons to support legislation to prohibit blanket exclusions by fidelity-bonding companies. The current exclusions remove a substantial number of jobs from the market available to ex-offenders. The limited available evidence suggests that ex-offenders may not pose any greater risks than some employees currently employed. Legislation precluding the use of blanket exclusions and requiring individual assessments of risks would still leave considerable discretion with employers and fidelity-bonding companies and would not impose upon them any greater burden of individual assessment than is now routinely shouldered by employers in countless contexts.

What is the Federal Bonding Prorgam and how does one apply for coverage?

The United States Department of Labor developed the Federal Bonding Program as a means of offering fidelity-bonding coverage to qualified job applicants who cannot otherwise obtain it. While the program is not exclusively directed at ex-convicts, it includes them. To be bonded under this program, an individual must be suitable for the job in question and not commercially bondable.

The jobseeker or the prospective employee may seek fidelity-bonding coverage at any local office of a state employment service. These offices are found everywhere in the United States and its possessions and territories, including Puerto Rico, the Virgin Islands, and Guam. The bonds are issued in units of $500 and the maximum coverage per month is $20,000. While coverage is normally limited to one year, it may be extended if the employer cannot make other bonding arrangements.

Do labor unions discriminate against ex-convicts?

Yes. A comprehensive 1969 report prepared for the Manpower Administration of the U.S. Department of Labor reported that discrimination by labor unions seriously hindered the employment of ex-convicts.[22]

One study provides an excellent example of the problem

facing an ex-convict seeking to enter an apprenticeship program in New York.[23] New York Labor law requires that apprentices in approved programs "shall be selected on the basis of qualifications alone, as determined by objective criteria which permit review, and without any direct or indirect limitation, specification, or discrimination as to race, creed, color, or national origin."[24]

"Yet," according to this study, "approved apprenticeship programs are permitted to require proof that an applicant has no police record and to reject an applicant who has an arrest record."[25]

Do private employment agencies discriminate against ex-convicts?

Yes, private employment agencies mirror private employers. The President's Commission on Law Enforcement and Administration of Justice reported that 75 percent of the employment agencies surveyed in the New York City area would not refer any applicant with a criminal record, even if it were an arrest not followed by conviction.[26]

Do ex-convicts face other problems in securing employment?

Possibly. Many jobs require the employee to have a driver's license, and many ex-convicts who are on parole or probation are prohibited from obtaining a driver's license by their parole or probation officer. Other jobs, especially in defense industries, require employees to obtain a security clearance, which an ex-offender, regardless of the nature of his criminal background, may not be able to obtain.

OCCUPATIONAL LICENSING

Thousands of occupations in the private sector are licensed and regulated by government. Many of these occupations are closed to ex-convicts because statutes, regulations, or municipal ordinances set forth standards for obtaining a license which make ex-convicts ineligible. For example, some establish "good moral character" or "professional conduct" as standards and equate convictions with bad character or unprofessional conduct. Others specifically state that conviction makes the applicant ineligible for the license.

What is an occupational license?

An occupational license is a permit to engage in a particular occupation that is regulated by government. Licenses are granted by government at the federal, state, or local level to qualified applicants. A person does not have an absolute right to be licensed for a particular occupation, but licenses may not be denied or withdrawn arbitrarily. Unlicensed participation in a regulated occupation may lead to criminal prosecution.

Occupational licensing varies considerably among the states and even among the occupations regulated within one state. An ex-convict may be barred from a certain occupation in one state, but may not in another state. Or an ex-convict may be precluded from some licensed occupations but not others within the same state. Or some licensing regulations may make the exclusion of ex-convicts mandatory, while others make it discretionary. Some jurisdictions have statutes which mitigate the effect of a conviction by, for example, making an ex-convict eligible for some licensed occupations after a fixed period of time has passed since the conviction.

As a general matter, does the state have the authority to regulate an occupation by licensing?

Yes. The Supreme Court has held that a state may, consistent with constitutional principles, regulate an occupation by licensing in order to protect the lives, health, property, and morals of the citizenry. What the Supreme Court stated in the last century in *Crowley v. Christenson* holds true today:

> It is undoubtedly true that it is the right of every citizen of the United States to pursue any lawful trade or business, under such restrictions as are imposed upon all persons of the same age, sex and condition. But the possession and enjoyment of all rights are subject to such reasonable conditions as may be deemed by the government authority of the country essential to the safety, health, peace, good order and morals of the community.[27]

The state has considerable latitude in deciding whether to regulate a particular occupation.[28] As a result, government at one level or another regulates over 350 occupations, such as doctors, lawyers, accountants, teachers, psychologists, funeral directors, barbers, billiard operators, electricians, chauffeurs, landscape architects, peddlers, radiologists, social workers, plumbers, and junk dealers. And the number of occupations licensed by government is expanding. However there have been a few cases in which courts have ruled that the regulation of a certain industry was outside the scope of the police power.[29]

Why do governments regulate occupations?

The generally accepted justification of government regulation of occupations is the protection of the public's health, safety, morals, and welfare. With many occupations, this justification is appropriate and sufficient. But as government has sought to impose licensing restraints on more occupations, the tie between the newly regulated occupation and the public's health, safety, morals, and welfare has become sufficiently tenuous to raise a doubt as to the need for regulation.

Who grants occupational licenses?

Federal and state statutes and municipal ordinances grant licensing authority to administrative agencies such as licensing boards and boards of examiners. Some licensing boards grant licenses only for a particular occupation. More often, one licensing board has jurisdiction over several related occupations.

While some licensing authority is vested in a single official, more often a licensing board is composed of several members from the regulated occupation. The licensing agency theoretically has two dominant functions. It establishes standards and qualifications for entrance into an occupation; it defines and enforces the standards of practice required of the licensed practitioner through such disciplinary action as suspension or revocation of the license.

The licensing agency has broad discretion in performing its duties, but the discretion is not unlimited. An agency may not, for example, deny, suspend, or revoke a license arbitrarily, and if it does, the aggrieved individual should seek judicial review. Courts will readily reverse agency decisions which are arbitrary. Courts are very reluctant, however, to substitute their judgment for an agency decision with which an individual may disagree, but which is not arbitrary.

Although some federal statutes require occupational licensing by a federal authority, most licensing is by state statute or municipal ordinance. There is some speculation that local licensing laws have a greater impact on employment opportunities than state licensing laws.[30] In some states, for example, the power of municipalities extends to the licensing of exhibitions, trade, business, vocations, occupations, and professions conducted within the municipality.[31]

Do licensing laws affect ex-offenders?

Yes. In fact, no member of society is more likely to be excluded from a licensed occupation than a convicted criminal. The number of occupations regulated by governmental licensing is increasing and those occupations are in an expanding sector of the economy. Today the federal government, every state, and innumerable municipalities account for over 2,000 restrictions affecting the licensing of ex-convicts. The 2,000 licensing regulations pertain to about 350 occupations employing about 10,000,000 people.

Some of these occupations are professions such as accountant, doctor, dentist, lawyer, and teacher, for which most ex-convicts would not have the necessary occupational skills. The vast majority of licensed occupations and jobs, however, are either semi-skilled or unskilled, such as ambulance attendant, barber, beautician, billiard-room employee, chauffeur, peddler, and taxi driver, and a large portion of ex-offenders could qualify.

The difficulty for ex-offenders stems from the fact that the licensing regulations often contain blanket exclusionary requirements that disqualify ex-offenders. As a result, a significant number of former convicts are barred from innumerable employment possibilities.

What are the grounds for excluding an ex-convict from a licensed occupation or revoking a license of an individual convicted of a crime?

While the specific statutory grounds for excluding ex-convicts from licensed occupations or revoking their licenses vary, the grounds generally fall into three broad categories: (1) lack of good moral character; (2) conviction of a crime; (3) unprofessional conduct. The vagueness of these terms gives the licensing agencies broad discretion, which they have generally protected by failing to define these terms in detailed and specific regulations. Courts have generally sanctioned this broad discretionary power by failing to strike these terms as unconstitutionally vague or to insist that licensing agencies promulgate detailed regulations that would limit their discretionary power.

What is "good moral character"?

The most common ground for excluding ex-convicts from a licensed occupation is the lack of "good moral character." An American Bar Association survey of licensing provisions, for example, found that over 1,800 of the 2,000 different licensing provisions affecting ex-offenders contain a requirement of or similar to "good moral character."[32] (Other similar terms require that the applicant be "capable of inspiring confidence," be of "good repute," and be "morally fit.") Moreover, courts have generally authorized licensing agencies to imply a requirement of good moral character even if it is not explicitly provided for in the authorizing statute.[33] Theoretically, the broad and vague requirement of good moral character is justified by the need to protect the public from individuals of bad character who would be likely to abuse the position of trust extended to them by the occupational license.

Besides being the most common ground for excluding an ex-offender from a licensed occupation, the requirement of good moral character is the most limiting. Licensing boards, with approval by the courts, tend to equate conviction of a crime, whether it be a misdemeanor or a felony, with bad moral character.[34] This is a much broader exclusionary category than that which excludes an ex-convict on the grounds of a conviction, for those statutory provisions are limited to felony crimes or crimes of moral turpitude. However, licensing agencies do not specifically define the term "good moral character," and courts have often had considerable difficulty deciding on the meaning of the term.[35]

A widely accepted, though undocumented, impression is that the requirements of the term vary with the degree of professionalism of the occupation in question. The more professional the occupation, the more stringent the character requirements. Thus, it is generally believed that licensing boards responsible for the professions of higher status involving a greater degree of public trust have more difficult character requirements. As a general rule, the burden is on the applicant for a license to prove his good moral character whether the occupation is a professional or nonprofessional one.

There are three serious problems with the requirement of good moral character:

First, the term is very vague. It could mean almost anything and case law suggests that it has in fact meant almost anything. Courts have found the requirement valid in a wide variety of vocations and have not required licensing authorities to define the term. Its vagueness allows an agency to be arbitrary and to place an applicant, especially one of limited resources, in the very difficult position of having to shoulder the burden of challenging an official ruling of a governmental agency in court.

Second, licensing agencies impose the requirement of good moral character in many occupations where the character requirement seems peripheral to the reasonable and satisfactory performance of the occupation. As a result, ex-offenders are excluded from occupations for which they have the skills and which they could perform consistent with the public interest. Courts have sanctioned this undue extension of the good-moral-character requirement by failing to strike it as an arbitrary requirement when it is not reasonably related to the nature of the occupation.

Third, there is some evidence that licensing agencies apply the good-moral-character requirement almost exclusively to persons with an arrest or conviction record.[36] This wooden and specialized use of the term subverts the term's theoretical justification.

Does the conviction of a crime regularly bar a person from obtaining an occupational license?

Yes. The second most common ground for excluding an

ex-convict for a licensed occupation is the conviction of a crime. The American Bar Association survey of licensing restrictions, for example, identified 410 statutory provisions which prohibit the granting of a license on the grounds of a conviction.[37]

These statutes vary as to the type of crime which will trigger the licensing disability. Some provisions refer only to felonies, others to crimes involving moral turpitude, and a few enumerate a specific list of crimes. In some cases a conviction by a military court or a discharge from the armed services on a less than honorable basis have served to bar an applicant from obtaining an occupational license. The classification of a crime as a misdemeanor, felony, or a crime involving moral turpitude is normally done by the law of the licensing jurisdiction.

Statutory provisions which make reference to felonies or enumerated offenses present no interpretational problems. Those provisions, however, which refer to crimes involving moral turpitude are vague, grant licensing agencies broad authority, and invite uneven application. Usually a misdemeanor involving moral turpitude may exclude an offender from licensed occupation as well as a felony conviction.

May a license be withdrawn because of unprofessional conduct?

Yes. A less important, but nevertheless possible, ground for excluding an ex-convict from a licensed occupation is unprofessional conduct. A doctor, lawyer, teacher, or accountant could have his license revoked or suspended because of unprofessional conduct. Courts have upheld the vague term "unprofessional conduct" as constitutional against challenges that it was unconstitutionally vague, and have sustained the suspension or revocation of a license on grounds of unprofessional conduct because of the conviction of a crime.[38] A license may even be revoked on this ground even though the criminal proceedings are dismissed.[39]

Do the statutory provisions setting forth exclusionary grounds generally include mitigating provisions?

No. Licensing statutes which automatically bar an applicant because of a conviction or failure to have good moral character generally fail to contain any mitigating clauses which might curb the impact of the exclusionary provisions. Mitigating clauses might limit the exclusion by:

1. insisting that there be a direct relationship between the nature of the crime for which the applicant was convicted and the nature of the occupation for which the applicant seeks a license;
2. requiring the licensing agency to consider the age of the offender and surrounding circumstances at the time of the offense;
3. prohibiting a licensing agency from considering a particular conviction once a set period of time has elapsed after the time of conviction;
4. requiring the licensing agency to consider the overall behavior of an individual from the time of conviction to the time of application for a license.

The general failure to include such mitigating provisions and to temper the harshness of inflexible exclusionary rules make the broad exclusion of ex-convicts from licensed occupations unfair and counterproductive to broad social goals.

Does an acquittal, suspension of sentence, pardon, or expungement automatically make an ex-convict eligible for a license for which he was previously ineligible?

Not necessarily. While an acquittal would seem to leave an individual with the same legal status as though no criminal charges were ever pressed, licensing boards occasionally insist on being able to review the circumstances of a criminal charge in order to determine the moral character of the applicant or licenseholder.

As a general rule, a suspension of sentence following a conviction will not prevent the denial of an application or revocation of a license.

A pardon is generally an ineffective remedy for making an ex-offender eligible for a license which depends on a character assessment, for licensing authorities will examine the criminal record despite the pardon.[40]

Even in states that provide for expungement of the criminal record, it is generally held that this relief does not extend to licensed employment.[41] Moreover, expungement, as a remedy for disabilities, has been criticized on the grounds that the process of concealment is often unworkable and unenforceable and to the extent that it permits an individual to deny a criminal record, it institutionalizes an untrue assertion.[42]

Is licensing policy coordinated with correctional training programs?

Often not. Another aspect of the problem that intensifies the employment difficulties facing ex-convicts is the inadequate prison job-training programs. They tend to be make-work, keep-busy programs or programs providing a service utilized only by a state, such as making license plates. Even where there is a useful prison employment-training program, its usefulness may be substantially impaired because state licensing laws may bar ex-convicts from employment in that field.[43]

B. THE RIGHT TO EMPLOYMENT

THE RIGHT TO PUBLIC EMPLOYMENT AND OCCUPATIONAL LICENSING

Should there be a rational relationship between a licensing and employment qualification and the nature of the occupation to be licensed or job to be performed?

Yes. A person has a constitutional right to insist that there be a rational relationship between licensing and employment qualifications and the nature of the occupation licensed and job to be performed. This right is rooted in several constitutional doctrines which are discussed below.

Is it unconstitutional to bar an ex-convict from public employment or an occupational license because of qualifications unrelated to the job or license in question?

Yes. The due process clause of the Fourteenth Amendment requires that there be a rational relationship between the qualifications and standards for a particular license or job and the nature of the job.

The leading case defining and applying this rule is *Schware v. Board of Bar Examiners*.[44] Schware, who had been charged but never tried or convicted of a crime, was denied a license to practice law in New Mexico in the mid-1950s. The basis of the denial was a finding that he lacked good moral character, which in turn rested on evidence which fell into three categories: (1) his use of aliases from 1934 to 1937 in order to avoid employment discrimination and to improve his effectiveness as an organizer; (2) several arrests in 1934 and 1940; (3) his membership in the Communist party from 1932 to 1940. The Supreme Court's majority opinion, written by Justice Black, stated that these facts, which Schware himself had divulged, did not justify a finding, especially when compared to the evidence relating to Schware's life since 1940, that Schware lacked good moral character. The Court, however, did not invalidate the good-moral-character requirement. Rather, it found that the evidence relied upon by state officials to deny Schware a license was not rationally related to the requirement.

The court presented the appropriate rule as follows:

A State cannot exclude a person from the practice of law or from any other occupation in a manner or for reasons that contravene the Due Process or Equal Protection Clause of the Fourteenth Amendment. . . . A State can require high standards of qualification, such as good moral character or proficiency in its law, before it admits an applicant to the bar, but any qualification must have a rational connection with the applicant's fitness or capacity to practice law. . . . Even in applying permissible standards, officers of a State cannot exclude an applicant when there is no basis for their finding that he fails to meet these standards, or when their action is invidiously discriminatory.[45]

Courts have applied this rule in a variety of contexts involving ex-convicts. For example, courts have invalidated the denial of a vendor's license to ex-offenders;[46] a city ordinance forbidding city employment for military veterans with less than an honorable discharge;[47] a statute which made specific crimes permissible grounds for denying a bookstore license;[48] a regulation which provided for automatic revocation of a license to drive interstate commercial vehicles upon conviction of an offense related to alcohol.[49]

In these cases, courts are not prohibiting the denial of a license or public employment on the grounds of a conviction. To give these cases that interpretation would be an error. Rather these courts are insisting that licenses and public employment not be denied to an individual merely because of a conviction. They insist upon some rational relationship between the license or occupation and the conviction if the conviction is to be used as a basis for denying the license or employment.

Does the equal-protection clause also make irrelevant job and licensing qualifications unconstitutional?

Yes. The equal-protection clause of the Fourteenth Amendment to the U.S. Constitution prohibits any state from denying any person the equal protection of the laws. The Supreme Court has held that a similar set of restraints are placed on the federal government through the due-process clause of the Fifth Amendment.

The equal-protection clause does not require government to treat every person the same. It permits government to make distinctions between groups or classes of people, provided that the distinctions are related to a legitimate state interest and the groups or classes are defined carefully.

The intensity with which a court reviews a classification varies. Essentially, there are two tests the court will use, although some commentators argue for a more flexible approach.[50]

First, there is the more demanding compelling-state-interest or strict-scrutiny test, which is applied in two contexts: (1) when a class is discriminated against on the basis of suspect criteria such as race;[51] (2) when the discrimination treads upon fundamental individual rights such as the right to travel or vote.[52]

Second, there is the rational-relationship test, which is applied unless a court finds the discrimination encroaches upon a suspect classification or a fundamental right. Although the rational-relationship test is less demanding than the compelling-state-interest test, it is nevertheless a test of some substance. As one court has noted: "Recent Supreme Court cases have made it quite apparent that simply discerning any legislative

THE RIGHT TO EMPLOYMENT

reason, however plausible, will not serve to satisfy the rational basis requirement."[53]

It is unlikely that a court will utilize the compelling-state-interest test in reviewing an automatic bar to the licensing or employment of ex-convicts. A classification based on a criminal record is not a suspect classification,[54] and although employment is vital to individuals there is no precedent supporting the view that the right to work is a fundamental one as that term is used in the cases.

There is one important exception to this broad rule. If an ex-offender is a member of a minority group and if the evidence supports the claim that the differing treatment of ex-convicts has a discriminating impact on a minority group, the compelling-state-interest test would be appropriate. Although this approach is possible, the burden of proof on a party is quite substantial.[55] Most challenges under the equal-protection clause to employment discrimination by the government will be evaluated by the rational-relationship standard. A couple of examples best illustrate the strength of the standard.

In *Butts v. Nichols*,[56] an Iowa statute prohibiting the employment of convicted felons in civil-service positions was challenged on several grounds, including a denial of equal protection. The court found the purpose of the statute to be protective, as is commonly the case:

> The defendants contend that municipal employees occupy a position of special trust, and since convicted felons have displayed their disregard for their fellow citizens, they should not be placed in a position to disregard the right of their fellow citizens again. In addition, the defendants contend that convicted felons do not possess the moral qualities and characteristics which are essential for public employment, and that they do not possess those habits of industry, obedience and fidelity which are essential qualifications for public employment. In essence, defendants assert that convicted felons cannot be relied upon to preserve the public trust.[57]

The court found the purpose valid and stated that "no doubt" the state could "logically prohibit and refuse employment in certain positions where the felony conviction would directly reflect on the felon's qualifications for the job."[58] But the court found that the Iowa statute embodied an

> "across-the-board" prohibition against the employment of felons in civil service positions. There is simply no tailoring in an effort to limit these statutes to conform to what might be legitimate state interests.
>
> Without a more precise relationship of the means utilized by . . . [the statute] to achieve the desired legislative end, this statute clearly violates the tenet of Equal Protection analysis that the exclusion [or inclusion] of members in a class is "necessary to achieve the articulated state goal."[59]

The court went on to argue that the blanket exclusion created a "clearly anomalous" result. For example, persons convicted of desertion of a spouse or leading a life of lewdness would be felons and hence would not be eligible for civil service employment, no matter the nature of the job. In contrast, an individual convicted of a crime of dishonesty, such as petty larceny, would not be a felon, and hence would be eligible for many civil service jobs where such "criminal propensities" would threaten the public. Accordingly, the court struck the statute as violating the equal-protection clause.

Smith v. Fussenich[60] provides another good example of the application of an equal-protection clause to an employment barrier. A three-judge district court invalidated a Connecticut statute which barred felony offenders from employment with licensed private detective and security guard agencies.

Using an equal-protection analysis, the court found the statute overly broad in that it failed to recognize "the obvious differences in the fitness and character of those persons with felony records." The statute was irrational because it barred felons but did not bar misdemeanants convicted of larceny, false entry, or rioting from becoming detectives. It was also irrational by comparison to another Connecticut statute which prohibited state agencies other than law-enforcement departments from rejecting applications for licenses "solely because of a prior conviction of a crime."

Lastly, the court stated that the statute failed to pass muster under the rational relationship test because its "across-the-board disqualification fails to consider probable and realistic circumstances in a felon's life, including the likelihood of rehabilitation, age at the time of conviction, and other mitigating circumstances related to the nature of the crime and degree of participation."[61]

Does it violate the irrebuttable-presumption doctrine to bar automatically an ex-offender from a government job or an occupational license?

Yes. Automatic employment barriers disqualify all ex-convicts without considering the individual differences among members of the excluded group. Such a presumption, which is not rebuttable, is called an irrebuttable presumption. Irrebuttable presumptions are generally disfavored and have been held to be unconstitutional in a variety of contexts.[62]

Few cases have squarely challenged employment disability statutes as unconstitutional because they establish an irrebuttable presumption. If they were, and if the courts did not shy from applying the irrebuttable-presumption doctrine, statutes with automatic employment barriers would be invalidated.

In *Pordum v. Board of Regents*, the Second Circuit Court of Appeals ruled that a tenured teacher, who had been suspended from employment due to a felony conviction, was not entitled to continue teaching pending a hearing concerning his fitness.[63] The Court of Appeals, in commenting on the claim that the sole function of the post-suspension hearing would be to show that Pordum had indeed been convicted of a crime, stated in part,

> If the hearing were to proceed in this manner, with the irrebuttable presumption that a person who has been convicted of committing a crime and who is on probation is unfit to teach in the public schools, it might raise serious constitutional difficulties . . . where no such legislative finding is present, exclusion from a profession can be justified only after a de-

tailed and particularistic consideration of the relationship between the person involved and the purpose of exclusion.[64]

Are these decisions against automatic employment barriers consistent with the Supreme Court's decision in DeVeau v. Braisted?

Yes. *DeVeau* was a special case in which the Supreme Court upheld the absolute disqualification of felons from office in waterfront labor organizations.[65] Before passing the statute challenged in *DeVeau*, federal and state legislatures held extensive and unusually careful hearings that had uncovered "a notoriously serious situation [which needed] drastic reform"[66] and found "impressive . . . evidence that the presence on the waterfront of ex-convicts was an important contributing factor to the corrupt waterfront situation."[67] On this record, the Supreme Court held that the automatic bar challenged in *DeVeau* was valid.

Circumstances similar to those found by the legislatures on the waterfront are not likely to be often repeated in other contexts.

Does a person have a constitutional right to insist that the government apply an otherwise valid qualifying standard fairly to his application for a job or license?

Yes. A licensing agency or public employer may apply a lawful standard unequally and thus create classes that do not promote the state interest that gave rise to the standard initially. In such cases, the unequal application of an otherwise valid standard runs afoul of the equal-protection clause.

The leading case illustrating this point is *Muhammad Ali v. Division of State Athletic Comm*.[68] Following his conviction for refusing induction into the U.S. Armed Forces, the New York State Athletic Commission suspended Muhammad Ali's boxing license. After failing to invalidate this suspension on the ground that a suspension due to a conviction was not rationally related to any legitimate state interest, Ali attacked the suspension on the ground that the defendants unequally applied this otherwise valid standard to him. Ali claimed and was able to prove that the defendants licensed many professional boxers who had been convicted. On this narrow ground, the court invalidated the suspension of Ali's boxing license.

This effective approach may not have wide application. Agencies which refuse to license or employ ex-convicts are usually consistent in their discriminatory practice. And when they are not, the evidence may be much harder to come by than it was in Ali's case.

Is the rational-relationship test a fair and effective test?

Standard-setting groups have made a number of legislative proposals pertinent to the issue. The National Advisory Commission on Criminal Justice Standards and Goals accepted the "direct-relationship" test proposed by the Special Project of the Vanderbilt Law Review.[69] The American Law Institute proposed limiting denial of licenses to circumstances where "the conviction is reasonably related to the competency of the individual to exercise the right or privilege."[70] A Model Civil Service provision proposed by the Georgetown Law Institute requires consideration of three factors: (1) the relationship between offense and the job sought; (2) the rehabilitation of the offender; and (3) the time lapse since conviction.

Standards relating to the Legal Status of Prisoners (Tentative Draft 1977)[71] argues that the direct relationship test does not "provide sufficient guidance for employers or ex-offenders. It tends to focus on the offense rather than on the particular offender. The interest served by refusing employment on the basis of the conviction requires an analysis of the offense, the offender, and the employment."[72] As a substitute, it proposes:

> Barriers to employment of convicted persons based solely on a past conviction should be prohibited unless the offense committed bears a substantial relationship to the functions and responsibilities of the employment. Among the factors which should be considered in evaluating the relationship between the offense and the employment are the following:
>
> (i) the likelihood the employment will enhance the opportunity for the commission of similar offenses;
>
> (ii) the time elapsed since conviction;

(iii) the person's conduct subsequent to conviction;

(iv) the circumstances of the offense and the person that led to the crime and the likelihood that such circumstances will recur."[73]

May an employer evaluate the circumstances surrounding a conviction in determining an applicant's suitability for employment?
Yes. But there is a considerable difference between an across-the-board policy prohibitinig the employment of ex-convicts and a review of the circumstances in a particular case to determine the suitability of an individual applicant. The first seems fair, the second is not.

THE RIGHT TO PRIVATE EMPLOYMENT

Are private employers subject to the restraints of the due process and equal-protection clauses?
No. The restraints of those clauses apply only to governmental actions. Private employers are subject to restraints imposed by federal and state statutes.

Do any federal statutes prohibit private employers from discriminating against ex-offenders?
Only indirectly. Title VII of the Civil Rights Act of 1964 focuses on employment discrimination.[74] As a general matter, it is intended to create an effective remedy for those discriminated against on grounds of race, color, religion, sex, and national origin. It does not prohibit discrimination on the basis of a criminal record. However, because minorities are disproportionately arrested and convicted, a strong argument can be made that employers should not adopt a policy of rejecting applicants solely because of a criminal record.[75]

Have any states adopted statutes that seek to protect ex-convicts from discrimination by private employers?
Yes. New York, for example, has a statute which seeks to protect ex-offenders from unfair discrimination in securing public or private employment or an occupational license.[76] According to New York's statute, an ex-offender

may not be denied employment or a license because of a conviction unless there is a "direct relationship" between the conviction and the specific license or employment sought, or unless the granting of the license or employment would involve an "unreasonable risk" to persons or property. The statute specifically defines "direct relationship" as meaning "that the nature of criminal conduct for which the person was convicted has a direct bearing on his fitness or ability" to perform the duties or responsibilities "necessarily related to the license or employment sought."

The statute directs that a private employer or public agency shall consider several factors in reviewing an ex-offender's application including the time elapsed since the crime was committed; the offender's age when the crime was committed; the seriousness of the offense; and any evidence of mitigation or rehabilitation produced by the offender. The statute also requires a public agency and a private employer to provide upon request "a written statement setting forth the reasons for such denial" if it denies an ex-offender's application.

Lastly, the statute specifically provides that it may be enforced by an ex-offender or the New York State or City human rights commission.

May a private employer inquire if a person has ever been arrested?

No. The Equal Employment Opportunity Commission has held that such an inquiry violates Title VII. It reasons that the mere request may discourage applicants or induce an individual to give false information, thus opening himself to be penalized.[77]

May an employee be discharged for giving false information in response to a question regarding previous arrests or convictions?

Before exploring the answer to this problem, let some ex-cons explain the heartache everyone with a record experiences:

> Now if you're out there on the bricks and looking for work, Joe, don't bother applying for any of those jobs I told you about and you'll save yourself a bundle of

heartaches. Whenever you apply for any jobs my advice is not to mention your record. That's right, lie to 'em. If they have a place on the employment application where it asks you if you've ever been convicted of a crime, put down N-O, no! If you don't you're screening yourself out of 75 percent of all jobs, and damned near 100 percent of the better jobs. You have to look ahead too, Joe. Big Willie, the trustyland barber, has a brother working for one of the big steel companies. A friend got him the job, white collar too. That was seven, eight years ago. He's still on the same job, but the guys who have only been with the company two or three years are moving right up the line to higher job classifications and better pay. Why? His boss told him why. He's got a record, and the company knows it's on his original employment application. His boss told him he was terribly sorry, that it wasn't his fault, but the higher-ups passed him up because fifteen years ago he served two years in prison. See, Joe, crime don't pay, because they ain't never going to let you up once they got you down. That's just the way it is.

Go ahead and tell 'em if you want to, Joe. You're taking a chance no matter what you do. If you tell 'em, you don't get the job most of the time. If you don't tell 'em, and they find out, they fire you. You know Louie, the cellhouse clerk? He got a job and didn't tell 'em about his record. Louie's parole officer came around checking on him and blowed the job for Louie. How do you like them apples? And Gabby, the four block runner, went out and got a job that'll knock you out. He was hired as a credit investigator! Yah, handling confidential financial reports all day long. While he was still on parole too. His parole officer was an o.k. guy and said more power to 'im. Well, it took about two months because the employment application investigation isn't handled by regional offices but is done by the main office in New York. One day his boss calls him in, red-faced and all, and says to him, why didn't you tell us? Louie says, if I'd told you, would you have hired me? His boss says, of course not! Louie was canned.[78]

Case law appears to prohibit an employer from refusing employment to everyone with a criminal record. From this perspective, an individual might feel confident about disclosing his record. Yet, as every ex-convict knows, what the law says and what people do are often very different, and the difficulty in enforcing the law often means that theoretical rights do not become reality.

Accordingly, many people with a criminal record seek to hide the past, and when they do they often get fired for falsifying an employment application. A recent decision of the United States Court of Appeals for the Eighth Circuit permitted such a firing.

In *Jimerson v. Kisco Company, Inc.*[79] Jimerson, a black male, stated that he had not been arrested or convicted after 1963, when he had in fact been arrested in 1971. When his employer discovered the 1971 arrest, Jimerson was fired for "falsifying his police record." Jimerson sued, claiming that his dismissal constituted racial discrimination in violation of Title VII. The court denied the claim, holding that Jimerson failed to sustain his burden of proof, which was "to show that blacks as a class were excluded for falsifying their arrest records at a higher rate than whites."

The *Jimerson* result is anomalous. It authorizes an employer to discharge an employee who fails to reveal an arrest even though the employer was not permitted to inquire into arrests in the first place.

NOTES

1. Published in 1969 and distributed by National Technical Information Service. *Also see* NEW YORK CITY COMMISSION ON HUMAN RIGHTS, THE EMPLOYMENT PROBLEMS OF EX-OFFENDER: (1972); H. MILLER, THE CLOSED DOOR: THE EFFECT OF A CRIMINAL RECORD ON EMPLOYMENT WITH STATE AND LOCAL PUBLIC AGENCIES, distributed by National Technical Information Service (1972); RCA INSTITUTES, THE INVISIBLE PRISON: AN ANALYSIS OF BARRIERS TO INMATE TRAINING AND POST-RELEASE EMPLOYMENT NEW YORK AND MAINE (New York, 1972); D. GLASER,

THE EFFECTIVENESS OF A PRISON AND PAROLE SYSTEM (Bobbs-Merrill. 1964) (abridged edition).
2. N.Y.C. COMMISSION, EMPLOYMENT PROBLEMS, *supra* note 1, at 18.
3. MILLER, THE CLOSED DOOR, *supra* note 1, at 95.
4. *Ibid.*, at 95–99.
5. CONTACT RESEARCH CORPORATION, AN ANALYSIS OF THE FEDERAL BONDING PROGRAM, *Summary* (Belmont, Mass., 1975).
6. *See* MILLER, THE CLOSED DOOR, *supra* note 1, at 49; Cohen and Rivkin, *Civil Disabilities: The Forgotten Punishment*, FEDERAL PROBATION (January 1969).
7. RCA, THE INVISIBLE PRISON, *supra* note 1, at ix.
8. GLASER, THE EFFECTIVENESS OF A PRISON AND PAROLE SYSTEM, *supra* note 1, at 330–31.
9. *Ibid.*, at 220–21.
10. *See* Chapter IV.
11. Meltsner, Caplan, and Lane, *An Act to Promote the Rehabilitation of Criminal Offenders in the State of New York*, 24 SYRACUSE L. REV. 885, 888 (1973).
12. PRESIDENT'S TASK FORCE ON PRISONER REHABILITATION, THE CRIMINAL OFFENDER—WHAT SHOULD BE DONE? 10 (1970).
13. 5 U.S.C. § 7313.
14. 29 U.S.C. § 504(a).
15. *See Employment of the Rehabilitated Offender in the Federal Service*, 35 FEDERAL PROBATION 52 (1971). Two positive policies of the U.S. Civil Service Commission deserve mentioning. Candidates for federal employment are not required to answer affirmatively questions pertaining to offenses committed before the applicant's twenty-first birthday in which the charge was adjudicated in a juvenile court or under a youth-offender law. Juvenile and youth offenders, however, must still meet the general requirement that all persons entering the federal service be of good moral character. Arrests not followed by conviction are not required to be shown on Civil Service applications. But the circumstances surrounding an arrest may be evaluated when determining an applicant's suitability for employment.
16. 10 U.S.C. § 3253(a)
17. *Ibid.*
18. MILLER, THE CLOSED DOOR, *supra* note 1, at 36–39.
19. Portnoy, *Employment of Former Criminals*, 55 CORNELL L. REV. 306, 310 (1970).
20. *Ibid.*, at 307.
21. *Ibid.*, CHAMBER OF COMMERCE OF THE UNITED STATES,

Marshaling Citizen Power to Modernize Corrections, 15 (1972).
22. G.A. Pownall, Employment Problems of Released Prisoners, *supra* at 18, distributed by National Technical Information Service (1972).
23. Meltsner, Caplan, and Lane, *An Act to Promote Rehabilitation*, *supra* note 11, at 885, 891–2.
24. N.Y. Lab. Law § 815.
25. Meltsner, Caplan, and Lane, *An Act to Promote Rehabilitation*, *supra* note 11, at 891–2.
26. President's Commission on Law Enforcement and Administration of Justice, Challenge of Crime in a Free Society, 75 (1967).
27. 137 U.S. 86, 89 (1890).
28. Day-Brite Lighting, Inc. v. Missouri, 342 U.S. 421 (1952); Schmidlinger v. Chicago, 226 U.S. 578 (1913).
29. *See, e.g.*, State v. Ballance, 51 S.E. 2d 731 (N.C. 1949) (photography); Livesay v. State Board of Examiners in Watchmaking, 322 S.W. 2d 209 (Tenn. 1959) (watchmaking).
30. Miller, The Closed Door, *supra* note 1, at 17. There are, however, no studies of local licensing laws.
31. Special Project, *The Collateral Consequences of a Criminal Conviction*, 23 Vand. L. Rev. 929, 1004, n. 490 (1970).
32. American Bar Association, Removing Offender Employment Restrictions: A Handbook on Remedial Legislation and Other Techniques for Alleviating Formal Employment Restrictions Confronting Ex-Offenders, 9–10 (1976) (distributed by Clearinghouse on Offender Employment Restrictions, Washington, D.C.).
33. Barton Trucking Corp. v. O'Connell, 165 N.E. 2d 163, 169, 197 N.Y.S. 2d 138, 148 (1959).
34. Note, *New Approaches to the Civil Disabilities of Ex-Offenders*, 64 Kentucky L. Rev. 382, 389 (1975).
35. *See, e.g.* Application of Brooks, 355 P.2d 840 (Wash. 1960); *In Re* Duntarelli, 66 N.E. 2d 83, 86 (Ill. 1946).
36. ABA, Removing Offender Employment Restrictions, *supra* note 32, at 9.
37. *Ibid.*, at 10.
38. *See, e.g.*, Irwin v. Board of Regents, 304 N.Y.S. 2d 319 (Sup. Ct. App. Div. 1969).
39. *See, e.g.*, Meyer v. Board of Medical Examiners, 34 Cal. 2d 62, 206 P.2d 1095 (1949).
40. *See, e.g.*, Page v. Watson, 140 Fla. 536, 192 So. 205 (1938); Stone v. Oklahoma Real Estate Commission, 369 P.2d 649 (Okla. 1962); State Board of Dental Examiners v. Breeland, 208 S.C. 469, 38 S.E. 2d 644 (1946).

41. Copeland v. Department of Alcoholic Beverage Control, 241 Cal. App. 2d 186, 50 Cal. Rptr. 452 (1966).
42. ABA, REMOVING OFFENDER EMPLOYMENT RESTRICTIONS, *supra* note 32 at 112–13.
43. MILLER, THE CLOSED DOOR, *supra* note 1, at 52.
44. 353 U.S. 232 (1957). For a helpful summary of the law pertinent to employment barriers see PLOTKIN, CONSTITUTIONAL CHALLENGES TO EMPLOYMENT DISABILITY STATUTES, published by the National Clearinghouse on Offender Employment Restrictions, Washington, D.C.
45. *Ibid.*, at 238-39.
46. Miller v. D.C. Board of Appeals and Review, 294 A.2d 365 (D.C. APP. 1972).
47. Thompson v. Gallagher, 489 F.2d 443 (5th Cir. 1973).
48. Perrine v. Municipal Court, 488 P.2d 648, 97 Cal. Rptr. 320 (1971).
49. Whelen v. Volpe, 348 F. Supp. 1235 (D. Minn. 1972), *vacated* 379 F. Supp. 1143 (D. Minn. 1973).
50. Gunther, *In Search of Evolving Doctrine on a Changing Court: A Model for a Newer Equal Protection*, 86 HARV. L. REV. 1 (1972).
51. *See, e.g.*, Loving v. Virginia, 388 U.S. 1 (1967) (race).
52. *See, e.g.*, Bullock v. Canter, 405 U.S. 134 (1972) (right to vote); Shapiro v. Thompson, 394 U.S. 618 (1969) (right to travel).
53. Butts v. Nichols, 381 F. Supp. 573, 579 (S.D. Iowa 1974).
54. Upshaw v. McNamara, 435 F.2d 1190 (1 Cir. 1970); Smith v. Fussenich, 440 F. Supp. 1077 (D. Conn. 1977) (three-judge court).
55. *See e.g.*, Butts v. Nichols, 381 F. Supp. 573 (S.D. Iowa 1974).
56. *Ibid.*
57. *Ibid.*, at 579–80.
58. *Ibid.*, at 580.
59. *Ibid.*
60. 440 F. Supp. 1077 (D. Conn. 1977) (three-judge court). *See also* Miller v. Carter, 547 F.2d 1314 (7th Cir. 1977), *aff'd. by an equally divided court*, 46 U.S.L.W. 4087 (1978).
61. These cases are not consistent with *Hawker v. New York* (170 U.S. 187 [1878]), but that case is probably no longer vital even though it has not been overruled. Moreover, *Hawker* is distinguishable from these cases on the ground that the critical issue under consideration in *Hawker* was whether a law forbidding felons from medical practice violated the *ex post facto* clause of the U.S. Constitution (art. I § 10) when applied to a doctor convicted before the statute was enacted. For a recent application of the

equal protection doctrine in a related field, see *New York City Transit Authority v. Beazer,* 47 U.S.L.W. 4291 (1979).
62. *See, generally,* Cleveland Board of Education v. LaFleur, 414 U.S. 632 (1974); Stanley v. Illinois, 405 U.S. 645 (1972). For a critical review of the irrebuttable presumption doctrine, *see* Note, *The Irrebuttable Presumption Doctrine in the Supreme Court,* 87 HARV. L. REV. 1534 (1974).
63. 491 F.2d 1281 (2nd Cir. 1974), *cert. denied* 419 U.S. 843 (1974).
64. *Ibid.,* at 1287, n. 4.
65. 363 U.S. 144 (1960).
66. *Ibid.,* at 147.
67. *Ibid.,* at 159–60.
68. 316 F. Supp. 1246 (S.D.N.Y. 1970); compare with 308 F. Supp. 11 (S.D.N.Y. 1969).
69. National Advisory Commission on Criminal Justice Standards and Goals § 16.17 (1973); *see also* FLA. STAT. ANN. § 112.011 (Supp. 1975).
70. AMERICAN LAW INSTITUTE, MODEL PENAL CODE § 306.1 (1962 Draft).
71. Joint Committee on the Legal Status of Prisoners, *The Legal Status of Prisoners* (tentative draft), printed in 14 AM. CRIM. L. REV., No. 3 (1977).
72. *Ibid.,* at 616, commentary following Standard § 10.4.
73. *Ibid.,* at § 10.4(a).
74. 42 U.S.C. § 2000 *et seq.*
75. *See generally,* Gregory v. Litton Systems, Inc., 472 F.2d 631 (9th Cir. 1972).
76. *See, e.g.,* N.Y. CORREC. LAW art. 23-A (McKinney 1977–78).
77. *See, e.g.,* EEOC Decision, 74–25, 10 FEP 260. (1973).
78. GRISWOLD, MISENHEIMER, POWERS, and TROMANHAUSER, AN EYE FOR AN EYE, 265–66 (1970).
79. 542 F. 2d 1008 (8th Cir. 1976).

VIII

Property, Insurance, Pensions, Contracts, and Miscellaneous

Is a convicted person divested of his property?

Property divestment upon conviction is almost a nonexistent concept, and where it does exist, it is generally not enforced.

The nonimprisoned convicted defendant is not threatened with property divestment, and the convicted defendant who is imprisoned for a term of years is generally not divested of his property.[1]

A convicted defendant imprisoned for life is not divested of his property unless a statute expressly requires divestment and Hawaii may be the only state which has such a statute. That statute provides, "All property given or in any manner whatsoever accruing to a convict shall vest in his guardian . . . or if he is sentenced for life, shall vest in his heirs."[2] But according to one commentator, the Hawaii statute and others similar to it are not enforced.[3]

Generally does a convicted felon lose his right to inherit?

No. In the United States today, the convicted criminal's capacity to acquire property by inheritance is governed by state statutes of descent and distribution which usually do not deny an ex-convict inheritance.

This rule permitting convicted felons to inherit is even true in the few states which retain civil-death statutes,[4] for those statutes are construed as depriving a convicted criminal only of civil rights specifically enumerated or sanctioned by prior judicial holding.[5] Since felons had the right to inherit at common law, they have the right to inherit under civil-death statutes unless they expressly provide otherwise.[6]

A civil-death statute may, however, prevent inheritance indirectly. *In Re Lindewall's Will*, decided by the New York Court of Appeals in 1942, illustrates this point well.[7] A convicted felon sentenced to life imprisonment was deemed civilly dead under New York's civil-death statute and was not permitted to inherit as a surviving spouse, because his marriage was terminated as a matter of law when the life sentence was imposed.

Are there any circumstances under which a convicted felon may lose his right to inherit?

Yes. A few.

The first and most significant circumstance arises when the offender has been convicted of the felonious killing of the person from whom he would have inherited. This rule barring a convicted felon from inheriting his victim's estate rests on the broadly accepted equitable policy that no one should profit by his own wrong.

In order to implement this policy, courts have had to employ two lines of argument to circumvent the constitutional and statutory provisions prohibiting forfeiture of an estate. First, they have argued that a conviction for felonious murder precluded vesting the estate in the felon.[8] According to this view, a killer's property was not forfeited; instead a killer was prevented by his wrongdoing from acquiring any new interest. The second approach employed the concept of the constructive trust.[9] Under this approach, courts argued that the killer took bare legal title but was denied the beneficial use and enjoyment of the victim's estate.

Nearly every jurisdiction follows this rule barring a killer from inheriting from his victim. Most states embody the rule in statutes which are generally believed to be constitutional,[10] although courts tend to construe them narrowly on the ground that they serve a penal purpose.[11] In other states, courts have interpreted the descent and distribution statutes to reach the same result.[12]

The crimes which will bar a convicted felon from inheriting from his victim vary considerably. Just about every jurisdiction that has the rule will bar a person convicted of having "murdered"[13] his victim. Some also bar felons convicted of "feloniously taking the life of another;"[14] or of willful,"[15] "unlawful,"[16] or "intentional" homicide.[17] Some jurisdictions deny inheritance to those who "procure"[18] the killing of another or are guilty of "aiding and abetting," "conspiracy," or being an "accessory" to, an unlawful killing.[19] Some states have statutes which exempt those guilty of accidental killing or of homicide committed in self-defense, and those who were insane when the crime was committed, from being denied their inheritance.[20]

These statutes present many questions of interpretation and procedure. If a statute specifies that a murderer should not inherit from his victim, does this apply to an heir guilty of a lesser offense such as manslaughter?[21] Must a person be criminally convicted prior to the civil adjudication of his inheritance rights?[22] Should a civil court determining inheritance rights be bound by the criminal court outcome regarding guilt or innocence?[23] These important questions require the attention of anyone whose inheritance right is threatened by the general rule that a convicted felon should not inherit from his victim.

There is a second circumstance which may serve as a basis for denying inheritance. In some states, a spouse guilty of abandonment, nonsupport, adultery or bigamy cannot inherit from the aggrieved spouse.[24] This is not the rule in most states, and because the noninheritance is triggered by misconduct rather than by a conviction, just drawing attention to it is sufficient for our purposes.

Are there any restrictions on an ex-convict's management of his property?

No. Once he has been released from prison, there are no restrictions on a convicted person's ability to supervise and manage his property interests. However, a prisoner may well experience difficulties in supervising and managing his property while in prison, and those problems deserve to be briefly reviewed.

Most states have provisions permitting the appointment of a fiduciary representative to supervise and manage the property of different groups,[25] but prisoners are not generally included. In the minority of states that have such provisions, the representative, who may be called an "administrator,"[26] "committee,"[27] "guardian"[28] or "trustee,"[29] is generally empowered to take whatever action is necessary to protect the prisoner's property. Some of these statutes, however, limit the appointment of a fiduciary representative in ways which make it difficult for a prisoner's property to be fully safeguarded. Examples of these limitations are: (1) limiting the appointment of a fiduciary representative only to prisoners serving a specified prison term; a prisoner serving a term other than the one specified is not eligible for the appointment of a fiduciary representative; (2) limiting the appointment of a fiduciary representative only to certain persons; (3) limiting the purpose of the appointment; generally this is invoked only to reach a debtor prisoner's property or for litigation purposes.

Statutes authorizing the appointment of a fiduciary representative to protect a prisoner's property sometimes raise another problem which occasionally diminishes a prisoner's right. These statutes are sometimes construed as giving the representative sole authority over a prisoner's property. Under this view, all legal acts by the convict must be made through the appointed fiduciary, and any direct act of the prisoner will be invalid.[30] This substantially reduces a prisoner's rights, even though that particular state may not have a civil-death statute. If a statute is not considered exclusive, a prisoner may carry out all legal acts except those for which a representative must be appointed.[31]

In a state which does not permit the appointment of a fiduciary representative to protect a prisoner's property, a prisoner may nevertheless be able to protect his property by creating a revocable private trust,[32] bailment or agency relationship.[33] These legal relationships are complex and may subject a prisoner to liability; they should be entered into only after a thorough review of the legal consequences of taking such a step.

A prisoner's right to protect his property during imprisonment can hardly be disputed. Yet few states have taken steps to permit such protection. There are at least three reasons for this: prisoners have little political influence; state legislators and prison officials are uninterested in the economic consequences of imprisonment for the prisoner; and most prisoners are poor.

May an ex-convict make a will?

Yes. There are no restraints on an ex-convict who wishes to make a will. Even a prisoner in a civil-death state apparently may make a will.

May an ex-convict contract for life insurance?

Yes. Every state appears to permit persons convicted of crimes to obtain life insurance. But the policy of insurance companies may present an ex-convict some difficulties.

According to a survey of thirty-four insurance companies conducted by the staff of the *Vanderbilt Law Review* in 1970,[34] few major insurance companies have an express policy against insuring a former convict once all prison and parole terms have been completed. An ex-convict may be required to pay a higher than average premium, but he most likely will be able to obtain life insurance.

In contrast, most companies refuse to insure a convicted defendant while he is still imprisoned and may refuse to write insurance while a person is on parole.[35] Of course, although an insurance company may be willing to insure a prisoner, a person imprisoned in a state that limits the capacity of prisoners to contract may be incapable of entering into an insurance contract, unless there is a provision permitting a fiduciary representative to enter into an insurance contract in his behalf.

Will an insurance company cancel the life insurance of a person convicted of a crime?

Apparently insurance companies do not cancel the life-insurance policy of a convicted offender, even if imprisoned.[36]

Is a person deemed civilly dead for the purpose of a life-insurance policy?

No. A life-insurance policy on a person imprisoned in a civil-death state is not payable until the prisoner is physically dead. Any other result would be contrary to the intent of an insurance contract which contemplates physical death. A civilly dead prisoner, however, may have difficulty using the insurance policy to secure a loan or to cash it in for its surrender value.[37] These difficulties are reduced in states that authorize a fiduciary representative to act for a prisoner.

Will a conviction interfere with a person being entitled to beneficiary rights under the policy insuring the life of another?

A convicted person's right to receive the insurance on another's life is ordinarily not altered by conviction or imprisonment.[38] But this is not the rule when the beneficiary kills the insured.[39] Public policy in those cases normally bars the beneficiary from receiving the insurance on the ground that a person should not benefit from an intentional illegal act. A beneficiary insane at the time he kills the insured, however, may be able to recover the insurance.[40]

Is an ex-convict permitted to obtain automobile insurance?

Yes. At least as a matter of law. Most insurance companies, however, are often unwilling to insure an ex-convict because they believe that the mere existence of a criminal record is so prejudicial that it reduces the insurer's ability of successfully defending a claim against its insured.[41] In such circumstances, an ex-convict may be forced to resort to "high-risk" companies and pay a higher premium or enter the high-risk pool from which standard insurance companies draw. An ex-convict will be in a better position to obtain ordinary automobile insurance in those states that have adopted no-fault insurance.

Will a conviction prevent a person's receiving his pension benefits?

Possibly. But this important area is too complicated to review here completely. What follows is a brief review of the basic issues.

A conviction may directly or indirectly cause a person to be found ineligible for a pension. A direct disqualification results when a specific term of the pension plan or pertinent statute or regulation governing public pension plans expressly ties ineligibility to a conviction.[42] An indirect disqualification results because a conviction may either cause a person to be suspended or discharged from employment or may cause a finding of dishonorable service during employment.[43]

It is possible that a person convicted of a crime will be disqualified from receiving a pension, whether that person is retired and already receiving the pension, eligible for the pension but still employed, or employed but not yet eligible for the pension. This may be the result whether or not a person is convicted of a crime arising from the employment or whether the crime occurred while the person was employed or retired. The types of crime that make a person ineligible for a pension vary widely from state to state.[44]

A person disqualified from receiving a pension may lose not only superannuated allowances but also the amounts already deducted from his paycheck and placed in the pension fund.[45] Some states, however, refund the employee his contribution and accrued interest.[46] Others allow the pension benefits to be reallocated to a convicted employee's dependents or spouse.[47]

If the board of trustees or commissioners who administer a pension fund decide that a person is ineligible for the pension, the decision is reviewable by a court. The outcome of judicial review may well depend on one of two issues:

First, a court will have to decide whether the board had the discretionary authority under the terms of the pension plan or pertinent statutes to deny a pension on the basis of a conviction. It is not always certain that a board has been vested with such broad authority, and under such circumstances a court may not be willing to assume that it has been so vested.[48]

Second, a court will have to decide whether a pension fund creates a contractual right in an employee or whether it represents only a gesture of appreciation by an employer to an employee for conscientious service. A decision that a pension fund is to be governed by contract law will enhance the claim of an employee and tend to restrict the discretionary power of a board. A decision that a pension fund is merely an employer's gesture will have the opposite impact.[49]

Are broad disqualification provisions terminating pension benefits fair?

No. To disqualify a person from receiving pension benefits because of a conviction resulting from a crime committed after retirement and unrelated to the person's past employment is wholly unjustified. Nevertheless, this result is possible. In addition, the employee may not be given a sum equivalent to his contribution to the pension fund. To reduce this unfairness does not mean that a criminal conviction should never disqualify an employee from receiving a pension. Rather a disqualification for a pension should be limited to crimes which bear a direct relationship to the person's employment and which are committed before a person becomes eligible for the pension benefits. In addition, an employee disqualified under these more limited circumstances should be refunded his contributions and accrued interest.

Will a conviction terminate a person's receipt of workmen's-compensation benefits?

Most states do not suspend workmen's-compensation benefits upon conviction of a crime.[50] In New York, which discontinues workmen's-compensation benefits upon conviction, it is implied in the cases that the benefits will be reinstated once the prisoner is paroled and his civil rights are reinstated.

May an ex-convict collect unemployment insurance?

Yes. An ex-convict who satisfies a state's unemployment-eligibility requirements may collect unemployment insurance.

May an ex-convict make a contract?

Yes. An ex-convict's right to contract is the same as nonoffenders'. As with the right to litigate, this question arises only because of the bar preventing prisoners to contract in a civil-death state. Although that bar still exists in the remaining few civil-death states, it may not be as absolute as it once was, and it may be successfully challenged in the courts. In any event, the bar does not apply to ex-convicts.[51]

Does an ex-convict have the right to act as an executor or an administrator of an estate?

Possibly. An executor is a person named in a will to oversee the administration of an estate. When a person dies without a will, the court will appoint an administrator to oversee the estate.

Several states have expressly forbidden an ex-convict convicted of a felony,[52] infamous crime,[53] or crime of moral turpitude[54] from acting as an administrator or executor. Normally, these prohibitions are explicit and leave a court no discretion. However, in the case of the appointment of an executor, a court may use what little discretionary authority it has to appoint the designated person so as to carry out the will of the deceased.[55] In states where statutes do not expressly prohibit ex-convicts from serving as an executor or administrator, courts tend to use their discretion to exclude ex-convicts from serving as an administrator or executor.

May an ex-convict be a guardian?

Theoretically yes. A guardian is a person responsible for the affairs of a physically or mentally incompetent person. He occupies a position of trust like an executor or administrator.

Although a few states disqualify ex-convicts from being guardians, most state statutes only require that a guardian be "suitable,"[56] "competent,"[57] or "fit"[58] and leave it to the courts to apply those terms in a particular context. Courts have gone both ways on the issue: some bar, others permit ex-convicts to be guardians.

May an ex-convict serve as a trustee responsible for administering a trust?

As a practical matter, yes. All that is required to be a trustee is that a person be able to take and hold property and administer a trust. An ex-convict can do that. However, the appointment standards found in some state statutes may bar an ex-convict's appointment.[59]

Are ex-convicts eligible for government benefit programs?

Yes. Ex-convicts are as eligible as nonoffenders to receive the benefits of government programs such as public assistance, food stamps, medicaid, and medicare. Each of these and other government programs have a variety of eligibility standards that an applicant must satisfy, but those standards do not discriminate against ex-convicts. It is unlikely that such discrimination would be constitutional.

Two areas require special attention. The first is education. Many offenders upon release from prison wish to improve their employment prospects by continuing their education. For a variety of reasons, including financial, they return to state-sponsored college and university systems. Some of these systems have responded to the ex-offenders' need for assistance by establishing special programs designed to help and support the ex-offender while a student.

A state educational system is not obligated to give special attention to ex-offenders, but it may not unreasonably discriminate against them. A policy or practice of refusing to accept ex-offenders would be unconstitutional.

The second area deserving brief special mention is public housing. Unlike public assistance or food stamps, which provide benefits to every eligible person, public housing programs have too few units to accommodate all financially eligible applicants. As a result, public housing agencies use nonfinancial eligibility standards to screen public-housing applicants. These standards may expressly discriminate against ex-convicts.

A presumption against ex-offenders applying for public housing may well be unconstitutional, especially if there were no way to rebut it. Anyone found ineligible for public housing because of a past conviction should consult a lawyer.

Does an ex-convict have equal access to the courts?

Yes. An ex-convict has a constitutionally protected right of access to the court which permits him to sue, or to defend himself if he is sued, in state or federal court. The strength of this right is the same regardless of whether the ex-convict's claim raises a constitutional, contract, tort, or property claim.

A question as to an ex-convict's right to sue or defend himself arises only because of the civil-death concept. In the past, a civilly dead prisoner lacked the capacity to litigate during the imprisonment term regardless of the nature of the lawsuit. Although a few states retain statutes which expressly provide that a prisoner is incompetent to initiate suit, they are most likely unconstitutional.[60]

May an ex-offender visit a relative in prison?

Yes. An ex-offender's conviction record should not be considered by prison officials in deciding whether he qualifies as a proper visitor. Prison officials may not unreasonably discriminate against ex-offenders any more than any other public official. A blanket prohibition against ex-offenders as visitors would constitute unreasonable discrimination.

May an ex-convict own a weapon?

Yes, in states that do not forbid it. But some states limit by statute an ex-convict's right to own a pistol or rifle unless his civil rights have been restored. This restraint is in conflict with the traditional right to bear arms secured by the Second Amendment to the U.S. Constitution. A resolution of the conflict requires a balancing of interests between the public good and private rights; and many courts might uphold the restraint. But an across-the-board prohibition applicable to everyone convicted of a crime might be constitutionally infirm.

Will a past conviction prejudice the treatment of a person charged or convicted of a new crime?

Yes. A past criminal record will have a significant impact on a person charged or convicted of a new crime. A past conviction may affect the setting of bail, availability of pretrial diversion programs, the availability of probation, or the length of prison sentence imposed if convicted. Moreover, a defendant may refuse to take the stand for fear of cross-examination based on a prior conviction. A past conviction may affect a prisoner's classification or eligibility for work release, furlough, and parole.

While there are arguments in favor of limiting the use of past convictions within the criminal justice system, their use is generally thought to be constitutional.

Is ignorance of the law an adequate defense for an ex-convict who violates a civil-disability prohibition?

Very possibly. Ordinarily the maxim "ignorance of the law is no excuse" imposes a burden on an individual to know what is prohibited by the criminal law. Under this rule, an action that violates the criminal law will subject that person to criminal penalties even though the person was unaware that his action constituted a crime.

Nevertheless, knowledge of the restrictions imposed by

civil disabilities is required in most cases if a person is to be criminally liable for violating a specific prohibition.[61]

NOTES

1. *See* Davis v. Superior Court, 175 Cal. App. 2d 8, 345 P.2d 513 (1959) (written material produced by a prisoner during the period of his confinement is owned by the prisoner even in the absence of the warden's consent). But see 27 OP. CAL. ATT'Y GEN. 241 (1959), which requires the warden's consent for all other property. See also MICH. STAT. ANN. § 25.104 (1957), which provides that the wife of a convicted person sentenced to more than three years in prison is entitled to dower.
2. HAW. REV. STAT. § 353-38 (1968).
3. Special Project, *The Collateral Consequences of a Criminal Conviction*, 23 VAND. L. REV. 929, 1183 (1970).
4. *See, e.g.*, In re Shaffer, 184 Misc. 855, 56 N.Y.S. 2d 568 (Sup. Ct. 1945); Grooms v. Thomas, 93 Okla. 87, 219 P. 700 (1923).
5. *See, e.g.*, In Re Fein, 51 Misc. 2d 1012, 274 N.Y.S. 2d 547 (N.Y. City Civ. Ct. Rec. 1966); Grooms v. Thomas, 93 Okla 87, 219 P. 700 (1923).
6. *See, e.g.*, In re Estate of Dickenson, 51 Cal. App. 2d 638, 125 P.2d 542 (1942); Kenyon v. Saunders, 18 R.I. 590, 30 A. 470 (1894).
7. 287 N.Y. 347 (1942).
8. *See, e.g.*, Weaver v. Hollis, 22 So. 2d 525 (1945); Price v. Hitaffer, 165 A. 470 (1933).
9. Bryant v. Bryant, 137 S.E. 188 (1927).
10. *See, e.g.*, Wilson v. Bates, 231 S.W. 2d 39 (1950); Egelhof v. Presler, 44 Ohio L. Abs. 376 (Franklin County P. Ct. 1945); Hamblin v. Marchant, 175 P. 678 (1918), *aff'd on rehearing*, 180 P. 811 (1919).
11. Bird v. Plunkett, 95 A.2d 71 (1953); Blanks v. Jiggetts, 64 S.E. 2d 809 (1951).
12. Perry v. Strawbridge, 108 S.W. 641 (1908).
13. *See, e.g.*, CONN. GEN. STAT. ANN. § 45-279 (Supp. 1978); COLO. REV. STAT. § 15-11-803 (1973); VA. CODE § 64. 1-18 (1968).
14. *See, e.g.*, KAN. STAT. § 59-513 (1976); KY. REV. STAT. ANN. § 381.280 (1976).
15. MISS. CODE ANN. § 91-1-25 (1972); R.I. GEN. LAWS § 33-1.1-1 (1962).
16. *See, e.g.*, N.C. GEN. STAT. § 31A-3(3) (1976); WASH. REV. CODE ANN. § 11.84.010 (1967).
17. *See e.g.*, IND. CODE ANN. § 29-1-2-12 (Burns, 1953)

18. See, e.g., OKLA. STAT. tit. 84 § 231 (1970); OR. REV. STAT. §§ 112.455 to .555 (1969); R.I. GEN. LAWS: § 33–1.1–1 (1962).
19. See, e.g., IND. CODE. ANN. § 29–1–2–12 (Burns, 1953); N.C. GEN. STAT. §§ 31A–3 to –15 (1976); WASH. REV. CODE ANN. §§ 11.84.010 to .900 (1967).
20. GA. CODE ANN. § 113–909 (Supp. 1969); TENN. CODE ANN. § 31–117 (1977).
21. The majority view holds that the estate is allowed to pass. See, e.g., In re Daniel's Estate 260 P. 2d 991 (1953); contra, McGhee v. Banks 154 S.E. 2d 37 (1967).
22. The majority view holds that it is not. See Legette v. Smith 85 S.E. 2d 575 (1955); contra, Smith v. Greenburg 218 P.2d 514 (1950).
23. The majority view holds that a prior criminal judgment should not be given evidentiary weight. See, e.g., 290 S.W. 2d 439 (1956).
24. See, e.g., Simms v. Kirk 144 N.E. 146 (1924); In re Barnes Estate, 267 N.Y.S. 634 (Sup. Ct. 1943); In re Mehaffey's Estate 156 A. 746 (1931).
25. For example, children and persons who are incompetent to handle their own affairs.
26. R.I. GEN. LAWS § 13–6–4 (1969).
27. N.Y. CORR. LAW § 320 (McKinney 1977).
28. ME. REV. STAT. tit. 18, § 3601 (3) (1964) as amended, (Supp. 1978).
29. KAN. STAT. § 59–1901 (1977).
30. New v. Smith 84 P. 1030 (1906); Commissioners of Rice County v. Lawrence, 29 Kan. 158 (1883). The exclusive provision in these cases was repealed by the Act of July 1, 1939, ch. 180, § 280 (1939) Kan. Laws, repealing KAN. REV. STAT. § 62–2002 (1923).
31. Hewson v. State, 27 App. Div. 2d 358, 279 N.Y.S. 2d 790 (1967); Kugel v. Kalik 176 Misc. 49, 25 N.Y.S. 2d 327 (Sup. Ct.), aff'd., 262 App. Div. 823, 28 N.Y.S. 2d 734 (1941).
32. A private express trust is a device whereby a prisoner may provide support for his family and protection of his property by creating a trust for his property and appointing a trustee who during the life of the trust has legal title to the property.
33. A bailment generally involves the giving of the property to a friend, relative, or other person for safekeeping. An agency relationship commonly involves the power of attorney, whereby the attorney is authorized to act for the prisoner.
34. Special Project, The Collateral Consequences of a Criminal Conviction, supra 1110, 1111, n. 316.

35. *Ibid.*
36. *Ibid.*
37. *See* Sullivan v. Prudential Ins. Co., 160 A. 777 (1932).
38. *See* Shapiro v. Equitable Life Assurance Soc'y, 182 Misc. 678, 45 N.Y.S. 2d 717 (Sup. Ct. 1943), *aff'd on other grounds*, 249 N.Y. 743, 61 N.E. 2d 745 (1945).
39. A number of states statutorily preclude a beneficiary from participating in the proceeds when he causes the death of the insured. *See, e.g.,* OKLA. STAT. tit. 84, § 231 (1970); OR. REV. STAT. §§ 112.455 to .555 (1969). *See also* Annotation, 27 A.L.R. 3d 794 (1969) for a complete collection of the cases.
40. Holdom v. Grand Lodge of Ancient Order of United Workmen, 43 N.E. 772 (1895); Ohio State Life Ins. Co. v. Barron, 263 N.W. 786 (1935); Campbell v. Ray, 245 A. 2d. 761 (Ch. N.J. 1968) *aff'd. mem.*, 259 A.2d 473 (App. Div. N.J. 1969).
41. Special Project, The Collateral Consequences of a Criminal Conviction, *supra* 1122 nn. 405–407.
42. *See, e.g.,* 5 U.S.C. §§ 8312–15 (annuity and retirement pay to civil and uniformed services); 42 U.S.C. § 402(u) (social security); CAL. GOV'T. CODE § 50883 (West 1966) (police & firemen); ILL. ANN. STAT. ch. 108½, §§ 8–251 (1963) (municipal employees), 9–235 (county employees), 11–230 (laborers), 12–191 (park employees), 13–221 (sanitary district employees), 15–187 (university employees), 16–199 (teachers), 18–163 (judges), 19–103 (house of correction employees), 19–203 (library employees).
43. *See* Hozer v. State Police & Firemen's Pension Fund, 230 A.2d 508 (App. Div. N.J. 1967); Plunkett v. Bd. of Pension Comm'rs., 173 A. 923 (Sup. Ct. N.J. 1934), *aff'd.*, 176 A. 341 (Ct. Err. & App. N.J. 1935); Fromm v. Bd. of Directors of Police and Firemen's Retirement Sys., 195 A.2d 32 (App. Div. N.J. 1963).
44. *See, e.g.,* CAL. GOV'T. CODE § 50883 (1966) (felonies); PA. STAT. ANN. tit. 53 §§ 39323, 65599 (Supp. 1978) (misdemeanors); MASS. ANN. LAWS ch. 32 § 15(3) (1966) (offense relating to pensions); N.J. STAT. ANN. §43:1–2 (1962) (moral turpitude).
45. *See* Sally v. Firemen's & Policemen's Pension Fund Comm'n., 124 A.2d 244 (Sup. Ct. N.J. 1940); Walter v. Police & Fire Pension Comm'n., 198 A. 383 (Sup. Ct. N.J. 1938).
46. *See, e.g.,* D.C. CODE § 1–319(c) (1966); N.J. STAT. ANN. § 43: 15A–41(a) (Supp. 1977); PA. STAT. ANN. tit. 53, § 13438 (1957).
47. *See, e.g.,* OKLA. STAT. tit 11, § 370 (1959); WASH. REV.

CODE ANN. § 41.18.130 (1969); N.J. STAT. ANN. § 43.1-2 (1962); TEX. REV. CIV. STAT. ANN. art. 6243e.1, § 15 (Supp. 1978).
48. Hinman v. Bd. of Trustees of Firemen's Relief & Pension Fund, 74 P.2d 475 (1937).
49. Compare Ballurio v. Castellini, 102 A.2d 662 (App. Div. N.J. 1954), with Skaggs v. City of Los Angeles, 275 P.2d 9 (1954).
50. For the minority rule, see Pallas v. Misericordia Hosp., 291 N.Y. 692, 52 N.E. 2d 590 (1943); Boatwright v. State Indus. Accident Comm'r, 244 Or. 140, 416 P.2d 328 (1966).
51. But see Rosman v. Cuevas, 176 Cal. App. 2d 867, 1 Cal. Rptr. 485 (App. Dep't Super. Ct. 1959), in which a California court held that even a parolee could not contract for the purchase of an automobile.
52. See, e.g., NEV. REV. STAT. §§ 138.020(1) (b), 139.010 (2) (1973); TEX. PROB. CODE § 78 (c) (Supp. 1978).
53. See, e.g., ALA. CODE tit. 61 § 69 (1960).
54. See, e.g., N.M. STAT. ANN. § 31–1–6(1975); WASH. REV. CODE ANN. § 11.36.010 (1967).
55. See, e.g., In re Johnson's Will, 202 Misc. 751, 112 N.Y.S. 2d 866 (Sur. Ct. 1952); In re Duncan's Estate, 181 Okla. 407, 74 P.2d 117 (1937); In Re Raynor, 48 Misc. 325, 96 N.Y.S. 895 (Sur. Ct. 1905).
56. See, e.g., MICH. STAT. ANN. § 27.3178 (299) (1962); W. VA. CODE § 44–10–3 (1966).
57. See, e.g., VA. CODE § 31–5 (1969).
58. See, e.g., ILL. ANN. STAT. ch. 37, § 705–7 (Smith-Hurd Supp. 1970).
59. See, e.g., CONN. GEN. STAT. ANN. § 45–84 (1958); OKLA. STAT. tit. 60, § 175.39 (1971).
60. See Thompson v. Bond, 241 F. Supp. 878 (W.D. Me. 1976); Bush v. Reid, 516 P.2d 1215 (Alaska 1973); Bilello v. A.J. Eckert Co., 42 A.D. 2d 243, 346 N.Y.S. 2d 2 (1973); Delorme v. Pierce Freightlines Co., 353 F. Supp. 258 (D. Or. 1973).
61. See Lambert v. California, 355 U.S. 225 (1957). Also compare United States v. Mancuso, 420 F.2d 556 (2d Cir. 1970) with People v. DeStefano, 64 Ill. App. 2d 389, 212 N.E. 2d 357 (1965), cert. denied, 385 U.S. 821 (1966).

IX

The Right to Serve as a Juror*

What is a jury?
A jury is a group of people summoned and sworn to decide on the facts at issue in a civil or criminal trial. Juries are supposedly composed of one's peers or a cross-section of the community.

How many types of juries are there?
There are two types of juries: a grand jury and a petit or trial jury.

A grand jury usually consists of twenty-three people summoned to determine at the outset of the criminal process whether there are sufficient grounds to justify a criminal indictment.

The purpose of a petit or trial jury is to determine issues of fact in a civil or criminal trial. Traditionally, trial juries are composed of twelve persons. The United States Supreme Court, however, has recently held that six-person juries are constitutionally permissible in state criminal trials.[1]

For the balance of this chapter, the term "jury" is used to include both types of jury, unless one type is specified.

How are juries selected?
Persons who sit on a jury are generally selected by an appointed commission or clerk of the court from local lists

---

*This chapter is based on research done by Noel Dennis.

of voters or taxpayers. The commissioners or clerk often have the responsibility of making initial inquiries into the qualifications of a prospective juror by questionnaire, personal interview, or other means.[2] Once enough qualified persons are found, the names of all these persons are placed on a "jury wheel" and selected at random for assignment to jury duty.[3] Unless excused, persons summoned to appear for jury duty who fail to appear may be criminally liable.[4]

Whatever the selection process, however, it may not discriminate on the basis of race,[5] sex,[6] or on any other classification not reasonably based.[7]

Who establishes the qualifications for jurors?

State legislatures establish the qualifications for jurors. Qualifications are usually addressed to a person's citizenship, length of residency in the state, age, educational ability, and good character.

The U.S. Supreme Court has held that the Constitution grants legislatures broad authority in setting juror qualifications.[8] As long as the exclusions are not arbitrary or racially or sexually discriminatory, legislatures may "restrict, abridge, deny or enlarge the right and duty of jury service. . . ."[9]

What are some typical juror qualifications?

A majority of states mandate one or more of the following requirements:

- citizenship in the state for a certain period of time;[10]
- minimum and/or maximum age requirements;[11]
- an ability to read, write, speak and understand English[12] or have a fair education;[13]
- residency in the county in which the jury shall sit;[14]
- no mental or physical disability which would prevent a prospective juror from serving;[15]
- registered elector or taxpayer;[16]
- good character or approved reputation;[17]
- freedom from past criminal conviction.[18]

Do states exclude ex-convicts from serving as a juror?

Yes. Most states have express statutory or constitutional provisions which exclude ex-convicts from serving as jurors. These provisions have evolved from the common law and generally remain effective unless a person's civil rights have been restored. At least two state courts have held that the common-law rule disqualifying convicted persons is applicable even in the absence of an express statutory provision.[19]

For what kinds of crimes will a person be excluded from serving on a jury?

As in other areas, variation is enormous. About three-fourths of the states exclude persons who have been convicted of specific crimes from jury service.[20] More states than not exclude anyone convicted of a felony.[21] Some states mandate disqualification if a person has been convicted of an offense involving "moral turpitude"[22] or an "infamous crime."[23] Still others disqualify anyone convicted of a crime punishable by imprisonment.[24]

Here are some specific examples. Maryland disqualifies anyone against whom a charge is pending or who was convicted of a crime "punishable by a fine of $500.00 or more, or by imprisonment for more than six months, or both" and who has not been pardoned.[25] Delaware disqualifies anyone against whom there is a pending charge or conviction for a crime punishable by imprisonment for more than one year.[26] New Jersey's stringent law disqualifies anyone who has been convicted of any crime.[27] Florida disqualifies a person convicted of bribery, forgery, perjury, or larceny, and anyone convicted of a felony under Florida law or its equivalent in any other jurisdiction.[28] Federal law disqualifies a person against whom there is a pending charge or a conviction in a state or federal court for a crime punishable by imprisonment for more than one year.[29]

May a person be ineligible for jury service if he is under indictment?

Yes, in some states. Louisiana disqualifies anyone indicted for a felony[30] and Pennsylvania bars persons indicted for felonies or misdemeanors.[31] Under federal law, a person is excluded who is indicted for a charge punishable by imprisonment for more than one year.[32]

May an ex-convict be challenged for cause as a juror?

Yes. Most states permit an individual to be excluded

from a jury without requiring the party making the challenge to use one of its few peremptory challenges.[33] A party making this kind of challenge must ground it upon some statutory provision.[34] When a challenge is made on some ground other than that authorized by statute, the trial judge has wide discretion in passing on the motion.[35] It is conceivable that a challenge could be overcome in the absence of express disqualifying language barring ex-convicts from jury duty.[36]

If there is no express statutory disqualification, are there any other means by which a convicted person can be excluded from jury service?

Yes. Many jurisdictions require jurors to be selected from a list of registered voters.[37] Because many states bar ex-convicts from voting, they are excluded from jury duty as well. Although this method of jury selection has been challenged, most courts have held it proper.[38] Thus in states like Arizona and Connecticut which do not expressly disqualify ex-convicts from jury duty, an ex-convict may nevertheless be excluded because he is disfranchised.

Further, many jurisdictions require jurors to be of "good character" or "approved integrity."[39] For example, New Hampshire denies jury service to a person because "of vicious habits or other sufficient cause."[40] These vague standards are used to disqualify convicted persons from jury duty,[41] and have been upheld by the courts against charges that they were vague and lent themselves to discriminatory application.[42]

May an ex-convict who has been granted a pardon or amnesty or whose civil rights have been restored qualify for jury service?

Yes, if it is so provided in a statute. For example, the United States Code allows a person convicted of a crime punishable by one year imprisonment to qualify as a prospective juror if "his civil rights have . . . been restored by pardon or amnesty."[43] Florida allows a convicted person to qualify if his civil rights have been restored.[44] Arkansas prohibits a convicted felon from qualifying unless he has been pardoned.[45] Other jurisdictions have similar provisions.[46] However, at least one state court has

THE RIGHT TO BE A JUROR

stated in its opinion that a pardon will not cure one's ineligibility as a juror and that person is forever barred.[47]

Does an ex-convict have a constitutional right to serve on a jury?

No court has ever so held.

Do statutes excluding convicted persons from jury service violate a person's constitutional right to a trial by an impartial jury?

The U.S. Supreme Court has not decided the question and no court has ever held this. In 1970, however, the Massachusetts Supreme Court held that it is not necessary to seat convicted persons on a jury in order to achieve an adequate cross-section of the community.[48] More recently, a federal district court in Oregon held that the exclusion of convicted felons from jury service, regardless of peer status, does not violate a person's rights under the Sixth Amendment to the U.S. Constitution.[49]

Is it fair to disqualify all ex-convicts from jury duty?

No. Laws disqualifying ex-convicts from jury service appear based on the assumption that ex-convicts cannot be fair and impartial. The law should not treat a past conviction as an indelible badge of dishonesty and partiality. Peremptory and for-cause challenges to jurors could remove individuals who could not in fact be fair and impartial.

NOTES

1. Williams v. Florida, 399 U.S. 78 (1970).
2. PA. STAT. ANN. tit. 17, § 1252(b).
3. DEL. CODE tit. 10, § 4507(a) (b).
4. 28 U.S.C. § 1864 (b).
5. Brown v. Allen, 344 U.S. 443 (1953); Carter v. Jury Comm'n, 396 U.S. 320 (1970).
6. Duren v. Missouri, — U.S., —, 58 L. Ed. 2d 579 (1979); Taylor v. Louisiana, 419 U.S. 522 (1975); Ballard v. United States, 329 U.S. 187 (1946). The U.S. Supreme Court has held that women may be exempted from jury service if the exemption is reasonably based and rationally applied. Hoyt v. Florida, 363 U.S. 57 (1961).

7. Hoyt v. Florida, 368 U.S. 57 (1961).
8. Carter v. Jury Comm'n, 396 U.S. 320 (1970) ("The States remain free to confine the selection to citizens, to persons meeting specified qualifications of age and educational attainment, and to those possessing good intelligence, sound judgment and fair character.")
9. People *ex rel.* Denny v. Traeger, 372 Ill. 11, 22 N.E. 2d 679 (1939).
10. FLA. STAT. ANN. § 40.01.
11. N.J. STAT. ANN. § 2A:69–1.
12. PA. STAT. ANN., tit. 17, § 1252(c).
13. CONN. GEN. STAT. ANN. § 51–217.
14. ARK. STAT ANN., 39–101 (Supp. 1975).
15. DEL. CODE tit. 10, § 4506.
16. ARIZ. REV. STAT. § 21–201.
17. ALA. CODE, tit. 30, § 21 (Supp. 1973).
18. FLA. STAT. ANN., §40.01(2).
19. Queenan v. Territory, 11 Okla. 261, 267, 71 P. 218, 219–20 (1901), aff'd, 190 U.S. 548 (1903); Watkins v. Baltimore and Ohio R.R., 43 S.E. 2d 219, 223 (1947).
20. Special Project, *Collateral Consequences of a Criminal Conviction,* 23 VAND. L. REV. 929, 1053 (1970). *See* Mo. ANN. STAT. §§ 557.490 (perjury or subornation of perjury), 559.470 (crimes against persons), 560.610 (crimes against property).
21. *See, e.g.,* ARK. STAT. ANN. § 39–102(e) (Supp. 1975); FLA. STAT. ANN. §40.01(2); KY. REV. STAT. § 29.025(1); PA. STAT. ANN. tit. 17, § 1279(c).
22. ALA. CODE tit. 30, § 21 (Supp. 1973).
23. MISS. CODE ANN. §§ 1762, 1762–02 (Supp. 1968).
24. N.D. CENT CODE §§ 27–09, 1–08(2)(e).
25. MD. ANN. CODE § 8–207.
26. DEL. CODE tit. 10, § 4506(b)(5).
27. N.J. STAT. ANN. § 2A:69–1.
28. FLA. STAT. ANN. § 40.01(2).
29. 28 U.S.C. § 1865(5).
30. LA. REV. STAT. ANN. § 13.3041 (1968).
31. PA. STAT. ANN. tit. 17, § 1333 (3rd Class Counties).
32. 28 U.S.C. § 1865(5).
33. *Collateral Consequences,* Collateral Consequences of a Criminal Conviction, *supra* 110, 111, n. 316.
34. Robinson v. Territory, 85 P. 453 (Okla. 1905).
35. Stone v. Pettus, 103 S.W. 413 (Tex. Civ. App. 1907).
36. *See* Commonwealth v. Wong Chung, 71 N.E. 292 (Mass. 1904).
37. *See* ARIZ. REV. STAT. § 21–201; ARK. STAT. ANN. § 39–101; CONN. GEN. STAT. ANN. § 51–217; PA. STAT. ANN. tit. 17, § 1279(c).

38. Chance v. United States, 322 F. 2d 201 (5th Cir. 1963), *cert. denied*, 379 U.S. 823 (1964).
39. *See* ALA. CODE tit. 30 § 21; FLA. STAT. ANN. § 40.01(3).
40. N.H. REV. STAT. ANN., § 500.29.
41. Grant v. N.Y. Herald Co., 138 App. Div. 727, 123 N.Y.S. 449 (1910).
42. Carter v. Jury Comm'n, 396 U.S. 320 (1970); People v. Ferguson, 286 N.Y.S. 2d 976 (Sup. Ct. 1968).
43. 28 U.S.C. § 1865 (5).
44. FLA. STAT. ANN., § 40.01 (2).
45. ARK. STAT. ANN., § 39–102(e) (Supp. 1975).
46. *See, e.g.*, DEL. CODE, tit. 10, § 4506(b) (5); KY. REV. STAT., § 29.025(1); MD. ANN. CODE, §8–207(5).
47. Anderson v. State, 40 Ala. App. 509, 517, 120 So. 2d 397, 404 (dictum), *cert. denied*, 270 Ala. 575, 120 S.2d 414 (1960), *rev'd on other grounds*, 366 U.S. 208 (1961).
48. Commonwealth v. Martin, 257 N.E. 2d 444 (Mass. 1970).
49. U.S. v. Armstrong 408 F. Supp. 1130 (D.C. Or. 1976).

X

The Right to Be a Witness*

What is a witness?
A witness is a person who testifies under oath in court to what he has seen, heard, or otherwise observed.

May an ex-convict be a witness?
In most instances, yes. At common law, a person who had been convicted of a felony, treason, or a crime involving fraud or deceit was disqualified as a witness. Today, the legislatures of many states have enacted statutes which completely override this disqualification and provide that ex-convicts may not be excluded as witnesses.[1] A few states, including Alabama, however, have retained the common-law disqualification for persons convicted of certain designated offenses, most notably perjury or subornation of perjury.[2] But these exclusions do not apply to an accused in a criminal case, who has a constitutional right to testify on his own behalf.[3] As discussed below, prior convictions may be used to impeach or challenge a witness's credibility.

Does it make sense to prohibit ex-convicts from being witnesses?
No. In some cases, this prohibition may injure the offender; in others it may adversely affect the case of a third party. The disability is imposed on the assumption that

---
*This chapter is based on research done by Karen Goldstein.

a convicted person will not be honest. Many offenses have little if any bearing on a person's willingness to tell the truth. Some offenses, such as perjury, may have some reasonable relationship to concerns of false testimony. But impeachment of a witness should be an adequate safeguard. The outright ban on giving testimony should be abolished.

What does it mean for a witness's credibility to be impeached?

A witness is supposed to provide evidence relevant to the disputed factual questions at issue in trial. The trier of fact—either a judge or a jury—is usually presented with conflicting evidence and must judge each witness's credibility. Thus, a person taking the stand places his credibility in issue. The process of challenging a witness's credibility is called *impeaching the witness*. A traditional way to impeach a witness is to introduce evidence of prior convictions.

Are all witnesses subject to impeachment?

Except as discussed below, yes.

May the conviction of any crime be used to impeach a witness?

Possibly. Most states have enacted statutes which delineate those crimes which may be used for impeachment purposes. Because these statutes are often vague and subject to differing judicial interpretations, they must be analyzed in the context of a state's developing case law.

Many states permit any crime to be used to impeach a witness.[4] Courts in these states generally permit proof of misdemeanors as well as felonies, regardless of the nature of the crime involved. Some states, such as California, have statutes permitting only felonies to be used for the purpose of attacking the credibility of the witness.[5] Others permit only an infamous crime to be used to impeach a witness.[6] Still other states limit the class of crimes that may be used for impeachment to those bearing on the honesty or veracity of the witness, such as perjury or fraud. For example, Kansas law provides that only convictions of crimes involving dishonesty or false statements are admissible for impeachment purposes.[7] In a number of states, only the conviction of a crime involving moral turpitude may be used to impeach the credibility of a witness.[8] Finally, some states do not specify which crimes are admissible for impeachment purposes.[9] In those states, the admissibility of a past conviction is left to the discretion of the trial judge.

May a witness be impeached by a conviction which is being appealed?

Most states permit a witness to be impeached by a conviction on appeal or for which a motion for a new trial is pending, on the grounds that the conviction has not yet been set aside.[10] A few states hold that a conviction from which an appeal is pending is not final and may not be used to impeach the credibility of a witness.[11]

May a witness be impeached by a conviction even if he was not imprisoned?

Usually, yes. A conviction is admissible even though the sentence has been commuted or suspended or for which the sentence was probation, since these developments do not change the fact of conviction.[12]

May a witness be impeached by a conviction for which he has been pardoned?

A conditional or unconditional pardon does not usually bar impeachment through the use of a conviction.[13] However, the pardon itself has been held admissible as evidence in a majority of the few cases in which the question has arisen. A few jurisdictions, including California, have enacted statutes that specifically provide that crimes which have been pardoned may not be used to attack the credibility of a witness.[14]

Is a conviction ever too stale to be used for the purpose of impeachment?

Probably not. A majority of the courts that have considered this question have refused to fix time limits to exclude remote convictions,[15] although numerous cases have held that the determination of remoteness is within the discretion of the trial court.[16] A few jurisdictions have statutes that prohibit the use of a conviction that does not fall within the indicated period. A typical statute reads, "The conviction of a crime involving moral turpitude within fifteen years shall be the only crime admissible in evidence given to affect the credibility of a witness."[17]

May an indictment or an arrest be used to impeach a witness?
Ordinarily not.[18]

May a plea of nolo contendere be used to impeach a witness?
Yes, in the majority of states that have considered the question.[19]

May a conviction in one state be used to impeach a witness testifying in a court of a second state?
Generally, yes.

May a record of juvenile delinquency be introduced into evidence for impeachment purposes?
Probably not. Many states expressly prohibit using juvenile records for this purpose. A typical statute noted by one court provides that "such an adjudication shall not be deemed a conviction . . . and that the disposition of a child . . . shall not be admissible as evidence against the child in any case or proceeding in any court other than the juvenile court."[20] In a majority of the remaining states, courts have held juvenile conviction records inadmissible for the purpose of impeaching a witness in a subsequent action.[21]

Does impeachment through prior convictions present special problems for the criminal defendant?
Yes. Generally, prior convictions may be used to impeach the credibility of a criminal defendant in the same way they are used to impeach the credibility of any witness in a civil or criminal action. But, at least theoretically, a prior conviction may not be considered by a jury in determining a defendant's guilt of the offense for which he is being tried. This is a difficult distinction to maintain, and many defendants decide not to testify on their own behalf out of fear that the distinction will be blurred in the jury's mind. A defendant's decision not to take the

stand, however, may be equally damaging, for a jury, regardless of the admonitions from the judge, may infer guilt from the defendant's decision not to testify.

In some jurisdictions, the trial court has the discretion to exclude proof of prior convictions, if its admission would have an unduly prejudicial effect on the outcome of the trial. For example, in New York a trial judge may make a ruling, before trial, as to a prosecutor's use of prior convictions for the purpose of impeaching the defendant's credibility.[22] In reaching its decision, a New York court will weigh the risk of undue prejudice, the relevance of the evidence to the defendant's credibility, and the effect of the evidence in discouraging the accused from taking the stand. In a few states, including Kansas, statutes prohibit the defendant's credibility from being impeached by prior convictions unless he first introduces evidence to establish his credibility.[23]

Are the rules of evidence permitting the impeachment of a person by a prior conviction generally in need of reform?

Yes. The majority rule today which permits impeachment has little or no relationship to veracity, and harms the administration of justice and the former offender. A defendant in a criminal case may be deterred from taking the stand because of an old, unrelated conviction or may have his case badly prejudiced because his chief witness was once convicted. The same circumstances might arise in a civil action. The fact that the courts instruct juries that prior convictions are introduced for the limited purpose of impeachment hardly eliminates the resulting prejudice. As Justice Jackson observed: "The naive assumption that prejudicial effects can be overcome by instructions to the jury . . . all practicing lawyers know to be unmitigated fiction."[24]

The use of a conviction for impeachment purposes should be limited to crimes that directly bear on veracity. The laws of evidence generally do not permit the introduction of irrelevant facts as evidence. There is no reason why irrelevant facts should be admitted for impeachment purposes. The existing rules of evidence are too broad to accomplish their legitimate purpose and have a highly prejudicial effect.

NOTES

1. *See, e.g.,* ARIZ. REV. STAT. §12–2201(b) (1956); N.C. GEN. STAT. §8–49 (1969).
2. ALA. CODE tit. 7, §434 (1958).
3. Farley v. State, 226 P.2d 1002 (Okla. 1950); Lowe v. State, 58 Okla. Crim. 233, 52 P.2d 115 (1935).
4. *See, e.g.,* FLA. STAT. ANN. §90.08 (1960); LA. REV. STAT. ANN. §15.495 (1967).
5. CAL. EVID. CODE §788 (West 1966).
6. *See, e.g.,* State v. Miller, 23 Conn. Supp. 294 (1962).
7. KAN. STAT. § 60–421 (1976).
8. *See, e.g.,* Hartford Acci. & Indem. Co. v. Williams, 516 S.W. 2d 425 (Tex. 1974); Pond v. Carter, 126 Vt. 299, 229 A.2d 248 (1967).
9. *See, e.g.,* State v. Johnson, 254 N.W. 2d 114 (S.D. 1977); State v. Olsen, 83 S.D. 260, 158 N.W. 2d 526 (1968).
10. *See, e.g.,* United States v. Empire, 174 F.2d 16 (7th Cir. 1949), *cert. denied,* 377 U.S. 959 (1949); People v. Thompson, 48 Ill. 2d 41, 268 N.E. 2d 369 (1971).
11. *See, e.g.,* Adkins v. Commonwealth, 309 S.W. 2d 165 (Ky. 1958); Fletcher v. North British and Mercantile Ins. Co., 425 S.W. 2d 159 (Mo. 1968).
12. *See, e.g.,* Burson v. State, 511 S.W. 2d 948 (Tex. 1974).
13. *See, e.g.,* Robson v. United States, 526 F.2d 1145 (1st Cir. 1975); Richards v. United States, 192 F.2d 602 (D.C. Cir. 1951).
14. CAL. EVID. CODE §788 (West 1966).
15. *See, e.g.,* Olds v. Pennsalt Chemicals Corp., 432 F.2d 1033 (6th Cir. 1970); United States v. Platz, 361 F.2d 958 (7th Cir. 1966).
16. *See, e.g.,* Brown v. State, 370 F.2d 242 (D.C. Cir. 1966); Dillard v. Smith, 153 Tex. Crim. 134, 218 S.W. 2d 476 (1949).
17. VT. STAT. ANN. tit. 12 §1608 (Supp. 1969).
18. *See, e.g.,* Ruffalo's Trucking Service v. National Ben-Franklin Ins. Co., 243 F.2d 949 (2d Cir. 1957); Judy v. McDaniel, 247 Ark. 409, 445 S.W. 2d 722 (1969).
19. *See, e.g.,* Reynolds v. People, 471 P.2d 417 (Colo. 1970); Lacey v. People, 166 Colo. 152, 442 P.2d 402 (1968); Commonwealth v. Sciullo, 169 Pa. Super. Ct. 318, 82 P.2d 695 (1951).
20. Rivus v. State, 501 S.W. 2d 918 (Tex. 1973).
21. *See, e.g.,* Shropshire v. State, 288 Ind. 39, 279 N.E. 2d 225 (1972); State v. Reynolds, 41 N.J. 163, 195 A.2d 443 (1963); *cert. denied,* 377 U.S. 1000 (1964).

22. People v. Sandoval, 34 N.Y. 2d 371 (1974).
23. KAN. STAT. §60–421 (1964).
24. Krulewitch v. United States, 336 U.S. 440, 453 (1949) (concurring opinion).

XI

Criminal-Registration Statutes*

What is a criminal-registration statute?

Any municipal or local ordinance or state statute which requires an ex-convict to register with the local police on or shortly after arrival in that locality, and to furnish them with information regarding his prior criminal history and present activities.

Are criminal-registration statutes the same as probation or parole?

No. A person on parole or probation is still serving his sentence. He is required to report regularly to an appropriate officer as a condition of being on parole or probation. Normally such a person must secure the permission of his parole or probation officer if he wishes to leave his immediate community.

A person is subject to a criminal-registration requirement even though he has completed his sentence. Thus an ex-convict who arrives in an area with a criminal-registration statute must report to the local police. Failure to do so might result in criminal liability.

What is the purpose of a criminal-registration statute or ordinance?

The stated purpose is to aid local police in preventing criminal activity and apprehending those who commit

*This chapter is based on research done by Noel Dennis.

crimes by knowing the names and addresses of ex-convicts newly arrived in the area. While these are laudable goals, it is most unlikely that the assumption is valid. There is no evidence for the assumption that registration will deter crime or that a person who intends to commit a crime will register. Moreover, laws assume that persons previously convicted continue to be sufficiently dangerous to warrant the requirement that they register.[1] Criminologists and sociologists, however, are not able to say with any certainty that an individual's prior conviction is by itself a sufficient criterion for predicting future criminality.

One known by-product of criminal-registration statutes is that they make it easier for police to annoy and harass known ex-convicts.[2]

How common are these ordinances?

More common than anyone might guess. The most comprehensive study to date was conducted in 1969.[3] The study surveyed all 381 cities with a population of 50,000 or more and found that 52 cities in 22 states had some kind of criminal-registration statute on the books. Arizona, California, Florida, Nevada, and Ohio also had state criminal-registration statutes.

Who must register under the statutes?

Criminal-registration ordinances require individuals who have been convicted of a specified crime to register. Normally a single conviction is sufficient to place a person within the ambit of a criminal-registration statute. A person merely arrested or indicted is not required to register. Some statutes, however, like the Ohio Habitual Sex Offenders law,[4] require two or more convictions in separate criminal actions.

What kinds of crimes will normally subject a person to a criminal-registration statute?

Criminal-registration statutes normally apply to persons convicted of a felony, sex offense, or narcotics offense.

The statute or ordinance usually specifies the offenses for which registration is required. For example, California's statute requiring sex offenders to register defines sex offender as one who is convicted of assault with intent to commit rape, the infamous crime against nature, or sodomy under Section 220, or of any offense defined in . . . Section 266 [Inveiglement or enticement of an unmarried female under 18 for the purpose of prostitution, etc.], Section 267 [Abduction of a person under 18 for prostitution], Section 268 [Seduction under promise of marriage], Section 285 [Incest], Section 286 [Sodomy], Section 261 [Rape].[5]

Statutes requiring registration of convicted felons are broadly defined. For example, the Florida statute requires registration of any person convicted of (1) a felony in any court of the state, or (2) a crime in any federal court or in any court of a state other than Florida, which would be a felony if committed in Florida.[6]

Some criminal-registration laws specify offenses which are not felonies or sex or narcotics offenses. For example, Nevada requires registration of any person convicted of any of the fifty-seven misdemeanors—some of which are of questionable constitutional validity.[7]

Might a person who appears to be covered by a criminal-registration statute be exempted?

Possibly. Exemptions from registering would be defined in the statute. Typical exemptions include:

1. full restoration of a person's civil rights by a court;
2. a full pardon for the offense;
3. passage of a specified time period since the last conviction during which the person has not been convicted of a new offense—generally from three[8] to ten[9] years.

How soon after entering a given locality must a person register?

Some statutes call for "immediate" registration; others require registration "promptly"; still others require registration within twenty-four hours, or forty-eight hours, or up to thirty days.[10]

Where must the person register?

Usually a person must register with the local police, sheriff, or bureau of criminal identification.

What information is required when a person registers?

The following information is typically required:
- name, any aliases, and occupation;
- a complete physical description;
- places of criminal conviction;
- date of conviction;
- name and location of any jail or prison of confinement;
- address of residence or stopping place;
- description of the kind of residence;
- projected length of stay;
- any other "helpful" information;
- a full set of fingerprints;
- a set of photographs.

Are criminal-registration records kept confidential?

Not likely. Some statutes contain clauses which seek to limit dissemination of criminal-registration records to law-enforcement agencies. Presumably public inspection of these records is not allowed under these provisions. Many statutes, however, do not limit dissemination of criminal-registration records. None of the provisions have adequate safeguards to assure a reasonable degree of confidentiality.

Does a person have a right to have his criminal-registration record returned to him upon leaving the jurisdiction?

Not unless it is authorized by the local ordinance or statute—and none of them so provide.

Are criminal-registration statutes enforced by the criminal law?

Yes. Any person who must register has a duty to register with the proper authority or be potentially vulnerable to criminal prosecution. Once a person has registered, he may be required to inform the proper authority of any change in address, and he may have a continuing duty to furnish timely statements. Failure to provide truthful information when required is in most cases a direct violation of the statute and leaves the person open to criminal prosecution.

What penalties may be imposed for failure to comply with a criminal-registration statute?

Failure to comply with a criminal-registration statute is usually a misdemeanor. Penalties are usually in the form of monetary fines, if imposed at all. Conviction for a misdemeanor, however, may be punished by a jail sentence in most jurisdictions.

May a person be convicted for violating a criminal-registration statute where he had no knowledge of his duty to register?

No. In *Lambert v. California*, the U.S. Supreme Court held, "Where a person did not know of his duty to register and where there was no proof of the probability of such knowledge, he may not be convicted consistently with due process."[11]

Lambert involved a section of the Los Angeles municipal code making it a criminal offense for a person convicted of what would be a felony in California to be present in Los Angeles without registering with the police. The defendant had been convicted of forgery, a felony, and had been living in Los Angeles for seven years without registering. She was charged with violating the ordinance. At trial, the municipal court refused to accept her offer of proof that she had no knowledge of the registration requirement and thus was denied due process of law. Defendant was convicted and appealed.

The Supreme Court found that while the statute validly fell within the scope of the municipality's police power, which is "one of the least limitable," the notice requirement of the due process clause places some limits on that power. There must be notice to satisfy due process, especially where the person is unaware of any wrongdoing and where the violation is unaccompanied by any activity save that of mere presence in the city. Thus the Court concluded that "actual knowledge of the duty to register, proof of the probability of such knowledge and subsequent failure to comply are necessary before a conviction under the ordinance can stand."[12]

Has any state or federal court ever held a criminal-registration statute unconstitutional?

No court has ever held a criminal-registration requirement to be unconstitutional. They are generally upheld on the ground that they serve a valid governmental purpose and thus fall within the broad scope of a state's or municipality's police power.[13] But criminal registration statutes have been found to be unconstitutional as applied to specific persons.[14] Thus, in every case, important constitutional rights may be involved which may render the application of a criminal-registration statute unconstitutional in a particular case.

Might criminal-registration statutes be unconstitutional?

Yes. It could be argued that a criminal-registration violated a person's First Amendment right to travel.[15] This argument depends on showing that the registration requirement chills the exercise of the right to travel. This cause-and-effect relationship might be difficult to prove.

It might also be argued that criminal-registration statutes are an irrational requirement in violation of the due-process and equal-protection clauses of the Fourteenth Amendment. These clauses require that there be a rational relationship between the registration requirement and the purpose served by the requirement. Since there is no empirical evidence that demonstrates that mere registration advances the value of either public protection or crime control, a court might well hold the registration requirement to be irrational and hence unconstitutional.

Might a criminal-registration statute be invalid on nonconstitutional grounds?

Yes. At least one state, California, has found criminal-registration ordinances invalid on the grounds that the city lacked the power to legislate in a field already preempted by the state.[16] The state court held that the state penal code (§290) had fully occupied the field of criminal registration, leaving no room for municipal action.

NOTES

1. Note, *Criminal Registration Ordinances: Police Control over Potential Recidivists*, 103 U. PA. L. REV. 60, 100 (1954).
2. "But even assuming that the theory of these ordinances is valid . . . the actual practices show that the theory is merely the facade for police harassment of individuals who have been convicted of a crime." *Ibid.*, at 102.
3. DREHER AND KAMMLER, CRIMINAL REGISTRATION STATUTES AND ORDINANCES IN THE UNITED STATES—A COMPILATION (Center for the Study of Crime, Delinquency and Corrections, Carbondale, Ill., 1969).
4. OHIO REV. CODE ANN. §2950.01.
5. CAL. PENAL CODE, §290 (West).
6. FLA. STAT. ANN., §775.13.
7. NEV. REV. STAT. §207.080 *et. seq.* In Nevada, one of the enumerated statutes requires a person to register if he has been convicted of *Nev. Rev. Stat.* §201.420 (Keeping a Disorderly House), which states in pertinent part that "any person who shall keep any disorderly house, or any house of public resort, by which the peace, comfort or decency of the immediate neighborhood, or any family thereof, is habitually disturbed, or who shall keep an inn in any disorderly manner, shall be guilty of a misdemeanor."
8. DREHER AND KAMMLER, CRIMINAL REGISTRATION, *supra* note 3, at 14.
9. FLA. STAT. ANN., §775.13(5)(c).
10. DREHER AND KAMMLER, CRIMINAL REGISTRATION, *supra* note 3, at 11–15.
11. Lambert v. California, 355 U.S. 225 (1957).
12. *Ibid.*, at 229.
13. State v. Ulesky, 100 N.J. Super. 287, 241 A.2d 671 (1968).
14. *See* note 16, *infra*.
15. *See* Shapiro v. Thompson, 394 U.S. 618 (1969). This argument was rejected in State v. Ulesky, 100 N.J. Super. 287, 241 A.2d 671 (1968).
16. Abbott v. City of Los Angeles, 53 Cal. 2d 674, 349 P.2d 974 (1960). *See also Ex Parte* Digiuro, 100 Cal. App. 2d 260, 223 P.2d 963 (1950).

XII

The Restoration of Lost Rights

So far we have focused on the rights lost as a result of a conviction. It is now time to shift our attention to the procedures for restoring those forfeited rights.

Every state and the federal government provides one or more procedures by which an offender may apply for a restoration of the civil rights that he forfeited upon conviction. Prior to reviewing these procedures, a few general remarks are appropriate.

The importance of restoring an ex-convict's rights is a direct consequence of the broad brush stroke used in curtailing the rights in the first place. If fewer rights were curtailed initially, and if the ones curtailed were carefully tailored to the offender's offense, the restoration of rights would not be so critical a problem. Besides reducing the unfairness caused by original stripping of rights, the restoration of rights helps an ex-offender live a normal, law-abiding life. This is particularly true in eliminating artificial barriers to employment.

As helpful as current restoration devices are for removing disabilities, they are not adequate for three reasons. Most states do not automatically restore the rights of ex-convicts upon the completion of a set of conditions. Instead, they have procedures whereby a governor, an administrative body, or the judiciary is granted discretionary authority to grant or deny an individual's application to have his rights restored. Because this broad grant of discretionary authority is not usually exercised in accordance with specific written guidelines, the evaluation of those applicants is not always evenhanded and fair. Furthermore, many ex-offenders do not know of these procedures nor know how to apply for them.

Although restoration devices which restore rights automatically are much better, only a minority of states have them, and they appear to make no effort to inform ex-convicts of them. Thus, some ex-convicts may not utilize rights they may have, for they are unaware that their rights have been restored.

More importantly, automatic and discretionary procedures do not restore all rights. For example, because restoration procedures do not preclude a finding of bad moral character, an ex-convict may be denied an occupational license, or be barred from holding public office. Nor do restoration procedures erase the social stigma surrounding a conviction.

A recognition of the limits of restoration procedures argues for three changes:

First, the number of disabilities arising out of a conviction should be sharply curtailed. The remaining few civil-death statutes should be repealed. Disabilities imposed on an offender should be directly related to the nature of the criminal behavior underlying the conviction, and procedures should be available for removing all other disabilities under appropriate circumstances.

Second, laws prohibiting unreasonable discrimination against ex-offenders by public and private parties should be adopted. These laws should seek to assure offenders fair treatment by government and private employers, insurance companies, bonding companies, public-housing agencies and private landlords, pension boards, and the like.

Third, every state and the federal government should adopt automatic restoration procedures restoring a breadth of civil rights. Prisoners and ex-convicts should be made aware of these procedures.

What is executive clemency?

Every state and the federal government offers some form or another of executive clemency, such as pardon, amnesty, remission of fines and forfeitures, reprieves, and commutations. Although only a pardon and an amnesty restore an ex-convict's rights, it is worth briefly defining each term.

A *pardon* is an exercise of sovereign prerogative relieving the person on whom it is bestowed from further punishment and from legal disabilities arising from the conviction.

An *amnesty* is a general pardon extended to a group without regard to special, individual circumstances. (Courts generally give the same legal effect to amnesty and pardon. Because a pardon is the far more commonly used procedure of the two, only it will be explored.)

By the *remission of fines and forfeitures,* all or part of a fine may be remitted as long as the money remains in the possession of the court or its officers.

A *reprieve* is a postponement of the execution of a sentence, usually granted in order to permit consideration of an application for a pardon. The most common use of reprieve has been to stay execution of the death penalty.

A *commutation* lessens the punishment of the original sentence. Its main purposes are to make a prisoner eligible for parole consideration or to substitute a life-imprisonment sentence for a death penalty.

Are there different types of pardons?

Yes. There are two basic types of pardons. There is a *full, free and absolute pardon,* which is the type that former President Gerald R. Ford gave to his predecessor Richard M. Nixon.[1] Full and absolute pardons are very rare; historically they have been given only to a person subsequently shown to be innocent of the crime for which he had been convicted.[2] The full and absolute pardon granted to Mr. Nixon was unique in many ways, including the fact that it was granted prior to a conviction.

A *conditional pardon* is the more common type and contains a precedent or subsequent condition, the performance of which is essential to the validity of the pardon.[3] Former President Nixon gave a conditional pardon to James R. Hoffa, former president of the International Brotherhood of Teamsters, which conditioned Hoffa's release from prison on the condition that he refrain from union management. Conditional pardons imply guilt, and their acceptance is generally viewed as a confession of guilt.[4]

Are pardons available in every jurisdiction?

Just about. The U.S. Constitution vests the President with the exclusive power to grant clemency to individuals convicted of federal crimes.[5] Thirty-two states vest the governor with virtually exclusive power to grant pardons.[6] Ten states vest the pardoning power in an administrative body, usually called a board of pardons.[7] In seven states, the governor grants a pardon only after a recommendation by the board of pardons.[8] In Rhode Island, the only state without a pardoning procedure, the legislature may restore an offender's right to vote or hold public office.[9]

For what reasons may a pardon be granted?

A pardon may be granted for many reasons, such as to correct an unduly severe sentence, to correct errors in the judicial system, to prevent the execution of a prisoner sentenced to death, or to satisfy the public interest.

A pardon may also be granted to restore an offender's civil rights after release from prison. Although this is perhaps one of the more common purposes today for granting a pardon, it is not effective for restoring an ex-convict's civil rights. This is true because very few pardons are given; only a small percentage of offenders apply for a pardon; and most offenders lack the resources of knowledge necessary to navigate the pardoning procedures. In addition, as in New York, a pardon is not granted to restore civil rights if a disability may be removed by another procedure.[10]

Are there any legal restrictions on the granting of pardons?

No. The pardoning authority is vested with essentially unchecked discretionary authority, which has been abusively exercised on occasion. The legislature and judiciary usually do not have any authority to restrict, compel, or interfere with the exercise of the pardoning authority.[11] The few restrictions commonly imposed on the pardoning authority are: (1) the pardoning power is unavailable in cases of treason or impeachment;[12] (2) the granting of a pardon must be publicly reported to the legislature;[13] and (3) a pardon may be granted only after conviction.[14]

May an individual compel the granting of a pardon?

No. Pardons are granted at the discretion of the pardoning authority. Neither the legislature or the judiciary has the authority to compel the pardoning authority to grant a pardon, regardless of the strength of the evidence supporting the claim that the pardon is withheld for malicious or arbitrary reasons.

May a person refuse to accept a pardon?

Yes. A person offered a pardon may accept or refuse it. Because pardons imply guilt, a party claiming innocence may refuse a pardon for fear that its acceptance will be viewed as a confession of guilt. There are only a few reported instances where a pardon has been refused.

How does one apply for a pardon?

The procedures vary from state to state. A state may require the applicant to make the application public by publishing a notice in a newspaper; may provide an application form; may conduct an independent evaluation of each applicant; may limit the frequency of one person's applications; and may provide a hearing. A person wishing to apply for a pardon should write the governor or board of pardons of the state from which he wishes to be granted a pardon.

Does a pardon blot out guilt?

The U.S. Supreme Court has answered this question both ways. In *Ex parte Garland,* the Court stated:

> A pardon reaches both the punishment prescribed for the offense and the guilt of the offender . . . it releases the punishment and blots out of existence the guilt, so that in the eye of the law the offender is as innocent as if he had never committed the offense . . . it removes the penalties and disabilities and restores him to all his civil rights.[15]

But in *Burdick v. United States,* the Court noted that there is a "confession of guilt implied in the acceptance of a pardon."[16] Although these conflicting authorities have created confusion, the majority of courts have held that a pardon neither obliterates the conviction nor reestablishes the offender's good character.[17] But a pardon does restore most civil rights forfeited on conviction.[18]

The uncertainty as to whether a pardon blots out guilt appears to result from the failure of courts to distinguish between the reasons for which the pardon was granted.[19] A pardon granted because of innocence should have the effect of an acquittal. It should, in other words, blot out guilt. A pardon granted for reasons other than innocence removes the consequences flowing from the underlying conviction, but not the guilt itself. Accordingly, the Supreme Court's statement in *Garland* is too broad and should be limited only to pardons granted for innocence.

What civil rights are restored by a pardon?

This question cannot be answered precisely. The rights restored by a pardon vary from state to state and may not be known with certainty within a state.

Sometimes the rights restored by a pardon may be expressly enumerated in a pardon. Other times the statute defining the disability will provide that the disability lasts until the right is restored by pardon. And on still other occasions, a court must determine whether a pardon restores a particular right.

A pardon usually restores a person's right to vote, contract, litigate, serve as juror, be a witness, and inherit property. It will also prevent the deportation of an alien convicted of a crime after legal entry into the United States.[20]

A pardon usually does not restore a person to a public office forfeited at the time of conviction.[21] But it may make a person eligible to hold public office in the future.[22]

A pardon does not automatically restore a person to a licensed profession or occupation which was forfeited at the time of conviction.[23] Most courts have held that a pardoned offender is ineligible for an occupational or professional license that, by statute, can be issued only to persons without a criminal record.[24] A pardon may, however, measurably assist in persuading a licensing authority to grant a license or a private employer to hire a particular person.

A pardon not granted on grounds of innocence does not usually restore a person's "good moral character." Thus, benefits extended only to individuals of good moral character may be denied to one convicted of a crime irrespective of a pardon.

A pardoned offender appearing as a witness may have his character impeached.

A pardon may not prevent a pardoned offender convicted of a new offense from being given a more severe sentence as a second felony offender or habitual offender.[25] Nor does a pardon restore a marriage dissolved because of a conviction or property rights which have vested in a third party as a result of the conviction.

Despite these limitations, a pardon reduces the stigma arising out of a conviction and cuts the prejudice normally sparked by a conviction. Thus, even though they do not restore all rights, pardons are worth having.

Is a pardon granted by one jurisdiction respected by another?

This question has three parts. First, is a pardon granted by the jurisdiction where the offender was convicted effective in restoring an offender's civil rights in another jurisdiction? The general rule is that a pardon granted by the convicting jurisdiction will be honored in other jurisdictions.[26]

Second, what is the effect of a pardon where the pardoning state is different from the convicting state? Generally, a pardoning authority can restore the civil rights lost in that state, but that does not effect the penal sanction imposed by the convicting jurisdiction.

Third, does a pardon granted by the President of the United States restore civil rights under state law? This difficult question is not precisely answerable under current case law.

If the intent of a presidential pardon granted to a person convicted of a federal offense is to remit all further punishments and liabilities imposed by a conviction, state-imposed disabilities that survive the pardon would infringe on a power granted exclusively to the President by the Constitution. On the other hand, to hold that a presidential pardon restores state civil rights infringes on recognized state sovereignty.

These interests were recently discussed by the Seventh Circuit Court of Appeals in *Bjerkan v. United States*,[27] and decided in a way that represents a significant departure from previous case law. Bjerkan, convicted of refusing to report for induction, collaterally attacked his sentence under 28 U.S.C. § 2255. By the time his appeal was heard by the Seventh Circuit, he had been released from federal custody by action of the Presidential Clemency Board and had received a full and unconditional presidential pardon. The issue on appeal to the Seventh Circuit was whether a full and unconditional presidential pardon rendered the case moot.

The Supreme Court had already decided in *Carafas v. LaValler*[28] that the disabilities arising out of a conviction were sufficient to satisfy the case and controversy requirements of Article Three of the U.S. Constitution. Thus, if the Seventh Circuit found that state-imposed disabilities survived a presidential pardon, it would have found the *Bjerkan* case not moot. But the Seventh Circuit dismissed the *Bjerkan* case as moot and in so doing found that a presidential pardon restores state civil rights. However desirable that outcome may be, it ignored the state disabilities that actually survive a presidential pardon.

The *Bjerkan* case could stand for the view that disabilities are not infringements upon rights of sufficient importance to justify federal jurisdiction, or that disabilities are not "punishments" that intrude upon the constitutional authority of the President. Either rationale, however, deprived Bjerkan of an adjudication of his claims against the legality of his sentence and conviction. And by implication, the result minimized the importance and reality of continuing disabilities.

In a different vein, it is worth noting that the pardoning authority of the President of the United States does not authorize the President to pardon a state offender.

Are civil rights ever restored automatically?

Yes. Over a dozen states provide for the automatic restoration of civil rights upon the fulfillment of conditions enumerated in the statutes.[29] These procedures were enacted to facilitate the restoration of the criminal's civil rights and to make the administration of restoration more efficient and economical. Although these conditions vary, typical examples provide for the restoration of rights upon release from prison, the completion of parole, final discharge from a sentence, or the expiration of a fixed period of time following discharge from a sentence.

Unlike pardons that must be applied for and are granted in the discretion of the pardoning authority, an offender does not apply for the restoration of rights under an automatic-restoration procedure. Unfortunately, offenders are frequently not informed of these statutes and thus do not know that their rights have been restored.

What is the effect of automatic-restoration statutes?

The few cases discussing the effect of automatic-restoration statutes make it clear that the rights restored by those statutes and by pardons are similar.[80] Accordingly, traditional rights such as the right to vote or serve on a jury are generally restored by automatic-restoration statutes, but the right to receive a professional or occupational license or hold public office are probably not restored. Also, like a pardon, automatic restoration does not restore "good moral character."

What does it mean to expunge or annul a criminal record?

About a dozen states have expungement or annulment statutes.[81] These statutes are designed to protect an offender against discrimination caused by the conviction by concealing the conviction from public view. Unlike pardons or automatic-restoration procedures, the objective of these statutes is to eliminate penalties imposed by public opinion rather than to remove legal disabilities arising from a conviction.

An offender may have his conviction expunged or annulled only upon the fulfillment of specific conditions. In the main, only an offender who has successfully completed a sentence of probation is eligible to have his record expunged or annulled.

Generally, courts have held that expungement restores an offender's right to vote or hold public license, but that it does not restore "good moral character" or automatically make an offender eligible for an occupational or professional license.

May a court authorize expungement in the absence of a statute authorizing it?

Yes, at least at the federal level. Even though no federal statute provides for the expungement of an arrest record, expungement lies within the equitable discretion of the court, but it is allowed only in "extreme circumstances."[32] In determining whether such circumstances exist, courts consider the "delicate balancing of the equities between the right of privacy of the individual and the right of law enforcement officials to perform their necessary duties."[33]

Such extreme circumstances have been found and records ordered to be expunged where procedures of mass arrests rendered judicial determination of probable cause impossible;[34] where the court determined that the sole purpose of the arrests was to harass civil-rights workers;[35] where the police misused the police records to the detriment of the defendant;[36] and where the arrest was proper but was based on a statute later declared unconstitutional.[37]

Should expungement be primarily limited to persons sentenced to probation?

No. Limiting expungement to probationers limits this procedure to those offenders who least need it in readjusting to society. The difficulties encountered by those released from prison are far more extensive than those experienced by probationers. Perhaps it was fair, when expungement was first tried, to limit it to those who presented the least risks. But expungement is no longer an experiment. Additional punishment is the only consequence of withholding expungement from those sentenced to confinement.

Besides pardons, automatic restorations, and expungement, are there other procedures for restoring civil rights?

Yes. A number of states have restoration procedures besides those already discussed.[38] Generally, under these procedures an offender must apply for a restoration of rights, and the approval of the application is largely at the discretion of the granting authority, which may be the governor, legislature, judiciary, or an administrative body. These procedures usually require an offender to have completed probation, a prison term, or a specified period after the end of the sentence before being eligible to apply for the restoration of rights.

These restorative procedures generally restore voting and other traditional rights, but they do not necessarily make one eligible for occupational or professional licensing or public office, nor do they signify the restoration of "good moral character."

Unfortunately, not many offenders know of these procedures and take advantage of them.

New York has two separate procedures which fall within this category. A Certificate of Relief from Disabilities is granted at the discretion of a court or the parole board to anyone convicted of one or more misdemeanors and not more than one felony.[39] A Certificate of Good Conduct is granted at the discretion of the parole board to any offender at least five years after the completion of his sentence.[40] Both certificates permit an ex-convict to apply for a job or license previously denied because of a conviction. However, these certificates do not restrict an employer or a licensing agency from exercising its discretion in denying a job or license.

Does the granting of probation or parole to an offender restore his rights?

Generally not. The granting of probation or parole to an offender does not remove the collateral consequences of a conviction. A probationer or parolee is more akin to a nonconvicted citizen than a prisoner, and in that sense has more "rights" than a prisoner. But those enlarged rights are due to the fact that he is not imprisoned, not to the diminution of disabilities.

There are, however, two major exceptions to this rule. In civil-death states, the granting of parole to a civilly dead prisoner does restore many basic civil rights. And an automatic-restoration statute may condition the restoration of rights upon the granting of parole.

Are current restoration devices adequate?

No. No state restores all civil rights. Regardless of the restoration procedures utilized, some disabilities remain effective for an offender's life. Most states do not have automatic-restoration devices or expungement statutes. States make little or no effort to inform prisoners and ex-convicts of the restoration devices, so that even the available devices are not fully used.

Reform is needed. Automatic-restoration devices and expungement statutes should be adopted. States should engage in extensive public education programs so that prisoners and ex-convicts know what they can do to regain their rights. Few if any disabilities should remain effective five years after an offender begins probation or parole or is released to the community.

NOTES

1. Proclamation 4, 311, Granting Pardon to Richard Nixon, 39 Fed. Reg. 32,601 (1974).
2. C. NEWMAN, SOURCEBOOK ON PROBATION, PAROLE AND PARDONS, 57 (3d ed. 1968).
3. *Ex parte* Wells, 59 U.S. (18 How.) 307, 311 (1855).
4. Burdick v. United States, 236 U.S. 79, 91 (1915).
5. U.S. CONST. art. II, §2.
6. These states are: Alaska, Arkansas, California, Colorado, Florida, Hawaii, Indiana, Illinios, Iowa, Kansas, Kentucky, Maine, Maryland, Michigan, Mississippi, Missouri, New Hampshire, New Jersey, New Mexico, New York, North Carolina, Ohio, Oklahoma, Oregon, South Dakota, Tennessee, Vermont, Virginia, Washington, West Virginia, Wisconsin, Wyoming.
7. These states are: Alabama, Connecticut, Georgia, Idaho, Minnesota, Nebraska, Nevada, North Dakota, Utah.
8. These states are: Arizona, Delaware, Louisiana, Massachusetts, Montana, Pennsylvania, Texas.
9. R.I. GEN. LAWS §13–6–2 (1956).
10. Rothman, *The Pardoning Power: Historical Perspective and Case Study of New York and Connecticut*, 12 COLUM. J. L. AND SOC. PROB. 149, 171–73 (1976).
11. *Ex parte* Garland, 71 U.S. (4 Wall.) 333 (1867); *Pollack v. Bridgeport Steamboat Company*, 114 U.S. 411 (1885); *Ex parte* Swain, 88 Okla. Cr. 235, 202 P.2d 223 (1949); State *ex rel.* Rowe v. Connors, 166 Tenn. 393, 61 S.W. 2d 471 (1933).
12. RUBIN, LAW OF CRIMINAL CORRECTION, ch. 16 §26 (student edition) (1973).
13. *Ibid.*, ch. 16 §31.
14. *Ibid.*, ch. 16 §28.
15. 71 U.S. (4 Wall.) 380 (1866).
16. 236 U.S. 79, 91 (1915).
17. 3 U.S. DEPT. OF JUSTICE, THE ATTORNEY GENERAL'S SUR-

VEY OF RELEASE PROCEDURES: *Pardon* 268, 292–93 (1939). *See, e.g.,* Mason v. State, 39 Ala. 1, 103 So. 2d 337, *aff'd*, 267 Ala. 507, 103 So. 2d 341 (1956); Hozer v. State, 95 N.J. Super. 196, 230 A.2d 508 (App. Div. 1967).

18. Adamany, *Executive Clemency in Wisconsin*, 36 WIS. B. BULL. 54, 59 (1963); Special Project, *The Collateral Consequences of a Conviction*, 23 VAND. L. REV. 929, 1145 (1970).

19. *See* Weihofen, *The Effect of Pardon*, 88 U. PA. L. REV. 177 (1939).

20. 8 U.S.C. §1251.

21. *See, e.g.,* Hulgan v. Thornton, 205 Ga. 753, 55 S.E. 2d 115 (1949).

22. *See, e.g.,* Slater v. Olson, 230 Iowa 1005, 299 N.W. 879 (1941); State *ex Rel.* Cloud v. Election Bd., 169 Okla. 363, 36 P.2d 20 (1934). *But compare* Ridgeway v. Catlett, 238 Ark. 323, 379 S.W. 2d 277 (1964); Comm'r of the Metro Dist. Comm'n v. Dir. of Civil Serv., 348 Mass. 184, 203 N.E. 2d 95 (1964).

23. *See, generally* Welch, *The Effect of a Pardon on License Revocation and Reinstatement*, 15 HASTINGS L.J. 355 (1964).

24. RUBIN, LAW OF CRIMINAL CORRECTION, ch. 16 §41.

25. *Ibid.*, at §40.

26. *Ibid.*, at §46.

27. 529 F.2d 125 (7th Cir. 1975). For a discussion of this case, *see* Bryant, *Effect of Presidential Pardon—State Civil Rights Restored*, 14 AM. CRIM. L. REV. 335 (1976); Comment, *Presidential Clemency and the Restoration of Civil Rights: Appraising the Consequences of a Full Article II Pardon*, 61 IOWA L. REV. 1927 (1976).

28. 391 U.S. 234 (1968).

29. *See, e.g.,* COL. CONST. art. 7, §10 (1974); KAN. STAT. §62–2252 (1964); MINN. STAT. ANN. §640.53 (1945); MO. ANN. STAT. §216.855(3) (1966); NEB. REV. STAT. §29–2634 (1964); N.H. REV. STAT. ANN. §607–A:5(I) (Supp. 1969); OHIO REV. CODE ANN. §2965.17 (Baldwin 1964); OR. REV. STAT. §137.250 (1967); PA. STAT. ANN. tit. 19, §893 (1964); S.D. COMPILED LAWS ANN. §23–57–7 (1967); WASH. REV. CODE ANN. §9.96.050 (Supp. 1969); WIS. STAT. ANN. §57.078 (1957); WYO. STAT. §7–311 (1957).

30. *Cf.* United States *ex rel.* Consola v. Karnuth, 27 F. Supp. 461 (W.D.N.Y. 1939); United States *ex rel.* Malesevic v. Perkins, 17 F. Supp. 851 (W.D. Pa. 1936), *aff'd*, 99 F.2d 255 (3rd Cir. 1938).

31. CAL. PENAL CODE §1203.4 (West 1956); DEL. CODE tit. 11, §4332(i) (Supp. 1968); IDAHO CODE §19–2604 (Supp.

1969); MICH. STAT. ANN. §§28.1274 (101) to (103) (Supp. 1969); MINN. STAT. ANN. §§242.31, 638.02 (Supp. 1970); NEV. REV. STAT. §176.225 (1967); N.J. REV. STAT. §2A:164–28 (1953); N.Y. CRIM. PROC. LAW §160.50 (McKinney Supp. 1976); N.D. CENT. CODE § 12–53–18 (1960); TEX. CRIM. PROC. CODE ANN. art. 42.12 & 7 (1966); UTAH CODE ANN. §77–35–17 (1953); WASH. REV. CODE ANN. §9.95.240 (1961); WYO. STAT. §7–315 (1957). For a discussion of expungement, *see* Comment, *Criminal Records of Arrest and Conviction: Expungement from the General Public Access*, 3 CALIF. W. L. REV. 121 (1967); Note, *The Effect of Expungement of a Criminal Conviction*, 40 S. CALIF. L. REV. 127 (1967).

32. United States v. Rosen, 343 F. Supp. 804, 807 (S.D.N.Y. 1972). *See also* United States v. Linn, 513 F.2d 925 (10th Cir. 1975).
33. United States v. Rosen, 343 F. Supp. 804, 806 (S.D.N.Y. 1972), *quoted approvingly in* United States v. Schnitzer, 567 F.2d 536, (2nd Cir. 1977).
34. Sullivan v. Murphy, 478 F.2d 938 (D.C. Cir. 1973).
35. United States v. McLeod, 385 F.2d 734 (5th Cir. 1976).
36. Wheeler v. Goodman, 306 F. Supp. 58 (W.D.N.C. 1969).
37. Kowall v. United States, 53 F.R.D. 211 (W.D. Mich. 1971).
38. *See e.g.*, CONN. GEN. STAT. ANN. §9–48 (1958); ILL. ANN. STAT. ch. 38, §124–2(b), 49 (1964); MISS. CODE ANN. §4004–27 (1956); N. H. *Const.* pt. 1, art. 11.; N.C. GEN. STAT. §§13–1 to –2, 13–5, 13–7 (1969); TENN. CODE ANN. §40–3701 (1955).
39. N.Y. CORREC. LAW §§701–03 (McKinney 1968).
40. N.Y. EXEC. LAW §242(3) (McKinney Supp. 1969).

XIII
Changing the Law

The current collateral consequences of a conviction are harsh, unfair, and counterproductive. They hinder the successful reintegration of the offender into the community, needlessly harm innocent third parties, and fail to advance legitimate governmental purposes. As a whole, they do not border on the irrational; they fall over the edge.

Current disabilities defy understanding unless viewed historically, Rooted in such crude concepts as attainder and civil death, current disabilities are largely without present justification, but yield slowly to reason. This phenomenon was described by Justice Oliver Wendell Holmes:

A very common phenomenon, and one very familiar to the student of history, is this. The customs, beliefs, or needs of a primitive time establish a rule or a formula. In the course of centuries the customs, belief, or necessity disappears, but the rule remains. The reason which gave rise to the rule has been forgotten, and ingenious minds set themselves to inquire how it is to be accounted for.[1]

What is the trend of the law?
The trend is the right way. States are reducing the number of disabilities applicable to ex-convicts and improving restoration devices; a few have adopted anti-discrimination statutes. But change has been difficult and slow and may

continue to be so, even though current disabilities lack a defender and are criticized by scholars, study commissions, and anyone else who has taken an interest in the field.

What kind of reforms are necessary?
This book has already made numerous specific suggestions for reform; they cluster into three dominant themes.
- Reduce the scope of current disabilities.
- Improve restoration devices.
- Prohibit by statute unreasonable discrimination against ex-convicts in the public and private sector.

How can the law be changed?
Statutes imposing civil disabilities can be changed by persuading a court to invalidate them or a legislature to repeal them.

What can the courts do?
When an issue is politically unpopular, it is often easier to change laws by turning to the courts rather than the legislatures. Many issues may be framed as legal disputes which can be properly presented to the courts. Using state or federal grounds, a court might well invalidate a disability the legislature is too shy to alter.

The route to the judiciary has been worn smooth by many groups too politically weak to secure relief from the legislature. Racial and ethnic minorities, mental patients, aliens, juvenile delinquents, prisoners, parolees, students, and religious minorities have often turned to the courts for relief and received it.

So far, ex-convicts have had only minimal success in the courts, and that has been mainly recently. Courts resist viewing disabilities as punishment, and they stretch to define a legitimate rationale that might justify a particular disability. Nevertheless, ex-convicts should continue to resort to the courts. The kind of success achieved in recent years should continue, and as it does, it may help create an overall climate that will assist in the repeal of disabilities. Also, some of this litigation may result in a few landmark decisions, which may speed developments along.

What are some of the difficulties in using the courts as an avenue for social reform?

There are many, but three deserve a brief mention:

First, constitutional litigation is complicated and requires a lawyer. Most people cannot afford a private lawyer and must turn to public-interest organizations for assistance. These organizations have limited resources and cannot meet the demand made for their services. Thus, many individuals eager to challenge particular disabilities may find it difficult to obtain a lawyer.

Second, courts decide only cases which present a real controversy between the parties. Many problems do not boil down to strict legal controversies, and those that do may not be of importance to many people. Moreover, when faced with a legal controversy, courts are usually more able to stop something from being accomplished than to require that something new be instituted.

Third, it is often difficult to implement judicial decisions. A hard-won court order may not result in the breadth of change it appears to imply.

These cautionary words should not discourage litigation. But litigation is no panacea. Reformers must look to the legislature as well as the courts as vehicles for change.

What can the legislatures do?

Legislatures are not subject to the same restrictions that courts are. Because the purpose of a legislature is to fashion the broad rules which govern society, it is not limited like the courts are to correcting the problem faced by one individual. It can make sweeping changes if it chooses to do so. It can repeal civil disabilities, adopt better restoration procedures, and restrict and penalize unfair discrimination against ex-convicts.

But legislatures are difficult to influence for politically weak or unpopular group like ex-convicts. Legislators are often unwilling to risk the loss of political support on behalf of ex-convicts. Thus, the legislature offers a greater capacity for change than the courts, but it may be very difficult to obtain.

Will a change in the law change the way ex-offenders are treated?

Generally yes, especially when specific rights such as voting, holding public office, and occupational licenses are at stake.

Moreover, current disabilities support the stigma that now attaches to a conviction and subjects an ex-convict to broad social prejudice.

And while reform of current disabilities will not eradicate that stigma and prejudice, it may weaken social prejudices and help usher in a new day when ex-convicts are not unfairly haunted at every turn by the past. The act of enhancing individual rights and dampening social prejudices is law functioning at its noble best.

NOTE

1. O. HOLMES, JR., THE COMMON LAW 5 (1881).

Appendix A
Voting Rights*

Deciding whether an ex-convict has the right to vote is a very complex problem. The pertinent state law may be both statutory and constitutional, and there may be several provisions of each. These provisions may be scattered throughout a state's body of law, causing a researcher to doubt whether it all has been found. Moreover, provisions which restore the right to vote are often separate from those which withdraw it and often appear to have been drafted without having fully considered the disfranchisement provisions.

The results of this complexity is that it is difficult to summarize the state of the law with precision. Establishing categories that make summaries possible requires glossing over the subtleties that distinguish one state from another. This disadvantage, however, seems offset by the advantages of presenting the pertinent law in table form.

Two tables follow. The first summarizes the law pertinent to disfranchisement. The second summarizes the law pertinent to restoration of rights. In order to determine a state's law, both tables must be consulted. Thus Table I reveals that Maine, Massachusetts, Pennsylvania, and Ver-

---

*This appendix is based upon the research of Bobbi Bonfeld. The charts used in the appendix are modeled after those contained in the *amicus curiae* brief filed in the U.S. Supreme Court by the American Bar Association in *Richardson v. Ramirez*, 418 U.S. 24 (1974).

mont disfranchise only because of election-law offenses and that thirty-six other states disfranchise because of any felony conviction whether or not it is related to the election process. Table II shows that twenty-two states automatically restore the right to vote upon the completion of certain conditions, and that five states (Alaska, Alabama, Iowa, Michigan, and New Mexico) restore the franchise only if the convicted person obtains a pardon.

Following the two tables is an alphabetical listing of the states with citations to a state's constitutional and statutory provisions pertinent to the withdrawal and restoration of the franchise.

TABLE I
STATE DISFRANCHISEMENT PROVISIONS

State	Felony	Infamous Crimes	Crimes Involving Moral Turpitude	Specified Offenses	Election Crimes	Treason	Crimes Punishable by Incarceration	While Incarcerated or Under Sentence
Alabama			✓	✓	✓	✓	✓	
Alaska	✓		✓	✓			✓	✓
Arizona	✓					✓		✓
Arkansas	✓							
California	✓			✓				
Colorado								✓
Connecticut	✓			✓	✓			
Delaware	✓				✓			
D.C.	✓							
Florida	✓							✓
Georgia			✓	✓		✓	✓	
Hawaii	✓							✓
Idaho	✓	✓		✓	✓	✓		✓
Illinois	✓						✓	✓
Indiana	✓	✓			✓			✓
Iowa	✓	✓						
Kansas	✓			✓			✓	✓
Kentucky	✓				✓		✓	✓
Louisiana	✓							✓

TABLE I (Cont'd)
STATE DISFRANCHISEMENT PROVISIONS

State	Felony	Infamous Crimes	Crimes Involving Moral Turpitude	Specified Offenses	Election Crimes	Treason	Crimes Punishable by Incarceration	While Incarcerated or Under Sentence
Maine					√			
Maryland		√		√				
Massachusetts					√			
Michigan								√
Minnesota	√			√		√		
Mississippi				√				
Missouri	√			√	√		√	
Montana	√							√
Nebraska	√							√
Nevada	√			√		√		
New Hampshire	√			√	√	√		√
New Jersey					√	√		√
New Mexico	√							
New York	√			√	√			
North Carolina	√							
North Dakota	√					√		
Ohio	√							
Oklahoma	√						√	√
Oregon	√							√

TABLE I (Cont'd)
STATE DISFRANCHISEMENT PROVISIONS

State	Felony	Infamous Crimes	Crime: Involving Moral Turpitude	Specified Offenses	Election Crimes	Treason	Crimes Punishable by Incarceration	While Incarcerated or Under Sentence
Pennsylvania								
Rhode Island	✓	✓			✓			
South Carolina				✓	✓			
South Dakota	✓			✓				✓
Tennessee								✓
Texas	✓	✓		✓				✓
Utah								
Vermont					✓	✓		
Virginia	✓	✓			✓			
Washington								
West Virginia	✓	✓			✓	✓		
Wisconsin	✓	✓		✓	✓	✓		✓
Wyoming	✓	✓						

TABLE II
STATE PROVISIONS FOR RESTORATION OF VOTING RIGHTS

State	Automatic Restoration	Disfranchisement For a Determinate Period	Disfranchisement For a Determinate Period: Only Certain Offenses	Pardon by Governor	Other Procedures
Alabama					
Alaska					✓
Arizona				✓	✓
Arkansas				✓	
California				✓	✓
Colorado	✓				
Connecticut	✓			✓	✓
Delaware			✓		
D.C.		✓		✓	✓
Florida	✓			✓	✓
Georgia				✓	✓
Hawaii	✓			✓	
Idaho				✓	✓
Illinois	✓				
Indiana		✓		✓	
Iowa	✓			✓	
Kansas				✓	
Kentucky			✓	✓	

TABLE II (Cont'd)
STATE PROVISIONS FOR RESTORATION OF VOTING RIGHTS

State	Automatic Restoration	Disfranchisement For a Determinate Period	Disfranchisement For a Determinate Period; Only Certain Offenses	Pardon by Governor	Other Procedures
Louisiana					
Maine	√				
Maryland		√		√	
Massachusetts				√	
Michigan		√		√	
Minnesota	√			√	
Mississippi					√
Missouri			√		√
Montana	√			√	
Nebraska	√			√	√
Nevada				√	√
New Hampshire	√			√	
New Jersey		√		√	
New Mexico				√	
New York	√			√	
North Carolina	√			√	
North Dakota				√	√

*The restoration provision in these states apply only to first felony offenders.

TABLE II (Cont'd)
STATE PROVISIONS FOR RESTORATION OF VOTING RIGHTS

State	Automatic Restoration	Disfranchisement For a Determinate Period	Disfranchisement For a Determinate Period; Only Certain Offences	Pardon by Governor	Other Procedures
Ohio	√				
Oklahoma				√	
Oregon	√			√	
Pennsylvania	√	√		√	
Rhode Island				√	√
South Carolina					√
South Dakota	√			√	
Tennessee			√	√	
Texas		√		√	√
Utah					
Vermont		√			
Virginia				√	√
Washington	√			√	
West Virginia	√			√	
Wisconsin	√				
Wyoming	√			√	

CONSTITUTIONAL AND STATUTORY CITATIONS ON VOTING RIGHTS, BY STATE.

1. ALA. CONST. art. VIII, §182; ALA. CONST. amend. 38; ALA. CODE tit. 17, §15 (1959); ALA. CODE tit. 42, §16 (1959).
2. ALASKA CONST. art. III, §21; ALASKA CONST. art. V, §2; ALASKA STAT. §15.05.030 (1976); ALASKA STAT. §33.20.070 (1962).
3. ARIZ. CONST. art. V, §5; ARIZ. CONST. art. VII, §2; ARIZ. REV. STAT. §13–1653 (1956); ARIZ. REV. STAT. §13–1744 (Supp. 1976–77); ARIZ. REV. STAT. §16–101(5) (1975); ARIZ. CRIME. PROC. RULES 29.1 (1973); ARIZ. REV. STAT. ANN. §31–402 (1976); ARIZ. REV. STAT. ANN. §31–443 (1976).
4. ARK. CONST. amend. 8, art. 3, §1; ARK. CONST. amend. 51, §11; ARK. CONST. art. 6, §18; ARK. STAT. ANN. §12–300(m) (1968).
5. CAL CONST. art. II, §4; CAL. CONST. art. V, §8; CAL. ELEC. CODE §500 (Supp. 1977); CAL. PENAL CODE §232 (Supp. 1977); CAL. PENAL CODE §228 (1970); CAL. PENAL CODE §2600 (Supp. 1977); CAL. PENAL CODE §4852.17 (Supp. 1977); CAL. PENAL CODE §4853 (1970); CAL. PENAL CODE §1203.4 (Supp. 1977).
6. COLO. CONST. art. IV, §7, COLO. CONST. art. VII, §10.
7. CONN. CONST. art. VI, §3; CONN. GEN. STAT. ANN. §9–46. (Supp. 1977); CONN. GEN. STAT. ANN. §9–46a (Supp. 1977).
8. DEL. CONST. art. V, §7; DEL. CONST. art. V, §2; DEL. CONST. art. VII, §1; DEL. CODE tit. 15, §1701 (1975); DEL. CODE ANN. tit. 11, §4347 (1975).
9. D.C. CODE §1–1102 (Supp. 1976–77); D.C. CODE ANN. §1–220 (1966).
10. FLA. CONST. art. 4, §8; FLA. CONST. art. 6, §4; FLA. STAT. ANN. §97.041 (Supp. 1977); FLA. STAT. ANN. §940.01 (1973); FLA. STAT. ANN. §940.05 (1973).
11. GA. CONST. §2–3011; GA. CONST. §2–501; GA. CODE ANN. §34–609 (Supp. 1976); GA. CODE ANN. §27–2701 (1972).
12. HAW. CONST. art. II, §2; HAW. CONST. art. IV, §5; HAW. REV. STAT. §831–2 (Supp. 1975); HAW. REV. STAT. §831–5 (Supp. 1975).
13. IDAHO CONST. art. VI, §3; IDAHO CONST. art. IV, §7: IDAHO CODE §34–403 (Supp. 1976); IDAHO CODE §20–240 (Supp. 1976).

14. ILL. CONST. art. §3, 2; ILL. ANN. STAT. ch. 46, §3–5 (Supp. 1977).
15. IND. CONST. art. II, §8; IND. CONST. art. V, §17; IND. CODE ANN. §3–1–32–8 (1972); IND. CODE ANN. §3–1–21–4 (1972); IND. CODE ANN. §3–1–32–64 (1972); IND. CODE ANN. §3–1–32–65 (1972).
16. IOWA CONST. art. II, §5; IOWA CONST. art. IV, §16; IOWA CODE ANN §48.31 (Supp. 1977–78); IOWA CODE ANN. §248.12 (1969).
17. KAN. CONST. art. 1, §7; KAN. CONST. art 5, §2; KAN. STAT. §21–4615 (1974); KAN STAT. §22–3722 (1974); KAN. STAT. §22–3701 (1974).
18. KY. CONST. §77; KY. CONST. §145; KY. REV. STAT. §160.991 (1971); KY. REV. STAT. §432.350 (1975).
19. LA. CONST. art. 1, §10; LA. CONST. art. 4, §5; LA. REV. STAT. ANN. §15:572 (Supp. 1977).
20. ME. CONST. art. II, §1; ME. CONST. art. V, §11; ME. CONST. art. IX, §13; ME. REV. STAT. tit. 21. §245 (Supp. 1976–77).
21. MD. CONST. art. 1, §2; MD. CONST. art. II, §20; MD. ANN. CODE art. 33, §3–4(c) (1976); MED. ANN. CODE art. 41, §118 (1971).
22. MASS. CONST. amend. art. III; MASS. CONST. pt. 2, ch. 2, §1, art. 8; MASS. ANN. LAWS ch. 51, §1 (Supp. 1977–78); MASS. GEN. LAWS ANN. ch. 55, §42 (Supp. 1977–78); MASS. GEN. LAWS ANN. ch. 127, §152 (1958).
23. MICH. CONST. art. 2, §2; MICH. CONST. art. 5, §14; MICH. COMP. LAWS ANN. §168.10 (1967).
24. MINN. CONST. art. 5, §7; MINN. CONST. art. 7, §1; MINN. STAT. ANN. §200.02 (Supp. 1977); MINN. STAT. ANN. §609.165 (Supp. 1977).
25. MISS. CONST. art. 12, §241; MISS. CONST. art. 12, §253; MISS. CODE ANN. §23–5–85 (1972); MISS. CODE ANN. §23–5–35 (1972); MISS. CODE ANN. §99–19–35 (1973).
26. MO. CONST. art. IV, §7; MO. CONST. art. VIII, §2; MO. STAT. ANN. 111.021 (Supp. 1977); MO. ANN. STAT. §113.040 (Supp. 1977); MO. ANN. STAT. §129.920 (Supp. 1977); MO. ANN. STAT. §222.030 (1962); MO. ANN. STAT. §560.610 (Supp. 1977); MO. ANN. STAT. §216.355 (1962).
27. MONT. CONST. art. IV, §2; MONT. CONST. art. VI, §12. MONT. REV. CODE ANN. §23–2701 (Supp. 1975).
28. NEB. CONST art. VI, §2; NEB. REV. STAT. §29–112 (1975); NEB. REV. STAT. §29–2264 (1975); NEB. REV. STAT. §83–1118 (Supp. 1975).
29. NEV. CONST. art. II, §1; NEV. CONST. art. V, §§13, 14; NEV. CONST. art. XV, §3; NEV. REV. STAT. §293.540.
30. N.H. CONST pt. 1, art. 11; N.H. REV. STAT. ANN. §607–A:2 (1974).

31. N.J. CONST. art. II, §7; N.J. REV. STAT. §19:4–1 (Supp. 1977–78); N.J. REV. STAT. §19:34–25 (1964); N.J. REV. STAT. §2A:167–5 (1971).
32. N.M. CONST. art. VII, §1; N.M. CONST. art. V, §6; N.M. STAT. ANN. §40A–29–14 (1972); N.M. STAT. ANN. §40A–29–21 (1972).
33. N.Y. CONST. art. II, §3; N.Y. CONST. art. IV, §4; N.Y. ELEC. LAW §§152, 462 (McKinney Supp. 1976–77).
34. N.C. CONST. art. III, §5(6); N.C. CONST. art. VI, §2(3); N.C. GEN. STAT. §13–1 (Supp. 1975); N.C. GEN. STAT. §163–55 (1976).
35. N.D. CONST. art. III, §76; N.D. CONST. art. V, §127; N.D. CENT. CODE §16–01–04 (1971); N.D. CENT. CODE §12–55–05 (1976); N.D. CENT. CODE §12–55–24 (1976).
36. OHIO CONST. art. III, §11; OHIO CONST. art. V, §4; OHIO REV. CODE ANN. §2961.01 (1975); OHIO REV. CODE ANN. §2967.16 (1975).
37. OKLA. CONST. art. III, §1; OKLA. CONST. art. VI, §10; OKLA. STAT. tit. 26, §4–101 (Supp. 1976–77); OKLA. STAT. tit. 57. §§332, 345 (1969).
38. OR. CONST. art. II, §3; OR. CONST. art. V, 14; OR. REV. STAT. §137.280 (1975).
39. PA. CONST. art. VII, §7; PA. CONST. art. IV, §9; PA. STAT. ANN. tit. 19, §893 (1964); PA. STAT. ANN. tit. 25, §3552 (1963).
40. R.I. CONST. amend. 24, §4; R.I. CONST. amend. 38; R.I. CONST. amend. 2; R.I. GEN. LAWS §17–23–5 (1970).
41. S.C. CONST. art. II, §7; S.C. CONST. art. IV, §14; S.C. CODE §23–62(5)(b) (Supp. 1975); S.C. CODE §16–61 (1962); S.C. CODE §55–642 (1962).
42. S.D. CONST. art. IV, §5; S.D. CONST. art. VII, §2; S.D. COMPILED LAWS ANN. §23–48–35 (1967); S.D. COMPILED LAWS ANN. §23–57–7 (1967); S.D. COMPILED LAWS ANN. §24–5–2 (1967); S.D. COMPILED LAWS ANN. §23–59–1 (1967).
43. TENN. CONST. art. I, §5; TENN. CONST. art. IV, §2; TENN. COST. art. III, §6; TENN. CODE ANN. §40–3501 (1975); TENN. CODE ANN. §40–3701 (1975).
44. TEX. CONST. art. IV, §11; TEX. CONST. art. VI, §1; TEX. CONST. art. XVI, §2; TEX. ELEC. CODE tit. 5 §5.01 (Supp. 1976–77); TEX. CRIM. PROC. CODE tit. 48 §48.01 (1966).
45. UTAH CONST. art. IV, §6; UTAH CONST. art. VII, §12; UTAH CODE ANN. §77–62–3 (Supp. 1975).
46. VT. CONST. ch. 11, §55; VT. CONST. ch. 11, §20.
47. VA. CONST. art. II, §1; VA. CONST. art V, §12; VA. CODE §24.1–42 (1973).
48. WASH. CONST. art. I, §3; WASH. CONST. art. III, §§9, 11; WASH. REV. CODE ANN. §9.95.160 (1961); WASH. REV.

CODE ANN. §9.96.010 (1961); WASH. REV. CODE ANN. §9.96.050 (Supp. 1976).
49. W. VA. CONST. art. IV, §1; W. VA. CONST. art. VII, §11; W. VA. CODE §3-1-3 (Supp. 1976); 51 OP. W. VA. CONST. art. IV, §1 (not to prohibit a convicted person from voting after completion of sentence); W. VA. CODE §5-1-16 (1971).
50. WISC. CONST. art. III, §§2, 6; WISC. CONST. art. V, §6; WISC. STAT. ANN. §6.03 (1967); WISC. STAT. ANN. §57.078 (Supp. 1976-77).
51. WYO. CONST. art. 4, §5; WYO. CONST. art. 6, §6; WYO. STAT. §6-4 (1959); WYO. STAT. §7-311 (1959); WYO. STAT. §7-386 (1959).

Appendix B
Licensing Restrictions

This Appendix is a duplicate of one prepared by the American Bar Association Clearinghouse on Offender Employment Restrictions and published in *Removing Offender Employment Restrictions: A Handbook on Remedial Legislation and Other Techniques for Alleviating Formal Employment Restrictions Confronting Ex-Offenders* (March 1976).

The following is a list of the occupations that have licensing restrictions against former offenders. The nature of the statutory restriction is indicated by a number:
1: A criminal offense is grounds for denying a license.
2: The applicant must have good moral character.
3: The applicant must have good moral character and not have a criminal record.

A word of caution about this chart is appropriate. Many categories in the chart plainly overlap as do hairdresser, beautician and cosmetologist. This is undoubtedly due to the fact that different states use different terms to mean the same thing. On the other hand, different states may very well use the same term, but define it differently. Thus, although the chart is a result of hours of research and dramatically illustrates the employment barriers facing ex-offenders, it should be considered as a guide to a state's prohibitions and not a substitute for its laws.

THE RIGHTS OF EX-OFFENDERS

OCCUPATION	TOTAL	Ala.	Alaska	Ariz.	Ark.	Calif.	Colo.	Conn.	Del.	D.C.	Fla.	Ga.	Hawaii	Idaho	Ill.	Ind.	Iowa
1 Abstractor	3																
2 Accountant (or CPA)	48	2	2	2	2	1		2	2	2	2	2	2		3	3	2
3 Agricultural Chemical Applicator	1																
4 Agricultural Produce Broker	1					3											
5 Agricultural Produce Dealer	2								2								
6 Agricultural Processor	1											2					
7 Agricultural Produce Merchant	1								2								
8 Aircraft Broker	1	2															
9 Aircraft Pilot	2					1											
10 Alcoholic Beverage Dealer	9			2	2			3								1	3
11 Alcoholic Beverage Employee	7			2	1	1										1	
12 Alcoholic Beverage Manufacturer	3				3	1											
13 Alcoholic Beverage Retailer	6				3			3								1	3
14 Alcoholic Beverage Transporter	8				3												
15 Amusement Operator	1																
16 Animal Dealer								2						2			
17 Apprentice	1																
18 Architect	42	2	2			3	2	2		2	2	2	2		2	3	3	2
19 Artificial Inseminator	2	2	2														3
20 Artist Manager	1					2											
21 Astrologer	1											2					
22 Attorney		2	2	2	2	2	2	2	2	2	2	2	3		2	2	2
23 Auctioneer	10								2			2					
24 Auctioneer—Livestock	1																
25 Automobile Dismantler	1					3											
26 Babcock Test Operator	1								2								2
27 Barber	47	2	3	3	3	2	2	2	2	2	2	2	3	3	3	3	3

LICENSING RESTRICTIONS

State	1	2	3	4	5	6	7	8	9	10	11	12	13	14	15	16	17	18	19	20	21	22	23	24	25	26	27
Wyo.	2																2			2							2
Wis.	2																2			3							3
W.Va.	2																2			2							2
Wash.	3																2			2							2
Va.	2	3															2										2
Vt.	2																2			2							2
Utah	3																2			3							2
Tex.	2																2			2							2
Tenn.	2														3		2			2		2					3
S.Dak.	2																2			2							2
S.C.	2																2										2
R.I.	2																2			2							2
Pa.	2																2			2		2					2
Oreg.	2																3			2		2					3
Okla.	2																2			2							2
Ohio	2																2			2		2					3
N.Dak.	2																3			2							3
N.C.	2																2			2		2					2
N.Y.	2									1	1	1	1				2			2							2
N.Mex.	2	2															2			2							2
N.J.	3									1	1	1	1				2			2							3
N.H.	2	3						2									2			3							2
Nev.	2																2			3		1					3
Nebr.	2	2							2								2			2							3
Mont.	2																2		2								
Mo.	2										1	3	3	3			2			2		2	1				
Miss.	2							3									2			2		3					3
Minn.	2																2			2		2					3
Mich.	2	2															2			2		2					3
Mass.	2																2	2		2							2
Md.	3																2			2							2
Maine	2																2	2		2		2					2
La.	2	2																2		3							2
Ky.	2	2															2	2		3		2					3
Kan.	2	2																		3		3					3

THE RIGHTS OF EX-OFFENDERS

OCCUPATION	TOTAL	Ala.	Alaska	Ariz.	Ark.	Calif.	Colo.	Conn.	Del.	D.C.	Fla.	Ga.	Hawaii	Idaho	Ill.	Ind.	Iowa
28 Barber Apprentice	8									2	2	3			3	3	3
29 Barber Instructor	6	2							1		3	3				3	3
30 Barber Manager/Owner	12				2		2										
31 Barber School	1											3					
32 Beautician	29	3	2	3		3				3	3	3			3	3	3
33 Beauty Culturist	1																
34 Beauty School	2																
35 Beauty-Shop Owner	12										2						3
36 Beer Retailer/Wholesaler	1																
37 Billiard Operator	3	3															
38 Bingo Operator	1							2									
39 Bioanalytical Lab Operator	2					3											
40 Biochemist	1																
41 Boiler Inspector	1																
42 Bondsman—Bail	11					3	3	3				3					
43 Boxer/Wrestler	6					2											
44 Boxing Promoter	2					2											
45 Broker—Business Chance	1																
46 Broker—Insurance	18		2	3		3	3			2		2			3	3	3
47 Broker—Investment	1																
48 Broker—Personal Property	2					2											
49 Broker—Real Estate	46	3	3		2	2		2	2	2	2	2		2	3	3	3
50 Broker—Savings and Loan	1			2													
51 Broker—Surplus Line Insurance	9							2									
52 Burial-Association Agent	1											3	2	3			
53 Business-School Operator	2			2													3
54 Butcher	1																

LICENSING RESTRICTIONS 175

State	28	29	30	31	32	33	34	35	36	37	38	39	40	41	42	43	44	45	46	47	48	49	50	51	52	53	54
Wyo.																											
Wis.																						1	2				
W.Va.					3	3		2															2	3			
Wash.			2																				2				
Va.																											
Vt.	2		2		2	3		2							2	3						2	3	3			
Utah			2	2	2	3		2														2	2	3			
Tex.					2	3											2	2				2	2				
Tenn.					1	2		3									2					2	2				
S.Dak.															3							2	2				
S.C.																						2	2				
R.I.						2	2													2		2	2				
Pa.						2	2	3														2	2				
Oreg.			3																3			2	3				
Okla.					2	2									3								3	3			
Ohio																			2	3	3	3	3				
N.Dak.		3																									
N.C.							2	2							3	3											
N.Y.	2		2												1	2											
N.Mex.											3																
N.J.			3		3			3		3												2	3	3			
N.H.	3																					3	2	3			
Nev.					2	2				2									2			3	2	3			
Nebr.			2		3	2		2																2			
Mont.																						2	2				
Mo.																						3	3	3	2		
Miss.																						3	3	3			
Minn.													2														
Mich.		2	2		3		2	3		2																	
Mass.															2	2	2					2	2				
Md.																						2	2	2			
Maine					2			2														2	3	2			
La.																		2	2			2	2	2			
Ky.			3																			2	2	2		1	
Kan.					2	3																					2

#	OCCUPATION	TOTAL	Ala.	Alaska	Ariz.	Ark.	Calif.	Colo.	Conn.	Del.	D.C.	Fla.	Ga.	Hawaii	Idaho	Ill.	Ind.	Iowa
1	Cattle Dealer	3																
2	Cemetery Salesman	7							2									
3	Chauffeur	12												3		3		2
4	Check Casher/Seller	9				2	2											
5	Child Day-Care Operator	3																
6	Chiropodist	36				2	3	3	2			3	2	2		2	3	2
7	Chiropractor	43	1	3	3	3	3	2	2	3		3	3	2		3	3	3
8	Cigarette Dealer																	
9	Cigarette Manufacturer	1																
10	Civil Engineer																	
11	Cleaning-Plant Operator	1																
12	Clinical Chemist	1					3											
13	Clinical-Lab Director	1					3											
14	Clinical-Lab Technologist	1					3				2							
15	Coalmine Examiner	2					3											
16	Collection Agent	1																
17	Commercial Driving School	15		3	3		3	3	3							1	1	3
18	Commission Merchant	1		2														
19	Contractor (Builder)	1																
20	Correspondence-School Rep.	1																
21	Cosmetologist	24	3	2		2	2		2	3	2		2			3		
22	Cosmetology Instructor	3		2												3		
23	Cotton Classer	1	2															
24	Dairy-Product Distributor	2										2						
25	Dairy Products—Buyer/Processor	3					2					2						
26	Day-Care Operator	2																

LICENSING RESTRICTIONS

State	1	2	3	4	5	6	7	8	9	10	11	12	13	14	15	16	17	18	19	20	21	22	23	24	25	26
Wyo.				2		2	2									2					3					
Wis.			2	2		2	2		3							3	2									
W.Va.			2	2		3	3																			
Wash.					2	3																				
Va.					3		3																			
Vt.				1		3	3														3	3				
Utah						2	3														3	3				
Tex.						3	3																			
Tenn.						2	3														2					
S.Dak.						2	3																			
S.C.																										
R.I.			2			2	2																			
Pa.				2		2	3																			2
Oreg.						3	3									3					3					
Okla.																										
Ohio			2	2		2	3																			
N.Dak.						3	2																			
N.C.						3	2														2					
N.Y.	3		3	3																						
N.Mex.						3	3									3										
N.J.	2			3		3	3									3										
N.H.						2	3																			
Nev.						2										2	3									
Nebr.			2	2		3	3									2	3				3					
Mont.			3		2	2	3	2								2					2	2				2
Mo.						3	3														2	2				
Miss.																										
Minn.			2	1		3	1				1											3				
Mich.						3	1										2				2	2				
Mass.						3	3										2		2	2						
Md.						2	3														2					
Maine							3																			
La.						3	3			2											3					
Ky.			2			3	2																			
Kan.						3	2														2					

THE RIGHTS OF EX-OFFENDERS

OCCUPATION	TOTAL	Ala.	Alaska	Ariz.	Ark.	Calif.	Colo.	Conn.	Del.	D.C.	Fla.	Ga.	Hawaii	Idaho	Ill.	Ind.	Iowa
27 Dealer—Livestock/Poultry	2																
28 Dealer—Tobacco/Soft Drink	2																
29 Debt Adjustor	2							3									
30 Debt Management Business	1																
31 Dental Hygienist	48	3		2	2	2	2	3		2	2	2	2	2	3	1	2
32 Dental Specialist	1																
33 Dentist	47	3		2	2	2	2	2	1	2	2	2	2	2	1	3	3
34 Detection of Deception Examiner	1																
35 Detective Agent	2																
36 Detective-Agency Operator	1																
37 Disposal-Plant Operator	1															2	
38 Distilling-Certificate Broker	1																
39 Dog Racing																	
40 Driver	2													3			
41 Driving Instructor	8																
42 Driving-School Operator	2																
43 Drug Dealer/Wholesaler	3																
44 Dry Cleaning	1																
45 Egg Dealer																	
46 Electrician	2					2											
47 Electrical Worker	1					2											
48 Electrologists	10				2	2											
49 Electrology Instructor	1					2											
50 Elevator Craftsman/Helper	1							2									
51 Elevator Inspector																	3
52 Embalmer	46	2								2	3	3	2	2	3	3	3
53 Emigrant Agent	2																3

LICENSING RESTRICTIONS   179

	27	28	29	30	31	32	33	34	35	36	37	38	39	40	41	42	43	44	45	46	47	48	49	50	51	52	53
Wyo.				2	2																					2	
Wis.							3						1	3												2	2
W.Va.				2	3	2	3																		2	3	
Wash.				2	2	2	2								2											2	3
Va.				2	2	2	2						3					2							3	3	
Vt.				2	2	2	2																		2	3	2
Utah			3	2	2	3	3																			2	
Tex.				1	2		3		3																	3	3
Tenn.	1					2								2		2									3	3	3
S.Dak.				2	2	2	2																				
S.C.		2		2	2	2	2			2															2	3	
R.I.				2	2	2	2																		2	3	
Pa.												2															
Oreg.				2	2	2	2																			3	
Okla.				2	2	2	2							2								3	3		2	3	3
Ohio				2	2	2	2															3	3		2	3	
N.Dak.		2		2	2	2	2																		2	3	
N.C.				2	2	2	3																		2	3	3
N.Y.	3			2	2	2	2																		2	2	3
N.Mex.				3	2	2	3												2								
N.J.				2	3	2	2															3			2	3	
N.H.				2	2	2	2																		2	2	
Nev.				2	2	2	2							2	2	2									3	2	
Nebr.				2	2	3	2															2			3	3	
Mont.				3	2	2	3																			3	
Mo.				2	2	2	2																			2	3
Miss.				2	2	2	2																		2	3	
Minn.				2	2	2	2																		3	3	3
Mich.				2	2	2	2														2	2			3	3	3
Mass.																	3										
Md.				2	2	2	2								2										1	3	3
Maine																											
La.				2	2	3	2																				
Ky.				2	3			3																	3	3	3
Kan.		2																1									

THE RIGHTS OF EX-OFFENDERS

OCCUPATION	TOTAL	Ala.	Alaska	Ariz.	Ark.	Calif.	Colo.	Conn.	Del.	D.C.	Fla.	Ga.	Hawaii	Idaho	Ill.	Ind.	Iowa
1 Employment-Agency Operator	11	2	2			2		2				2				2	2
2 Engineer	43	2	2		3	3	2	3	2	2	2	3	2	3		3	1
3 Engineer in Training	2																2
4 Escrow Agent	1															1	
5 Explosives Dealer	2			2													
6 Explosives Manufacturer/Distributor	2					2									1		
7 Explosives Handlers	1																
8 Exterminator	4					2						2	1	2			
9 Farm-Products Broker	1																
10 Farrier	1																
11 Feeder Swine Dealer	2														1	3	
12 Financial Planner	1														3		
13 Finger Weaver	1					2											
14 Firearms Dealer	1																
15 Fishing Boat Operator	1											1					
16 Florist	1															2	
17 Foreign-Exchange Dealer	1															1	
18 Forester	3																
19 Fortune Teller	1																
20 Fraternal-Society Agent	1											2					
21 Frozen-Foods Dealer	1																
22 Fumigator	1										1						
23 Fund Raiser	1																
24 Funeral Director	45	2	3	2	1	3	1	3		3	2	3		3	3	3	3
25 Fur Dealer/Breeder	1																

LICENSING RESTRICTIONS

State	1	2	3	4	5	6	7	8	9	10	11	12	13	14	15	16	17	18	19	20	21	22	23	24	25
Kan.		2	3																					3	
Ky.	3	3																						3	1
La.		2																				2			
Maine																									
Md.	2	2																						3	
Mass.		2																2						3	3
Mich.	2	2	2																					3	
Minn.		2	2	2																					
Miss.		2	2																					3	3
Mo.	2	2	2						2															3	3
Mont.	3	2	2																					3	3
Nebr.		2						2																3	3
Nev.											2													2	2
N.H.		2																						2	2
N.J.		2	2			3																		2	2
N.Mex.		2	2											3										2	2
N.Y.		2			1														2					2	3
N.C.																								3	
N.Dak.	2	2																							
Ohio	2	2	3																2					3	3
Okla.																			2						2
Oreg.		2																						3	3
Pa.						1																			
R.I.		2				1													2					2	3
S.C.		2																						3	3
S.Dak.		2	2																					3	3
Tenn.		2																						3	3
Tex.	3																							3	3
Utah		2																						3	2
Vt.		2	2																2					2	3
Va.		2	2																2					3	3
Wash.		2	2																					2	3
W.Va.		2	2																					2	3
Wis.		2	2																					2	
Wyo.		2																						2	

181

THE RIGHTS OF EX-OFFENDERS

OCCUPATION	TOTAL	Ala.	Alaska	Ariz.	Ark.	Calif.	Colo.	Conn.	Del.	D.C.	Fla.	Ga.	Hawaii	Idaho	Ill.	Ind.	Iowa
26 Gambling Operator	1																
27 Game Breeder	3	2															
28 Game Warden	1																
29 Geologist	1			2													
30 Guard	5																
31 Guide	4				3												
32 Guide (Hunting, Fishing)	1					2											
33 Guide Outfitter	1												3				
34 Gun Dealer	1										2						
35 Gunsmith	1																
36 Hairdresser	12							2									
37 Hairdressing Instructor	1							2									
38 Harbor Pilot	7	2									2	2					
39 Hawker	3																
40 Hearing-Aid Dispensor	10				3												
41 Hearing-Aid Fitter	2																
42 Healing-Arts Practitioner	1																
43 Home-Improvement Salesman	1																
44 Homeopath	1																
45 Horsemeat Processor	1																
46 Horse Racing	6														3		
47 Horse-Racing Personnel	2													3			
48 Horseshoer	1														2		
49 Horse Trainer	1																
50 Hospital Operator	1				2												
51 Hunting Guide	1				2												
52 Hypertrichnologist	1					3											

LICENSING RESTRICTIONS 183

	26	27	28	29	30	31	32	33	34	35	36	37	38	39	40	41	42	43	44	45	46	47	48	49	50	51	52
Wyo.				1	2																						
Wis.										2																	
W.Va.																											
Wash.									2																		
Va.								2	3																		
Vt.								2	2																		
Utah																											
Tex.					3																						
Tenn.										2																	
S.Dak.		2																									
S.C.				2						3	3																
R.I.																											
Pa.	2			3						2	2																
Oreg.									2	2																	
Okla.																				3							
Ohio									2	2																	
N.Dak.																											
N.C.								2	2																		
N.Y.										2																	
N.Mex.								2	2	2																	
N.J.									3	2										1	3						
N.H.									2																		
Nev.	2								2	2										2	2						
Nebr.																											
Mont.					2					2											1						
Mo.																											
Miss.																											
Minn.																											
Mich.									1																		
Mass.				3					2	2			2		3												
Md.																											
Maine									2	2							2										
La.																			3								
Ky.																											
Kan.																											

184 THE RIGHTS OF EX-OFFENDERS

OCCUPATION	TOTAL	Ala.	Alaska	Ariz.	Ark.	Calif.	Colo.	Conn.	Del.	D.C.	Fla.	Ga.	Hawaii	Idaho	Ill.	Ind.	Iowa
1 Industrial Alcohol	1																
2 Inhalation Therapist	1				3												
3 Insurance Adjuster	15				2							3	3				
4 Inspector	1																
5 Insurance Agent/Broker	42	3		2	3	2				2		3	1	3	2	2	
6 Insurance Agent—Fire	1	2															
7 Insurance Agent—Life	3																
8 Insurance Agent—Life and Health	2	2															2
9 Insurance Counselor	1										2						
10 Insurance Manager	1										3						
11 Insurance Rater	1																
12 Investment Agent	5																
13 Jockey	1																
14 Journeyman (Limited)	1						2										
15 Junk Dealer	4								2								
16 Junkyard Operator	1																
17 Labor Agent	1																
18 Landscape Architect	6						2	1			2	2					
19 Land Surveyor	32	2			2		2	2			2	2		3	1	2	2
20 Lightning-Rod Salesman	2													3	2	1	
21 Limburger Cheese Maker	1																
22 Limited Contractor	1							2									
23 Live Poultry Dealer	1																
24 Livery Service	1							2									
25 Livestock Dealer	7															2	3
26 Livestock Producer	1																

LICENSING RESTRICTIONS

State	1	2	3	4	5	6	7	8	9	10	11	12	13	14	15	16	17	18	19	20	21	22	23	24	25	26
Wyo.																			2	2						
Wis.																			2	2		2				
W.Va.				3															2	3						
Wash.				2	2														2	2						
Va.				2															2	2	2					
Vt.				3	3						1				2		2		2	2				2		
Utah			2	2	3																					
Tex.				2	2																					
Tenn.				1	2	2													2	2					1	
S.Dak.				2	1	2													2	2						
S.C.																										
R.I.				2	2																					
Pa.									2		2						2									
Oreg.			3	3	3														3							
Okla.			3	3	3																					
Ohio				2	2													1	2							
N.Dak.				3	3														2							
N.C.				2	2	2																				
N.Y.		1												1					2	3						
N.Mex.				2	2						3								2	2	2					
N.J.				3	3														2	2						
N.H.																		2								
Nev.			3	3	3														2	2					1	
Nebr.				3	2	3													2	2	2					
Mont.			2	2	3		2				2	1	1						2	2						
Mo.				3	2	2																				
Miss.			3	3	2														2	2						
Minn.				2	2														2	2						
Mich.				2	2	2																				
Mass.			2	2	2	2									2				2	2						
Md.				2	2																			2		
Maine			2	2																	2					
La.																										
Ky.			2	2	2		2					1							2	2						
Kan.																										1

THE RIGHTS OF EX-OFFENDERS

OCCUPATION	Iowa	Ind.	Ill.	Idaho	Hawaii	Ga.	Fla.	D.C.	Del.	Conn.	Colo.	Calif.	Ark.	Ariz.	Alaska	Ala.	TOTAL
27 Loanmaker																	5
28 Lobbyist																	1
29 Lodging Housekeeper																	1
30 Logscaler										2							1
31 Manicurist	22	3					2	2	2	3		2	3	2	2	3	3
32 Marine Diver																	1
33 Marine Pilot	1	2															
34 Marriage Counselor	1									3							
35 Masseur	2							2	3					2			
35	12																
36 Medical Lab Technician	1																
37 Medical Technician	2	2									2						
38 Merchant Truck Man	1																
39 Midwife	16	2						2	2	2	2				3	3	
40 Milk Handler/Dealer	3																
41 Milk Plant Manager	1																
42 Milk Tester/Weigher	1																
43 Mine Foreman	4							2	2								
44 Mine Inspector	7								2								
45 Mineral, Oil, and Gas Broker	1										3						2
46 Mobile-Home Salesman	1																
47 Money Lender	1																
48 Money-Order Vendor/Forwarder	3									2							
49 Mortgage Broker	1											2					
50 Mortician	1																
51 Motor-Carrier Vehicle Operator	1																
52 Motor-Club Agent	2															3	

LICENSING RESTRICTIONS   187

	27	28	29	30	31	32	33	34	35	36	37	38	39	40	41	42	43	44	45	46	47	48	49	50	51	52
Wyo.					3								2						2							
Wis.					3	3																				
W.Va.					3	3							2													
Wash.																										
Va.																										
Vt.									2									2								
Utah					3																					
Tex.																										
Tenn.																		2								
S.Dak.																										
S.C.	2	2																								
R.I.	2	2			2																					
Pa.					2								3													
Oreg.																										
Okla.								3																		
Ohio													2													
N.Dak.																	2									
N.C.									3																	
N.Y.												2	2	2	2	2	2			2	2					
N.Mex.					3				3	2																
N.J.								3	3	2			3													
N.H.						2			2	2	1															
Nev.														2												
Nebr.																										
Mont.		2							2	3									2					3		2
Mo.					2				2	3																
Miss.																										
Minn.					2	3																				
Mich.									2				3													
Mass.		2											2					2								
Md.																										
Maine																										
La.					3	3							3					2								
Ky.														2												
Kan.																		2								

THE RIGHTS OF EX-OFFENDERS

OCCUPATION	TOTAL	Ala.	Alaska	Ariz.	Ark.	Calif.	Colo.	Conn.	Del.	D.C.	Fla.	Ga.	Hawaii	Idaho	Ill.	Ind.	Iowa
1 Motor Common Carrier	1							2									
2 Motor-Vehicle Dealer	17					3		2									
3 Motor-Vehicle Operator	12							2			2	3	1				
4 Motor-Vehicle Salesman	5												1				
5 Motor-Vehicle Used-Parts Dealer	1																
6 Naturopath	7			3		2				3	2						
7 Nurse—Practical/Vocational	48	2	3	3	3	3	2	2	2	2	3	2	2	2	3	3	2
8 Nurse—Professional/Registered	49	2	3	3	3	3	2	2	2	2	2	2	2	2	3	3	2
9 Nurse—Psychiatric	1																
10 Nurse-Psychiatric Technician	2				3	3											
11 Nursing-Home Administrator	14	2				2			2		3	2			3		
12 Nursing-Home Operator	1																
13 Nurseryman	3												2				
14 Nursery Stock Dealer					2	2											
15 Obstetrician	1																
16 Operating Engineer	1																
17 Opthalmic Dispenser	4																
18 Optician	11	2				3			2		3	3		2			
19 Optician—Assistant	1					2											
20 Optician—Assistant Mechanical	1					2											
21 Optician—Mechanical	1					2											
22 Optometrist	49	2	2	2	2	1	2	2	2	3	2	2	2	3	2	2	2
23 Orthopedist																	
24 Osteopath	44	2	2	2	3	1	3	3		2	2	3	1	3	3	3	2
25 Pawnbroker	11		2	2	2												

LICENSING RESTRICTIONS

State	1	2	3	4	5	6	7	8	9	10	11	12	13	14	15	16	17	18	19	20	21	22	23	24	25
Wyo.							2	2														3	3		1
Wis.				2			2	2			2											3	3		
W.Va.							3	3														3		3	
Wash.							2	2	2													2		2	3
Va.							2	2	2													2	2	3	2
Vt.		3				3	3	3														2	2	3	2
Utah						3	3	3														3	2	3	
Tex.							2	3			2	2						2				2	3	3	2
Tenn.							2	3														2	2	3	2
S.Dak.							2	3	2					2								2	3	3	2
S.C.							2	2	2								2	2				2	2	3	2
R.I.							2	2	2													2	2	3	2
Pa.				2			2	2	2													3	3	3	
Oreg.						3	2	2			2	2										2	2	3	2
Okla.		2	3				3	3	3													2	3	1	3
Ohio		2	3				3	3	3													3	2		2
N.Dak.		2	2		1		2	2	3													3	3	3	
N.C.							3	3														2	2	3	
N.Y.			2	2			2	3	2							2						3	3	3	
N.Mex.		2	3	2			3	3				3										2	3	3	3
N.J.			3				3	3	3													3	3	3	
N.H.							2	3	3													3		3	
Nev.		1	1				2	3	3		2	2					3	3				2	2	3	3
Nebr.		1	3		1		2	3														3	3	3	
Mont.											2	2										2	3	2	3
Mo.																						3	3		
Miss.							2	3	2													2	2	3	2
Minn.							3	3														3	2	3	
Mich.				1			3	3														2	3	2	3
Mass.							2	2	3								1					2	2	3	2
Md.				1			3	3	3													2	2	3	3
Maine							2	3	3						2							3	3	3	2
La.		2	2	2			2	3	2		2											3	1	3	
Ky.			2				3	3									2					2	3	2	3
Kan.			2				3	3														3	3		

THE RIGHTS OF EX-OFFENDERS

OCCUPATION	TOTAL	Ala.	Alaska	Ariz.	Ark.	Calif.	Colo.	Conn.	Del.	D.C.	Fla.	Ga.	Hawaii	Idaho	Ill.	Ind.	Iowa
26 Peddler	1																
27 Pedicurist	1																
28 Pest Control	7			2	2						3						
29 Petshop Owner/Dog Dealer	1													1			
30 Pharmacist	47	2	3	2	3	3	3	2	2	2	2	3	3		2	3	3
31 Photographer	2										2						
32 Physical Therapist	47	3	3	3	3	3	3	2	3	3	3	3	2		2	3	3
33 Physician	50	2	2	3	3	3	1	3	2	3	3	3	2		3	3	3
34 Pilot—Ship	2																
35 Plumber	10	2							2	2							1
36 Podiatrist	26					3		2	2	2	2	3				3	2
37 Polygraph Examiner	1																
38 Poultry Technician	1																
39 Priest (for marriage)	1																
40 Private Investigator	25				3	3	2	3	3							3	3
41 Product Wholesaler	1																
42 Professional Planner	1							1									
43 Psychiatric Technician	1																
44 Psychologist	40	3		2	3	3	3	3	2	2	3	3	3		3	3	3
45 Public Adjuster	1																
46 Public Service Operator (Motor Veh.)	1					2											
47 Public Weigher	2					2											
48 Radiologist	1									2							
49 Real-Estate Salesman/Broker	45	3	3	3	2	2	2	3	2	2	2	3			2	3	3
50 Recreation-Hall Operator	1																
51 Remittance Agent	1								2								

LICENSING RESTRICTIONS

	26	27	28	29	30	31	32	33	34	35	36	37	38	39	40	41	42	43	44	45	46	47	48	49	50	51
Wyo.				2		2		2			2								3					2		
Wis.				2		2		2			2				3				3					2		
W.Va.				2		2	3	3			2								3					2	3	
Wash.			2	2		2	2	2	2		2								2					3		
Va.				2			3	3			3													2		
Vt.				2		2	3	3			3								3					2	3	
Utah					3	3	2	3		2									3					2		
Tex.					3	2	2	3			2	3							3					2		
Tenn.						2	2	2			2	3	3						3					2		
S.Dak.					3						2	3												2		
S.C.						2	2	2							2				2					2		
R.I.						2	3	3											3					2	2	
Pa.						2		3						2					3					2		
Oreg.						2	3	2											2					3		
Okla.			3			2	3	3											2					2		
Ohio					3	2	3	2							2	3			3					2		
N.Dak.				2											2	1			3					3		
N.C.						2	3	2							2				3					2		
N.Y.						1	2	2			2				3				2	3			2			
N.Mex.						2	3	3		2					2	3	2		3					3		
N.J.					3	2	3	3			2	3	3					2	3					3		
N.H.						2	2	3			2								3					2		
Nev.					3	3	3	2							3	3			2	3				3		
Nebr.					3	3	3	3							3				3	3				2		
Mont.						2	3	3								2			3					2		
Mo.					3	3	3	3																		
Miss.						2	3	2											3					3	3	
Minn.					3	3	3	3	2										3					3	3	
Mich.						3	3	3		2	2	3			3	1			2	2				2		3
Mass.							3	2			2	3							2	2				2		
Md.				2		2	3	2			2	2							3	2				2		
Maine				2	2	2	3	2			2	2							2	3				2		
La.				2		3	3	2											3					2	2	
Ky						2	3		2		3			2					2	2				2	2	
Kan.			1	2		3	3	2			3	3			2				2	2				2		

#	OCCUPATION	Iowa	Ind.	Ill.	Idaho	Hawaii	Ga.	Fla.	D.C.	Del.	Conn.	Colo.	Calif.	Ark.	Ariz.	Alaska	Ala.	TOTAL
1	Retail Drugs																	1
2	Roentgenologist										2						1	2
3	Safety-Deposit Box Agent			1														1
4	Sanitarian				2	2		3							2		2	14
5	Schoolbus Driver												3					4
6	Secondhand Dealer							2			2							3
7	Secondhand Dealer—Auto										2							2
8	Securities Agent/Broker/Salesman	1		2	2	2	2	1	2		3		2	1	3	1	1	34
9	Seller of Checks and Money Orders	2						2										1
10	Septic Tank Cleaner																	1
11	Ship Pilot																	1
12	Ship Port Pilot							2										1
13	Shorthand Reporter				2							2	2					7
14	Small-Loan Lender							2					2					6
15	Social Worker									2					3			6
16	Solid-Fuel Weigher																	1
17	Sprinkler Irrigation Fitter																	
18	Steam Engineer									2								1
19	Stevedores							2										1
20	Structural Pest Controller											1						2
21	Surveyors																	2
22	Tattoo Artist						2											1
23	Taxidermist																	1

LICENSING RESTRICTIONS

	1	2	3	4	5	6	7	8	9	10	11	12	13	14	15	16	17	18	19	20	21	22	23
Wyo.																							
Wis.								1															
W.Va.				2	2																		
Wash.								1															
Va.								2	1														
Vt.				2	3									3		2							
Utah				2				1	1				2										
Tex.																							
Tenn.								2															
S.Dak.								1	2	1	1												
S.C.																							2
R.I.												2	2	3									
Pa.								2	1	1	2		2	2									
Oreg.					3									2	1								
Okla.								3	2	1			2							3			
Ohio					2																		
N.Dak.								3	2	1	1												
N.C.					3																		
N.Y.													2			2							
N.Mex.					3	3							2		2								
N.J.																							
N.H.					2			1	1														
Nev.								3	1	1													
Nebr.						2																	
Mont.								3	1	1													
Mo.													2										
Miss.																					2		
Minn.				2																			
Mich.					2																		
Mass.								3	1					2									
Md.			1		2		1																
Maine						2		2												2			
La.																							
Ky.																							
Kan.													2										

OCCUPATION	TOTAL	Ala.	Alaska	Ariz.	Ark.	Calif.	Colo.	Conn.	Del.	D.C.	Fla.	Ga.	Hawaii	Idaho	Ill.	Ind.	Iowa
24 Taxi Driver	1																2
25 Teacher	28	2				3	2				2	2	2	2		1	2
26 Television Repairman	1														3		
27 Television Technician	1																
28 Ticket Broker	1																
29 Transportation Broker	1																
30 Tree Expert	1														3		
31 Tree Surgeon	2																
32 Undertaker	1									3							
33 Used Car Dealer	1																
34 Vendor	4					2				2	2						
35 Veterinarian	47	2	2	2	3	3	2	2	2	2	3	2	2	2	3	3	2
36 Warehouseman	11	2															
37 Watchmaker											2					3	2
38 Watchman	5																
39 Water-Treatment Plant Operator	1																
40 Water-Well Contractor	1																
41 Weatherman	2																
42 Weighmaster	5							2									
43 Well Driller/Contractor	2														3		
44 X-Ray Technician	3																

LICENSING RESTRICTIONS

	24	25	26	27	28	29	30	31	32	33	34	35	36	37	38	39	40	41	42	43	44
Wyo.												2									
Wis.		2	2								3	2	2	1				2	2		
W.Va.			2									2	2	2							
Wash.												2	2								
Va.		3																			
Vt.																					
Utah			2	2								2	2								
Tex.			2	2			2				3	3	3		3						
Tenn.			2	2							3	2	3		3				2		
S.Dak.		3		3								2	2						2		
S.C.		1	3									3	3					2	2		
R.I.												2	1	2							
Pa.		2	2				2					2	2	2					2		
Oreg.		3	3									2	2		2				2		
Okla.		2	1	2								3	2	2					2		
Ohio																					
N.Dak.												3	2					2	2		
N.C.																					
N.Y.		2										2	2		3				2	2	
N.Mex.												2	2								
N.J.								2													
N.H.												3	2							2	2
Nev.																					
Nebr.		2	2								3	3	3								
Mont.		2	2								3	3	2								
Mo.		2	2	2							3	2	3				2				
Miss.		2	2									2	2								
Minn.												2	2		2	2					
Mich.												2	2		2						
Mass.		3	3								3	3	3			3					
Md.					2			2													
Maine		2	2	3																	
La.																					
Ky.		2										3	2		2	2					
Kan.												2	3		2	2					

Appendix C
Legal Assistance

Good lawyers able to provide effective legal assistance without charge are difficult to find. The following list of ACLU state affiliates may be helpful in locating such assistance.

ALABAMA

Alabama CLU
P.O. Box 1972
University, Ala. 35486
(205) 758-2301

ALASKA

Alaska CLU
230 Charles St.
Fairbanks, Alaska 99701
(907) 479-7227

ARIZONA

Arizona CLU
822 A Mill Ave.
Tempe, Ariz. 85231
(602) 966-3374

ARKANSAS

ACLU of Arkansas
P.O. Box 5045
North Little Rock, Ark. 72119
(501) 374-8892

CALIFORNIA

ACLU of Northern California
593 Market St.
San Francisco, Calif. 94105
(415) 433-2750

ACLU of Southern California
633 S. Shatto Place
Los Angeles, Calif. 90005
(213) 487-1720

COLORADO

ACLU of Colorado
1711 Pennsylvania St.
Denver, Colo. 80203
(303) 825-5176

CONNECTICUT

Connecticut CLU
57 Pratt St., Rm. 713
Hartford, Conn. 06103
(203) 246-7471 or 72

FLORIDA

ACLU of Florida
7210 S. Red Rd., Rm. 213
So. Miami, Fla. 33143
(305) 373-2052

GEORGIA

ACLU of Georgia
88 Walton St.
Atlanta, Ga. 30303
(404) 523-5398

HAWAII

ACLU of Hawaii
217 S. King St.
Suite 211
Honolulu, Hawaii 96813
(808) 524-5177 or 7373

ILLINOIS

Illinois Division, ACLU
5 South Wabash Ave.
Suite 1516
Chicago, Ill. 60603
(312) 236-5564

INDIANA

Indiana CLU
445 North Pennsylvania St.
Suite 604
Indianapolis, Ind. 46204
(317) 635-4056

Calumet Chapter
P.O. Box 2521
Gary, Ind. 46403

IOWA

Iowa CLU
1101 Walnut St.
Des Moines, Iowa 40309
(515) 282-0923

KANSAS

Kansas CLU
3926 E. First St.
Wichita, Kans. 67208

KENTUCKY

Kentucky CLU
134 Breckenridge Lane
Louisville, Ky. 40207
(502) 895-0279

LOUISIANA

ACLU of Louisiana
606 Common St. Rm. 302
New Orleans, La. 70130
(504) 522-0617

MAINE

Maine CLU
193 Middle Street
Portland, Maine 04111
(207) 774-5444

MARYLAND

ACLU of Maryland
1231 North Calvert St.
Baltimore, Md. 21202
(301) 685-6460

MASSACHUSETTS

CLU of Massachusetts
100 Franklin St.
Boston, Mass. 02108
(617) 227-9469

MICHIGAN

ACLU of Michigan
808 Washington Blvd. Bldg.
234 State St.
Detroit, Mich. 48226
(313) 961-4662

MINNESOTA

Minnesota CLU
628 Central Ave.
Minneapolis, Minn. 55414
(612) 332-1708 or 2032

MISSISSIPPI

ACLU of Mississippi
520 North President St.
Jackson, Miss. 39201
(601) 355-7495

MISSOURI

ACLU of Eastern Missouri
8011 Clayton Rd., Suite 216
St. Louis, Mo. 63117
(314) 721-1215

ACLU of Western Missouri
823 Walnut, Rm. 608
Kansas City, Mo. 64106
(913) 782-2500

MONTANA

ACLU of Montana
625½ Ave. "E"
Billings, Mont. 59102
(406) 656-8695

NATIONAL CAPITAL AREA, WASH., D.C.

ACLU of the National Capital
3000 Connecticut Ave., N.W.
Suite 437
Washington, D.C. 20008
(202) 483-3830

NEBRASKA

Nebraska CLU
P.O. Box 81455
Lincoln, Nebr. 68501
(402) 432-8091

NEVADA

ACLU of Nevada
P.O. Box 8947
Reno, Nev. 89507
(702) 784-6718

NEW HAMPSHIRE

New Hampshire CLU
3 Pleasant St., Rm. 7
Concord, N.H. 03301
(603) 225-3080

NEW JERSEY

ACLU of New Jersey
45 Academy St., Rm. 203
Newark, N.J. 07102
(201) 642-2084

NEW MEXICO

ACLU of New Mexico
510 Second St., N.W.
Albuquerque, N.M. 87101
(505) 842-1448

NEW YORK

New York CLU
84 Fifth Ave., Suite 300
New York, N.Y. 10011
(212) 924-7800

NORTH CAROLINA

North Carolina CLU
P.O. Box 3094
Greensboro, N.C. 27402
(919) 273-1641

OHIO

ACLU of Ohio
203 E. Broad St., Suite 200
Columbus, Ohio 43215
(614) 228-8951

Greater Cleveland Chapter
2108 Payne Avenue, Rm. 825

Cleveland, Ohio 44114
(216) SU 1-6276

Cincinnati Chapter
177 Section Rd.
Cincinnati, Ohio 45237
(513) 631-3737

OKLAHOMA

Oklahoma CLU
P.O. Box 799
Oklahoma City, Ok. 73101
(405) 235-0946 or 427-0626

OREGON

ACLU of Oregon
309 Senator Bldg.
Portland, Or. 97204
(503) 227-3186

PENNSYLVANIA

ACLU of Pennsylvania
260 South 15th St.
Philadelphia, Pa. 19102
(215) 735-7103

Pittsburgh Chapter
237 Oakland Ave.
Pittsburgh, Pa. 15213
(412) 261-5160 or 391-7210
ext. 1541

Delaware Chapter
2409 West 17th St.
Wilmington, De. 19806
(302) 654-3966

RHODE ISLAND

Rhode Island CLU
55 Eddy St., Suite 508
Providence, R.I. 02903
(401) 831-7171

SOUTH CAROLINA

ACLU of South Carolina
2016½ Green St., Rm. 3
Columbia, S.C. 29205
(803) 799-5151 or 799-3767

TENNESSEE

ACLU of Tennessee
P.O. Box 91
Knoxville, Tenn. 37901
(615) 524-1787

TEXAS

Texas CLU
600 West Seventh St.
Austin, Texas 78701
(512) 477-5849 or 4335

Houston, Texas 77006
905 Richmond
Houston, Texas 77006
(713) 524-5925

UTAH

ACLU of Utah
211 E. 3rd South
Salt Lake City, Utah 84111
(801) 521-9289

VERMONT

Vermont CLU
43 State St.
Montpelier, Vt. 05602
(802) 223-6304

VIRGINIA

ACLU of Virginia
10 South 10th St.
Insurance Bldg.
Richmond, Va. 23219
(804) 644-8022

WASHINGTON

ACLU of Washingtgon
2101 Smith Tower
Seattle, Wash. 98104
(206) 624-2180

WEST VIRGINIA

West Virginia CLU
1332 Washington Blvd.
Huntington, W Va. 25701
(304) 525-3951

WISCONSIN

Wisconsin CLU
1840 North Farwell Ave.
Rm. 1, Lower Level
Milwaukee, Wis. 53202
(414) 272-4032

In addition to the ACLU offices, the following organizations might prove helpful.

The National Prison Project of the ACLU Foundation
1346 Connecticut Ave., Suite 1031
Washington, D.C. 20036

The NAACP Legal Defense Fund

10 Columbus Circle
New York, N.Y. 10019

The Legal Action Center
19 West 44th St.
New York, N.Y. 10036

Appendix D

Organizations Providing Job Assistance to Ex-Offenders

This directory was prepared by the Clearinghouse on Offender Employment Restrictions of the National Offender Service Coordination Program sponsored by the American Bar Association.

ALABAMA

Birmingham

Community Acceptance Program
2121 8th Ave., N., Suite 1524
Birmingham, Ala. 35203
(205) 251-5934

National Alliance of Businessmen*
935 Daniel Bldg.
Birmingham, Ala. 35233
(205) 254-1696
(job-ready ex-offenders)*

Mobile

National Alliance of Businessmen*
1509 Government St., Suite 501
Mobile, Ala. 36604
(205) 690-2166

ALASKA

Anchorage

National Alliance of Businessmen*
121 W. Fireweed Ln., Suite 240
Anchorage, Alaska 99503
(907) 272-9479

New Start Center
207 E. 4th Ave.
Anchorage, Alaska 99501
(907) 274-5525

Juneau

Alaska Jaycees, Inc.
Box 1065
Juneau, Alaska 99801
(907) 798-0841 ext. 164
(gives preference to Alaskan residents)

ARIZONA

Phoenix

Adult Probation Department
500 S. 3rd Ave.
Phoenix, Ariz. 85003
(602) 262-3488
("Find jobs for those persons placed on Adult Probation by the Superior Court, Maricopa County")

Ex-Offender Program
Dept. of Economic Security
1535 W. Jefferson
Phoenix, Ariz. 85007
("Only if incarcerated in an Arizona institution")

National Alliance of Businessmen*
111 W. Monroe St., Suite 720
Phoenix, Ariz. 85003
(602) 261-4901

Phoenix 7th Step Chapter
715 N. 7th Ave.
Phoenix, Ariz. 85003
(602) 254-6218

Tucson

Ex-Offender Program
Pima College
2202 W. Anklam Rd.
Tucson, Ariz. 85709
(602) 884-6991

ARKANSAS

Little Rock

National Alliance of Businessmen*
512 Continental Bldg.
Little Rock, Ark. 72201
(501) 374-3755

CALIFORNIA

Bakersfield

National Alliance of Businessmen*
P.O. Box 978
210 K Street Mall
Bakersfield, Calif. 93302
(805) 327-8665

Berkeley

Ex-Offender Skills Bank
739 Allston Way
Berkeley, Calif. 94701
(415) 464-0304

Chico

Prisoners' Support Group
218 Chestnut St.
Chico, Calif. 95926
(916) 895-5817

Colton

National Alliance of Businessmen*
12139 Mt. Vernon Ave.
Colton, Calif. 92324
(714) 825-1490

Downey

Ex-Offender Employment Program of the L.A. County Probation Dept.
9150 E. Imperial Hwy.
Downey, Calif. 90242
(213) 923-7721 ext. 2851
("Adult ex-offenders referred primarily by probation—local and U.S.—and parole agencies and federal correctional institutions in County")

Fresno

Ex-Offender Community
    Resource Council
P.O. Box 1902

Fresno, Calif. 93718
(209) 266-2032
(assists inmates returning to Fresno County from all institutions)

National Alliance of Businessmen*
2220 Tulare St., Suite 923
Fresno, Calif. 93721
(209) 266-2032

SER
Jobs for Progress
843 East Fern
Fresno, Calif. 93728
(209) 237-5555

Hayward

Adult Freedom 7th Step House
475 Medford Ave.
Hayward, Calif. 94541

Youth Group 7th Step House
27787 Haldane Ct.
Hayward, Calif. 94545

Ex-Offender Skills Bank
24790 Amador
Hayward, Calif. 94544
(415) 782-4700

Los Angeles

Career Planning Center
1623 S. LaCienega
Los Angeles, Calif. 90035
(213) 273-6633

Los Angeles 7th Step Chapter
2900 W. Third St.
Los Angeles, Calif. 90020
(213) 387-6139

National Alliance of Businessmen*
450 N. Grand Ave., Suite G-106
Los Angeles, Calif. 90012
(213) 626-5121

Modesto

Golden Chain 7th Step Chapter
1926 Chelsea Ave.
Modesto, Calif. 05359
(209) 524-1660

Oakland

Alameda County Ex-Offenders Skills Bank
1925 Brush St.
Oakland, Calif. 94612
(415) 464-1246
("Ex-offender residents of Alameda County")

National Alliance of Businessmen*
2218 Webster St.
Oakland Calif. 94612
(415) 839-9460

Orange

National Alliance of Businessmen*
1 City Blvd. West, Suite 316
Orange, Calif. 92668
(714) 547-5923

Pasadena

PSCS-Project JOVE II
812 N. Fair Oaks Ave.
Pasadena, Calif. 91103
(213) 792-2151 or 681-4676
("Eighteen years or older, incarcerated 6 months or longer")

Redwood City

San Mateo County Probation Dept.
Hall of Justice
Redwood City, Calif. 94063
(415) 364-5600 ext. 2322
("Generally to those persons on probation to this county—but willing to help others as possible")

Service League of San Mateo
    County
505 Middlefield Rd.
Redwood City, Calif. 94063
(415) 364-4664

Richmond

Richmond Service Center
Office of Employment
Development Dept.
217 10th St.
Richmond, Calif. 94801
(415) 237-5500

Sacramento

National Alliance of Businessmen
2322 J St.
Sacramento, Calif. 95816
(916) 440-3151

Sacramento Resource Council,
    Inc.
2322 J St.
Sacramento, Calif. 95816
(916) 440-3151

7th Step Foundation
Central Valleys Chapter
1812 J St., Suite 11
Sacramento, Calif. 95814
(916) 442-0085

San Diego

Project J.O.V.E.
1196 Broadway
San Diego, Calif. 92101
(714) 233-6572
("Three months minimum incarceration or men & women on parole")

San Francisco

Bay Area Quest Program
2238 Vallejo St.
San Francisco, Calif. 94123
(415) 922-7174
("Women offenders")

Forum Project West
1187 Franklin St.
San Francisco, Calif. 94109
(415) 776-1827

Northeast Drug Division Program
15 Boardman Pl.
San Francisco, Calif. 94103
(415) 863-1967
("Referrals from the Probation Department")

Northern Calif. Service League
28 Boardman Pl.
San Francisco, Calif. 94103
(415) 863-2323
("Inmates San Francisco County jails & ex-offenders")

Parole & Pre-Release Employment
2948 16th St.
San Francisco, Calif. 94102
(415) 557-0539

Work Out Program
8114 Market St.
San Francisco, Calif. 94102
(415) 863-6819
("Ex-offenders released from the county jail—S.F.")

San Jose

ESO
1460 Koll Circle
San Jose, California 95112
(408) 287-5230

Ex-Squared Foundation
235 E. Santa Clara St., Suite 408
San Jose, Calif. 95113
(408) 292-2873

Project Re-Entry
1460 Koll Cir.
San Jose, Calif. 95112
(408) 998-3020

San Leandro

East Bay 7th Step Chapter
(National Headquarters)
1155 E. 14th St.
San Leandro, Calif. 94577

San Pedro

Pre-Release Community Re-Entry Project
Box 7
Terminal Island
San Pedro, Calif. 90731
("Inmates of Terminal Island—F.C.I.")

San Rafael

Committee for Prisoner Humanity and Justice
1414 4th St.
San Rafael, Calif. 94901
(415) 454-5700

Santa Barbara

National Alliance of Businessmen*
3868 State St., 2nd Fl.
Santa Barbara, Calif. 93105
(805) 687-6481

Santa Clara

National Alliance of Businessmen*
P.O. Box 251
Santa Clara, Calif. 95052
(408) 249-0501

Susanville

Inmate Resource Center
P.O. Box 790
Susanville, Calif. 96130
(916) 257-2183 ext. 45

Ukiah

First Offenders Project
P.O. Box 112
Ukiah, Calif. 95482
(707) 462-6643
("No more than one felony conviction; priority to property offenders")

Van Nuys

7th Step Training Center
8780 Van Nuys Blvd.
Van Nuys, Calif. 91350

Ventura

Unified Corrections Project Clearinghouse
40 N. Fir
Ventura, Calif. 93001
(805) 648-6131 ext. 2891

COLORADO

Colorado Springs

Employ-Ex
25 N. Spruce
Colorado Springs, Colo.
(303) 572-3994

National Alliance of Businessmen*
111½ E. Pikes Peak
Colorado Springs, Colo. 80903
(303) 636-3331

Denver

Colorado 7th Step Chapter
700 Washington St., #910
Denver, Colo. 80203

Employ-Ex
1117 Cherokee
Denver, Colo. 80204
(303) 572-8616

J.O.I.N., Inc.
Denver Juvenile Probation Dept.
770 Grant St.
Denver, Colo. 80205
(303) 837-1944
("Youth 10–18 years")

National Alliance of Businessmen*
818 17th St., Suite 810
Denver, Colo. 80202
(303) 534-4641

Golden

Employ-Ex
The Gold Bldg.
607 10th St.
Golden, Colo. 80401
(303) 278-2735

Pueblo

Employ-Ex
c/o Pueblo Manpower Administration
720 N. Main St.
Pueblo, Colo. 81002
(303) 545-7837

CONNECTICUT

Bridgeport

Co-Op
10 Fairfield Ave.
Bridgeport, Conn. 06604
(203) 367-8441

National Alliance of Businessmen*
Metro Bank Bldg.
180 Fairfield Ave.
Bridgeport, Conn. 06604
(203) 333-0176

Danbury

Interchange Youth Service Bureau
80 Main St.
Danbury, Conn. 06810
(203) 748-1249 or
(203) 743-5529

Derby

Team Offender Program
256 Main St.
Derby, Conn. 06418
(203) 735-9388

East Hartford

Connecticut Jaycees Institutional Assistance Program
135 Burnside Ave.
East Hartford, Conn. 06108
(203) 528-9623

Hartford

Catholic Family Services
244 Main St.
Hartford, Conn. 06106
(203) 522-8241

Connecticut Prison Assoc.
340 Capitol Ave., Rm. 101
Hartford, Conn. 06115
(203) 566-2030

National Alliance of Businessmen*
250 Constitution Plaza
Hartford, Conn. 06103
(203) 525-4451

Poor People's Federation
1229 Albany Ave.
Hartford, Conn. 06112
(203) 278-7570

New Britain

New Britain Human Resources Agency
35 Court St.
New Britain, Conn. 06052
(203) 225-8601

New Haven

National Alliance of Businessmen*
195 Church St.
New Haven, Conn. 06510
(203) 562-5194

Project MORE
Hill Neighborhood Corp.
P.O. Box 7005

611 Congress Ave.
New Haven, Conn. 06510
(203) 777-6371

New London

New Directions
253 Captain's Walk
New London, Conn. 06320
(203) 447-3041

Stamford

Community Return
First Congregational Church
Latham Park, Rm. 307
Stamford, Conn. 06901
(203) 325-0416

Torrington

Catholic Family Services
132 Grove St.
Torrington, Conn. 06790
(203) 482-5558

Waterbury

Adult Re-Direction
NOW, Inc.
215 S. Elm St.
Waterbury, Conn. 06704
(203) 757-1256

National Alliance of Businessmen*
c/o Chamber of Commerce
32 N. Main St.
Waterbury, Conn. 06702
(203) 757-0701

DELAWARE

National Alliance of Businessmen*
300 Delaware Ave., Suite 1014
Wilmington, Del. 19801
(302) 571-6106

DISTRICT OF COLUMBIA

Bureau of Rehabilitation
666 11th St., N.W., Suite 520
Washington, D.C. 20001
(202) 637-6955

D.C. Department of Manpower
500 C St., N.W., Rm. 241
Washington, D.C. 20001
(202) 393-6151 ext. 210 or 211
("offenders recently released or paroled")

Human Resources Development Institute
AFL-CIO National Office
815 16th St., N.W.
Washington, D.C. 20006
(202) 638-3912
("Poor, unemployed, minorities, low income, ex-offender, underemployed")

National Alliance of Businessmen*
1129 20th St., N.W. 2nd Flr.
Washingtmn, D.C. 20036
(202) 833-8190

Social Services for the Criminal Bar
6616 32nd Pl., N.W.
Washington, D.C. 20015
(202) 244-9142 or 363-7397

Wider Opportunities for Women
1649 K St., N.W.
Washington, D.C. 20036
(202) 638-4868
(Supported employment program for women probationers)

FLORIDA

Hollywood

Active House, Inc.
515 S. 21st Ave.
Hollywood, Fla. 33020
(305) 920-4315
("Offenders, ex-offenders & their families")

Jacksonville

National Alliance of Businessmen*
4019 Woodcock Dr., Suite 212
Jacksonville, Fla. 32207
(904) 791-3511

Walnut House Ex-Offender Program
1450 E. 11th St.
Jacksonville, Fla. 32206
(904) 633-4059 or 633-4069
("Persons on probation, parole, MCR, and expirationists")

Work Furlough
Office of the Sheriff
515 Victoria St.
Jacksonville, Fla. 32202
(904) 633-4084
("Job development & placement limited to program participants")

Miami

National Alliance of Businessmen*
c/o Fla. State Employment Service
P.O. Box 520684
Miami, Fla. 33152
(305) 379-7052

Transitions, Inc.
1150 S.W. 22nd St.
Miami, Fla. 33129
(305) 856-9740

Orlando

National Alliance of Businessmen*
3191 Maguire Blvd., Suite 180
Orlando, Fla. 32803
(305) 894-1851

Office of the Court Alternatives
1 N. Orange, Suite 606
Orlando, Fla. 32801
(305) 299-0905 or 420-3695

Pensacola

National Alliance of Businessmen*
c/o Vince Whibbs Pontiac
3401 Navy Blvd.
Pensacola, Fla. 32507
(904) 433-7671

St. Petersburg

National Alliance of Businessmen
300 Bldg. East, Suite 629
300 – 31st St., N.
St. Petersburg, Fla. 33713
(813) 893-3500 to 3509

Tampa

Women's Resource Center
Treatment Center
706 Franklin St., Suite 605
Tampa, Fla. 33602
(813) 223-4997

GEORGIA

Atlanta

Achievement Training Opportunities
848 Peachtree St., N.E.
Atlanta, Ga. 30308
(404) 881-0828

Assistance to Offenders, Inc.
848 Peachtree St., N.E., Rm. 218
Atlanta, Ga. 30308
(404) 881-0821

National Alliance of Businessmen*
235 Peachtree St., N.E., Suite 1214
Atlanta, Ga. 30303
(404) 526-6347

Augusta

National Alliance of Businessmen*
First National Bank Bldg.
801 Broad St., Suite 606
Augusta, Ga. 30902
(404) 722-5532

Columbus

National Alliance of Businessmen
c/o Ga. DOL
1328 Second Ave.
Columbus, Ga. 31902
(404) 327-4381

Macon

Bibb County Probation Office
Bibb County Courthouse, Rm. 405
Mulberry St.
Macon, Ga. 31201
(912) 745-8667
("Only assist probationers from the state superior court, not federal probationers")

Dept. of Offender Rehabilitation
Probation/Parole Office
204 Spring St., Suite E
Macon, Ga. 31201
(912) 744-6092

HAWAII

Honolulu

Model Ex-Offender Program
2119 N. King St., Rm. 207
Honolulu, Hawaii 96819
(808) 848-1766

National Alliance of Businessmen*
200 N. Vineyard Blvd., Suite 503
Honolulu, Hawaii 96817
(808) 536-6922

ILLINOIS

Belleville

St. Clair County MEP
1 S. Church St.
Belleville, Ill. 62220

Cairo

Project HAND
2110 Sycamore St.
P.O. Box 108
Cairo, Ill. 62914

Chicago

Chance
Irving Park United Methodist Church
3810 N. Keeler St.
Chicago, Ill.
(312) 283-6262

Chicago Urban League
4500 S. Michigan Ave.
Chicago, Ill.
(312) 285-5800

Dept. of Corrections
Employment Program
260 N. LaSalle St., 16th Flr.
Chicago, Ill.
(312) 793-2673

Dept. of Corrections
Human Relations & Special Services
160 N. LaSalle St., 4th Flr.
Chicago, Ill.
(312) 793-2956

FREE, Inc.
1926-28 N. Humboldt Blvd.
Chicago, Ill. 60647
(312) 384-8447
("Latino offenders")

Just Jobs, Inc.
4429 N. Broadway
Chicago, Ill.
(312) 784-4555

Model Ex-Offender Program
120 S. Riverside Plaza, Suite 1016
Chicago, Ill. 60606
(312) 454-1560

National Alliance of Businessmen
6 N. Michigan Ave., Suite 1000
Chicago, Ill. 60602
(312) 782-5096

Operation Dare
343 S. Dearborn St.
Chicago, Ill. 60504
(312) 322-4700 or 922-5163

Operation PUSH
930 E. 50th St.
Chicago, Ill.
(312) 373-3366

Options, Inc.
1301 S. Wabash Ave.
Chicago, Ill. 60605
(312) 341-9450
("Applicants with six months of prison release or convictions")

PACE Institute
2600 S. California
Chicago, Ill. 60608
(312) 927-3840
("Provides services only to those trained in PACE program")

St. Anthony's Inn Inc.
105 W. Madison St.
Chicago, Ill. 60602
(312) 782-9660
("all ex-offenders in regard to employment opportunities")

St. Leonard's House
2100 W. Warren Blvd.
Chicago, Ill.
(312) 738-1414

Still Doing Time
4545 S. Drexel Blvd.
Chicago, Ill. 60653
(312) 268-7505

7th Step Foundation
4546 S. Lake Park
Chicago, Ill. 60653
(312) 536-6088

Tri-Faith, Central Office
116 S. Michigan Ave.
Chicago, Ill.
(312) 641-1030

Tri-Faith, Lawndale
1449 S. Keeler
Chicago, Ill.
(312) 277-2240

Tri-Faith, Uptown
4407 N. Broadway
Chicago, Ill.
(312) 561-7310

Tri-Faith, W. Garfield
3932 W. Madison St.
Chicago, Ill.
(312) 826-5515

Urban Progress Center
4622 S. King Dr.
Chicago, Ill.
(312) 548-6700

YMCA Metropolitan Chicago
19 S. LaSalle St.
Chicago, Ill.
(312) 222-8150

Decatur

Vocational Alternative Program
140-142 W. Wood St.
Decatur, Ill. 62521
(217) 423-6119

East St. Louis

East St. Louis MEP
234 Collinsville Ave.
East St. Louis, Ill. 62201

ORGANIZATIONS PROVIDING JOB ASSISTANCE

Edwardsville

Madison-Bond MEP
103 W. Purcell, Rm. 500
Edwardsville, Ill. 62025

Geneva

Community Correctional Services
P.O. Box 143
Geneva, Ill. 60134

Joliet

Will County MEP Program
81 N. Chicago St., Rm. 402
Joliet, Ill. 60435

Peoria

National Alliance of Businessmen
301 S.W. Adams St., Suite 1022
Peoria, Ill. 61602
(309) 674-9343

Tri-County (Peoria) Urban League
Model Ex-Offender & People in Transition Programs
317 S. MacArthur Hwy.
Peoria, Ill. 61605
(309) 673-7474

Pontiac

Career Development Program for Offenders
P.O. Box 99
Pontiac Correctional Center
Pontiac, Ill. 61764
(815) 844-7144

Rockford

HOPE
401 S. Main St., Suite 213
Rockford, Ill. 61101
(815) 987-5720

National Alliance of Businessmen
107 N. 3rd St.
P.O. Box 830
Rockford, Ill. 61105
(815) 987-7261

Northern Ill. Federation for Offenders
304 N. Main St.
Rockford, Ill. 61101
(815) 963-1570

Rock Island

Operation DARE—1
718 24th St.
Rock Island, Ill. 61201
(309) 786-7711

Springfield

New Start, Inc.
714 E. Capitol St.
Springfield, Ill. 62701

Sangamon County Correction MEP Program
918 E. Capitol St.
Springfield, Ill. 62701

Waukegan

Lake County Correction MEP Program
213 Water St.
Waukegan, Ill. 60085

INDIANA

Anderson

Re-Entry, Inc.
Box 815
Anderson, Ind. 46015
(317) 644-3566

Evansville

National Alliance of Businessmen
c/o Hulman Bldg.

22-24 N.W. 4th St.
Evansville, Ind. 47707

Fort Wayne

National Alliance of Businessmen*
826 Ewing St., Suite 301
Fort Wayne, Ind. 46802
(219) 742-1361

Gary

National Alliance of Businessmen*
504 Broadway, Suite 928
Gary, Ind. 46402
(219) 883-1857

Indianapolis

Indiana Dept. of Corrections
Manpower Program
804 State Office Bldg.
100 N. Senate Ave.
Indianapolis, Ind. 46204
(317) 633-4165
("Limited only to offenders & ex-offenders")

National Alliance of Businessmen*
320 N. Meridian St., Suite 1020
Indianapolis, Ind. 46204
(317) 632-1316

P.A.C.E.
1505 N. Delaware St., Rm. 7
Indianapolis, Ind. 46202
(317) 639-2545
("All currently incarcerated or ex-offenders, no nonoffenders")

Michigan City

PACT Community Resource Center
Prisoner & Community Together, Inc.
P.O. Box 177
431 Willard Ave.
Michigan City, Ind. 46360
(219) 872-9139
("Limited to prisoners & ex-offenders")

South Bend

National Alliance of Businessmen*
320 W. Jefferson
Box 807
South Bend, Ind. 46624
(219) 234-0051

IOWA

Anamosa

Operation Assist
Box B
Anamosa, Iowa 52205
("Inmates of this reformatory and others")

Des Moines

Community Assistance Program for Ex-Offenders
Residential Correctional Facility
Bldg. 65
Gruber St.—Fort Des Moines
Des Moines, Iowa 50315
(515) 244-3202

National Alliance of Businessmen*
800 High St., Suite 7740
Des Moines, Iowa 50307
(515) 283-2161

Fort Madison

7th Step Foundation
727 Ave. F
Fort Madison, Iowa 52627
(319) 372-2224
("Ex-offenders, probationers, people still in prison, soon leaving")

KANSAS

Kansas City

Mid-America 7th Step Chapter
1216 N. 76 Terrace
Kansas City, Kan. 66101

Topeka

Topeka 7th Step Chapter
P.O. Box 634
Topeka, Kan. 66601
(913) 232-8203

Wichita

National Alliance of Businessmen*
111 W. Douglas, Suite 600
Wichita, Kan. 67202
(316) 265-8644

Wichita 7th Step Chapter
P.O. Box 819
Wichita, Kan. 67201
(316) 265-2301

KENTUCKY

Lexington

Bluegrass Employment & Training Program
(CETA)
190 N. Upper St.
Lexington, Ky. 40507

Bureau of Rehabilitation Services
Blackburn Correctional Complex
Route 8—Spurr Rd.
Lexintgon, Ky. 40505

Clearinghouse for Ex-Offenders
Court Square Bldg., #208
107 Cheapside
Lexington, Ky. 40508
(606) 259-0487

Employment Readiness Program
Blackburn Correctional Complex
Route 8—Spurr Rd.
Lexington, Ky. 40505

Volunteers in Corrections
302 W. Main St.
Lexington, Ky. 40507
(606) 254-3822

Louisville

Clearinghouse for Ex-Offenders
Republic Bldg., Rm. 208
429 W. Walnut
Louisville, Ky. 40202
(502) 588-4521
("Individuals convicted of felonies who have residence in the Louisville & Jefferson County, Kentucky area.")

The 7th Step Foundation
Kentucky Towers
5th & Walnut Streets
Louisville, Ky. 40202
(502) 583-2753

National Alliance of Businessmen*
1015 W. Chestnut St.
Louisville, Ky. 40203
(502) 584-2403

LOUISIANA

Baton Rouge

Community Correction & Rehabilitation Center, Inc.
Male Residential Facility
500 River Rd.
P.O. Box 3593
Baton Rouge, La. 70821
(504) 344-3788

Female Residential Facility
855 S. Ferdinand St.
P.O. Box 3593
Baton Rouge, La. 70821
(504) 344-7674

DeQuincy

Helping Hand/LCI Jaycees
Box 1056
DeQuincy, La. 70633

Lafayette

National Alliance of Businessmen*
109 Industrial Pkwy.
Lafayette, La. 70501
(318) 232-0562

New Orleans

Volunteers of America
Community Residential Center
1002 Napoleon Ave.
New Orleans, La. 70115
(504) 891-5831
("federal offenders")

National Alliance of Businessmen*
2025 Canal St., Suite 203
New Orleans, La. 70112
(504) 821-2887

Shreveport

National Alliance of Businessmen*
3808 Southern Ave.
P.O. Box 6289
Shreveport, La. 71106
(318) 226-5009

MAINE

Bangor

National Alliance of Businessmen*
324 Harlow St.
Bangor, Maine 04401
(207) 945-6434

Portland

National Alliance of Businessmen*
142 Free St.
Portland, Maine 04101
(207) 772-2811

South Windham

Job Developers Project
Division of Probation & Parole
102 High St.
South Windham, Maine 04082
(207) 892-2266

MARYLAND

Annapolis

Offender Aid & Restoration
P.O. Box 365
Annapolis, Md. 21404
(301) 244-1239
Washingcon—261-1650 ext. 1238
Baltimore—269-1350 ext. 1238

Baltimore

Mayor's Office of Manpower Resources
701 St. Paul St.
Baltimore, Md. 21202
(301) 396-5586

Model Ex-Offender Program
2506 N. Charles St.
Baltimore, Md. 21218
(301) 383-6060

National Alliance of Businessmen*
1100 N. Eutaw St.
Baltimore, Md. 21201
(301) 728-2383

State of Maryland Division of Parole & Probation
2100 Guilford Ave., Rm. 204
Baltimore, Md. 21224
(301) 383-3789

Bethesda

Second Genesis, Inc.
4720 Montgomery Ln., Suite 800

ORGANIZATIONS PROVIDING JOB ASSISTANCE

Bethesda, Md. 20014
(301) 656-1545
("Services for Second Genesis inpatients only. Primarily inpatient program for drug offenders")

Cumberland

National Alliance of Businessmen
141 Baltimore St.
Cumberland, Md. 21502
(301) 724-8833
(job-ready ex-offenders)

Hagerstown

Breathedsville Jaycees, Inc.
Maryland Correctional Training Center
R.F.D. #3, Box 3333
Hagerstown, Md. 21740

National Alliance of Businessmen*
138 E. Antietam St., Suite 208
Hagerstown, Md. 21740
(301) 797-5800

MASSACHUSETTS

Boston

Brookehouse Drop-In Center
79 Chandler St.
Boston, Mass. 02117
(617) 482-2520

Dept. of Corrections
Office of Manpower Development
Leverett Saltonstall Bldg.
Government Center
100 Cambridge St.
Boston, Mass. 02202
(617) 727-3950
(people on parole, probation & pretrial diversion)

Law Offender Services Division
Charles F. Hurley Bldg.
Government Center
Boston, Mass. 02114
(administrative office: teams in statewide offices)

Mass. Half-way Houses, Inc.
P.O. Box 348
Back Bay Annex
Boston, Mass. 02117
(617) 261-1864

Mass. Parole Board
100 Cambridge St.
Boston, Mass. 02202
(617) 727-3279

National Alliance of Businessmen
50 Federal St., Suite 204
Boston, Mass. 02110
(617) 482-6513
(job-ready ex-offenders)

Self Development Group
14 Somerset St.
Boston, Mass. 02108
(617) 996-3395
(adult offenders)

Lowell

National Alliance of Businessmen*
176 Church St.
Lowell, Mass. 01852

New Bedford

National Alliance of Businessmen*
422 Mt. Pleasant St.
New Bedford, Mass. 02746
(617) 996-3395

North Grafton

Spectrum House
211 Westboro Rd.
P.O. Box 545
North Grafton, Mass. 01536

Springfield

Hampden County Jail & House of Correction Model Inmate Employment Project
79 York Street
Springfield, Mass. 01103
(413) 734-4792 or 781-1560

National Alliance of Businessmen
25 Harrison Ave.
Springfield, Mass. 01103

Worcester

National Alliance of Businessmen*
370 Main St., Suite 822
Worcester, Mass. 01608

MICHIGAN

Ann Arbor

Inmate Rehabilitation Program
Washtenaw County Bldg., Rm. 2
P.O. Box 645
Ann Arbor, Mich.
(313) 994-2990
("Priority Washtenaw County Jail inmates")

Detroit

Committee for Rehabilitation & Reinvolvement of Ex-Offenders
19 Clifford
Detroit, Mich. 48201

National Alliance of Businessmen*
1200 6th St., Suite 234
Detroit, Mich. 48226
(313) 237-0130

Operation HELP
1404 Gratiot
Detroit, Mich. 48207

Team for Justice
1035 St. Antoine
Detroit, Mich. 48226
(313) 965-3242

Flint

Genessee County Jail Treatment Program
917 Beach St.
Flint, Mich. 48503
(313) 232-3161

National Alliance of Businessmen*
444 Church St.
Flint, Mich. 48502
(313) 232-0196

Grand Rapids

National Alliance of Businessmen*
1133 Michigan St., N.E.
Grand Rapids, Mich. 49503
(616) 451-8358

Kalamazoo

National Alliance of Businessmen
438 W. South St.
Kalamazoo, Mich. 49006
(616) 342-0254

Lansing

Michigan Dept. of Corrections
Stevens T. Mason Bldg.
Lansing, Mich. 48913
(517) 373-0287

National Alliance of Businessmen*
505 W. Washtenaw St., Suite 301
Lansing, Mich. 48933
(517) 371-1610

Saginaw

National Alliance of Businessmen*

107 S. Washington, Suite 410
Saginaw, Mich. 48605
(517) 753-6361

MINNESOTA

Duluth

National Alliance of Businessmen
205 Sellwood Bldg.
Duluth, Minn. 55802
(218) 722-3363

Pre-Trial Services
17 N. Fourth Ave., West
Duluth, Minn. 55802
(218) 723-3298

Minneapolis

HIRE
1009 Nicollet Ave.
Minneapolis, Minn. 55403
(612) 348-8560

Multi-Resource Center, Inc.
1900 Chicago Ave., S.
Minneapolis, Minn. 55404
(612) 871-2402

National Alliance of Businessmen*
628 Nicollet Mall
Minneapolis, Minn. 55402
(612) 333-2317

Saginaw

North East Regional Corrections
Rt. 1, Box 119
Saginaw, Minn. 55779
(218) 729-8673

Sandstone

Sandstone Vocational School
P.O. Box P
Sandstone, Minn. 55072
(612) 245-2226
("Employment services to incarcerated felons only")

St. Paul

National Alliance of Businessmen*
170 Wabasha St., Suite 300
St. Paul, Minn. 55102
(612) 222-5561

MISSISSIPPI

Jackson

National Alliance of Businessmen*
733 N. State St., Suite 3
Jackson, Miss. 39201
(601) 355-6468

MISSOURI

Cape Girardeau

Cape Girardeau Corrections Service Center
703 Broadway
Cape Girardeau, Mo. 63701
(314) 334-6093
("Ex-offenders; primary interest: flat time")

Carthage

Community Corrections Program
400 E. 4th St.
Carthage, Mo. 64836
(417) 358-8177

Columbia

Columbia Community Service Center
512 Cherry St.
Columbia, Mo. 65201
(314) 443-0413
("Ex-offenders; primary interest: flat time")

Jefferson City

Model-Ex-Offender Program
Division of Corrections
Community Services Unit

911 Missouri Blvd.
P.O. Box 236
Jefferson City, Mo. 65101
(Serves parolees, flat-timers, and work releasees recently released from a Missouri penal institution)

Kansas City

Dismas House of Kansas City
3000 Campbell St.
Kansas City, Mo. 64109
(816) 753-1334

Employment & Training Systems/Project Option & Court Intervention Project
306 E. 12th St.
Kansas City, Mo. 64106
(816) 471-0170
("Offenders under supervision by local law-enforcement agencies")

Kansas City Community Corrections Service Center
4612 Troost
Kansas City, Mo. 64110
(816) 561-7324
("Flat-timers—those who commutate their sentence—are given first priority, but we do work with people on probation, parole")

Manpower Service Systems
3030 Prospect Avenue
Kansas City, Mo. 64128
(816) 861-9373

National Alliance of Businessmen*
114 W. 11th St.
Kansas City, Mo. 64105
(816) 374-2536

Springfield

Springfield Corrections Service Center
320 E. Pershing St.
P.O. Box 1326-SSS
Springfield, Mo. 65805
(417) 866-1996
("Ex-offenders; primary interest: flat time")

St. Louis

National Alliance of Businessmen*
710 N. 12th St., Suite 702
St. Louis, Mo. 63101
(314) 421-2234

St. Louis Corrections Service Center No. 1
4100 Page Blvd.
St. Louis, Mo. 63113
(314) 652-0360
("Ex-offenders; primary interest: flat time")

St. Louis Corrections Service Center No. 2
818 Olive St., Suite 643
P.O. Box 596
St. Louis, Mo. 63188
(314) 231-2211
("Ex-offenders; primary interest: flat time")

NEBRASKA

Omaha

National Alliance of Businessmen*
4470 Farnam St.
Omaha, Nebr. 68131
(402) 551-3090

7th Step Foundation
5351 No. 30th
Omaha, Nebr. 68131
(402) 453-7808

NEVADA

Carson City

Job Seeking Skills Project
1100 E. Williams

Carson City, Nev. 89701
(702) 885-4425

Reno

Entitaas Foundation
16020 S. Virginia St.
Reno, Nev. 89502
(702) 826-4037

NEW HAMPSHIRE

Concord

Vocational Rehabilitation Unit
State Prison
Concord, N.H. 03301
(603) 224-6654

NEW JERSEY

Asbury Park

National Alliance of Businessmen*
601 Bangs Ave., Suite 905
Asbury Park, N.J. 07712
(201) 776-6670

Camden

Camden County Work Release Program
603 Federal St.
Camden, N.J. 08101
(609) 541-9331

National Alliance of Businessmen*
1800 Davis St., Suite 313-314
Camden, N.J. 08104
(609) 962-6501

Hopewell

New Jersey Jaycees Criminal Justice Program
Millstone River Apts., Apt. H-7
Hopewell, N.J. 08525
(609) 466-0400 ext. 208

Jersey City

National Alliance of Businessmen*
1 Exchange Pl., Suite 919
Jersey City, N.J. 07302
(201) 547-7487

Vocational Service Center
111 Storms Ave., 9th Flr.
Jersey City, N.J. 07306
(201) 433-8530 or 8532

Morristown

Morris County Chaplaincy Council
26 South St.
Morristown, N.J. 07960
(201) 540-1600
("N.J. state prisons & county jails")

Newark

Integrity, Inc.
97 Lincoln Park
Newark, N.J. 07102
(201) 623-0600
("Drug abusers & alcoholics")

National Alliance of Businessmen*
50 Park Pl., Suite 730
Newark, N.J. 07102
(201) 642-2713

New Brunswick

The Morrow Projects of the State of N.J. Association on Corrections
118 Church St.
New Brunswick, N.J. 08901
(201) 247-2770
("Adult ex-offender—over 18 years of age")

Paterson

Passaic County Probation Dept.
129 Market St.

Paterson, N.J. 07505
(201) 525-5000 ext. 356
("Those under supervision of Passaic County Probation Department")

Perth Amboy

Middlesex County Job Bank
262 State St.
Perth Amboy, N.J.
(201) 826-8587
("Restricted to probationers of Middlesex County with no pending charges")

Trenton

Garden State School District
1901 N. Olden Ave. Ext.
Trenton, N.J. 08618
(609) 292-8690

Morrow Projects of the N.J. Association of Correction, Clinton House
21 N. Clinton Ave.
Trenton, N.J. 08609
(609) 396-9186
("Limited to adult inmates & ex-offenders")

National Alliance of Businessmen*
28 W. State St., Rm. 614
Trenton, N.J. 08608
(609) 396-2323

New Jersey Bureau of Parole
Community Resource Specialist Project
P.O. Box 1237
Trenton, N.J. 08625
(609) 292-4256
("Parolees & ex-offenders")

Woodbridge

National Alliance of Businessmen*
655 Amboy Ave.
Woodbridge, N.J. 07095
(201) 634-8770

NEW MEXICO

Albuquerque

Alternative House, Inc.
109 Elm St., S.E.
Albuquerque, N.Mex.
(505) 247-0173

The Halfway House
(for ex-offenders)
P.O. Box 6617 Station B
Albuquerque, N.Mex. 87107
(505) 842-3204
("Those on parole & probation to the State of New Mexico")

National Alliance of Businessmen*
111 Carlisle Blvd., S.E.
Albuquerque, N.Mex. 87106
(505) 266-5963

Santa Fe

JUNTOS, Inc.
621 Old Santa Fe Trail, #10
Santa Fe, N.Mex. 87501
(505) 982-4624 or 4625
("Ex-offenders, intervention [court referrals], youth & their families")

NEW YORK

Albany

National Alliance of Businessmen*
3 Computer Drive
Albany, N.Y. 12205
(518) 458-7406

Binghamton

Probe
86 Hawley St.
Binghamton, N.Y. 13901
(607) 772-8912

National Alliance of Businessmen

ORGANIZATIONS PROVIDING JOB ASSISTANCE 221

19 Chenango St., Suite 407
Binghamton, N.Y. 13901
(607) 722-4274

Buffalo

National Alliance of Businessmen*
Niagara Frontier Bldg., Suite 912
290 Main St.
Buffalo, N.Y. 14202
(716) 852-5654

Fairport

Seven Lakes 7th Step Chapter
47 Alwick Rise
Fairport, N.Y. 14450
(716) 223-2422

Jericho

National Alliance of Businessmen
131 Jericho Turnpike
Jericho, N.Y. 11753
(516) 333-9315
("Excludes persons convicted of sex crimes or repetitive assaults, not drug-free, & persons with serious mental disorders")

New York City

Argus Community, Inc.
578 E. 161 St.
Bronx, N.Y. 10456
(212) 665-7943

Harlem Confrontation House, Inc.
2027 7th Ave.
New York, N.Y. 10027
(212) 663-8300

Legal Aid Diversion Project
11 Park Pl., Room 1610
New York, N.Y. 10007
(212) 233-4947

NAACP—Project Rebound
270 W. 96th St.
New York, N.Y. 10025
(212) 663-7600

National Alliance of Businessmen*
380 Madison Ave., 14th Flr.
New York, N.Y. 10017
(212) 573-9500

The Prison Apostolate
Catholic Charities
Archdiocese of N.Y.
1011 First Ave.
New York, N.Y. 10022
(212) 371-1000

Private Concerns, Inc.
477 Madison Ave.
New York, N.Y. 10022
(212) 644-1630

Querer, Inc.
391 E. 149th St.
Bronx, N.Y. 10455
(212) 665-9660

Womens' Prison Assn. & Hopper Home
110 Second Ave.
New York, N.Y. 10003
(212) 674-1163
("Women")

Port Washington

Long Island Friends of Fortune
382 Main St.
Port Washington, N.Y. 11050
(516) 883-2365

Rochester

National Alliance of Businessmen*
25 N. State St., Suite 283
Rochester, N.Y. 14604
(716) 232-2600

Rochester Area Parole Office
75 Clinton Ave., N.
Rochester, N.Y. 14604

(716) 232-5464
("Individuals under parole supervision")

Syracuse

National Alliance of Businessmen*
677 S. Salina St.
Syracuse, N.Y. 13202
(315) 474-6476

Project Re-Entry
309 S. Franklin St.
Syracuse, N.Y. 13202
(315) 476-5396

Utica

National Alliance of Businessmen*
185 Genessee St., Suite 1405
Utica, N.Y. 13501

NORTH CAROLINA

Charlotte

National Alliance of Businessmen*
500 E. Morehead St., Suite 220
Charlotte, N.C. 28202
(704) 372-4491

Fayetteville

Fayetteville Youth Services Bureau
239 Robeson St.
Fayetteville, N.C.
(919) 485-3161

Greensboro

Greensboro Urban Ministry
316 S. Spring St.
Greensboro, N.C. 27401
(919) 273-6916

National Alliance of Businessmen*
1105 E. Wendover Ave.
P.O. Box 6987
Greensboro, N.C. 27405
(919) 275-0783

Raleigh

Second Chance, Inc.
1109 Raleigh Bldg.
5 West Hargett St.
Raleigh, N.C.
(919) 832-0768

NORTH DAKOTA

Bismarck

Dept. of Parole & Probation
East of Bismarck
Bismarck, N.Dak. 58501
(Adult offenders on probation or parole)

Model-Ex-Offender Program
Governor's Office
State Capitol
Bismarck, N.Dak. 58505
(701) 224-2790

N.Dak. State Penitentiary
East of Bismarck
Box 1497
Bismarck, N.Dak. 58501

State Youth Authority
Social Service Board
State Capitol Bldg.
Bismarck, N.Dak. 58501
(juvenile offenders placed under their jurisdiction by the courts)

Fargo

National Alliance of Businessmen*
321 N. 4th St.
P.O. Box 829
Fargo, N.Dak. 58102
(701) 293-5830

Mandan

N.Dak. State Industrial School
Mandan, N.Dak. 58554

OHIO

Akron

PREP Program
Goodwill Industries
36 S. College St.
Akron, Ohio 44308
(216) 762-8421 ext. 248

National Alliance of Businessmen*
150 E. Market St.
Akron, Ohio 44308
(216) 253-4434

Cincinnati

Bob Huddleston 7th Step Chapter
2644 Colerain Ave.
Cincinnati, Ohio 45214
(513) 681-5880

Community Action Commission
801 Linn St.
Cincinnati, Ohio 45203
(513) 241-1425

COSOAP (Talbert House)
1632 Central Pkwy.
Cincinnati, Ohio 45210
(513) 579-9300
(job preparation for ex-offenders living in Cincinnati area)

National Alliance of Businessmen*
309 Vine St., Suite 510
Cincinnati, Ohio 45202
(513) 381-3160

Vedanta House
2214 Vine St.
Cincinnati, Ohio 45243
("Offenders with drug-related problems")

(juvenile inmates just prior to release)

Cleveland

Bur Metro Office
2728 Euclid Ave., Suite 400
Cleveland, Ohio 44115
(216) 579-6680
("Only those who are Bur clients")

Cleveland Vocational Education Project
2301 E. 65th St.
Cleveland, Ohio 44104
(216) 361-3500

Cuyahoga County 7th Step Chapter
2108 Payne Ave., Rm. 815
Cleveland, Ohio 44114
(216) 621-5660

National Alliance of Businessmen*
1375 Euclid Ave., Suite 510
Cleveland, Ohio 44115
(216) 861-6100

Columbus

Central Ohio 7th Step Chapter
993 E. Main St.
Columbus, Ohio 43205

Comprehensive Employment & Training Program (CETA)
720 E. Broad St.
Columbus, Ohio 43215
(614) 461-7373

Columbus Youth Bureau
1465 E. Broad St.
Columbus, Ohio 43205

National Alliance of Businessmen*
8 E. Long St., Suite 210
Columbus, Ohio 43215
(614) 224-9154

Traynor House Halfway House
225 King Ave.
Columbus, Ohio 43201

(614) 299-7374
(for female offenders)

Volunteers in Probation
926 E. Broad St. Suite 203
Columbus, Ohio 43215
(614) 252-1156

Woman to Woman
935 E. Broad St.
Columbus, Ohio 43205
(614) 235-0936

Dayton

National Alliance of Businessmen
225 S. Main St.
Dayton, Ohio 45402
(513) 228-4145

Pre-Trial Release Program
333 W. 1st St., Suite 334
Dayton, Ohio 45402
(513) 228-9696

Elyria

Lorain County 7th Step Chapter
Investment Plaza Bldg., #206
538 Broad St.
Elyria, Ohio 44035

Lorain

National Alliance of Businessmen*
707 Broadway
Lorain, Ohio 44054
(216) 244-2228

Marion

Marion County 7th Step Chapter
132 Church St.
Marion, Ohio 43302
(614) 382-5714

Toledo

National Alliance of Businessmen*
P.O. Box 309
Toledo, Ohio 43691
(419) 476-7588

Youngstown

Mahoning County Residential Treatment Center
1764 Market St.
Youngstown, Ohio 44507
(216) 744-5143

National Alliance of Businessmen*
2026 S. Ave., P.O. Box 198
Youngstown, Ohio 44501
(216) 744-5201

OKLAHOMA

Oklahoma City

Council of Resocialization for Ex-Offenders
505 N.E. 46th St.
Oklahoma City, Okla. 73105
(405) 521-9761

HOPE
431 S.W. 11th
Oklahoma City, Okla. 73124
(405) 272-0271
("Ex-prisoners & families of prisoners")

National Alliance of Businessmen*
4401 Classen Blvd., Suite 400
Oklahoma City, Okla. 73118
(405) 525-8525

Tulsa

National Alliance of Businessmen*
2651 E. 21st St., Suite 109
Tulsa, Okla. 74114
(918) 747-3636

ORGANIZATIONS PROVIDING JOB ASSISTANCE

OREGON

Eugene

National Alliance of Businessmen*
220 Seneca Rd.
P.O. Box 185
Eugene, Oreg. 97401
(503) 485-8574

SPONSORS, Inc.
380 W. 13th
Eugene, Oreg. 97401
(503) 485-8341

Portland

International Lifeliners Assoc.
1506 S.E. 21st St.
Portland, Oreg. 97214
(503) 233-5691

Job Therapy, Inc.
1535 N.E. 17th St.
Portland, Oreg. 97232
(503) 288-5525

National Alliance of Businessmen*
403 Pittock Block
921 S.W. Washington St.
Portland, Oreg. 97205
(503) 226-4063

Offender Career Placement & Diversion Program
313 Portland Labor Center
201 S.W. Arthur St., Room 411
Portland, Oreg. 97201
(503) 223-2193
(Pretrial intervention service for first offenders, misdemeanor/minor cases)

Urban Indian Program
2326 N.W. Westover Rd.
Portland, Oreg. 97210
(503) 248-4562
("American Indian clientele only")

Salem

Manpower Consortium
672 Church St., N.E.
Salem, Oreg. 97301
(503) 588-6369

Model Ex-Offender Program
2575 Center St., N.E.
Salem, Oreg. 97301
(503) 378-2144

Oregon Indian Comm.
445 Union St., N.E.
Salem, Oreg. 97310
(503) 378-2377
(American Indian & alcohol and/or drug abusers)

PENNSYLVANIA

Allentown

National Alliance of Businessmen*
1411 Union Blvd.
Allentown, Pa. 18102
(215) 435-9025

Harrisburg

Public Offender Program
Labor & Industry Bldg.
Harrisburg, Pa. 17121
(717) 787-4326

National Alliance of Businessmen*
114 Walnut St.
Harrisburg, Pa. 17101
(717) 233-5796

Johnstown

National Alliance of Businessmen*
443 Washington St.
Johnstown, Pa. 15901

Lancaster

National Alliance of Businessmen*

c/o Lancaster Area Manufacturing Assoc.
30 W. Orange St.
Lancaster, Pa. 17604

Philadelphia

Adult Probation/Diversion Services
1317 Filbert St.
Philadelphia, Pa 19107
(215) LO3-4745

Area Manpower Planning Council
Penn Square Bldg., 7th Flr.
1317 Filbert St.
Philadelphia, Pa. 19107
(215) MU6-2100

National Alliance of Businessmen*
3 Penn Center Plaza, Suite 607
Philadelphia, Pa. 19102
(215) 665-0254

Project INCITE
OIC of America
100 W. Coulter St.
Philadelphia, Pa.
(215) 849-3010

Task Force II
United Church of Christ
150 N. Second
Philadelphia, Pa. 19106
(215) 922-2713

Vocational Counseling & Job Referral Program of the Philadelphia Adult Probation Dept.
1 N. 13th St.—Mezzanine Level
Philadelphia, Pa. 19107
(215) 686-7466
("Serve adult offenders on probation & parole under the Court of Common Pleas of the City & County of Philadelphia")

Pittsburgh

CETA
2400 E. Carson St.
Pittsburgh, Pa. 15203
(412) 481-9300

Community Release Agency, Inc.
400 Manor Bldg.
564 Forbes Ave.
Pittsburgh, Pa. 15219
(412) 391-8848
("Pre-trial arrestee living in the poor and black communities of Allegheny County")

National Alliance of Businessmen*
911 Penn Ave., 4th Floor
Pittsburgh, Pa. 15222
(412) 565-2762

Pennsylvania Program for Women/Girl Offenders
906 Fifth Ave.
Pittsburgh, Pa. 15219
(412) 281-7380
("Female offenders")

Urban League of Pittsburgh, Inc.
Ex-Offender Program
200 Ross St.
Pittsburgh, Pa. 15219
(412) 261-6010 ext. 385

Urban Talent Development
5604 Baum Blvd.
Pittsburgh, Pa.
(412) 687-7500
("Male & female offenders & ex-offenders")

Reading

National Alliance of Businessmen*
443 Washington St.
Reading, Pa. 19601
(215) 376-4879

ORGANIZATIONS PROVIDING JOB ASSISTANCE

Wilkes-Barre

National Alliance of Businessmen*
32 E. Union St.
Wilkes-Barre, Pa. 18701
(717) 825-7511

York

National Alliance of Businessmen*
35 N. George St.
P.O. Box 2212
York, Pa. 17405
(717) 854-5596

PUERTO RICO

San Juan

Model Ex-Offender Program
G.P.O. Box 4452
San Juan, P.R. 00936
(809) 764-7676

National Alliance of Businessmen*
G.P.O. Box 2399
San Juan, P.R. 00936
(809) 764-2669

RHODE ISLAND

Providence

National Alliance of Businessmen*
2 Jackson Walkway, Suite 1
Providence, R.I. 02903
(401) 521-4747

SOUTH CAROLINA

Columbia

Alston Wilkes Society
P.O. Box 363
Columbia, S.C. 29202
(803) 799-2490
("South Carolina residents who desire to return to the state")

Pre-Trial Intervention
1311 Marion St.
Columbia, S.C. 29202
(605) 253-5301

Greenville

National Alliance of Businessmen*
252 Bldg., Suite 108
Greenville, S.C. 29607
(803) 233-2020

SOUTH DAKOTA

Sioux Falls

National Alliance of Businessmen*
101 W. 9th St.
Sioux Falls, S. Dak. 57102
(605) 338-0851

TENNESSEE

Chattanooga

Volunteers in Tennessee Corrections
3475 Brainerd Rd.
Chattanooga, Tenn. 37411
(615) 698-4447

Nashville

Tennessee Dept. of Corrections
Model Ex-Offender Program
618 Doctors Bldg.
Nashville, Tenn. 37219
(615) 741-1317

Middle Tennessee 7th Step Chapter
P.O. Box 40968
Nashville, Tenn. 37204
(615) 297-2547

Memphis

National Alliance of Businessmen*
42 S. Second St.

P.O. Box 224
Memphis, Tenn. 38103
(901) 523-8091

Transitional Center for Women
1842 Court Ave
Memphis, Tenn. 38104
(901) 276-4487

TEXAS

Austin

Development Assistance for Rehabilitation
1711-A E. First St.
Austin, Tex. 78702
(512) 476-0694

HEART—Model Ex-Offender Program
TDCA/Youth Services Division
210 Barton Springs Rd., 3rd Flr.
Austin, Tex. 78704
(800) 292-9642

State Jr. Bar of Texas
Volunteers in Parole
P.O. Box 12487
Austin, Tex. 78711
(512) 476-6823
("Parolees from TDC—others will be referred")

Corpus Christi

CETA
515 N. Carancahua St.
Corpus Christi, Tex 78401
(512) 883-5261
("Youth delinquents ages 16–22")

Nueces County Juvenile Dept.
2310 Gollihar
P.O. Box 7276
Corpus Christi, Tex 78415
("Juvenile offenders 10–17 years")

Dallas

Dallas 7th Step Chapter
2615 Joe Field Rd.
Dallas, Tex. 75229

National Alliance of Businessmen
1507 Pacific Ave., Suite 410
Dallas, Tex. 75201
(214) 749-7161

Salvation Army Welfare Center
2203 N. Akard St.
Dallas, Tex. 75201

The Way Back House, Inc.
526 Liberty St.
Dallas, Tex. 75204
(214) 827-2181
(housing, employment, counseling)

El Paso

National Alliance of Businessmen*
P.O. Box 682
El Paso, Tex. 79944
(915) 533-5434

Forth Worth

Fort Worth Center for Ex-Offenders, Inc.
2016 Evans Ave.
Fort Worth, Tex. 76104
(817) 921-0213

National Alliance of Businessmen*
819 Taylor St., Suite 7A25E
Fort Worth, Tex. 76102
(817) 334-2061

Tarrant County Manpower Dept.
Ex-Offender Program
Tarrant County Courthouse
100 W. Weatherford St.
Fort Worth, Tex. 76102
(males presently on Tarrant County probation, 21–28 and

ORGANIZATIONS PROVIDING JOB ASSISTANCE

older. Vocational counseling, job-development referral, on-the-job training, skill training)

Houston

National Alliance of Businessmen*
3637 W. Alabama St., Suite 340
Houston, Tex. 77027
(713) 627-9600

New Directions, Inc.
3520 Montrose, Suite 100
Houston, Tex. 77008
(housing, employment, counseling)

Prisoners' Personal Aid
6001 Gulf Freeway, Suite B-104
Houston, Tex. 77023
(housing, employment, counseling)

Women in Action
625 W. Alabama, #4
Houston, Tex. 77006
(713) 523-5339
("County jail residents & former residents")

San Antonio

Barrio Betterment & Development Corp.
P.O. Drawer 7467
San Antonio, Tex. 78207
(512) 224-1911

Blackburn Halfway House
201 E. Courtland
San Antonio, Tex. 78212
(512) 734-7084

National Alliance of Businessmen*
3355 Cherry Ridge, Suite 103
San Antonio, Tex. 78230
(512) 344-9738

Project Detour II
1017 N. Main, Suite 206
San Antonio, Tex. 78212
(512) 226-6321

San Antonio Community Correctional Center, Inc.
Kerper House
1639 W. Mistletoe
San Antonio, Tex. 78201
(512) 732-7191

Texas Vocation Rehabilitation Commission
414 S. Main
San Antonio, Tex. 78205
(512) 225-3281

UTAH

Salt Lake City

Comprehensive Employment & Training Act
431 S. 6th East
Salt Lake City, Utah 84120

Dept. of Employment Security
Job Service-Counseling
1234 S. Main
Salt Lake City, Utah 84110

National Alliance of Businessmen*
10 Exchange Pl., Suite 714
Salt Lake City, Utah 84111
(801) 328-4825

VERMONT

Burlington

Employment Adjustment
138 Church St.
Burlington, Vt. 05401
(802) 658-0423

Workout
14A Church St.
Burlington, Vt. 05401
(802) 658-4903 or 864-5737

St. Johnsbury

Orleans County Council of Social Agencies
129 Railroad St.
St. Johnsbury, Vt. 05819
(802) 748-5151

Winooski

Model Ex-Offender Program
Champlain Valley Work & Training
P.O. Box 185
Winooski, Vt. 05404
(802) 655-2334

VIRGINIA

Alexandria

Second Genesis, Inc.
1204 Prince St.
Alexandria, Va. 22314
(703) 683-4610

Arlington

Good News Mission
1036 S. Highland St.
Arlington, Va. 22204
(703) 979-2200
("Residents in its halfway house & inmates in jails served by its chaplains")

Probation & Parole in Service to Va.
1400 N. Uhle St.
Arlington, Va. 22207
(703) 528-6666
("Only ex-offenders who are on probation or parole in District 10")

Ettrick

7th Step Foundation, Inc.
20606 Third Ave.
Ettrick, Va. 23803

Fairfax

Offender Aid & Restoration of Fairfax County
4057 Chain Bridge Rd.
Fairfax, Va. 22030
(703) 691-3158
("Primarily adults")

Norfolk

Human Resources Development Institute
203 Executive Bldg.—Janaf
Norfolk, Va. 23502
(804) 461-4555

National Alliance of Businessmen*
Koger Executive Cir. Bldg. 5, Suite 201
Norfolk, Va. 23502
(804) 461-9396

STEP-UP Program
203 Executive Bldg.—Janaf
Norfolk, Va. 23502
(804) 461-4557

Richmond

Project Aid-Sir
312 E. Clay St.
Richmond, Va. 23220
(804) 644-3008
("Convicted felons & their families and ex-felons & their families. Clients must be drug-free & nonalcoholics")

Rubicon, Inc.
1208 W. Franklin St.
Richmond, Va. 23220
(804) 359-3257
("Offenders having drug history")

National Alliance of Businessmen*
201 E. Franklin St.
Richmond, Va. 23219
(804) 782-2708

ORGANIZATIONS PROVIDING JOB ASSISTANCE

Roanoke

National Alliance of Businessmen
2823 Williamson Rd., N.E.
Roanoke, Va. 24012
(703) 982-6286

WASHINGTON

Monroe

Multi-Service Center
Washington State Reformatory
P.O. Box 777
Monroe, Wash. 98272
(206) 794-8077 ext. 325 or 331

Olympia

Adult Probation & Parole
Capitol Center Bldg.
P.O. Box 1788
Olympia, Wash. 98504
(206) 753-1502

Corrections Clearinghouse
Dept. of Employment Security
Airdustrial Park, Bldg. 17
Olympia, Wash. 98504
(206) 753-1362

Seattle

Dept of Social & Health Services
723 United Pacific Bldg.
Seattle, Wash. 98102
(206) 464-6140

Job Therapy, Inc.
205 Smith Tower
Seattle, Wash. 98104
(206) 622-9620
("Adult felons")

PIVOT
1700 N.E. 150
Seattle, Wash. 98155
(206) 545-6768

Seattle King County New Careers Project, Inc.
1107 E. Columbia
Seattle, Wash. 98104
(206) 447-3910

Shelton

Washington Corrections Center
Pre-Release Program
P.O. Box 900
Shelton, Wash. 98584
(206) 426-4433 ext. 294

Tacoma

Tacoma Urban League
1301 S. Kay
Tacoma, Wash. 98405
(job search & development ex-offender placement service)

National Alliance of Businessmen
302 Broadway Terrace Bldg.
Tacoma, Wash. 98402
(206) 593-6521
("Economically disadvantaged Vietnam-era veterans, ex-offenders, and needy youth")

Seattle

Seattle–King County Public Defender
623 Second Ave.
Seattle, Wash. 98104
(206) 447-3910

WEST VIRGINIA

Belle

National Alliance of Businessmen*
901 W. Dupont Ave.
Belle, W. Va. 25015
(304) 949-4313

Huntington

National Alliance of Businessmen*
Prichard Bldg., Suite 1219

Huntington, W. Va. 25701
(304) 529-6069

WISCONSIN

Kenosha

Partners, Inc.
5825 Sixth Ave. Suite 301
Kenosha, Wis. 53140
(provides consulting services)

LaCrosse

LaCrosse County Jail Project
P.O. Box 597
LaCrosse, Wis. 54601
(608) 782-0704

National Alliance of Businessmen*
710 Main St.
P.O. Box 842
LaCrosse, Wis. 54601
(608) 784-7010

Madison

Center for Public Representation
520 University Ave.
Madison, Wis. 53703
(608) 251-4008
("Legal representation for group interests only")

Job Service
P.O. Box 1607
Madison, Wis. 53701
(608) 266-6996
("Focuses on service to parolees from state penal institutions, primarily southeast Wisconsin")

National Alliance of Businessmen*
615 E. Washington Ave.
Madison, Wis. 53703
(608) 255-9222

Milwaukee

National Alliance of Businessmen*
828 N. Broadway
Milwaukee, Wis. 53202
(414) 273-3000

Wisconsin Correctional Service
436 W. Wisconsin Ave.
Room 500
Milwaukee, Wis. 53203
(414) 271-2512

Racine

National Alliance of Businessmen*
300 Fifth St.
Racine, Wis. 53403
(414) 632-6114

Project Re-Entry
718-22 N. Memorial Dr.
Racine, Wis. 53404
(414) 637-9381 or 82
("For newly released offenders returning to this area from state institutions & county jails")

Richland Center

National Alliance of Businessmen*
P.O. Box 128
Richland Center, Wis. 53581
(608) 647-3966

NATIONAL ORGANIZATIONS

The following national organizations may also be able to provide information on whether there are offender job-assistance organizations in specific localities.

ORGANIZATIONS PROVIDING JOB ASSISTANCE

American Correctional Association
National Offender Services CONtact Center
P.O. Box 81826
Lincoln, Neb. 68501

Bureau of Recruiting and Examining
U.S. Civil Service Commission
Washington, D.C. 20415
(Information on employment opportunities for ex-offenders with the federal government)

Human Resources Development Institute
AFL-CIO
815 16th St., N.W.
Washington, D.C. 20006

John Howard Association
537 S. Dearborn St.
Chicago, Ill. 60605

Joint Action in Community Service, Inc.
1730 M St., N.W.
Washington, D.C. 20036

National Alliance of Businessmen
Ex-Offender Program
1730 K St., N.W.
Washington, D.C. 20006

National Center for Voluntary Action
1785 Massachusetts Ave., N.W.
Washington, D.C. 20036

National Council on Crime & Delinquency
411 Hackensack Ave.
Hackensack, N.J. 07601

National Information Center on Volunteerism
Boulder, Colo. 80302

National Urban Leauge
500 E. 62nd St.
New York, N.Y. 10021

One America, Inc.
1330 Massachusetts Ave., N.W., Suite 205
Washington, D.C. 20005
(Assistance to women offenders)

Volunteers in Probation
200 Washington Square Plaza
Royal Oak, Mich. 48067

7th Step Foundation National Headquarters
1155 E. 14th St.
San Leandro, Calif. 94577

*These and other offices of the National Alliance of Businessmen listed in this directory provide assistance to rehabilitated job-ready former offenders referred through transitional agencies as part of NAB's national ex-offender program effort.

Appendix E
Legal Standards on Civil Disabilities

The following standards are one part of a ten-part set of standards relating to the legal status of prisoners recommended by the Joint Committee on the Legal Status of Prisoners, a group sponsored by the American Bar Association. The entire set of standards, labeled "Tentative Draft," complete with commentary, may be found in volume 14, number 3, of the *American Criminal Law Review* (1977).

PART X. CIVIL DISABILITIES

10.1 Repeal of Mandatory Civil Disabilities
Except for those specifically preserved in this part, mandatory provisions imposing collateral disabilities or penalties, or depriving convicted persons of their civil rights should be repealed. Any collateral disability or penalty or deprivation of a civil right resulting from a criminal conviction should be imposed only after a determination in each individual case that the disability or penalty advances an important governmental interest.

10.2 Voting Rights
Persons convicted of any offense whether or not incarcerated should not be deprived of the right to vote, either by law, or by the practice of governmental officials. Prisoners should be authorized to vote at their last place of residence prior to confinement unless they can establish

some other residence in accordance with rules applicable to free citizens.

10.3 Judicial Rights
Persons convicted of any offense should be entitled to

(a) initiate and defend suit in any court in their own name under procedures applicable to free citizens;

(b) serve on juries except while actually confined;

(c) execute judicially enforceable documents and agreements; and

(d) except during actual confinement, serve as a court appointed fiduciary.

10.4 Employment and Licensing

(a) Barriers to employment of convicted persons based solely on a past conviction should be prohibited unless the offense committed bears a substantial relationship to the functions and responsibilities of the employment. Among the factors which should be considered in evaluating the relationship between the offense and the employment are the following:

(i) the likelihood the employment will enhance the opportunity for the commission of similar offenses;

(ii) the time elapsed since conviction;

(iii) the person's conduct subsequent to conviction;

(iv) the circumstances of the offense and the person that led to the crime and the likelihood that such circumstances will recur.

(b) *Private Employment and Occupational Licensing.* Each jurisdiction should enact legislation protecting persons convicted of criminal offenses from unreasonable barriers in private employment. Such legislation should officially govern (1) refusing employment; (2) discharging persons from employment; (3) refusing fair employment conditions, remuneration, or promotion; (4) denying membership in any labor union or other organization affecting employability; and (5) denying or revoking a license necessary to engage in any occupation, profession, or employment.

(c) *Elective and Appointive Office.* Past convictions should not bar a person from running for elected office, although jurisdictions may provide that conviction of specified offenses will result in the automatic forfeiture of elective office held at the time of conviction. A convention should not bar a person from holding appointive public office although the appointing official may require forfeiture of an office held at the time of conviction.

(d) *Public Employment.* Public employment should be governed by the same standards proposed for private employment.

(e) *Appointive Public Office and Public Employment Distinguished.* For purposes of this standard, "appointive public office" includes policy making positions. "Public employment" includes positions which are generally governed by civil service or personnel systems or are considered career appointments.

(f) *Regulated Activities Other than Employment.* Licensing or other governmental regulations should not exclude automatically persons convicted of any offense from participation in regulated activities. Persons should not be barred from regulated activity on the basis of a conviction unless the offense committed bears a substantial relationship to participation in the activity. In determining whether such a relationship exists, the factors listed in (b) should be considered.

10.5 Domestic Rights

(a) The domestic relationships of persons convicted of criminal offenses should be governed by rules applicable to free citizens. Conviction or confinement alone should not be sufficient to deprive a person of any of the following domestic rights:

(i) the right to contract or dissolve marriage;

(ii) parental rights, including the right to direct the rearing of their children;

(iii) the right to grant or withhold consent to the adoption of children;

(iv) the right to adopt children.

(b) Conviction or confinement alone should not constitute neglect or abandonment of a spouse or child and persons convicted or confined should be assisted in making appropriate arrangements for their spouse or child during periods of confinement. Correctional authorities should experiment with special facilities within correctional institutions that would allow prisoners to keep their children with them during confinement.

10.6 Property and Financial Rights

(a) *Property.* Persons convicted of any offense should not be deprived of the right to acquire, inherit, sell or otherwise dispose of real or personal property, consistent with the rule that a person should not profit from his own wrong. Persons unable to manage or preserve their property by reason of confinement should be entitled to appoint someone of their own choosing to act on their behalf.

(b) *Pension and Social Security.* Persons convicted of any offense or confined as a result of a conviction should not, for those reasons alone, lose any otherwise vested pension rights or become ineligible to participate in any governmental program providing relief, medical care, old age pension, or other assistance.

(c) *Insurance.* State departments of insurance should require companies to offer insurance of all kinds to persons who have been convicted of any offense and should insure that any rate differential based solely on a conviction is justified.

(d) *Credit Agencies.* Agencies that compile and report information used to determine a person's suitability for credit or employment should be prohibited from disclosing criminal convictions that from the date of parole or release antedate the report by more than five years.

10.7 Imposition of Disabilities

(a) When a collateral disability or penalty or deprivation of civil right resulting from a criminal conviction is imposed, the following should apply:

(i) The procedures for imposition of the disability should be comparable to the Model State Administrative Procedure Act.

(ii) A disability should be imposed for a stated period after which the person subject to the disability should be entitled to have the appropriateness of the disability reconsidered. Within the stated period of the disability, if a person can present evidence that the disability imposed upon him no longer effectuates an important governmental interest, he should be entitled to a reconsideration.

(iii) The burden of proving the appropriateness of the disability should be on those seeking to impose it except a convicted person should bear the burden of proving an allegation that his conviction has unfairly affected his application for or status in private employment.

(b) Jurisdictions should adopt appropriate mechanisms for the enforcement of prohibitions against barriers to private employment applicable to convicted persons.

10.8 Expungement of Convictions
Each jurisdiction should have a judicial procedure for expunging criminal convictions, the effect of which would be to mitigate or avoid collateral disabilities.

Are you a member?

The ACLU needs the strength of your membership to continue defending civil liberties. If you have not renewed, we urge you to do so today. If you are not a member, please join.

Fill out the membership form below and send, with the mailing label on the right, to: **American Civil Liberties Union, 22 East 40 Street, New York, N.Y. 10016. Att: Membership Dept.**

If you have already renewed, give this issue to a friend and ask them to join.

	Individual	Joint
Basic Membership	☐ $20	☐ $30
Contributing Membership	☐ $35	☐ $50
Supporting Membership	☐ $75	☐ $75
Sustaining Membership	☐ $125	☐ $125
Life Membership	☐ $1,000	☐ $1,000
☐ $5 Limited Income Member		☐ Other $_____

Enclosed is my check for $_____.
(Make your check payable to the American Civil Liberties Union.)

PLEASE PRINT
☐ Renewal of membership
☐ New membership

NAME_____

ADDRESS_____

CITY_____STATE_____ZIP_____

ACLU-H

ACLU HANDBOOKS

THE RIGHTS OF GOVERNMENT EMPLOYEES Robert O'Neil	38505	1.75
THE RIGHTS OF CANDIDATES AND VOTERS B. Neuborne and A. Eisenberg	28159	1.50
THE RIGHTS OF MENTAL PATIENTS Bruce Ennis and Richard Emery	36574	1.75
THE RIGHTS OF THE POOR Sylvia Law	28001	1.25
THE RIGHTS OF PRISONERS Rudovsky, Bronstein, and Koren	35436	1.50
THE RIGHTS OF STUDENTS (Revised Ed.) Alan H. Levine and Eve Cary	32045	1.50
THE RIGHTS OF SUSPECTS Oliver Rosengart	28043	1.25
THE RIGHTS OF TEACHERS David Rubin	25049	1.50
THE RIGHTS OF WOMEN Susan Deller Ross	27953	1.75
THE RIGHTS OF REPORTERS Joel M. Gora	38836	1.75
THE RIGHTS OF HOSPITAL PATIENTS George J. Annas	39198	1.75
THE RIGHTS OF GAY PEOPLE E. Boggan, M. Haft, C. Lister, J. Rupp	24976	1.75
THE RIGHTS OF MENTALLY RETARDED PERSONS Paul Friedman	31351	1.50
THE RIGHTS OF ALIENS David Carliner	31534	1.50
THE RIGHTS OF YOUNG PEOPLE Alan Sussman	42077	1.75
THE RIGHTS OF MILITARY PERSONNEL (Revised Ed. of THE RIGHTS OF SERVICEMEN) Robert R. Rivkin and Barton F. Stichman	33365	1.50
THE RIGHTS OF VETERANS David Addlestone and Susan Hewman	36285	1.75

Wherever better paperbacks are sold, or direct from the publisher. Include 25¢ per copy for postage and handling; allow 4-6 weeks for delivery.

Avon Books, Mail Order Dept.,
250 West 55th Street, New York, N.Y. 10019

ACLU 10-78